DATE DUE

INDONESIA

INDONESIA
PEOPLES AND HISTORIES

JEAN GELMAN TAYLOR

YALE UNIVERSITY PRESS / NEW HAVEN & LONDON

Published with assistance from the Mary Cady Tew Memorial Fund.

Designed by Mary Valencia.
Set in Adobe Garamond type by The Composing Room of Michigan, Inc.
Printed in the United States of America by Sheridan Books.

The Library of Congress has cataloged the hardcover edition as follows:

Taylor, Jean Gelman, 1944–
Indonesia : peoples and histories / Jean Gelman Taylor.
p. cm.
Includes bibliographical references and index.
ISBN 0-300-09709-3 (cloth : alk. paper)
1. Indonesia—History. 2. Indonesia—Ethnic relations—History. I Title.
DS634 .T39 2003
959.8—dc21

2002152348

A catalogue record for this book is available from the British Library.

The paper in this book meets the guidelines for permanence and durability of the Committee on Production Guidelines for Book Longevity of the Council on Library Resources.

ISBN 978-0-300-10518-6 (pbk. : alk. paper)

10 9 8 7 6 5 4 3

In memory of
JOHN R. W. SMAIL
with respect and affection

CONTENTS

CAPSULES

CAPSULES

CAPSULES

ILLUSTRATIONS AND MAPS

MAPS

PREFACE

My aim in this book is to place Indonesians at the center of their own story. But there is no single story or history, and the principals become Indonesians only in the telling of Indonesian histories. The historical context in which this book is written is the debate within Indonesia itself as to what regions and communities constitute the nation. It is not the distant argument of academics, but the subject of real conflict between and within Indonesian communities. The debate is carried through violence as well as through public discussion. Men, women, and children die, lives are disrupted, property is destroyed, and fear settles in public meeting places. In this book I have tried to establish links between Indonesian communities, to show why, historically, they have reasons to live together in one nation and, at the same time, to show histories of difference.

In the scholarly literature on Indonesia there is a long tradition of stressing Javanese "difference," particularly in the individual's approach to Islam as either "orthodox" or "syncretic." I find "folk Islam" a more helpful way of understanding approaches to religious belief and practice, because it links Javanese with all other Islamic communities of the archipelago and relates Indonesian Islams to the traditions and histories of Islam everywhere. In discussing Javanese difference, most scholars adopt the Javanese (and Dutch) perception that Indonesia is Java plus Outer Islands, that the core is Java and that the societies of the other islands form a fringe. Sometimes that fringe is called the Malay-Muslim zone, again indicating Java's difference.

For all historians there is a very real problem in how to write an Indonesian history that covers Java and somehow fits "the rest" in. Each community is its own center. It is possible to write a history that begins with Ternate and its water empire, or that takes Aceh as the organizing center, includes its vassal states on the Malay Peninsula and Sumatra, and follows the process of such polities becoming incorporated into a state based in Java. No center other than Jakarta was proposed by Indonesians in creating their nation in 1945. No one argued that Palembang in southeast Sumatra, site of the ancient kingdom of Srivijaya, should be the capital of the new country of Indonesia. Nor were there any proponents for Pasai, the first known sultanate to export Islam across the archipelago. Java and the Javanese have seemed to Indonesians to be the core of the nation. The Dutch city of Jakarta, heir to Muslim and Hindu pasts, was accepted as the appropriate site for the republic's capital.

Labels create problems in telling histories. There was no entity internationally recognized as "Indonesia" before 1949 or even thought of before the second and third decades of the twentieth century. The term "Indonesian" appears straightforward, but it covers citizens whose ancestors originated in the Indonesian archipelago, China, India, Arabia, and Europe. Political and religious passions often reserve the term Indonesian for those whose ancestors originated in Arabia and the archipelago. Designating an Indonesian as, for example, "Chinese" (as I do in this text) regrettably carries the implication, and reinforces it, that such persons are not "really" Indonesian. Some scholars use the term Chinese Indonesian. Logically, then, we should also say Minangkabau Indonesian, Arab Indonesian, Javanese Indonesian, and so on. Similarly, the term "Dutch" appears straightforward, meaning a person born in Holland. But in Indonesian histories, Dutch troops generally meant a company composed of a score of European men and hundreds of Balinese, Javanese, Batavians, Timorese, Buginese, and Ambonese soldiers. Nationalist, imperial, and postcolonial histories cast colonialism as a great drama of brown against white, but to ordinary men and women the drama was more complicated.

Dutch rule created a single political unit incorporating many sultanates. It circulated Muslim and Christian Indonesians through colonial space along roads, railways, and steamship routes. Dutch rule brought Indonesians into continuous relationships with each other, where before encounters were sporadic. The Dutch also played the role of agent for the introduction and application of technological inventions such as the printing press, the telegraph, and vaccinations. Indonesians rejected foreign rule, but there are no voices calling for an end to electricity and mechanized transport. Another lasting legacy of the Dutch was the emotional impact of rule by Christian Europeans. The boundaries of the Dutch-made state are today under challenge, limiting Christian space and Christian authority over Muslim Indonesians.

A major theme in this book is mobility, and especially the mobile man. Wandering holy men, traveling scholars, traders, porters, rebel princes, and thugs (sometimes called local heroes) journey through texts written by Indonesians and outsiders. The Dutch saw Indonesia as full of wild spaces where there were pirates at sea, roving gangs on land, troublesome seers. Indonesian stories tell of wandering heroes who fight their way through forest or journey over seas in their quest for holiness or a high-status bride or to retrieve a birthright. Exile and transmigration were devices of archipelago kings and Dutch governors-general, and they are the tools today of Indonesian presidents. Militias and paid mobs erupt from mountain hideouts and urban slums to plant their mark on society, to force it into new directions. Before, communities lived in parallel worlds, their lives touching at times. Today, some communities in Indonesia are being overwhelmed, the space for their difference shrinking. The worldwide web has brought profound change. Ideas that formerly could be trapped or stifled are now flung into space, where they jostle with everyone's ideas, and fuel angers and hatreds, nourish conspiracy seekers, and inspire idealists of every kind.

This work of an outsider to Indonesian histories may strike Indonesians as a strange and unfamiliar narrating of their own history, which is the learned history from the national curriculum and the personal experience of living through history. It can only touch lightly, if at all, on periods, events, and persons which strike others as all-important. I have tried to tell Indonesian histories through byways and minor characters, as well as through big events, to bring in ordinary lives, problems, and encounters. There are myriads of Indonesian histories. Only a sampling exists between the covers of this book.

This book combines a continuous narrative with short essays embedded within each chapter. These capsules treat themes, individuals, works of art, variant interpretations by scholars, and topics such as calendars, caliphs, and mosque design. Some essays link a theme to several time periods. Readers knowledgeable about Buddhism or the meanings of the public kiss in Indonesia can skip the essays on these topics. Those who want to learn about the politics of polygamy, or the history of coins, or the meanings of *merdeka* can go straight to the particular essays. The titles of the essays and page locations are listed following the table of contents.

The sources are arranged in the bibliography under chapter headings. For this book I have drawn mainly on English-language texts, since it is a general history, but I have also included some books and articles in Indonesian, Dutch, and French that I found particularly valuable.

The spelling of places and names conforms to modernized spelling systems. Older texts use Achin for Aceh, Djakarta for Jakarta, the Moluccas for Maluku, Malacca for Melaka, the Celebes for Sulawesi. I use Kalimantan to refer to the two-thirds of the island of Borneo that is part of Indonesia. West Irian has been renamed Papua, and the country of Timor Loro Sa'e succeeds the Indonesian province of East Timor. Terms from Indonesian and other languages are translated in the text the first time they appear. Those used more than once are listed alphabetically in the glossary.

The bibliography acknowledges my debt to scholars past and present. I want to name those to whom my special thanks are due, beginning with my teachers Jamie Mackie and John Smail for whom I have written this book. They created my interest in Indonesia and gave me ways of thinking about it. I thank Anthony Reid for proposing to Yale University Press that I write this book, and the staff of the Press for their patience, skills, and support. Over many years the staff of the Documentation Center of the Royal Institute of Linguistics and Anthropology of Leiden, The Netherlands, have allowed me to study its wonderful photograph collection. My thanks particularly to Gerrit Knaap and Dorothée Buur. I thank Jaap Anten for assistance in providing illustrations for this book. I thank also the Lontar Foundation of Jakarta and especially Hani Siti Hasanah and John H. McGlynn, for assistance and their gracious permission to reproduce the illustrations in the text.

The Arts Faculty of the University of New South Wales has supported this book by providing travel grants so that I could participate in international conferences and revisit Indonesia, and by awarding me study leave for research and writing. My colleagues in the School of History endorsed my plans, rearranged teaching schedules, and gave me encouragement. I particularly acknowledge Roger Bell, Ian Tyrrell, and my partners in Southeast Asian History, Ian Black, John Ingleson, and Mina Roces. I have drawn on the expertise of Rochayah Machali, David Reeve, and Edward Aspinall in the School of Modern Languages. I thank Margaret Astar, social sciences reference librarian, for her scholarly assistance and friendship.

My colleagues Barbara Watson Andaya, Charles Coppel, Robert Cribb, Nancy Florida, Tineke Hellwig, Clive Kessler, Ellen Rafferty, and Michael Van Langenberg have generously shared their rich knowledge. Donald Emmerson has carried on with me a conversation about Indonesia over many years and places. I thank him for detailed comments on Chapter 12 and continual encouragement. I thank Wolfgang Linser for his detailed comments on the early chapters. My profound thanks go to Laurie Jo Sears and to Ian Black. They read every word of this text and commented on it with grace, tact, and a devotion of time drawn out of full lives. Robert Cribb created the maps, and I thank him for contributing his unique skills and knowledge to this book.

Learning grows out of teaching as well as out of research, and here I want to thank Iskandar P. Nugraha and Kristarniarsi, whose doctoral studies, insights, and kindness have taught me so much. I especially thank Iskandar Nugraha and Tony B. Wurjantono who made possible for me a journey through time in Java. I thank Thomas and Mieke Nelwan for their hospitality, friendship of many years, and love for my family.

My son and husband called this the book that would not end. No female academic could have two more supportive men in her life. I thank Harry for his computer expertise and Howard for sustaining me with humor.

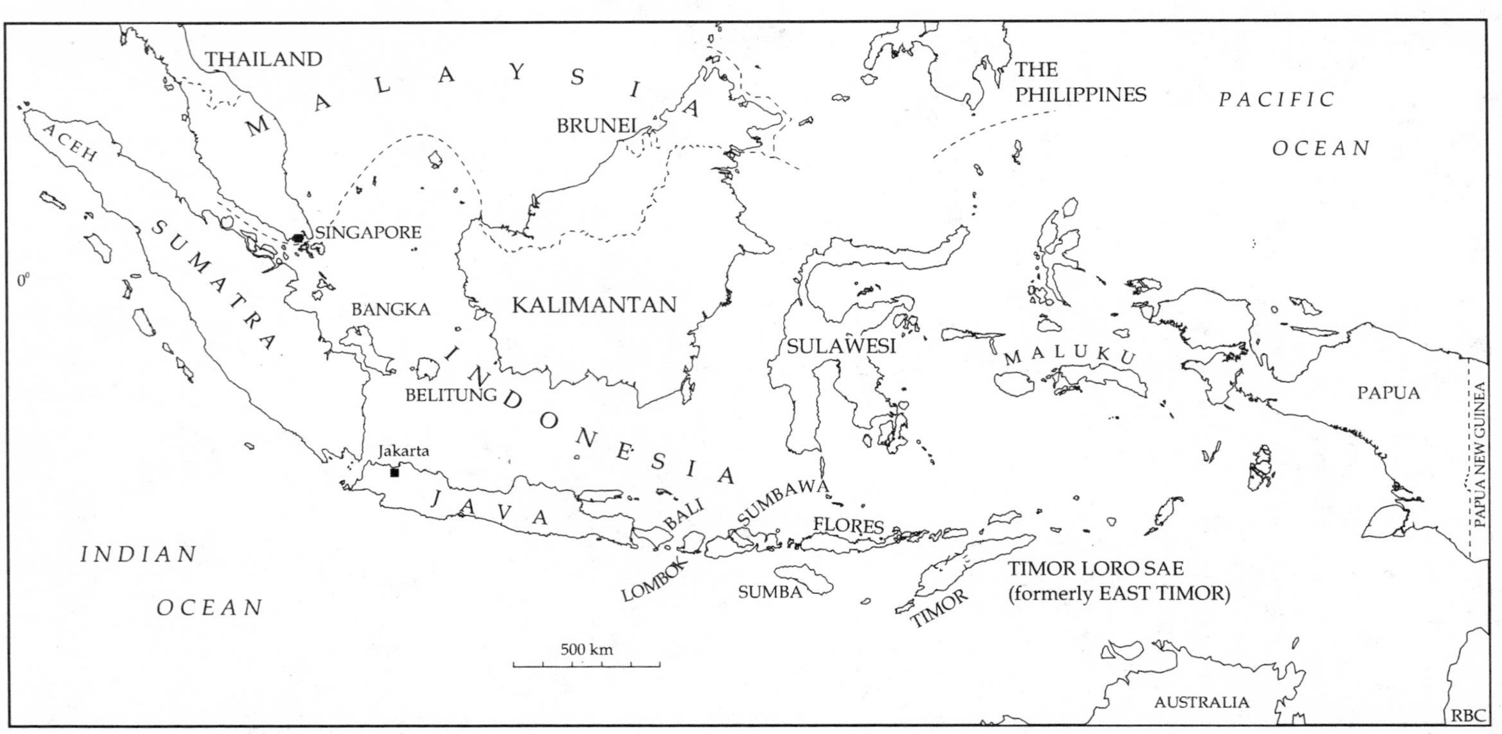

The Republic of Indonesia and Neighboring Countries

INTRODUCTION

Indonesia is the fourth largest country in the world. It is important as exporter of petroleum, natural gas, and manufactured goods, as consumer of Western and Japanese aid and investment funds, and as the world's largest Muslim nation. It is an archipelago country, made up of 17,506 islands, populated by 230 million people speaking more than three hundred languages. It has been an independent republic for more than fifty years, before that a colony of the Dutch and a zone of Islamic monarchies. The world's largest Buddhist temple survives from the ninth century in the heart of Java, and a form of Hinduism lives on in Bali. A fringe of Christian communities encircles Java.

Indonesia is a modern idea, conceived first in the minds of the Dutch military around 1850, adopted by Dutch civilian politicians in the 1890s, and realized by 1914. Indonesian youth who lived in the principal cities of the Dutch colonial state and studied in Dutch-language schools conceived the goal of making the colonial state the chief focus for everyone's identity but under self-rule. When they took up this ambitious project peoples' minds were already informed with the identity of Islam. This self-understanding had evolved in stages from identity as subjects of a Muslim king, to a conception of self as Muslims in a land ruled by an aristocracy of Muslims united in alliance with Christian Europeans. Promoters of Indonesian identity competed with other youths who wanted to arouse in Muslims an objection to rule by Christians. Some also wanted to wrest Islam from its local roots, to shed the distinctive features of Indonesian cultures celebrated by nationalists, and align Islam with Arabness.

This book is a social history more than a political one. It narrates journeys of peoples of the archipelago into today's republic. It aims to set the lives of men, women, and children in huts, workshops, and palaces, to present parallel histories, influenced and influencing, submerged but not obliterated by the big picture. The subtitle of the book is *Peoples and Histories* because many pasts have fused into the nation of Indonesia.

I believe that the past consists of facts about people and processes that are knowable and verifiable and that interpretations select and suppress facts according to the personality and moral judgments of each historian. Every writer has an agenda that emphasizes one class or one gender or one region. Individual authors may have an aptitude for economic or technological history, or a fascination with individuals in their settings. My approach to Indonesian histories grew out of an early interest in the meeting of Indonesian and Dutch in Asian settings. That interest led into other pasts and times before and since those encounters.

Modern Indonesia's presidents have ruled a state that has existed longer than the Dutch colony did in its final form. They have drawn on technologies available to the modern world to generate a profound identity of Indonesian through the state ideology of Panca Sila, whose ideal followers believe in one God, in one Indonesian identity, in a place in the world for Indonesia, in a homegrown solution to political organization, and in a just and prosperous society. This state philosophy competes with Islam and its commitment to Allah, Muhammad, Islamic law, and a place for Indonesia within the world Islamic community.

Sukarno, who was Indonesia's first president (in office 1945–1967), perceived Indonesia as a land of village republics with traditions of mutual aid, discussion, and consensus that could be applied to the national level. Maria Ulfah Santoso, Indonesia's first woman law graduate, viewed the same landscape and saw women wanting monogamy and the vote. In 1945 she advocated protection for all Indonesians through a bill of rights. Pakubuwono X, ruler of the princedom of Surakarta from 1893 to 1939, wanted to be acknowledged king of Java. The visionary Kartosuwiryo (1905–1962) accepted the title of *imam* from his followers, preached withdrawal, and launched his militias on campaigns to usher in an Islamic state. The communist activist Tan

Malaka (1897–1949) thought that ordinary Indonesians would never have lives worth living until hereditary kings, aristocrats, and colonial governors were swept aside.

The idea of an independent Indonesia has caused uprisings and wars. In 1926 and 1927 branches of the Indonesian Communist Party attempted to throw off Dutch rule. In 1943 members of paramilitary forces rebelled against Japanese occupation of the archipelago. In 1945 armed bands began the fight to prevent Holland from reimposing colonial rule following the collapse of Japan's wartime empire. In 1948 the Army of (the Muslim) God and Indonesian Communist troops attacked Republican troops in separate attempts to realize their own visions of Indonesia. So did rebels and separatists in Ambon, Sulawesi, Sumatra, and west Java in the 1950s. In 1965, in the cause of preserving the Republic of Indonesia from communism, General Suharto unleashed regular army units, local militias, and individuals against left-wing Indonesians. Armed and civilian opposition in East Timor challenged the idea of Indonesia from 1974 to 1999. Politicians and militias today challenge the idea of Indonesia in Aceh and Papua.

Indonesians today debate how they should be governed, which rights should be limited for the benefit of the whole, what direction the country should move in, and whether a nation of Muslims can create lasting democratic forms. The openness and vigor of these debates are attributable to the end of President Suharto's thirty-two-year rule in 1998. While groups campaign for human rights, an independent judiciary, and an accountable government, the Western press depicts Indonesia as a place hostile to a secular West, a land of Islamic militias intent on extinguishing the rights of those proclaiming difference.

Until recently Indonesia presented itself to the West not as a Muslim country but through Bali, a land of smiling faces, exotic dancers, paradisical landscapes. Western scholars once wrote about the stillness of Javanese interior life, the sophisticated tolerance of its philosophy. Now authors focus on violence in its many forms of state terror directed against dissenters and the public at large. Once Indonesia was presented as the world's crossroads because it straddles the great water highway that connects China to the West and because its peoples follow the world's religions: Islam, Buddhism, Hinduism, and Christianity. Now that crossroads is more often discussed as the province of people smugglers.

Within its home region Indonesia is a formidable presence. It is far more populous and exports its excess laborers to neighboring countries. Dissenters flee into the region to escape and to publicize ethnic, religious, and political conflicts. Indonesia's visionaries attract young men from the region to join religious causes; its popular culture beams to the region's Malay youth messages of modernity and "cool." Its timber, minerals, and cheap labor attract multinational companies, while Indonesia's wealthy invest in safer regional economies. Indonesia at times appears menacing to its neighbors, Timor Loro Sa'e, Malaysia, Singapore, Brunei, the Philippines, Papua New Guinea, and Australia.

Indonesia's history is not widely known even in its own region. Magazine articles and documentaries present fragments: environmental disasters of fire and flood, the installation of a woman as the Republic of Indonesia's fifth president in 2001, the demands in 2002 to expel non-Muslim foreigners and establish Indonesia as a country ruled by Islamic law.

Many Indonesian intellectuals, politicians, and journalists believe that foreigners (principally the West) do not understand Indonesia, have no grasp of the complex problems it faces, no sympathy for the struggles to find political forms that will suit the aspirations of Indonesians and bring ordinary people prosperity, peace, and justice. Many Indonesians believe that Western governments and international human rights' organizations seek the breakup of Indonesia by aiding opposition movements in the eastern and western ends of the archipelago. They point to the contradiction: the West lectures Indonesians on human rights and economic management while supporting and cooperating with the country's corrupt nexus of political, military, and business elites and overlooking the plight of internal refugees fleeing ethnic conflicts and natural disasters.

The context in which I write is the collapse of President Suharto's long rule and the rapid succession of three new presidents. Under Suharto's leadership an official policy of order, security, and economic development replaced fervor for Moscow or Mecca. Indonesia resumed its leadership position among nonaligned countries through its economic achievements: continuing expansion of schools and medical services for male and female, programs for attaining self-sufficiency in rice and for industrialization. In 1990, for the first time the value of manufactured goods exceeded raw materials in exports, and millions of Indonesians began to see their standard of living improve. The Asian monetary crisis abruptly reversed these gains in 1997 when banks and businesses collapsed, and more than half of all Indonesians fell into their government's definition of impoverishment. Suharto's presidency dissolved in a chaos of ethnically targeted killings, breakaway movements, and an army seemingly out of control. A new struggle for power and a contest of visions now mark Indonesia as pregnant with possibilities.

1

EARLY BEGINNINGS
Histories Through Material Culture

In the beginning there was no Indonesia. Land bridges connected the islands of Java, Sumatra, and Borneo to the Eurasian land mass. Bones discovered in the Solo valley are the only clue that ancestors lived 1.5 million years ago in Java. Human society reveals itself faintly from around 40,000 B.C.E. Descendants of early communities today live on the fringes of the Indonesian archipelago, in New Guinea, on the Melanesian islands, in Australia, and in the highlands of the Malay Peninsula and the Philippines. Until recent times they were tropical forest hunters, gatherers of tubers, and producers of flaked stone tools. In the Indonesian islands they were absorbed or displaced by peoples who entered the islands after their separation from the Asian mainland. The oldest sites in this island world where human remains, manufactured objects, and evidence of agriculture have been found together date to the sixth century B.C.E.

Older books speak of waves of migrations, evoking a powerful but misleading image of people gathering at fixed points on Asia's mainland to head to known destinations in lands to the south: this way to Vietnam; that way to Java. The variations observable among Indonesians today are not the result of separate migrations by different races. They are the product of a long, slow expansion within the archipelago of one ethnolinguistic group whose members adapted to various locales, mixed with existing communities, and responded in different ways and times to the influences of external civilizations. Today's

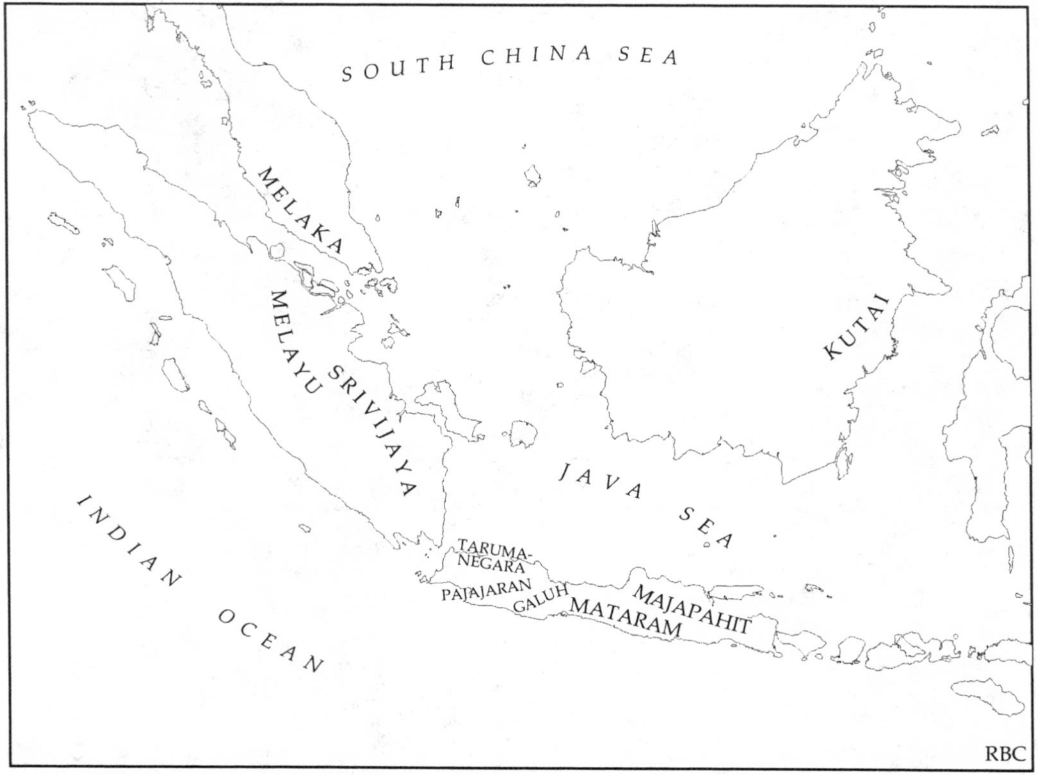

Early Kingdoms in the Western Archipelago

large populations of the archipelago share a common origin in southern China and speak a great variety of languages in the Austronesian family.

Around 4000 B.C.E., along the marshy coasts of China between the Yangzi Delta and South Fujian, pockets of peoples grew rice, had domesticated pigs and chickens, and made clay pots to store and boil grain. They used waterways as their footpaths, maneuvering small, flat-bottomed boats along rivers and among coastal sandbars. From around 3000 B.C.E. specialists worked in metal. By 1000 B.C.E., communities along the coasts of mainland Southeast Asia were raising rice in the flood areas of rivers, making pottery and stone tools, mining metal ores and casting objects in bronze. One theory endorsed by Pluvier places the origins of today's Indonesians in these settlements. Over generations, farmers of land and sea edged south from China, eventually moving into the Malay Peninsula and from there into the archipelago.

Bellwood argues that migrations into island Southeast Asia were by sea routes. South China coastal peoples sailed to the western shores of Taiwan, where they cultivated rice in swampland, passed on techniques of pottery making and spinning to their children, produced adzes with beveled edges, and put buffaloes to domestic use. Above all, they remained adept on water. To seafaring people, knowledgeable about wind and ocean, tree felling, and construction of boats, the South China Sea yielded islands and shores that reproduced a familiar habitat. Mangrove coasts abounded in fish and turtles, riverbanks gave shelter from storms of the open seas, forested lowlands produced woods and rattans for boats and huts, and cliff caves for shelter. Wind and water currents carried travelers to island stepping-stones in the sea. They reached the northern Philippine Islands by 3000 B.C.E., the islands of eastern Indonesia and Borneo by around 2000 B.C.E., and New Guinea, Java, and Sumatra between 1500 and 1000 B.C.E.

The evidence for migration along sea routes is linguistic. The languages spoken today in a region stretching from Taiwan, the Philippines, Indonesia, and Malaysia to the Cham-speaking areas of Vietnam are related and are distinct from languages spoken on the mainland.

Within the Indonesian archipelago, groups spread along shores and up rivers, engulfing the pre-Austronesian hunter-gatherers. The lives of Austronesian-speaking communities in the oldest settlements are known only from evidence yielded by excavated sites, for this era in Indonesian histories is without writing. The boat was house, vehicle, and site of production. Estuaries, rivers, lakes, and coasts provided regular supplies of food year round, so that groups who farmed Indonesian waters established land settlements to support their life on the water and divided their labor between land and sea. In fishing communities of the past few hundred years, for which there are written records, there is a division of labor by age and gender. Men caught near-shore varieties of fish with spears and nets; they selected and cut timbers to build and sail boats for deep-sea fishing; they hunted turtles and dived for mother-of-pearl; they mended fishing nets. Women and children gathered shellfish from the beds near seashores and reefs; they worked on boat and on shore; they preserved and stored marine foods for land use and sea journeys by drying them in the sun, smoking them over fire, boiling, or salting.

Hunting by boat and settling on shore allowed communities to venture into the forested coastline, plains, and hill slopes for food and building materials. In their long expansion through the islands of the archipelago, Austronesians relied on tubers growing in the floor of rain forests, gathered fruits, and hunted wild pigs. In the rain-soaked islands of the eastern archipelago, they harvested the sago palm for food and construction materials. Some archipelago communities in drier regions, using axes and fire, cleared small patches of the rain forest's dense undergrowth to broadcast seeds of rice and root vegetables. They hunted in the tangle of vegetation hemming their plots, and gathered plants growing wild, before moving on to clear another plot. Some groups adapted to inland waterways, sowing seeds along rivers whose soils were enriched by water periodically rising and flooding the banks. Other groups followed rivers upstream to settle in fertile mountain valleys and raise rice.

RICE

Rice is a staple for all classes in Indonesia today, but it has been incorporated into Indonesian diets only as people acquired the technology to grow it or were able to buy rice raised elsewhere. Remains of wild rice date from 3,000 B.C.E. in Sulawesi. Evidence for rice cultivation comes much later from Java, where eighth-century C.E. stone inscriptions record that kings levied taxes in rice. Scenes carved into the walls of the ninth-century Prambanan temples suggest a division of labor between animals, men, and women that could still be seen in Java in the twentieth century: a buffalo is harnessed to a plow; women plant seedlings in a field and pound rice; a man carries sheaves of rice at each end of a pole laid across his shoulders. In the sixteenth century, Europeans visiting the eastern archipelago noted that cooked rice was a new prestige food there, served to the ruling classes at ceremonies and feasts.

Rice requires exposure to the sun to ripen. The growing of rice in cleared fields is linked, in Indonesian histories, to the production of iron axes for clearing sites, domestication of the water buffalo, harnessing its strength for breaking up mud clods with iron-tipped plows, and using its manure as fertilizer. The expansion of rice cultivation over the past fifteen hundred years has slowly transformed Indonesian landscapes from dense forests to permanently cleared fields and concentrated settlements.

Many of the rivers which rise in the high mountains of Indonesia's islands make their way to sea down rocky cliffs, along beds strewn with huge boulders. They crash by waterfalls to lower ravines until they reach the coastal plains. There they divide into many branches and move sluggishly across a watery landscape where land and sea become indistinguishable in periods of heavy rainfall and storms, and where rivers become shallow in hot, dry spells. Such rivers could not be used as water highways connecting high interior to coast and sea-lanes. Travel combined paths cut through jungle and paths navigated on water. Many groups were made remote by their upland location, by shifts in settlement patterns of coastal peoples, by difficult terrain, and by an unequal contention with other inhabitants of wooded areas, particularly the tigers, wild pigs, and poisonous snakes. Long journeys were major undertakings of resourceful and healthy men.

People in coastal settlements had sporadic contact with semi-nomad farmers of the rain forest and with people of upland valleys, and more regular contact with peoples resident along other coasts. Communities living on boat and on land sailed within small spheres that linked into the travel circuits of other coastal communities. In Indonesia's histories, sea peoples have played important roles as traders, pirates, mercenaries, and slavers; they have taken the role of outsider, recorder, and supplier for land-bound communities. They go by various names in written sources: sea nomads, sea gypsies, sea hunters and gatherers, and the Indonesian term *orang laut* (people of the sea).

It is not knowable how many people lived on shore and on water in the thousand years for which the evidence of settlements is from excavated artifacts. Nor can the number of forest-dwelling communities that died out from disease, animal attacks, or wounds be known, or how quickly peoples whose ancestral origins were in southern China competed with, displaced, or absorbed the earlier pockets of humanity living in the archipelago's forests. What is known are the movements of twentieth-century inhabitants of rain forest on Borneo. In thirty years one group of Iban people traveled through three hundred kilometers of Sarawak forest, clearing and cultivating plots, and living off foods raised in any one clearing for one and two years.

Before writing, Indonesian histories can be dimly grasped through the lives of things. Objects explain how life was sustained, how humans struggled to acquire and preserve food, how they tried to protect physical and mental health, how they conducted their spiritual life. Objects reveal differences of wealth and destiny between people. Things, in their area of origin, in their area of discovery, in their construction, reveal the skills of a community at specific times in its history. Objects provide the record of technologies, of ideas, of human organization, of human needs and desires. They establish transport networks. Goods, technologies, and ideas traveled along land and sea paths, carried by people who moved outside their communities of birth, fostering wants, desires, knowledge, and a sense of others.

Early Indonesian histories are relayed through objects made of stone and of metal, which represent solutions people produced long ago to the practical problems posed by Indonesian landscapes of rain forest and waterways. Stone axes, picks, and knives extended human strength for clearing a patch of forest to plant food crops, for felling trees to build a boat, for digging a shallow pit to get at metal ores, for skinning an animal, or for cutting into a tree for its resin or food starch. Polished axes, produced from stone distinctive to areas in south Sumatra and west Java, spread to faraway communities along a myriad of overlapping sailing circuits.

From around 500 B.C.E. these circuits meshed with sailing routes that took archipelago peoples into the spheres of major civilizations developing in South and East Asia. An ancient history of human contact, of curiosity, desire, and recognition of the significance of new objects took place at sites where land and sea paths joined. By the third century B.C.E. the Chinese had developed smelting techniques that allowed them to produce a metal tough enough for hoes, axes, and the tips of wooden plows. They produced iron goods for Chinese markets and for export overseas in big blast furnaces. In the last centuries before the Common Era, metal goods were percolating through trade networks that extended into the Indonesian archipelago and were becoming desired objects.

Knowledge of how to detect metal deposits and of how to mine and work in metal also spread along archipelago seaways. Iron ores are found in soils in west Sumatra and south Sulawesi, copper ores in Sumatran and south Java soils, tin in the Bangka and Belitung islands, and gold in west Sumatra's highlands and the river banks of west Kalimantan. Extraction and working of ores required the skills and labor of many men and women in a community: makers of hoes, shovels, and baskets; miners; collectors and cutters of firewood, charcoal makers for heating furnaces; metalworkers to melt and beat ores into bars, smiths to fashion tools, weapons, and bracelets; traders to put goods made from metal into networks of buying and selling. All depended on farmers of sea and land for food hunted, grown, preserved, prepared, and served. Archipelago metal industries developed at sites with ores, forest, water highway, and sizable settlements of people.

In most of the archipelago there were no deposits of metals. Some communities obtained bars of copper, iron, and other metals through long chains of exchange that ultimately led to China and Japan. Technologies, artistic designs, and items circulated among outward-oriented, seafaring communities scattered along the coasts of Sumatra, Java, Bali, Kalimantan, and the smaller islands of Talaud, Sumba, Sumbawa, Flores, and Selayar. Their metalworkers made arrowheads, swords, armor, axes, knives, plowshares, and fish hooks, urns, incense holders, and dishes, rings, and bracelets.

Metal objects for work, war, storage, and decoration were introduced into distant regions of the archipelago by Chinese imports and by local industries. The curved blade of the dagger called *kris,* made by blacksmiths in Java, was shaped from bars of an iron-nickel alloy found only in the soils of Soroako in Sulawesi. Iron axes and knives, produced by mining communities in Belitung and Karimata in the western archipelago, traveled along water highways, passing through many hands. Some ended their journey as possessions of chiefs in settlements on the northwestern tip of New Guinea. Iron tools and weapons, vessels and jewelry made of bronze, silver, or gold were used by communities with developing social hierarchies of leaders, religious specialists, soldiers, artisans, farmers, and traders.

For their new owners, in settlements far distant from communities which manufactured and used metal goods, the possession of an object made from metal might be a sign of elevated status, and the object used to display the wealth and self-importance of a ruler. For instance, large drums made of bronze, cast by metalworking communities in northern Vietnam between 500 B.C.E. and 300 C.E., have been found in prehistoric sites in Sumatra, Java, and Bali. It is not possible to know if the owners of these drums valued them as musical instruments or for the beauty of their engraved surfaces. Drums were not objects to be shared or passed on. After the death of their owners the drums were placed in their graves. Musical instruments originating in Vietnam represent, in Indonesian societies, wealth hoarded and wealth withdrawn from the community.

Ancient things made from stone and metal carry Indonesian histories of belief in the infinite social distance between rulers and ruled. The makers of stone axes in sites in Sumatra, Java, Bali, Sumbawa, and Sumba also quarried huge stone slabs. They carved designs of animals and human heads on the slabs, then dragged them up the slopes of hills to raise them over the graves of their rulers. Burial sites provide evidence of a belief in the duty of ordinary people to serve, as well as belief in a future existence for rulers with the same privileges as they extorted on earth. Alongside the rings, bracelets, arrowheads, and daggers found in royal graves of the archipelago are the bones of people killed to serve bosses in their next life.

GRAVES AS HISTORY

Secure disposal of the dead is common to most human societies. Ritual burial tells us about local economies, levels of craftsmanship, patterns of trade, and local tastes, as well as about religious and class systems. The oldest burial sites yet found in Indonesia contain personal possessions alongside the deceased, and sometimes also human and animal bones. They establish a long history in the archipelago of belief in a life after death.

Disposal of the dead in the Indonesian archipelago covers a wide range of practices: interment of bones in pottery jars with beads (Bali, Tangir), interment beneath great stone slabs and pillars (Sumatra, Java, Bali), skull coffins made of stone in the shape of birds or mythological creatures (Nias), interment with heads of slain enemies in stone houses decorated with skulls and war scenes (Minahasa), interment under tombstones constructed according to Muslim and Christian prescription and designs, and cremation.

Solid monuments for the well-to-do and powerful attest to the enterprises of stonemasons, blacksmiths, iron founders, and toolmakers. Large blocks of stone are often the only reminder of the laborers who quarried them and hauled them to burial sites. The decoration of graves, their motifs, symbols, and epitaphs are evidence of other kinds of unremembered laborers: they reveal knowledge of theology, traditions, and alphabets. Fourteenth-century tombs from Trawulan, for instance, demonstrate the presence in east Java of stonemasons who could chisel words in Javanese and Arabic. Tombs from south Sulawesi bear inscriptions in Arabic and Buginese languages and writing systems.

Time and tropical climate have erased all trace of most people in life or death. The requirements of modern cities and of politics obliterate old gravesites. Many markers to Dutch people who lived in Java in the seventeenth and eighteenth centuries, for example, have been bulldozed, and only a few tombs are now preserved in Jakarta's Tanah Abang cemetery. Victims of war, pogrom, purge, and massacre have no individual markers. Hundreds of Indonesians disappeared during the war for independence, victims of rival armed gangs and group hysteria. Between one half and a million people were killed in the process of changing presidents between 1965 and 1966. The bones of more lie in mass graves in Aceh, Papua (Irian), and Timor Loro Sa'e. Rivers and the sea became graveyards for unknown numbers in local wars at the end of Indonesia's twentieth century.

Diffusion of metalworking and of metal goods within the Indonesian archipelago occurred because of local knowledge of the sea. Sailing techniques were based on observation of the power of wind and water currents. Accumulated experience produced patterns of sailing and timing of routes. Local products carried by local sailors forged connections between archipelago settlements. Products of the Indonesian landscape of forest and sea drew archipelago communities into the orbits of land-based civilizations. Archipelago sailors put forest and sea products into water-borne chains of exchange. Some of these products ended up in distant societies with different sets of cultural requirements and different inheritances of knowledge.

Pre-industrial communities far removed from each other in place, time, and culture had many uses for resins from Indonesia's rain forests. Archipelago people who grew their food and lived among trees had discovered how to get a tree's resin by collecting in baskets the sticky liquid which exuded from a cut made with a stone ax. They applied tree gums to glue together hefting points and blades of knives. They used tree resins to coat and repair waterproof containers, to seal carrying baskets, and to caulk boats to prevent leaks. They bound the planks of rafts with forest rattan and tree gum. They burned the damar resin in torches for interior light and for outdoor night performances. Essential oils of resins provided incense for religious ceremonies. Other tree saps were the source of lacquers and varnishes used to preserve and beautify furniture, screens, and containers made of wood. Some trees had fragrant barks used to perfume living spaces when burned. The resins and crystals produced by pine trees that grow on mountain slopes in northwest Sumatra and west Java were used as fungicides and fumigants and were applied to wounds to stop bleeding.

Trees were tapped while a community farmed an area, then abandoned when the group moved to clear and farm a new site. In large, semi-sedentary communities, resin collection was no longer random tapping but the regular gathering of resins, accompanied by the ownership of trees and inheritance of them. Extraction of resins and barks required local knowledge, tools of stone or iron, collecting baskets, and a portion of the time of people who lived in and from the forest. Resins and barks were easy to carry on river and sea journeys.

Land dwellers gathered resins, spices, and fragrant barks from trees. They harvested coconuts; they planted pepper vines among native trees. (Much later, as a result of contact with Europeans, they raised coffee and tea bushes, tobacco vines, and rubber trees in their forests.) They hunted forest-dwelling birds for their feathers. Indonesian peoples who lived more on sea than on land collected the nests of cliff-dwelling birds; they hunted turtles for their shell, dived for mother-of-pearl, fished for trepang, and extracted salt from seawater.

Sea and forest products made the archipelago important to foreigners, attracted them to its water lanes and jungle paths, and brought in new knowledge. Demand stimulated a change from sporadic gathering to regular cultivation and collecting. Exchange made local men rich and employers of foreign and local experts. Sea and forest products inserted Chinese and Indians into Indonesian histories in centuries before the beginning of the Common Era. These products brought Arabs into those histories from the seventh century and Europeans from the sixteenth. Oil, a product of Indonesian land and seabed, brought in Japanese and Americans in the twentieth. All these foreigners introduced into Indonesian networks products of their own industries. They spread their own technologies, systems of belief, and knowledge.

In the oldest burial site yet opened in the archipelago, glass beads of Indian origin were found alongside objects of metal. These goods made outside the region flowed into archipelago networks of exchange and became the coveted possessions of a man important to his community in north Bali in the first century C.E. There is no reciprocal evidence from Indian or Chinese soils of the Indonesian goods traded in exchange, for barks and birds' nests leave no remains, but other archaeological clues indicate that items originating in the Indonesian archipelago were flowing back along the same shipping routes.

Feathers and ships give hints of trade and archipelago lives. Plumes from the bird of paradise, which is native to New Guinea, are thought to be engraved on bronze drums cast by artisans working two thousand years ago in northern Vietnam, and so suggest a very old trade linking the easternmost part of Indonesia with the Asian mainland. Shipwrecks of boats, determined to be of Indonesian construction and dated to the second century B.C.E., lie along the southeast coast of India. Such remains hint at traffic in things from Indonesian forests and seas centuries before written evidence surfaces in Chinese documents of the fifth century C.E.

Archipelago sailors who put in at ports along India's southeast coast in the centuries before the Common Era interacted with coastal settlements in similar stages of development to their own. By the fifth century C.E., the agrarian Indian and Chinese states were very different from contemporary archipelago shore settlements because of the size of populations occupying cleared landscapes of farms, permanent villages, and factory work sites. Through taxes paid in grain and manufactured products of metal, cloth, and ceramics, Indian and Chinese peoples on the mainland supported city-based elites and hierarchies of officials who developed and spread religions and other branches of knowledge. The taxes of farmers and artisans paid for learning systems that stored information through writing and supported specialists whose webs of contact spread overland and by sea to other civilizations. Goods, knowledge, and technologies from Indian and Chinese states accompanied specialists on their travels. By the third century C.E., the major merchant and craft communities of India's southeast coast had established subsidiary settlements in ports of mainland Southeast Asia. They were Buddhists, and subjects of kingdoms in India whose ruling classes were devotees of Hindu gods and patrons of *brahmins* (or *brahmans*).

HINDUISM AND BUDDHISM

Hinduism is the term coined by Westerners to describe Indian religious beliefs and practices derived from a wide body of oral and written literatures and represented in temples, statuary, carvings, paintings, ritual, and social organization. Central to early Indian philosophical thought was belief in a soul that progresses through many forms of animal and human life until perfect comprehension grants it release from a chain of existences. Buddhism is a variant within Hinduism which teaches that the path to release from existence is through the shedding of desire and gaining of a knowledge derived from both book learning and intuitive insight. Hinduism emphasizes purity and its maintenance by avoidance of pollution; Buddhism emphasizes the ending of desire.

In India philosophers wrote in Sanskrit, which attained an elevated status as the language of learned communication, philosophy, ritual, and literature. Sanskrit literature covers philosophy, architecture, astronomy, art, metrical poetry, grammar, and medicine. Buddhism had its own literature in its own sacred language, Pali, that recorded the life and teachings of the Buddha, recounted his previous lives, stories of spiritually charged individuals and gods, and detailed rules for monastic living.

The concept of one god in many manifestations was structured by literary and artistic conventions. Each god had specific characteristics; there were rules for portraying them in statues and paintings, and distinct rituals for their worship. The Hindu gods lived on Mount Meru, a cosmic, holy hill surrounded by oceans. Specific places in the Indian landscape are associated with the descent of gods from Mount Meru and their worldly adventures in human forms. Places were also associated with the Buddha. Pilgrimage to holy sites inducted people of different social classes into different levels of knowledge.

Hindu and Buddhist temples were constructed in two forms: as enclosed space and as diagrammatic space. The enclosed space held a statue of the god. The form of the temple and its positioning along the lines of the compass represented in stone an intellectual perception of the universe. The temple was also an object of instruction. On its walls were carved scenes of the lives of gods and heroes and the consequences of choices between good and evil. Pilgrims walked around a temple with a guide who explained the stories carved in stone and the representative features of sculptures.

Buddhism was enveloped within Hinduism in India, but it took on a separate life in the diverse societies to which it spread. In Sri Lanka and in Myanmar, Thailand, Cambodia, and Laos it developed into a Buddhism for men in monasteries and a Buddhism for people living within families engaged in the business of earning a living. In China a folk Buddhism developed around devotional cults to gods and goddesses. Among Chinese elites Buddhism evolved into philosophical and speculative cults.

Hindu and Buddhist religious thought perceived humans as fundamentally unequal members in society at different stages in their spiritual development. In Hindu thinking, people were born into ranks of occupation and privilege (often called castes by Westerners) that reflected their religious attainment. The senior rank was that of the brahmins, who practiced rituals of purification most rigidly in dietary laws, occupations, and avoidance of physical contact (such as eating at a common table) with persons of other occupation groups. Buddhist thinkers also perceived spiritual, economic, and political inequalities, but emphasized release from all social conditions through withdrawal from society, rather than through rebirth into higher castes. In Southeast Asian variants of Buddhism, rebirth into a male body was one prerequisite in the long spiritual journey toward enlightenment.

Sailor-traders from ports in the Indonesian archipelago had intermittent acquaintance with Indian merchant communities and culture in Indian ports long before their own home ports were of sufficient importance to attract foreign merchants to establish offices in them. So long as trading networks carried only limited numbers of foreign luxury items, and so long as these rare goods were withdrawn from commerce by being buried in the graves of Indonesian chiefs, archipelago settlements were small places of no significance beyond their immediate neighborhood. When objects circulating in trade networks reflected the growing manufacturing capacity of Asian civilizations, they triggered a corresponding development in some archipelago communities on the coasts of Kalimantan, Sumatra, and Java. These communities grew into ports which specialized in collecting products from their immediate hinterland, from their neighbors, and from places that could be reached across water.

Foreign merchants found it worthwhile to visit places with regular supplies of regional specialties in their markets in sufficient quantities and variety. Major sellers relied on the local knowledge and contacts of a port's traders to obtain for them feathers, resins, and turtle shell, rather than themselves walking along hazardous jungle paths to settlements that might be able to supply only one or two kinds of products, and then unpredictably.

Indian merchants who made the long sea journey east to establish branch offices in archipelago trading centers were agents for colleagues based in mainland Asia. Visiting merchants applied to the prominent men of archipelago ports for the right to do business there and to erect buildings where they could live and store their goods. Payments they made to conduct their business took the form of fine cloth and jewelry, foreign objects of desire that had no local equivalent, and were too rare and expensive to be owned by anyone of lower rank. Cotton painted or stitched in gold and silk thread to be worn or displayed as wall hangings distinguished recipients in communities where people wore clothing made from bark. Foreign cloth and jewelry inducted their new owners into international fashion.

In cities in India businesses were run by guilds which were organized around devotion to specific gods, with their own temples and religious staff supported by guild members' contributions. Such temples also functioned as meeting halls for businessmen and attracted markets. Their regular calendar of religious festivals drew pilgrim-shoppers. Reproducing their business style overseas, Indian merchant communities built temples as well as market stalls. Their gifts to the local ruler secured them grants of land. Merchants imported builders who knew the designs and codes for temple architecture; they brought in artisans who could carve panels on temple walls and sculptors who knew religious conventions governing representation of Hindu and Buddhist gods. They brought in priests to sanctify the temple, to conduct the rituals prescribed for its god, and to train temple assistants.

Local rulers availed themselves of the services of these foreign specialists too. Experts' skills were portable and enabled them to work for multiple employers. Most probably did not travel directly from India to jobs in the Indonesian archipelago. They were an international set of men distinguished by their mastery of some branch of Sanskrit learning. They found jobs in palaces and religious communities as professional writers, flatterers, philosophers, librarians, vocational teachers, and guardians of devotional cults. Brahmin is the single term covering many paid occupations, all of them linked to literacy. The term includes men who were celibate and men who lived in families, holy men and men of affairs. Essential to the definition is the link to ruling families as paid employee, beneficiary, and sycophant.

The heads of archipelago ports who employed brahmins adopted titles and royal names used by princes of Indian states. These titles were familiar to the Indian merchants whom they allowed to settle in their ports. Archipelago men who took the Indian titles of *raja* or *maharaja*, and added the Indian royal suffix *-varman* to their names, advertised their position as ruler to newcomers. The origins of Indonesian states are located in the fifth century of the Common Era, because it is from this period that use of these titles can be established.

INDONESIAN MAHARAJAS

Heads of Southeast Asian ports who were the principal traders in their home region and who used royal titles and reign names in vogue in Indian kingdoms formed an international set. Inscriptions chiseled into seven stone pillars (called *yupa* posts) tell the story of the rise in fortune and pretensions of a local family that controlled territory near today's city of Kutai in east Kalimantan in the fifth century C.E. The pillars, erected on the command of King Mulavarman, record his victories in battle, his generosity to brahmins, and his princely genealogy. Inscriptions on stone from west Java, also in Sanskrit and also dated to the fifth century C.E., announce decrees of another archipelago member belonging to the club for royals, Purnavarman, king of Tarumanegara.

Yupa Post from Kalimantan, early fifth century C.E. Sanskrit words preserved on stone in Pallava script tell the story of a family that controlled territory near Kutai in east Kalimantan. King Mulavarman's victories, his generosity to brahmins, and his princely genealogy are recorded on seven yupa posts. National Museum, Jakarta, D 2 c. Photo courtesy of the Lontar Foundation.

By their pursuit and possession of Indian things, archipelago men transformed the hubs of commerce from which they operated. Principal traders used their new wealth to invent an imagined India. In port and countryside their wealth and contacts resulted in the construction of stone and brick temples modeled on temples in India, embellished with carvings inspired by Indian temple wall carvings, housing sculptures of gods carved out of stone according to the rules of Hindu or Buddhist iconography. Port rulers insti-

INDIANIZATION AND INDONESIA

Indianization is a term used by nineteenth-century European historians to explain discoveries in Java, Sumatra, and east Kalimantan of Sanskrit inscriptions, sculptures of Buddhist and Hindu gods, the design of temples constructed between the eighth and fifteenth centuries, versions of Indian epics in local languages, forms of dance and music, place-names, and the large body of Sanskrit vocabulary in languages spoken today in the Indonesian archipelago. This cultural heritage was considered the legacy of Indian conquest and colonization.

Scholars such as Coedès and Bosch argued that there was no evidence of large-scale migration from India. They thought Indian civilization provided the tools for archipelago societies to transform themselves from nomadic tribal groups into states supported by permanently settled agriculturalists. According to this theory, archipelago chiefs hired brahmins from India and sent some of their own staff to study at important centers of learning there. These chiefs turned themselves into kings by employing Indians who gave them royal Sanskrit titles and reenacted on Indonesian soil great Hindu ceremonies of sacrifice to legitimize the rule of their patrons.

Wolters and Wisseman Christie argue the opposite case: that state formation preceded Indianization. In their view, wandering tribal chiefs did not send for brahmins; rather, the process of transformation from head of a nomadic kin group to ruler of a defined territory took place before there was much contact with brahmins. Local rulers had to be sufficiently rich to attract and support scribes, architects, sculptors, and religious officials at their courts. Their growing involvement in international trade first acquainted local rulers with goods and merchants from distant places, brought them knowledge of other societies, made them keen to acquire itinerant foreigners' skills, and eager to enhance their own position and impress foreigners in their ports. They imported exotic objects, such as bronze drums and fine textiles, and esoteric knowledge, in the form of Hindu and Buddhist devotional cults that celebrated rulers as deputies or even incarnations of gods.

tuted the calendar of Hindu and Buddhist rites to organize local time and business. They made their ports known internationally by fancy Indian names. They adopted Indian manners as they imagined them to be. They mixed with and employed brahmins.

Most archipelago peoples did not speak or understand Sanskrit, which was not used for recording the commercial transactions which sustained archipelago ports. Sanskrit was used to celebrate gods and kings; it was used to convey instruction in the composition of literature; it was the language of manuals for the guidance of kings, and of technical books for engineers, masons, and artists. It was the route for studying the philosophies of Hinduism and Buddhism. The great pillars of stone erected in public spaces, chiseled with texts in Indian alphabets, were intended to be imposing, to dominate by their size and the mystery of their signs. The ability to unlock the meaning of their signs belonged to men who traveled to study and to work.

Mobile men put their knowledge at the disposal of their raja patrons and of men of their own kind. They did not put writing into the service of the forest-dwelling communities who lived in the hinterland of archipelago ports, or into the service of collectors of sea products, or of sailors. Professional writers served a cosmopolitan world anchored in ports of mainland and island Southeast Asia. Temples, sculptures, and texts in archipelago landscapes were primarily for the cosmopolitans. The labor of Indonesian men and women of land and sea communities paid for the scholars and religious foundations that were patronized by their rulers. The relation of Indonesians to this cosmopolitan culture was that of workers, spectators at ceremonies, and minor participants at festivals.

The international community of scholars doing the circuit of archipelago mini-Indias included men from China. From around the fourth century C.E., Chinese students of Buddhism made their way to centers of Buddhist learning and pilgrimage in India by the sea highway which runs through the western end of the Indonesian archipelago. Their ships put in at ports along the way for supplies of food and fresh water. As a result, travelers became knowledgeable about goods available in these ports and financed their journeys by trading as they went. By the fifth and sixth centuries C.E., Chinese annals refer to far-off trading centers in the seas to China's south. So far, archaeological evidence has not been found to link sites along Sumatra's east coast or Java's northwest coast to the vague reports that reached compilers of knowledge for the imperial court of China. But, from the seventh century, Chinese records specify among their southern sources of resins and pepper a port whose name, in its Chinese rendering of Shih-li-fo-shih, has been identified as the Indonesian harbor state of Srivijaya (or Sri Vijaya, Sriwijaya, Sri Wijaya).

Srivijaya was a trading center that, in the last decades of the seventh century C.E., bore signs of participating in the regional culture: Sanskrit place-name; rulers known by Sanskrit titles and reign names; inscriptions on stone;

CHINA, BARBARIAN STATES, AND RECORD-KEEPING

Ancient China's writers perceived China as the "middle kingdom," the center of the world, ruled by emperors in the name of Heaven. This middle kingdom had identifiable borders, within which were subjects who were speakers of Chinese language and culturally Chinese. This inner space was ringed by barbarian states whose peoples were to be dealt with by military conquest and assimilation. When the Chinese state expanded its territory, it settled soldiers, farmers, administrators, and artisans who were already socialized as Chinese in conquered lands. States separated from the middle kingdom by sea were considered distant vassals who were grateful to receive occasional visits from imperial envoys and to acknowledge the cultural and political superiority of China through paying tribute.

This conception of the universe conditioned Chinese administrative practice and behavior. China was the giver in international relations as inventor, manufacturer, exporter, and disseminator of useful knowledge to the inferior. Government departments gathered, analyzed, and recorded information useful to the center. The names of foreign rulers, their states, and products were entered into imperial files. Information, in the form of characters brushed or penned with inks on to paper, was preserved by the regular copying, correcting, and editing of existing documents.

No Chinese-language texts chiseled into stone have been found in the archipelago. Chinese texts concerning the archipelago were composed in China to serve Chinese purposes. They preserve a vision of barbarian vassal states ringing China.

royal patronage of a Buddhist religious foundation. Srivijaya was situated on the southeast coast of Sumatra, in a watery landscape of tributaries of the Musi River, islands, and sandbars. River and jungle paths connected Srivijaya to forest-dwelling communities and to communities at higher reaches of rivers in the Barisan Mountains. Sea circuits connected Srivijaya to ports dotting the Java Sea. Its extreme southern location meant that Srivijaya was not a natural putting in place for ships sailing down the Straits of Melaka or sailing from China. But the exertions of its land and sea populations made Srivijaya a showcase for archipelago produce from many areas. Its long-distance sailors carried samples as far as ports on China's south coast.

Evidence for this trade exists in Chinese records only. Foreign trade was a royal monopoly in China. China received ships, it did not send them out. Officials of the imperial bureaucracy charged with the supervision of ports on China's southern coast examined cargo of foreign ships. Trade goods which officials wanted to put into Chinese markets were labeled "tribute," gifts humbly presented by barbarians. The country understood by China's port officials to be supplying the goods was approved and granted official status as a vassal. The licensed vassal received seals of office and "gifts," that is, trade items in exchange for those brought into China. Chinese officials dictated the number of ships the vassal state could send. No other ships were allowed to proceed upriver, discharge their goods, and take on Chinese products for the return journey.

In this statement of relations, Srivijaya was designated a vassal state in the sixth century C.E. Chinese records show tribute missions (trade) in the sixth, seventh, and eighth centuries and again in the tenth and eleventh. Srivijaya's "tribute" consisted of pepper, resins, rattans, ivory, plumes, birds' nests, turtles, sea cucumber, and mother-of-pearl; "gifts" from China's emperors to Srivijaya were industrial dyes, iron, ceramics, and silk. In the Chinese presentation, for seven hundred years a Sumatran state is recognized as a vassal, which acts as intermediary for many barbarian archipelago harbor states, bringing their tribute to China along with Srivijaya's own. In Chinese presentation, the honor of being a vassal is conferred by China, and it is taken away by China when the vassal proves itself unworthy. In 1380, Srivijaya was stripped of its special relationship to China and the honor of being China's vassal was transferred to the Javanese kingdom of Majapahit. Srivijaya drops out of the named Chinese world to become an anonymous, minor barbarian state represented to China by Java.

Chinese vagueness in the location and name of Srivijaya may be explained in two ways. First, the imperial government did not license Chinese ships and

Chinese pilots to make the long journey south before the early fifteenth century. Crews sailing between the archipelago and China were Malay, not Chinese. Second, in the imperial conception, the location of China in the center was what mattered; the exact location of a vassal state within the barbarian fringe was of lesser importance. Influenced by this imperial Chinese conception of history, historians of Indonesia describe Srivijaya as a trading state with movable headquarters (Palembang to Jambi), or as a collection of ports all using the name Srivijaya.

The wealth generated by trade allowed Srivijaya's rulers to present themselves in their immediate region in a different manner. China's vassal took on Indian signs and appeared to its neighbors as a participant in the regional culture. Srivijaya's rulers indulged in support of international scholars devoted to exploring Buddhist doctrines. Srivijaya's reputation as a center for the study of Buddhism enticed Chinese scholars bound for India to make the long detour south. In Srivijaya they furthered their knowledge of Sanskrit grammar and of doctrine in preparation for more advanced studies at Buddhist centers in India itself. Within Chinese imperial records there is a direct reference to Srivijaya as site of a community of one thousand students of Buddhism. The Chinese scholar-pilgrim I Ching (or I Tsing) was temporarily a member of that community in 671, studying Sanskrit in preparation for the next stage of his journey, which was India.

Srivijaya can also be placed within a context of archipelago societies and histories. In an Indonesian context, Srivijaya is the site of the earliest written form of Malay yet discovered. Chiseled on to stone tablets, dated to the years 682–686 C.E., in an Indic script, is the language of the peoples of the western archipelago. The texts represent the king directly addressing his Malay-speaking subjects. Adorned by titles of Indian royalty, he calls himself the granter of eternal peace, records his victories over other kingdoms, his gifts, and prayers for success, his vow to pursue the path to Buddhahood. Inscribed, too, are the king's subjects, their existence preserved in the form of oaths that leaders of river communities and sea populations swore, binding them as clients to the Srivijayan ruling family.

These stones also testify to professional writers who, in the seventh century, applied their knowledge of Indian alphabets to the problem of rendering in written form the language spoken by their employer and his subjects. In this, Srivijaya's significance in Indonesian histories far surpasses the arguments of scholars as to the exact location of Srivijaya's capital or the extent and duration of its rule over archipelago peoples.

SRIVIJAYA AND INDONESIA

In Indonesian histories Srivijaya represents a past forgotten, a past recreated by foreign scholars, and a past recovered and packaged by intellectuals of the nationalist movement for Indonesian identity within an Indonesian state. Until the published research of the French scholar Coedès in the 1920s, neither Sumatrans of the Palembang area nor Indonesians anywhere else had ever heard of Srivijaya. Coedès's discoveries and interpretations were published in the colony's Dutch and Indonesian-language newspapers. In the nationalist imagining, Srivijaya became evidence of early greatness, of archipelago unities, of Sumatran importance, a great empire of the western archipelago to balance Java's Majapahit in the east. Srivijaya and Majapahit were packaged to prove the unity of Indonesian peoples prior to the Dutch colonial state.

A discoverable history of archipelago ports, known in textbooks by the collective name Srivijaya, is therefore the product of several histories: of common people whose taxes in forest and sea products supported the desires of their rulers for international status; of mobile men who wrote in Sanskrit and Malay, built temples, and developed a community of scholarship in archipelago ports; of Chinese officials whose intellectual training led them to locate Srivijaya within the Chinese vision of world center and vassals; and of Chinese scholars whose interest in the real India led them to the invented Indias of the archipelago.

The common thing that all foreigners injected into Indonesian networks of exchange was the alphabet. Writing and knowledge stored in writing slipped across networks of exchange. Lines written into stone in Malay thirteen hundred years ago reinforce what objects tell in Indonesian histories in the time before writing. Stone graves and their contents tell us people perceived a great gap between ruler and ruled; that the duty of commoner to lord was limitless; that ordinary men and women labored to support ruling families and their devotional cults. Objects and writing on stone give evidence of the meshing of communities on land and on sea, and of the reshaping of landscape.

2

COMMUNITIES AND KINGDOMS

Histories Through Writing and Temples

Indonesian landscapes are the invention of modern times: densely settled cities and plains, hills stripped of forest, bird, and animal life to make way for farming, mining, factories, and housing complexes; suburban landscapes of high-rise office and apartment blocks; countryside crisscrossed by toll roads and telephone lines and dotted with Internet booths. The archipelago's humid climate and centuries of natural and human cataclysms have obliterated most vestiges of ancient pasts. Urban Indonesians may briefly confront a past they would never suspect was around them, by reading in the newspaper of old objects turned up in the plowing of a field or seeing remains of stone temples or cemeteries in modern settings. They may experience the ninth-century Borobudur temple on a school or holiday excursion; they may notice the rubble of Hindu temples in the vicinity of Muslim holy places that they visit. Remains of other ancient pasts are in mountains beyond the easy reach of car and tour bus. Little survives from Majapahit or Srivijaya, the two kingdoms most important to nationalist historians in the construction of Indonesia's past.

In allocating funds for excavation and preservation, Indonesia's colonial and republican governments have favored Hindu and Buddhist sites in Java. There is less emphasis on preservation of sites associated with the early history of Islam in Indonesia. Indonesian funds, public and private, pay for the construction of new mosques, not the exploration of old ones. The past which is preserved and presented for tourism and in textbook photographs appears detached from histories experienced by citizens of the world's largest Muslim country.

With no visible past, we turn again to things made of metal and stone. Unlike the machetes, axes, and drums that tell earliest histories, these objects have words written on them. The soil of Indonesia's mountainsides, forests, and plains has thrown up texts on stone, gold, copper, ceramic, and bone. Inscribed objects often exist outside of a context, not in relation to any other object or to the remains of an ancient building such as a palace, library or monastery. The oldest written text from Indonesia is chiseled on seven stone pillars, the only evidence that has survived of the fifth-century Kalimantan king, Mulavarman, and his subjects. The contents of inscriptions provide snapshots of moments in the ongoing life of a community. Inscriptions cannot be taken to describe centuries or society in all its classes and concerns. Nor do the materials preserving Indonesia's ancient texts represent all forms of writing surfaces. Animal skins, tree bark, and leaves survive only from modern times. Even more durable writing materials may disappear. Rainfall and humidity wear away stones, and lichens and plants may render their surfaces unreadable. Stones may also be hauled away by later generations to build temples in honor of new gods.

Inscribed objects retrieved from Indonesia's modern landscapes convey histories of communities and kingdoms that were located at intersections of land and sea routes. They tell histories of itinerant men, of their employers, of communities stratified by wealth, occupation, physical mobility, and gender. They give a history of intellectual exchange and innovation, and a history of communities interacting within the archipelago and with cities on Asia's mainland.

WRITING, LANGUAGE, AND SCRIPT

Four components of writing are language, writing system, writing material, and content. The writing systems in which Indonesian languages are rendered tell of a history of contact with other societies, of training and travel by professional writers, and of their links to skilled workers such as stonemasons and metalsmiths. A writing system suggests histories of religious and intellectual exchange and of political hegemony. It also reveals what certain classes in a community may be presumed to know.

In human history very few writing systems have been invented. Indonesian languages are rendered in the writing systems that were devised by speakers of Sanskrit, Arabic, and Latin. For instance, Malay, in its long history as a written language, has been rendered in Indic, Arabic, and Roman writing systems. Javanese can be found written in the Nagari and Pallava writing systems of India, in an Arabic writing system modified to incorporate Javanese sounds called *pegon,* and in the Roman alphabet. Indonesia's languages have never been expressed in Chinese characters, although Indonesian place-names, personal names, and names of trade goods appear in reports and histories written for China's imperial courts.

Three thousand inscriptions from ancient Indonesian communities have been found dating from the fifth through the ninth centuries of the Common Era. The earliest are on stone pillars. In many ancient Indonesian cultures upright stones, troughs of stone, rice-blocks, and chests were erected, some carved with animals and birds. What was new about the Kalimantan pillars was that their surfaces were covered in words, and they resemble devotional pillars erected in Indian kingdoms that were contemporary with Mulavarman. The language boasting of this king's exploits is Sanskrit, the literary language of India; the writing system is modeled on the Pallava script of south India.

Two hundred and fifty inscriptions on stone and copper plates record the commands of royalty in Java from the fifth to the fifteenth century C.E. The earliest are also in the Sanskrit language. From the ninth century the language of inscriptions is in an archaic language that is today known as Old Javanese. Some inscriptions from Java are written in the Nagari script, which originated in north India. The Nagari script announced royal decisions in Bali, too. The oldest inscription yet discovered in Bali dates from 882 C.E. and is in an archaic form of the Balinese language. From the tenth century inscriptions found in Bali are in a mixture of Old Balinese, Sanskrit, and Old Javanese. The language of all inscriptions in Bali after 1016 C.E. is Old Javanese.

Pillars erected in public places were intended to publicize the royal presence and to awe. They were larger than the men who quarried and dragged them to the space designated. Their texts were hammered and chiseled on to front, back, and sides of the stone surfaces in large, elongated letters. These pillars were the focal point of ceremonies in open spaces; they were the site for gatherings of kings' men to swear oaths. Their contents were fixed in one place; people had to go to the writing. Archipelago kings who wished to communicate in writing with distant officials employed not stonemasons, but metalworkers, men who knew how to heat metal and beat it into thin sheets. To write on such a medium, the scribe needed a finely pointed tool, not a chisel, and had to squeeze the contents into sheets ten to twenty-five centimeters wide and twenty to twenty-five centimeters in length by making the letters small and rounded. Most plates could carry four lines of text only, so, unless the text was very brief, it continued on several plates. These portable plates carried a ruler's specific message to an individual or a village.

All known inscriptions from Indonesia are issued in the name of kings. The voice of the king is the voice of the giver of orders. Subjects must obey, they must pay taxes, they must perform specified duties, they must swear oaths binding them to their promises. The other voice on metal and stone is that of the writer. The writer sings praises to the king, compares him to Indian gods. The writer carefully establishes the date of the act of writing according to an Indian system for calculating time.

TIME, CALENDARS, AND DATES

Individual lives are passed within different understandings of time and methods for calculating it. Early kings of Java maintained a calendar based on the Hindu Saka era. Inscriptions issued in their name record decrees by date and hour, using Sanskrit terms. It is not known if these terms and concepts of measured time were widely used outside the courts, or whether farmers and artisans used different terms for time and other methods of measuring it. The first year of the Saka era corresponds to 78 C.E. in the Western calendar. All Java's kings set time within this register until they ordered their subjects' lives to be governed by Muslim time. Sultan Agung of Mataram introduced the Islamic system of reckoning in 1636. In this system, year 1 marks Muhammad's flight from Mecca to Medina and is equivalent to 622 in the Western calendar. In the Christian calendar of Western Europe, year 1 was the birth of Jesus. In today's world Europe's calendar is used in internation contact and is known as Common time.

The historical pasts of Indonesians have taken place in the sacred time of Hindu, Buddhist, Muslim, and Christian dating systems. They are dated, in this text, in the Common time calendar system of Before Common Era (B.C.E.) and Common Era (C.E.).

Writers were specialists, the paid employees of people who could not read or write: kings and the royal establishment of princes, princesses, officials, and commanders of armies. The Indic writing systems employed by scribes working for kings in the Indonesian archipelago were also used by their contemporaries working for kings in Indian states, in Sri Lanka, and in kingdoms of mainland Southeast Asia. Between the fifth and eighth centuries the formation of letters on clay tablets, stone slabs, and copper plates all over this vast region shows great uniformity. The common style of writing suggests that a set of writers circulated among centers of pilgrimage, monasteries, and courts, selling and teaching their skill. Professional writers were mobile men who sought appointments at royal courts or who, through royal patronage, settled permanently in a religious community to pursue a life of study, teaching, and preservation of manuscripts by copying them.

Starting in the middle of the eighth century C.E., letters in inscriptions made in Java look different from the "handwriting" of inscriptions in Indian alphabets elsewhere in Asia. The development of a Javanese regional style suggests that, by the eighth century, scribal communities in Java were homegrown. Candidates for the post of professional writer at courts in Java did not have to travel to Indian kingdoms to learn how to write. They studied from locally trained teachers who taught from locally produced texts. Around this time also, professional writers who lived among speakers of Javanese began to experiment with turning their spoken language into written words using the Indian writing systems that they knew. Samples survive from the ninth century of royal commands issued in language that the king's subjects could comprehend. Writers also were consulting their Sanskrit dictionaries, grammars, and style books to produce poetry in Javanese that retold stories they had learned from Sanskrit literature.

While these developments suggest fewer professional writers traveling the South and Southeast Asian circuit, and more locally produced scholars, Java's professional writers remained in touch with developments in Indian philosophy, ritual life, and literature. For a thousand years, Sanskrit language and literature were studied in the Indonesian archipelago. Sanskrit texts were brought from India, were circulated with commentaries in Javanese, and inspired compositions in Javanese. At the same time, Sanskrit language continued to be used for original compositions. Texts were compiled as teaching aids; dictionaries and grammars were also written and copied for the teaching of Sanskrit far from its home base. In the fifteenth century, rituals in vogue in India were being described in poetry composed in Java in the Javanese language.

KAKAWIN: POETRY AND PRINCES

Kakawin are long narrative poems composed in Old Javanese. Writers used a literary language, rather than the way it was spoken daily. The poems are in verse form with rhythms and meters derived from Sanskrit literature. Kakawins were composed at the courts of central and east Java kings between the ninth and the sixteenth centuries. The stories, drawn from India's *Ramayana* and *Mahabharata,* told of gods, goddesses, demons, holy men, and royals transplanted into a Javanese landscape.

Commoners rarely appear in these stories. Royal men, or men who are incarnations of gods, undertake quests for objects, for missing relatives, or for special knowledge. In their wanderings they have erotic adventures, fight in great battles, and receive instruction from gods on the meaning of human existence, which they later pass on to wives and followers. The authors of kakawins compare their royal patrons to the gods, apologize for their weaknesses in composition, and describe the act of writing as a spiritual journey they hope will lead them to ultimate knowledge.

Royal marriage is a dominant theme of many kakawins, which gives insight into prevailing customs and values. The ideal royal marriage was between cousins; the bride should be a virgin. As a wife she should be a virtuous role model for other women through loyalty and faithfulness to her husband. Queens are praised for following their husbands on to the funeral pyre. Kakawins depict princes making love in gardens, sighing for a lost love, feasting, enjoying jewels, gold, and fine textiles. Princes have many women who openly display their passions. Kakawins from this era of Java place illicit love affairs in a world of elite literacy, where love poems and letters are royal pastimes. Women are celebrated as devoting their thoughts, their confidences, and their actions to men; they are not praised as mothers.

The content and purpose of inscriptions from Java match the writing material. Hammered into stone were verses praising a king's piety as worshipper of Hindu gods. Stone texts speak of foreign priests and record royal gifts. The portable texts, engraved on small metal plates, contain charters defining boundaries of villages and regulating markets. There are legal documents that allocate to religious foundations the right to collect taxes from designated villages and forbid royal tax officials (sometimes identified by name) from entering those villages. Other inscriptions record royal gifts of gold, silver, and cloth made to holy men and temples, to officials and their wives. Some inscriptions give accounts of performances of dance, singing, and theater and the foods consumed at feasts. These inscriptions carry the date of the transaction and the name of the king and of the senior officials responsible for passing down the king's orders. Sometimes the name of the scribe is also recorded.

Texts on stone and metal from central and east Java tell us about societies whose members were of many classes and occupations. A great chain of officials linked king to commoner. There were ministers, counselors, and military commanders who were in charge of guarding roads. There were heads of districts, market officials, tax collectors, and village elders, surveyors of woods, and astrologers. Village men appointed or honored by the king were granted Sanskrit titles. This act drew commoners into a court-centered culture.

Individual villagers owned and sold land for a house and land planted with rice and fruit trees, according to ninth-century inscriptions, and could be allocated a share of village common land for dry crops and pasturage for their animals. Taxes levied reveal an array of occupations among villagers. There were people who made dyes, dyed cloth, and were weavers; there were makers of clay pots, and of bamboo screens and mats; there were processors of sugar cane and coconut oil. Some villagers were snarers of birds and animals, others were animal breeders. There were smiths, carpenters, and workers in gold, iron, copper, and bronze. Other men operated ferries at river crossings. Porters transported goods between markets that rotated among clusters of villages according to the five-day Javanese week. There were boatmen and fishermen, makers of charcoal and lime, water carriers, cooks, and tailors. Other occupations mentioned are washers of corpses, medical specialists, chanters of songs, musicians, drummers, organizers of cockfights, and cooks. There were also elephant riders, pike men, organizers of hunts, and overseers of foreigners and prostitutes.

Inscriptions reveal that professional vendors operated in commercial networks linking village markets with markets in ports. They were buyers of buffaloes, cows, goats, pigs, and rice. Rice, cotton, clothing, metals, salt, salted fish, and cooking oils were exchanged in local markets. Professional traders bulked goods, moved, and resold them. Their customers were smaller traders who purchased goods for local sale and foreign traders who imported metals and ceramics. Inscriptions from tenth-century Java identify foreign traders as Asians from the mainland: Chams, Khmers, Mons, Bengalis, and South Indians. Their agents operated in Javanese villages and were subject to extra taxes. Foreigners are also often mentioned as collectors of the king's revenue.

From inscriptions we learn that people grew bananas, cucumbers, onions, garlic, and ginger, and raised fish, ducks, geese, and chickens. They made many alcoholic drinks from palm and sugarcane. At feasts they ate rice, chicken, and vegetables on palm leaves. At ceremonies all ranks of men and women were seated in a circle facing the consecration stone recording the king's piety and gifts. Wives of officials are listed as recipients of royal gifts. The official performing the ceremony pronounced the curse against potential breakers of the king's decrees. Inscriptions included the curse formula, which often covered many lines.

Inscriptions from the kingdom of Kediri (eleventh to thirteenth centuries) show that kings were devotees of Visnu and praised as incarnations of the god. They record the king granting honors and titles to officials who were religious advisers, military and naval commanders, and handlers of elephants and horses. Armies were equipped with lances and arrows. Villages had militias under local commanders and their own banners. The inscriptions also tell us that Kediri kings computed fines in gold, and levied taxes on the sale of cattle, metal goods, salt, and oil, and on performances of song and dance. From inscriptions comes evidence of the use of writing itself: a Kediri king had guidance manuals on religious affairs and on the art of ruling.

The evidence of the inscriptions is that a web of palaces, temples, monasteries, markets, and villages spread over Java's countryside. The Indian gods Siva, Visnu, and Brahma lived above Java's mountains; their servants and demons walked below. Only the temples remain to validate the thousand-year Javan world conjured up in the inscriptions. Archaeological investigations show that between 700 and 900 C.E. thirty-three temples and temple complexes were constructed on the southern slopes of Mount Merapi in central Java. Between the mountain and the Indian Ocean 218 sites of human activity (religious buildings, inscriptions) have been identified. Only one site near Prambanan is possibly the remains of a palace compound and settlement that included a bathing place and meditation caves. It is known as Kraton Ratu Boko (King Boko's palace).

The mountains of central Java provided the volcanic rocks used to construct buildings that housed images of the gods who lived above. Teak forests provided the construction material for kings' residences, monasteries, pilgrims' dormitories, and libraries. Forests also were the source of rattan, bamboo, and palm leaves for the flimsy huts of farmers and their village meeting halls. Housing of kings and commoners alike disintegrated in the tropical climate. The soil is made fertile by lava flows, so that the area has been continuously settled and farmed for over a millennium, and objects bearing stories of the past have therefore been lost. Many ruined temples require an expert to discern the form these buildings once took. Others, in better state of preservation, have been robbed. Their inner chambers and altars are denuded of statues; wall niches are empty; gods are headless.

The dynastic families who inhabited the palaces and controlled the harvests of central Java's farmers put their wealth at the disposal of priests, architects, and builders to create temples honoring Hindu gods or the Buddha. After men had prepared rice fields, the tasks of planting, weeding, harvesting, and cooking could be left to women and children. Male labor could be drawn off the fields and put to quarrying and transporting stones. The part-time farmer-laborers shaped the stones into blocks of uniform size and laid them according to the directions of architects. Artisans transformed the rock faces into stories in stone and hollowed out niches for the statues carved by sculptors. Inscriptions do not give names to the laborers and skilled carvers. They tell us the supervisors of those laborers were men who inhabited an intellectual world that encompassed Southeast Asia and India. Architects in central Java had copies of the Indian Sanskrit text *Manasara Silpasastra,* which specified that temples be erected on fertile soil near water sources. Java's temples were sited in view of mountain peaks, on high foundations approached by steep and deep stone steps.

The inscriptions record a royal dynasty in central Java called Sailendra, whose members worshipped the Buddha, and a royal dynasty of Sanjaya, which followed Hindu gods. Inscriptions record a marriage between the two royal houses in 846 C.E. In Javanese tradition, the Sailendras commanded the construction of the Borobudur temple, the Sanjayas built the many temples of the Prambanan group that are dedicated to Hindu gods and whose wall pictures tell stories of Prince Rama, his wife Sita, the demon king Ravana, and the monkey Hanuman. The Sanjayas were also builders of the Buddhist temples Sewu and Plaosan.

When a righteous king allocated villages to a religious foundation, he ensured endless toil for the inhabitants, yet his action also stimulated village economic life. Holy men performed temple rites to audiences, trained new cadres of scribes, and generated business for local residents by drawing in scholars and pilgrims who had to purchase lodging, food, and souvenirs. Large religious foundations were ringed by markets, villages, and rice fields. There were also shrines in hermitages and at sacred places in the landscape that were remote from human habitation and difficult for pilgrims to reach.

THE DIENG PLATEAU TEMPLES

Twelve and thirteen hundred years ago Javanese laborers built stone temples to Hindu gods high up in the mountains in a volcanic hollow called the Dieng Plateau. Dieng comes from the Sanskrit words Di Hyang and means "place of the gods." Worshippers made the long walk from villages further down the slopes to congregate around shrines that the priests entered, treading up steep stairs and over a high entrance stone to face the altar and its image. Small pipes in temple walls brought water for the priests to bathe the sacred images. Inside, in the semi-obscurity, and invisible to the common people outside on the terraces, priests invited the gods to descend to animate their statues and communicate their messages for humans.

Today, some of the temples have been reconstructed; foundations of others remain, their upper sections in ruins. Children play in and around them, women sit on sections of fallen shrines, flocks of sheep graze. Farmers have stripped the mountain slopes of trees right up to the summit to plant every centimeter with food crops. A new, white mosque, with Arabic architectural forms of dome and minaret, far more imposing in size than the ancient buildings, is positioned in line with Dieng temples named Bima and Gatotkaca. Around the mosque are the houses and shops of the modern village that supports it. Arabic prayers and Indonesian language sermons broadcast on loudspeakers are the contemporary form of religious liturgy heard in Dieng. Perhaps the mosque, at the western end of a line of Hindu temples, is intended as the natural progression in the development of religious understanding; possibly it is in opposition to the past of Java's Indic gods and princes.

Mountain temple complexes, individual small shrines, and the numerous large-scale plains temples crowding this region of Java are products of extraordinary labor, building resources, management, and vision. Dominating the picture of Javanese pasts is the Borobudur, an enormous temple dedicated to worship of the Buddha and designed by its architects to represent Buddhist doctrines through its form, the carvings on its walls, and its sculptures. It is a mountain of human manufacture built within a ring of volcanic mountains in central Java. Its construction was begun around 760 C.E. and completed in 830. The Borobudur represents the pious intent of a dynasty of kings who re-created Indian pilgrimage sites in Java, and who were rich and powerful enough to harness the labor of their subjects to achieve their goal over a period of seventy years.

All classes were organized into realizing their rulers' dream. Unskilled laborers leveled the earth for the temple's foundation and terraced the hillside to produce the temple's four square stories. They hauled more than one million

Dieng Plateau: Hindu temples and mosque. Temples to Hindu gods of the seventh and eighth centuries C.E. seem to point toward the twentieth-century mosque. Photo courtesy of Iskandar P. Nugraha.

blocks of stone to the site. Stonemasons cut and fitted the blocks, and skilled craftsmen carved the designs that form a continuous narrative along the four lower levels. Other workers built the open passageways that go around each level and the steep staircases that lead up to higher levels. Sculptors carved statues of the Buddha for placing in niches along the passageways and for the three open, circular levels. They built the stone latticework *stupas,* bell-shaped structures that represent the lotus where the Buddha sat to meditate. (In Buddhist temple architecture the lotus symbolizes the Buddha.) On the Borobudur latticed stupas enclose statues of seated Buddhas and make them objects to be perceived only indistinctly by the pilgrim, reflecting the human struggle for understanding. The central stupa forms the apex of the worshipper's climb. It is solid, with only a small niche (now empty) for a sacred object, possibly a relic of the Buddha. The styles of the Buddha sculptures depicting him teaching and meditating, and the recounting of lives of the Buddha in the 1,460 narrative panels follow the requirements of Buddhist art as exemplified in temples in India and in Buddhist manuals. So, present at the building site were specialists in Buddhist history, theology, art, and architecture, as well as the overseers of all the different kinds of workers, and the organizers of food and work schedules.

The narrative panels tell the life of the sixth-century B.C.E. Buddha through a stylized rendering of the daily life of the privileged of eighth-century Java. The panels show gods, royals, their attendants, but contain few pictures of the daily life of laborers. The vital sea highway, which made contact with world centers of Buddhism possible and is so central to Indonesian histories, is only hinted at in two panels on which are carved masted ships with sails.

The Borobudur belongs to that era of Java's history when Indian civilization was being remade in a Javanese landscape. After the Borobudur was completed there was no need for the pious to make the long journey to India to worship at sites associated with the Buddha. The pilgrim made instead a shorter physical expedition and, by walking around and up the temple-mountain, made a symbolic journey into the spiritual meanings of the Buddha's teaching. Students of Buddhism could also consult texts composed in Java. The oldest Buddhist text found in central Java, written on gold plates sometime in the seventh or eighth centuries C.E., explains the Buddhist doctrine of human suffering, rebirth, and release. Its simplified Sanskrit language made it accessible to monks at the beginning of their studies, but the text also included mystical signs that advanced students of religion could ponder to accelerate their progression in knowledge and insight. A tenth-century text attaches explanations in Javanese to the Sanskrit verses of Buddhist doctrine.

Like modern tourists, visitors to the Borobudur purchased souvenirs to mark their pilgrimage and aid in their devotions. Many of these miniature clay models of stupas and small clay tablets stamped with Buddha images have been dug up near the Borobudur. They were possibly made by the women potters shown in a wall carving on the temple smoothing clay with a paddlelike tool, while men bring them fresh supplies.

THE BOROBUDUR: "DISCOVERY AND NEGLECT," RESTORATION AND SIGNIFICANCE

When Java's ruling classes converted to Islam they diverted tax revenues to the building of mosques and Islamic schools and for teachers. Java's Hindu-Buddhist temples ceased to be the focus of organized, public worship. They fell into disrepair when the priests were gone and kings no longer assigned workers to their maintenance. Creepers and trees grew in temple courtyards and passageways, dust and dirt covered the carvings, and rubble accumulated.

For the Muslim population, the temples retained an aura of illicit magical potency and connection to spirit forces of the pre-Islamic past. Rebels against Java's Muslim kings went to the Borobudur to gather spiritual strength. Frederik Coyett is the first European known to have visited the Borobudur. Understanding the temple to be abandoned, he had some of the Buddhas removed in 1733 and transported to the house he was constructing in Batavia. (The house later became the possession of Jakarta's Chinese community which made it into a temple for its Buddhas.)

The Borobudur and other temples from Java's pre-Islamic past were objects of great interest to British officials who operated European rule in Java between 1811 and 1816. The design and decorative motifs resembled temples the British had explored in India, and appeared to be of no concern to Java's ruling classes. Nine centuries had passed since the Borobudur was an active site of scholarship and worship. It took 200 men six weeks to cut and burn the vegetation that enveloped the temple-mountain and to clear away the dirt and rubble to reveal the shape of the structure and its carved panels. The Borobudur became a place of secular pilgrimage (tourism) for adventurous Europeans; in 1844 a teahouse was built on the top-most stupa that had once sheltered a relic of the Buddha.

The world's largest Buddhist monument was of peculiar interest to Siam's King Chulalongkorn, who ruled as a Buddhist monarch. After a visit to the excavated site in 1896, he asked his Dutch hosts for souvenirs. Eight cartloads of sculptures, wall panels, carved animals, and guardian kala heads were cut out of the Borobudur and shipped to Bangkok, where they remain in the national museum.

Related to the notion of discovery is that of neglect. Europeans convinced themselves that the Borobudur and other artistic treasures were left to decay because of the ignorance or laziness of Java's upper classes.

Java's elite did devote attention and money to the upkeep of holy sites, but only to those in use. Europeans could not pursue an interest in mosque design and embellishment because in Javanese conceptions of Islam, the admission of non-Muslims would pollute a holy place. For this reason, European scholarly interest was channeled to Java's older, pre-Islamic past.

The Borobudur was accorded world heritage status and restored with international funds from 1974 to 1983. Today, schoolgirls and their teachers, dressed in Indonesian versions of Islamic clothing, visit the Borobudur as part of history classes. Schoolboys use the latticed stupas as trashcans for their drink bottles.

Chulalongkorn, Siam's King Rama V, visits the Borobudur, 1896. The Buddhist king and his suite were accompanied by the twin pillars of colonial rule, Dutch civil servants and Javanese royalty. Photographic Archive, Royal Institute of Linguistics and Anthropology, Leiden, No. 9890. Photo courtesy of the KITLV.

The Borobudur was not constructed in isolation. Shrines housing a single large statue of the Buddha were also erected close by. The many temples consecrated to Hindu gods of the Prambanan complex also consumed huge amounts of labor. Surrounding the three principal temples, each built to enclose an image, were hundreds of smaller temples in regular lines. Their wall panels recount the Indian Rama stories in a Javanese landscape teeming with buffaloes, snakes, mice, geese, trees, densely entwining leaves, and flowers.

HUMAN SACRIFICE IN EARLY JAVA?

Excavations conducted on the site of the Prambanan complex of temples, dedicated to Siva and other Hindu gods, and in the grounds of Candi Sojiwan, a Buddhist temple a few kilometers to its south, revealed the existence of human bones. Deep shafts beneath the pedestals of statues were found to contain ritual deposits of gold and copper plates, the burned bones of animals and hens, coins and gems, and human remains. At the time of the excavations in the early twentieth century, scant attention was paid to the human skeletons. Human sacrifice did not sit with the idealized view of Java's ancient past cherished by Dutch archaeologists and their Javanese pupils and colleagues. The temples were thought to be funerary monuments built over the burned bones of kings.

Archaeologists at the time, impressed by the artistry of architecture and sculpture and their relation to Indian civilization, had no mental framework in which to consider the discoveries. The bones were removed by excavators, who left no description of how the bodies were placed. Contemporary scholars, more interested in the "indigenous" than the borrowed, are willing to argue that the human remains are evidence of sacrifice. They speculate that ancient Javanese sought to appease spirits before construction of buildings began and that this indigenous concept was incorporated by royal priests into Hindu rituals. Interpretation of archaeological evidence is bound to time and academic trends.

In the tenth century the palaces of wealthy kings and their temples were to be found in east Java. Temple-building on the scale of the previous two hundred years ended in central Java. The lives of central Java's inhabitants went unrecorded after around 900 C.E. because no authority drew on their labor to build temples and boast on stone slabs or copper plates of its actions.

Many of the temples in east Java's flatter landscape are constructed of bricks that are smaller than the building blocks of Mount Merapi's temples. The surviving temples are also smaller in conception: they enclose or set off a statue of a Hindu god or goddess, or they are memorial temples for deceased kings and queens, erected by their successors. The sculptors commissioned to carve funeral portraits in stone gave royals the same features, costume, and gestures that were conventional in portraying Visnu or the Buddhist goddess of mercy. The language preserved in contemporary inscriptions equates royals with divine beings.

East Java royalty consumed less of their subjects' time, energies, and resources in their temple building projects. Perhaps the population whose labor they could command was smaller than that living in the villages of central Java, or their labor was directed to a greater variety of tasks. The villages supporting central Java's early temples were all on the southern slopes of Mount Merapi, between it and the coast. Java's south coast has no harbors offering safety from the dangerous riptides of the Indian Ocean. Central Java's rulers concentrated on reproducing India in Java, on making travel unnecessary. They directed their wealth in labor and crops to building and supporting temple communities in their home base. By contrast, east Java's kingdoms were oriented to the sea-lanes of the archipelago. Their location on the Brantas River connected them to the north coast with its natural harbors, busy ports, and calm seas. East Java's kings exported the wealth of their subjects' labor and fostered international commerce. This orientation in the tenth century wrote east Java communities into discoverable histories and returned Javanese communities to the dynamic consequences of links between land and sea.

The carvings on walls of east Java temples, such as the twelfth-century Panataran, show something of this society. Around the chief figures of divine beings, royals, and their counselors are wheeled carts, houses, men riding horses using saddle and stirrups, and ordinary people enjoying fruit in the shade of thatched roofs supported by posts. The women, their hair in buns, wear long-sleeved blouses that reach below the knees and partially cover patterned skirts. A way for today's tourists to retrieve Indonesian histories, these wall panels also attracted visitors when they were freshly created. Temple guardians could conduct pilgrims around and through a religious building, explaining the meaning of each panel, giving instruction on the names of gods depicted, their special identifying characteristics, and their teaching. The phallic *lingga* symbol that is incorporated into temple design and embellishment represented the life force of the god Siva. The horrors of hell could be impressed on those who looked at panels showing torture by fire and water. Carvings of worshippers demonstrated to pilgrim crowds the proper way to sit and pay respect to divine beings. Good conduct and social relations were made plain to ordinary men and women who gazed at smiling queens bowing to royal husbands. Perhaps they saw themselves in all the servants shown in stone waiting, bringing trays of fruits, tending animals, and marching into battle. The scholars and royal establishment could engage in learned discussion of Buddhist philosophy, search difficult texts for hidden meanings, and enact esoteric rites to attain mystical union with the gods. Ordinary people (whose labor supported all this) could gain a personal understanding of Hinduism or Buddhism through visiting, seeing, and listening.

Few in ancient Indonesian societies could read, but everywhere there was writing, set down in verse to be chanted aloud. Professional singers, dancers, and musicians performed in open public places before audiences of royals, officials, attendants, and villagers. Troupes traveled the temple circuit according to the calendar of feast days; they followed royal processions to provide entertainment that drew songs and plays from Javanese translations of India's Sanskrit literature. Itinerant professionals spread a web of court-centered culture among the villagers who worked to support royalty and religious communities. Chanted poetry celebrated kings as gods and described their adventures in battle and love. Such poetry might validate a king's right to the throne in the minds of officials. For common people the poetry circulated a vocabulary and set of ideas about royalty that stressed the almost divine qualities of their rulers and their limitless rights, their personal beauty, and their opulent style of living. At the same time, the villages provided the court with new recruits for performing groups. The court provided an escape from hard labor in quarries for talented village youth; the court's performing companies also felt the impact of village tastes and styles.

In Java the adaptation of Indian writing systems to reproduce Javanese words and sounds was called *kawi.* Scribes employed in Javanese courts became the agents for transmitting Indic scripts and heritage of Hindu and Buddhist cultures to communities in other parts of the Indonesian archipelago. In this way Javanese scribes reproduced the intellectual role that brahmins in the international circuit had performed for them. They disseminated skills,

THE PANJI TALES

Folk memory of east Java kingdoms is preserved in Java, Bali, Banjarmasin, and Palembang through the Panji tales. In these stories there are four kingdoms—Kuripan, Daha (another name for Kediri), Gegelang, and Singhasari—and each kingdom is ruled by a brother. The eldest of the brothers is the king of Kuripan. His son, Raden Inu, is betrothed to his cousin, the princess of Daha, who disappears. Raden Inu adopts the name Panji and goes in quest of his missing princess. After many adventures the pair is finally reunited and marries. Panji represents a Javanese conception of the ruler as prince and warrior, a man able to attract followers, and a patron of Javanese arts.

knowledge, scholarly vocabulary, and tastes by their own travels, by their appointments at distant courts, by their production of texts, and by their schools. Many Indonesian communities first wrote their languages in scripts derived from kawi. They acquired parts of Sanskrit civilization, not directly from Indians or from Indian states, but from Javanese itinerant professionals. As a result, Java became important in Indonesian histories for its cultural and political impact. Java is inscribed in the local histories of many archipelago communities as the source of their traditions and forms of statecraft. Java's greatest impact was on Bali.

The island of Bali was one of the stopping points on the sea highway that connected eastern Indonesia's islands to ports in India. An ancient exchange of Indonesian spices and fragrant woods for Indian pottery brings Bali's north coast into world history. Archaeologists date the oldest settlements there to the first and second centuries C.E. Early evidence of human settlement at Gilimanuk on the northwest coast of Bali reveals a society that lived from fish, shellfish, domesticated pigs, dogs, and poultry, and that hunted wild pigs, birds, rats, and bats. Members produced earthenware pots in which they stored foods. They also created pots as receptacles for the burial of high-ranking members of the community. They gained metal goods such as axes and drums, pottery and glass beads through this contact with the sea highways.

Participating in the international set, Bali's chiefs appropriated the Indian title maharaja and employed some of the region's itinerant professionals to record their decrees. Inscriptions link royalty to tax revenues from rice fields, orchards, gardens, grasslands, animal breeding, and cock fighting. The Balinese, while surrounded by sea, were not the archipelago's sailors. Their web of society spread into the varied habitats of Bali, the dry north and east zones, and the central and fertile southern plains where crops were raised in both irrigated and dry fields.

Bali's chiefs employed the region's Sanskrit specialists to write down their king's commands in Old Balinese. These inscriptions, engraved on copper plates, date from 882 C.E. But the site of their island, just two and a half kilometers from Java's easternmost point, knitted the Balinese into the cultural and political world of Java. By the eleventh century most inscriptions found in Bali are in Old Javanese and they are written in kawi. Java's language superseded Balinese as the language of administration, religion, philosophy, and literature. Balinese writers copied Java's literature and composed original works in the language of Java's courts. Manuals on Sanskrit vocabulary and grammar from Bali preserve older versions that had been compiled in Java. The manuals list Sanskrit words for animals and plants, and Sanskrit epithets for gods, with their translation into Old Javanese; some give Balinese equivalents of words in Old Javanese; some set out the many grammatical forms of Sanskrit nouns and pronouns. For literary writers, these manuals provided a source of elevated words to dignify and embellish their texts. They also helped transport Java's Sanskrit-inspired literary culture further east to Balinese colonies in Lombok, and to maintain a Hindu inspiration in modern Indonesia's cultures.

WRITING ON LONTAR AND TREE BARK

The tradition of writing on lontar leaf is at least a thousand years old in Bali. Lontar resembles copper plates because the leaf produces a writing material of long, thin strips that contain typically four lines of writing. Sometimes the text consists of two lines of writing and drawings illustrating the contents.

The production of writing material from the palmyra palm was, until the twentieth century, a cottage industry. Mature leaves were harvested during the dry season, which occurs in Bali between May and October. A long process of washing, drying, pressing, smoothing, trimming, and polishing produces a medium for incising with an iron stylus. A black paste is smeared over the leaves, then wiped off, leaving the writing blackened and more easily seen against the brown color of the leaves. The leaves are perforated with three holes and bound together to keep the pages in sequence. Hard covers, often decorated, protect the leaves. Lontar manuscripts are placed in boxes or bags and kept in temples, special pavilions, or an offering shelf in the northeast corner of the owner's house.

Lontar manuscripts exist in Sanskrit, Old Javanese, and Modern Balinese languages. They can be quite short business documents, recording names of village council members, regulations on rice cultivation and irrigation, and instructions for cock-fighting. Some contain diplomatic correspondence between Bali's courts. There are manuals of rituals, medical knowledge, and explanations of the divination properties of letters of the alphabet. Longer texts recount family genealogies and the descent of kings, histories of kingdoms, and stories that derive from Indian epics.

Throughout the archipelago communities have made lontar from the leaves of various palm trees, such as the sugar and coconut palms which grow in rainy areas, as well as from leaves of the palmyra from the drier regions of the eastern archipelago. Some villages also produced a coarse paper from the inner bark of trees. Other writing materials were bamboo and the treated skins of goats. Letters were written on these materials either with a knife or with a pen fashioned from the rib of a leaf or bamboo. Writing with a pen required the manufacture of inks from soot and tree resins. Ink pots and book stands were also necessities for the professional writer. Paper made from tree bark was flexible for rolling into scrolls. Stories and illustrations were penned on scrolls, which were slowly unfolded to show listeners the pictures as the reader chanted the text, often to the accompaniment of a drum.

Palm leaves, best used in strips, were suitable for the regular lines of the kawi script. In reading sessions which have been observed and recorded over the past three hundred years, lontar leaves are laid flat on a low table or offering tray when they are read. A group of men take turns to recite or sing the contents and explain its meaning in everyday language. Rituals of making offerings, burning incense, and reciting special prayers precede reading as well as the copying of texts. Lontar manuscripts have a lifetime of about two hundred years. Damaged texts are disposed of by cremation.

The Balinese lontar tradition persisted into the twentieth century. In addition to copying and recopying old texts produced in Bali, Balinese writers preserved texts originally composed in Java by this same process of copying. Balinese lontar preserve selected texts from a Javanese cultural form after it ceased to exist in Java. Balinese lontar remind us that writing on perishable tree leaves existed side by side with writing on stone and metal. The surviving inscriptions from Java, therefore, probably represent only one part of a much larger written record.

Java's adventurers, professional writers, and craftsmen traveled west as well as east. The distinctive skills that they possessed made them attractive to local chiefs everywhere. In some cases, adventurers displaced local chiefs or married into their families. They represented themselves in the new style, using the Sanskrit titles of royalty in circulation in the archipelago and participating in the royal devotional cults fashionable in Java. The web of this Javanized Indian culture spread even into the mountains of central Sumatra. High in the Minangkabau heartland are brick shrines and thirty-five inscriptions on stone in kawi dating to the late fourteenth century. Shrines and inscriptions record the existence of a community of skilled workers and of laborers supporting a man who advertised his international connections through his reign name, Sri Maharaja Adityavarman, and through his patronage of a Tantric sect of Buddhism. He also added being Javanese as an ingredient in local conceptions of what made a person royal by locating his ancestry in Java. All later Islamic kings of Sumatra and of the Malay Peninsula, Sarawak, and Brunei claimed descent from Adityavarman and from Java's royal families. In April 2002

A Balinese Lontar telling the Nawaruci story. Sonobudoyo Museum, Yogyakarta L 13 1. Photo courtesy of the Lontar Foundation.

Adityavarman's Minangkabau heir recalled his ancestor's connection with Java by conferring on Yogyakarta's Sultan Hamengkuwono X the Sumatran title of Yang Dipertuan Maharajo Alam Sakti (Great Lord of the Universe).

The oldest evidence of sedentary communities on Java's north coast and of writing in Java actually comes from the western end of the island, from the region called Sunda. Makers of stone axes had a product valued by groups living in and close to rain forests who needed axes to fell trees before they could clear undergrowth by fire and sow seeds in rough clearings. Trade in axes brought west Java into regional trade networks. By the fifth century C.E. local leaders were using their wealth to emulate the set of men represented by Mulavarman in Kalimantan. Artisans in the pay of King Purnavarman recorded on stone, in the Pallava script, the royal gift of one thousand cows to the king's brahmins. Six hundred years later professional writers, living among communities of Sundanese speakers and employed by their kings, used a (now archaic) form of the Sundanese language. Like scribes at courts in central and east Java, they had turned from Sanskrit to the language of their region, aided by the model of kawi. The earliest inscription on stone in Old Sundanese written in kawi dates from 1030.

Sundanese scribes followed established trends in Javanese courts. They, too, made royal commands portable by writing on copper plates. The oldest examples found date to the fourteenth century and provide evidence for the Sundanese kingdom of Pajajaran (1344–1570s). Sundanese scribes also used tree leaves as a writing medium for many purposes. They explained Hindu and Buddhist beliefs and told stories of heroes and heroines of the kingdoms of Galuh and Pajajaran, and of a royal envoy who could fly through the air on missions to other states. Scribes constructed prestigious genealogies for leading families and set down calculations for auspicious times to undertake journeys and to marry. They preserved compilations of customs, myths, and magical sayings on lontar, charms for rain, for personal protection, curing, and love magic.

From Sundanese lontars also come evidence of female literacy. It is usual to suppose that those who could read and write in early Indonesian communities were men. The itinerant scribal class was male, and officials appointed to assess royal domains and collect taxes were men. But a lontar of thirty-seven leaves in Old Sundanese has been preserved whose author gave her name as Buyut Ni Dawit. She was a member of a religious community headed by Ni Teja Pura Bancana. Such communities were celibate, gave instruction to girls, and provided a refuge for palace women who were losers in court politics and a place for elite women to retire. They did not produce itinerant professionals.

When a kingdom's economic fortunes declined, a major port was reduced to a backwater and an existence that cannot now be discovered. A religious community, cut off from pilgrim tourists and deprived of a steady source of income from villages and royal gifts, dispersed. An impoverished royal family unable to employ professionals could no longer advertise its kingdom's advantages or leave a record more exact than what folk memory could preserve. Similarly, when royal patrons switched their allegiance to Islam or Christianity, establishments of kawi-writing scholars dispersed to seek employment elsewhere. They lost their skills when these could no longer be put to profitable use. Another mini-India gradually disappeared from the map of the big trader and the traveling brahmin.

By 1000 C.E. people lived everywhere across the archipelago, on land and sea, on the coast, on the plains, and in the high interior. Some communities moved seasonally across land and seascapes, while villages of farmers were tied to one place by forms of agriculture, by sentiment, and by powerful rulers. There were communities organized politically under kinship leaders, communities run by a handful of powerful families, and communities where hereditary monarchies had evolved. The most visible ancient Indonesian communities were those supporting kings, writers, and builders. So early Indonesian histories are staged in specific sites in Java, Bali, Sumatra, and Borneo, while all the islands to Java's north and east seem dark and empty, waiting for their history to begin. It is possible to discern outlines of a past that covers and connects archipelago societies by considering shipbuilding, farming, and housing. These fundamentals of daily life suggest how ordinary people lived and allow us to fill coast and interior of Indonesia's islands with peoples and their histories.

Before the nineteenth century, water routes were more important than land routes for the transport of people and their goods, and for establishing intellectual connections. A great variety of craft ferried people across rivers and carried them downstream to ports and across seas. Many peoples adapted to an archipelago environment by living on water, rather than on land. Bugis, Makasar, Mandar, Bajau, and Butung peoples, whose homelands are in and around Sulawesi, and Madurese, whose homeland is off Java's northeast coast, are Indonesia's maritime peoples. They have established colonies outside their original heartlands in many places in the archipelago and the Malay Peninsula, and historically performed sea functions for land-bound settlements in the archipelago.

Twelfth-century seafarers who entered the Straits of Melaka from the eastern end might spot a large inscription carved into the granite cliff alongside a series of vertical indentations. Some may have anchored off this point on the northwest coast of Karimun Besar Island in the Riau archipelago to take in water from a freshwater well, and to venerate the indentations as footprints of the Buddha. The inscription is in Sanskrit in the Nagari script of north India, and its carver called himself the "pundit from Bengal, the Mahayanist." Indonesian pilots plotted their course across the seas by reference to the stars, cliffs, promontories, coastal shrines, and unusual landmarks. Perhaps they clarified their position in the seas after sighting this inscription.

Indonesian ships were divided between those which carried people and goods and those which were specialized warships. Ships for trade stored goods in baskets, straw bags, and clay jars under mats of woven rattan. Markets were at river mouths where they opened into sheltered bays dotted with small islands and sandbars. Such markets were the first sight and destination of the sailor. Flat-bottomed boats or war canoes could sail right in to shore to disgorge cargo to waiting porters, or troops. Larger vessels anchored in deeper water in the bays, sheltered among the islands, and sent representatives and cargo ashore in small row boats. In some places local men rowed out to where larger ships were anchored and traded directly in foodstuffs and fresh water, and offered services, such as laundry and sex. Markets on shore were both at the landing site, where goods could be bought right off small boats or from local women with goods in baskets, and inside the town's walls, where the more substantial, covered stalls were. Markets were also at ferry crossings, at tollgates, near shrines and religious foundations, in district capitals, and at rural industrial sites for metalworking, lime making, and pottery.

Ship construction sites were located where suitable stands of timber, sheltered bays, and skilled workers—woodcutters, carpenters, shipwrights, sail makers—were to be found. Before 1500, large boats in the archipelago were imported from Bamo (in today's southern Myanmar). Archipelago centers of boat construction were in Bira in southeastern Sulawesi, in Java's teak forest districts of Rembang, Lasem, and Juwana, and in Aceh. Several factors shaped boat construction: an environment of islands linked by shallow seas and strong, predictable winds, and terrains of swamp, jungle, and mountain that made sea routes more efficient than land routes. Indonesian boat builders lashed planks of wood together with rattan ropes or bound them with wooden pegs. They sealed gaps between planks with resinous pitch. They hollowed boats from tree trunks, and transported to markets logs lashed together and floated on rivers as rafts. Already in the first millennium C.E. archipelago boat builders were constructing double outrigger canoes, sea craft with rudder, a support mast, and a fixed sail. This kind of ship can be seen carved in a wall panel of the Borobudur and in stone reliefs at Lau Biang, north Sumatra (dated to around 400–700 C.E.). By the sixteenth century Indonesian shipping included large oceangoing vessels that could carry up to one thousand men and many kilograms of goods. They had between two, three, or four masts and sails woven from rattan.

In the eastern archipelago ships were especially adapted for naval patrols, raids, and policing the seas. War boats of the rulers of Ternate were called *kora-kora.* They were powered by rowers (slaves or men paying their taxes through their labor), making the kora-koras independent of winds and also capable of sailing against the wind. Individual boats had a crew of two hundred men. Often fleets of kora-koras with crews of two thousand were assembled to police subject territories which, in this environment of clusters of small, mountainous islands, were situated across expanses of water. Because of their construction, these war ships could maneuver among shoals, sandbanks, reefs, and islands, and against currents and whirlpools. They were able to outperform European ships until the introduction into Indonesian waters of flat-bottomed, steam-powered ships in the 1850s.

WINDS AND WIVES

Winds blow between land and sea along Java's north coast, making year-round sailing possible, but for inter-island connections shippers were dependent on the cycle of the monsoon winds. From May to October, winds blowing from Australia sent Indonesian craft on voyages from the eastern archipelago to Java, Sumatra, and Melaka. This period coincides with the dry season in Java when farmers were harvesting and surrendering rice to collectors who moved it to ships. From November to April winds blew ships from Melaka to Java. Sailing time between Melaka and west Java was four weeks.

Sales, purchases, repairs, provisioning, and sailing times had to proceed according to a timetable dictated by the winds, so individual boats were anchored for weeks at a time. As a result, archipelago ports contained a migratory class of captains and crews. Wealthy traders established houses in the major ports of their operations and installed a wife in each port to manage household and business. Crewmen rented temporary wives during their brief stays or used the more limited services of prostitutes.

Rented women were slaves, part of the great mass of individuals who moved along trade routes to take up jobs in ports. By contrast, a wife was the daughter of a locally established family. Marriage to such a woman gave the foreign trader local in-laws. Brothers-in-law and fathers-in-law provided foreign traders with contacts for local commerce. Male relatives supplied assistants and partners and were a source of knowledge on local prices and specialties. Polygamy in this context was not a harem of many women, but separate households in different ports along the business route of the trader. Each household was headed by a wife who lived in a circle of her own kin and whose business interests were related to her husband's.

Throughout the archipelago, in agricultural and urban economies, semi-nomadic males were supported by fixed women. Women and children were home-based; they raised vegetables and rice, or were market sellers; they had part-time husbands and fathers. Men spent many months at sea or made trading expeditions on foot. This division of labor is often called *rantau.*

Trade routes had exposed scattered communities in the archipelago to metal objects and to knowledge of metalworking since around 500 B.C.E. Smiths who created metal objects out of gravel-bearing ores through fire, intense heat, and special tools perhaps seemed to possess magical powers. The objects they created, such as krises, gongs, machetes, and axes were in demand everywhere. In the late fifteenth century, traders from Java introduced to the Maluku Islands metal goods such as coins, krises, and gongs. Other seaborne traders had been visiting the Onin region of southwestern New Guinea at least since the fourteenth century, exchanging axes for bark from the massoy tree. Archipelago peoples used oil prepared from massoy bark in industries such as fixing dyes and making medicines, perfumes, and cosmetics. New Guinea coastal villagers were introduced into Indonesian histories through this exchange of a forest product for metal goods. The exchange allows a glimpse of Indonesian pasts in western New Guinea and in the small, seemingly isolated, island clusters of the eastern archipelago. Eastern Indonesia sailors performing the sea linkage for the land-bound cultures of New Guinea also introduced New Guinea products to international markets.

Sailors and traders carried food supplies for their personal consumption on long sea journeys, as well as for selling to archipelago communities that lacked reliable, year-round food supplies. They brought seeds, agricultural techniques, and knowledge of processing and cooking foods to archipelago

BIRDS OF PARADISE

The brilliantly colored plumage of the bird of paradise, native to New Guinea, was used for headdresses to identify a tribe's fighting men. Beyond New Guinea the feathers entered the collections of exotic goods that kings amassed as a sign and consequence of their wealth. They were part of the treasures of eighth-century kings in Sumatra and China. Trade in the plumes can be traced as far back as the first century B.C.E., and it continued until the 1920s, when the birds were almost extinct and fashions had changed.

Hunters in the area of New Guinea known as Bird's Head captured the brightly colored male bird of paradise by shooting it with bow and arrow. The entire bird was then skinned and its legs, skull, and coarse wing feathers removed. The inner cavity was treated with wood ash and the prepared bird was smoke-dried. Birds for export were stored in sealed bamboo tubes or palm leaf wrappings and hung near fireplaces to protect them from damage by insects. Sailors from Indonesia's Aru and Kai Islands, which lie off the Bird's Head promontory, exchanged baked sago loaves for the plumes.

By the time Portuguese traders sailed the seas of eastern Indonesia in 1512, they were witnessing intricate trade networks. Traders from the Aru and Kai islands brought bird of paradise feathers, parrot skins, and aromatic tree barks, together with their own locally processed sago loaves, to Banda. The Bandanese consumed sago as a food staple. They added the New Guinea products to their own nutmegs, coconuts, and fruit, then transported this cargo to the Maluku islands. Traders from south China and Indian ports sailed to Melaka and Java to pick up spices, aromatic woods, pearls, and feathers for imperial sales agents in China and markets in India. Arab traders who visited Indian ports carried the bird of paradise feathers and other jungle and sea produce to markets in the Middle East and, eventually, Europe. By the thirteenth century the feathers that formed the headdress of New Guinea warriors also adorned the helmets of knights in Europe's courts.

peoples who farmed by cultivating some crops in gardens and gathering food from trees and bushes growing wild. Cultivated seeds, unlike those growing in the wild, do not have to compete with other plants, leading to greater yields. Where rice was cultivated, for example, larger populations were possible. Until the sixteenth century, local and world demand for pepper, cloves, mace, and nutmeg could be met by gathering and processing plant produce that grew in the wild as a part-time occupation. Increased demands led archipelago rulers to organize the cultivation of clove trees and pepper bushes in gardens by a new kind of laborer. In place of the farmer who gathered a set amount of nuts for tax payment was the imported slave laborer or increasing numbers of female and child laborers to tend pepper bushes and dry the fruits of spice trees.

Plants native to one region of the world were disseminated to others by trade, conquest, travelers, and immigrants. Plants were often known in a region, but their systematic cultivation did not occur for many centuries, or else was developed in another region. Experiments in acclimatizing plants, seed selection, and cultivation techniques are part of the recorded history of Indonesia in its relationship to Europe. The same principles applied to plants indigenous within Asia and whose cultivation spread to the archipelago before the era of recorded history. This process was the result of the seafaring, commerce, and colonization of islands in the archipelago by Indonesian sailors.

PLANTS AND PLACE

Plants native to Indonesia are nutmeg, cloves, ginger, sago palm, and bananas. Bananas have been cultivated by archipelago farmers since 1500–1000 B.C.E. Many of the plants important in Indonesian histories as sustenance for local populations and as exports are native to other parts of Asia, Europe, the Middle East, and the Americas. Names of the farmers who tried raising food plants native to China (such as rice, a staple for most Indonesians today) or India (pepper) two thousand and more years ago cannot be known. In this ancient Asian history of experimental farming India is important as the source of many plants established in Indonesian landscapes. Indian plants had a dynamic impact on early Indonesian economies, just as Indian alphabets had on intellectual histories. Cotton, grown for clothing fiber, originated in India and was introduced into Java around 300 B.C.E. It later spread to north Bali, south Sulawesi, and Selayar. The palmyra palm, used for the manufacture of paper, was cultivated by the third millennium B.C.E in southern India and spread into the eastern archipelago. Pepper was domesticated in its native Mumbai region of India by 1000 B.C.E and cultivated in the western Indonesian archipelago from around 600 B.C.E Sugar, native to Southeast Asia, was cultivated by the third or second millennium B.C.E

Diffusion of plants is not always direct. In Indonesian histories, Europeans introduced coffee bushes from Yemen in the early eighteenth century, breadfruit from Polynesia, and cinnamon which is native to Sri Lanka. (Unlike the early history, the dates and names of many European introducers of foreign species are known, and experiments in cultivating introduced plants in Indonesia can be studied.) In the early twentieth century the Dutch also introduced mulberry bushes, which are native to southern China, to hilly areas of Sulawesi, especially Soppeng. European vegetables such as cabbage, carrots, lettuce, and legumes, and fruits such as strawberries and apples were brought to the archipelago, raised in hill stations, and entered the diet of local communities. From the Americas Europeans brought food plants which form the core of today's Indonesian diet and cookery: maize, sweet potatoes, cassava, capsicums, chilies, peanuts, and tomatoes. Indonesian farmers and cooks adopted them as mainstays for a population that did not have access to irrigated rice land. They also applied foreign plants to local needs. After oil was pressed out from peanuts, a cake remained which farmers used for manuring garden plots.

Also critical for the livelihood and health of Indonesians was tobacco, which was brought from South America to Indonesia by the Spanish. The modern colonial history of Indonesia is bound up with large-scale growing of tobacco for export to Europe. Since the sixteenth century Indonesian men, women, and children have also smoked and chewed it, and tobacco was of sufficient importance in people's lives for its introduction to be recorded in a Javanese epic, *Babad Jaka Tingkir* (Tale of Jaka Tingkir).

Forms of housing also provide clues as to how people live. The earliest evidence in the Indonesian archipelago, cave-dwellings, served as temporary shelter for nomadic hunters on land and sea. Around 2000 B.C.E., on the walls of the Pattae Cave near Maros in southwestern Sulawesi, a long-gone band painted the wild boar they tried to capture and left handprints asserting their struggle for life.

Excavations of dwelling sites from the fourth century B.C.E. establish the very ancient history of domestic housing built on piles. The contemporary Malay-style house found in Sumatra is on piles, has a deep roof, a verandah, and separate staircases for men and women. The allocation of the front, open part of the house as men's space, and the back and inner parts as women's is common in many parts of the archipelago and remains a characteristic of Indonesian domestic architecture today.

The house on stilts with curved roof was also the style in the ninth century Javanese village, as shown in carvings on the Prambanan and Borobudur temples, but by the fourteenth century a distinctive Javanese style had evolved for the residences of royalty and commoners. The house was built on the ground. Those built for the wealthy had four chief elements: a *pendopo,* an elevated platform with a roof resting on pillars and open for public receptions and entertainments; a *pringgitan,* an area for the (male) head of the house; a *dalem,* the private apartments of women and children; and a *sentong,* a place reserved for household ceremonies. A deep roof signaled the high status of the occupants.

The Balinese house is a series of small wooden structures within a stone-walled compound. Individual buildings serve different functions: bedrooms with verandahs, kitchen, bathroom, granary, family temple, and sometimes a workshop. The orientation and placement of buildings within the compound follow precise rules according to the occupants' caste, and are prescribed in building treatises preserved from fifteenth-century texts. Common to Balinese domestic architecture is a roof supported by a single pole with radiating beams.

In most other parts of the archipelago homes were built of bamboo and thatch on piles, often with multiple, steeply curved roofs, and they were adaptable for housing several generations. Decorative elements, such as buffalo horn roofs, and the representation of house lizards, horn bills, and rice-pounding appear in house design over many regions and centuries. Split gates and protective kala heads were common elements of public and private buildings in Java and Bali. Whatever the style of house, fixing the time of its construction, its orientation, and the approach or gateway was the work of specialists.

From around 1000 C.E. Indonesian lives began to feel the impact of a new set of men traveling the international circuit. There was in Indonesian waters a greater degree of travel, an increase in the numbers of foreigners at ports, and a conjunction of traders from Arabia, India, and China who were Muslim. These men valued the title of sultan over raja, consulted texts constructed in book form written in the Arabic alphabet, and stimulated in Indonesian societies the development of states organized as Muslim territories and of pilgrimage within landscapes shaped by Islam.

3

SULTANS AND STATES
Histories Through Islam

Indonesian communities located at stopping points on the sea highways connecting China, India, and Arabia were best placed to pick up new world trends in thinking, making, and doing. Leaders of these strategically placed archipelago communities called themselves rajas. The India they consciously connected themselves to was not a fossilized museum of ancient Sanskrit culture. Religious scholars and professional writers at Indonesian courts were in touch with Indian religious trends. They were familiar with Hindu devotional sects that rejected the practice of making gods visible through sculptures in stone and substituted the worship of one unseen god in place of many. They knew about cults devoted to achieving mystical union of the believer and the divine. Through their contacts with India, archipelago scribes and religious specialists also became aware of Islamic versions of these concepts.

Crews sailing from Indonesian harbors in the thirteenth, fourteenth, and fifteenth centuries sold goods in Indian ports controlled by merchants who were Muslim. In the same period, rural Hindu populations of Indian states became subjects of urban Muslim establishments of kings, military commanders, and religious leaders. In Indian cities, Muslim merchants diverted some of their wealth to the support of Islamic teachers and mosques. They also supported mosque communities in Indonesian ports where their agents did busi-

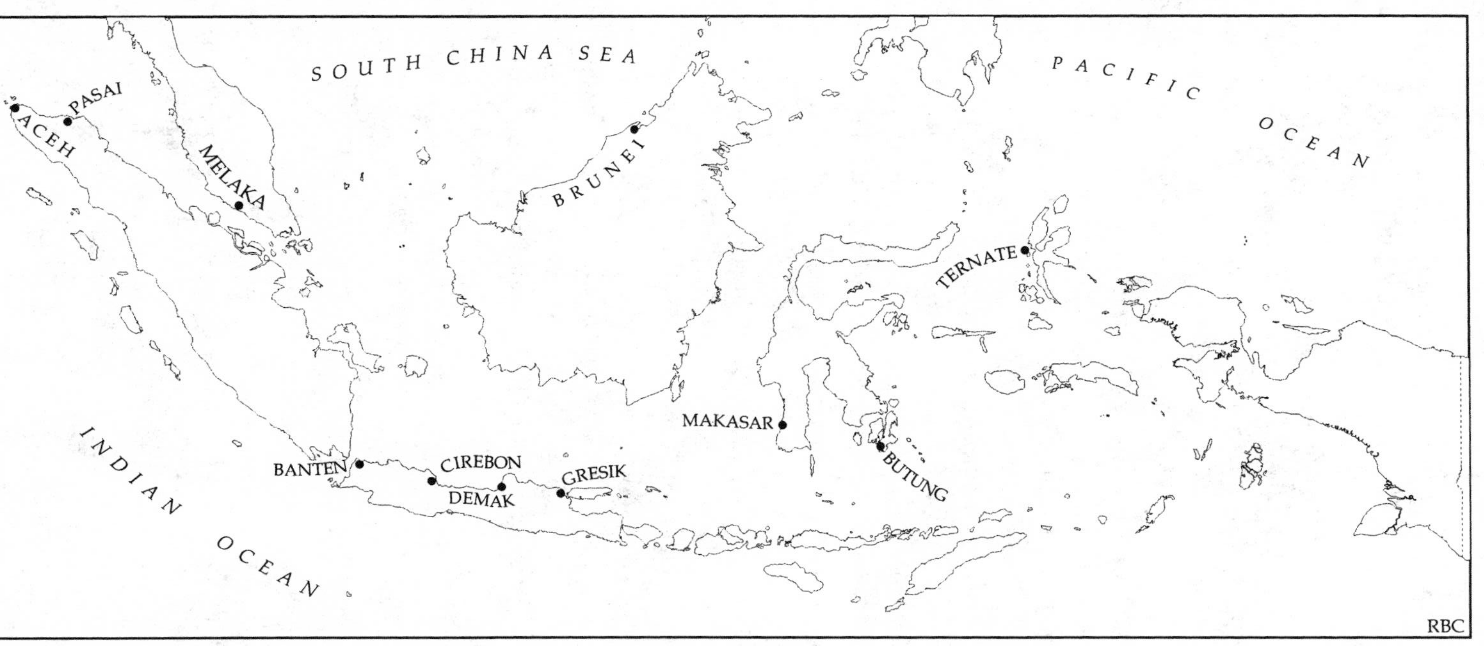

Early Sultanates

ness. In different ways Indonesian rajas, traders, scholars, artisans, and laborers became conscious of a web of civilization spreading out from the Islamic heartland of Arabia. Arabic was one of the international languages for diplomacy, trade, scholarship, and religion, so that port rulers hired scribes capable of reading and writing Arabic. Archipelago traders did business with Muslim men who were members of an international network of buyers and sellers. Local artisans learned new designs in textiles and costumes, new forms of art and architecture. Laborers in Indonesian ports were hired to construct buildings conforming to the tastes of Islamized businessmen.

Archipelago sailors carried Indonesian products to China as well as to India. Although much in contact with official China and its envoys, archipelago rulers never made themselves known through inscriptions written in Chinese or through adoption of Chinese titles and reign names. The reason for this was that Chinese political theory had only one center of the world and one emperor, so that envoys sent from Chinese courts did not flatter Indonesian kings by proposing to them the titles of emperor and son of heaven. Instead, envoys from China named archipelago kings vassals and awarded them honors which underlined their inferior status. For example, in 1375 the Hung Wu emperor incorporated the mountains and rivers of Srivijaya and Java into the map of China. Chinese civilization exerted a lesser appeal over island kings in comparison with Hindu, Buddhist, and Muslim civilizations.

At the same time, Arabs were putting in at northern ports in Sumatra. Many were from the southwest fringe of the Arabian Peninsula, which is known as the Hadramaut. For centuries Hadrami merchants exported rare spices and woods to ports on the Indian and East African coasts. From the ninth century C.E. a regular sea trade route took Arab merchants to Sumatran ports. There they purchased Indonesian varieties of resins, camphor, and fragrant woods to supplement the cargo they were carrying to China. By the thirteenth century there were settlements of Arab merchants in the major trading centers of the Indonesian archipelago.

Arabs supplying the China market also sold their skills in navigation and piloting to the Chinese, who starting in the twelfth century came to the archipelago rather than waiting in China for Indonesian ships to come to them. As a result, there were far more Chinese ships, crews, businessmen, and laborers in Indonesian ports. Archipelago communities anchored on sea routes received an overpowering impression of China's military and commercial might. They also perceived that some Chinese merchants were part of the new world network of Islam.

Over several centuries, residents of the archipelago's international ports

THE NANYANG: CHINA OFFSHORE

Migrations of Chinese by sea into regions to China's south created the Nanyang, a vast area which the Chinese thought of as a zone for Chinese offshore settlement and production, a fringe to China. The Yuan (Mongol) dynasty that controlled all China from 1271 to 1368 inherited the earlier Southern Song's orientation to the Nanyang. It sent emissaries to ports in Sumatra and Java, and outfitted oceangoing junks that held crews of 150 to 300 men. These ships were designed to sustain long voyages.

Mongol fleets carried diplomatic staff and armies to fringe territories to announce the new dynasty and establish its claims to homage and dues. Mongol soldiers from one fleet, landing in Java in 1293, became entangled in a power struggle between the kingdoms of Kediri and Singhasari. For Singhasari's Prince Wijaya, these agents of a foreign superpower presented the chance to gain allies and win the war against Kediri. In Javanese tradition, Mongol raiding in east Java's coastal villages led to the founding of the kingdom of Majapahit.

THE ZHENG HE VOYAGES: IMPERIAL CHINA AT SEA

In the first decades of the fifteenth century, the Chinese court experimented with a royal trade conducted by its agents in foreign ports, instead of having foreign traders sail to China. The Yung Le Emperor (r. 1402–1424) financed six fleets over the years 1405 to 1422. The first three sailed to ports on the central coast of Vietnam, east as far as modern-day Surabaya (northeast Java), then west to Palembang, through the Melaka Straits, stopping at Melaka and at Pasai on the Sumatran side, then to Sri Lanka and Calicut on India's southwest coast. The fourth and sixth expeditions followed the same route, but after Calicut they continued across the Arabian Sea, and entered the Straits of Hormuz, while the sixth reached the entrance to the Red Sea at Aden. The last great voyage was authorized by the Xuande (Hsuan Te) Emperor (r. 1426–1435) and set out in 1431.

These fleets imposed on the dispersed trading settlements in the Indonesian archipelago by their size, the numbers of ships, people aboard, and the quantities of merchandise they carried. Each expedition was like a floating country. There were water tankers and supply ships that carried food and building materials for repairs at sea, transport ships for cavalry horses, warships, patrol boats, and large, nine-masted junks. The largest ships, which carried China's merchandise, had four decks. The lowest was filled with stones and soil as ballast, a second deck served as living quarters and space for kitchens. Silk, cotton, tea, iron, salt, hemp, wine, and ceramics were stowed in another deck, and on the top deck were cannon and fighting platforms. Individual ships communicated with each other by flags, signal bells, drummers, gongs, lanterns, and carrier pigeon. Two hundred ships and twenty-seven thousand sailors, soldiers, officials, envoys, merchants, artisans, and artists on each expedition strained the abilities of Indonesian ports (populated by a few thousand) to receive them.

The expeditions have become known as the Zheng He (Cheng Ho) voyages, after their commander, a highly placed court official who died during the return voyage of the seventh fleet in 1433. Zheng He and his lieutenants lived on as mythologized cult figures in legends told in Java, Bali, Kalimantan, and Sumatra. Temples dedicated to their honor continued to attract worshippers into the twentieth century in Jakarta and Semarang. The historical Zheng He was a Muslim from Yunnan. He belonged to that group of China's border peoples who had become a part of the world Islamic community and who drew their knowledge from international Arab networks that crisscrossed Eurasia by land and sea. Zheng

He's Islamic connections were not remembered in Indonesian folk histories, but his expeditions left businessmen in the archipelago—Indonesian, Indian, Arab—with the conviction that there existed a huge market in China for their goods.

encountered foreign Muslims as a minority group in their cities. When a ship anchored, assistants of the harbormaster rowed out to it to inquire who owned and operated the ship, and what they wanted to buy. Gifts presented by the ship's captain and principal passengers to the harbormaster and ruler eased their way and advertised what they had to sell. If they were admitted to the ruler's presence they were questioned about their origins and the politics and state of business in the ports on their itinerary. Sometimes local rajas called on the foreign Muslims to contribute their medical knowledge or debate their beliefs. The foreigners requested permission to unload their cargo, to sell, to rent space, and to live and work on shore while they did their business. They employed Indonesian agents to assemble cargo for export; they contracted with Indonesian brokers to supply male and female laborers to carry goods, construct market stalls and warehouses, and supply food and sex. The formal procession of merchants for an audience with the ruler allowed a port's population to observe the foreigners' appearance, costume, and customs.

Specific conditions were necessary before the occasional visit by a foreign merchant ship led to the establishment of a permanent community. The local ruler had to want to grow rich from trade. Such a ruler created a predictable business environment for foreigners by maintaining a navy able to keep the sea approaches to his port free of raiders, and by heading an administration that guaranteed the safety of foreign merchants and their property in his port. There had to be enforceable standards for weights and measures of goods and for currencies. Then foreign merchants operating in an international network settled representatives in an archipelago port. Over time a community developed in the ward assigned it, distinguished by the religion and business methods of its members and the styles of their housing and religious buildings. A nucleus of local converts formed around the foreign Muslims: wives, in-laws, children, household servants, and others who had frequent dealings with the Muslim community, such as the mosque janitors and animal slaughterers in the market.

Linking Indian, Arab, and Chinese Muslims was a persistent concept of an Islamic community that was an expanding, global community. This understanding of Islamic space and community made it possible for learned men to travel from one end of the Islamic world to the other. Some settled in foreign ports to head mosques or set up a school. At every city where they stopped, religious scholars strengthened the common knowledge and Islamic consciousness of their minority culture. Indonesians living at the junction of local sea-lanes and international routes, therefore, had long experience of individual Muslims and Muslim neighborhoods. From around the 1280s, they had home grown Islamic communities in their midst as well.

The earliest Islamic states were in the far west of the Indonesian archipelago on the northern tip of Sumatra. By the 1430s Melaka's rulers were Muslim. At the eastern end of the archipelago, the ruler of Ternate converted to Islam around 1460. In Java Demak's ruler proclaimed it a royal Muslim city around 1470, while the nearby harbor cities of Tuban, Gresik, and Cirebon had Muslim rulers by about 1500. Around 1515 the port of Aceh had a Muslim ruler. Madura had a Muslim ruler by 1528. Gorontalo, on the northeastern arm of Sulawesi, had a Muslim ruling class by 1525 and Butung, lying off the southeastern arm, by 1542. In 1605 the rulers of Luwu, Tallo', and Gowa in southern Sulawesi converted to Islam and the whole peninsula had Muslim rulers by 1611. The ruler of Bima (Sumbawa) converted to Islam in 1615. All these places were small states and towns. In 1641 the ruler of the archipelago's largest kingdom, Mataram in Java, advertised his rule as Islamic by taking the title of sultan.

When small-scale rulers declared themselves to be Muslim and ordered their subjects to follow them, they had no big establishment to displace or displease. Over four centuries there developed a string of Muslim ports fringing Indonesian kingdoms of the plains and upland valleys with their Hindu and Buddhist establishments of royalty, priests, scribes, architects, artists, sculptors, artisans, and rice farmers. Islamic ports were far from the archipelago's many forest-dwelling communities. Familiarity with Islam and its representatives varied in the archipelago according to a society's geographic location and to historical time. Indonesia's Islamic states were formed within a context of difference.

Because the first homegrown Islamic societies were small, scattered ports, Islamization itself seems to begin in the empty places on the map. That is, Islamization occurred first not in the populated plains of central Java but in the extreme west and east of the archipelago, places that had not previously seemed to exist or to even to belong to the Indonesian islands. Furthermore, because the process occurred over several centuries, it brought some places, such as Siak and Banjarmasin, into Indonesian histories in the sixteenth century, other places, such as Balambangan (east Java), in the eighteenth. In the late twentieth century the process of expanding Islamic rule also brought into Indonesian histories peoples who had seemed to be part of quite other histories: the populations of interior mountain villages of West New Guinea and of East Timor.

"Islam" is an Arabic word meaning "surrender," in the sense of surrender to God, and "Muslim" means "one who surrenders." Islamic civilization encompasses the science, arts, written literature, musical and oral culture, costume, morality, and government in Muslim-ruled lands. All Muslims across the globe and in all periods of historical time believe that Islam is the final revelation of God and was delivered to Muhammad during periods of ascetic meditation in the seventh century in Arabia. Muslims believe that the divine revelations were reproduced, as God spoke them to Muhammad, in the Koran, and that the laws given to Muhammad are valid in all periods of time and in all places. Muslims accept five principal duties: acknowledgment of Allah as the sole God and Muhammad as God's prophet; ritual prayer at five set times each twenty-four hours; fasting during daylight hours of the month of Ramadhan to commemorate Muhammad's reception of the revelations; pilgrimage to sites in Mecca and Medina associated with Muhammad's spiritual and political life; and payment of taxes for support of religious officials, travelers, and the poor.

Muhammad was born around 570 C.E. In his lifetime he was a trader, prophet, war commander, and ruler of a new state with its capital in Medina. Following Muhammad's death in 632 conflicts developed over questions of interpretation and leadership. His followers sought to ensure their survival as an Islamic community by expanding the territory under the rule of Muslims. Raids against hostile Arab tribes quickly broadened into civil wars among Arabs and wars of conquest over non-Arabs. Over time Muhammad's revelations were systematized in theology, law, statecraft, ritual, and custom. Monarchy became the characteristic form of Islamic government. As Islam spread out of its heartland into non-Arab parts of the world, individual Muslims brought the influence of their native culture to their understanding and practice of Islam. But key features of Islam—Koran, Islamic law, leadership by religious experts, schools, mosque, mysticism, and pilgrimage to Arabia—remained permanent features of Islamic practice everywhere, and these features shaped the host societies in which Muslims lived.

THE KORAN, SHARIA, AND MEN LEARNED IN RELIGION

The Koran (alternative forms: Quran, Qur-an, Qur'an) is the written text of the words heard by Muhammad over a period of twenty-three years. It was assembled in its current form by the mid-seventh century. The text consists of 114 *surahs* (sections), whose length varies from a few verses to as many as 286 (surah 2). The content includes praises to God, exposition of correct behavior and belief, descriptions of paradise, sins, and punishments, and retelling of key stories from the Jewish Torah and the Christian New Testament. Sayings attributed to Muhammad by his followers and stories of his life were compiled in the Hadith in the ninth century. Koran and Hadith are Islam's key sources. Muslims believe the Koran was spoken by God in Arabic. The acts of reciting and hearing the Koran are considered to confer God's blessing. Religion classes commence with recitation. Indonesian kings paid for public recitations of the Koran on Thursday nights, in the evenings of Ramadhan, and at ritual occasions such as funerals.

Arising from the belief that the Koran is divine speech were requirements that all Muslims should learn Arabic and reluctance to translate the Koran into other languages. Its transmission was by recitation and by hand-copied pages bound into book form. Although the printing press reached Muslim lands from Europe in 1492, Muslim kings banned setting Arabic into type until the early nineteenth century. As a result, copies of the Koran were limited and study of the Koran confined to small numbers of men in Muslim communities. The first Koran printed in Arabic in Indonesia was published in Palembang in 1854. Commentaries on the Koran were composed in Arabic by native speakers of Indonesian languages. The first translation of the Koran into modern Indonesian was published in Jakarta by the Japanese military command in 1944. There is evidence of a seventeenth-century Malay translation made in Aceh and an eighteenth-century Koran with translation in the Bugis and Makasar languages following each line of Arabic.

The Koran has been known in the West through the polemics of Christian theologians since the seventh century. It was first printed in Arabic in Vienna in 1530. A Dutch-language translation of the Koran in the nineteenth century excited the anger of those Indonesians who felt it a disgrace to translate the Koran into a language of Christian Europe.

Islamic law, known by the Arabic word sharia (syaria in modern Indonesian spelling), codifies rules contained in the Koran and Hadith. Councils of senior religious scholars determine whether something not discussed in the Koran is lawful for Muslims and publicize the decision through a *fatwah.* Religious scholars are known by the Arabic word *ulama,* the plural form of the word *alim* (scholar) that has passed into the Indonesian language to mean one scholar and many. The duty of ulamas is to ensure that sharia is the basis of the state's administration, and to teach. Pious Muslims honor ulamas by kissing their hand. In Javanese Muslim culture drawing near to an ulama is believed to confer God's blessing. In theory, as men learned in the Koran, ulamas were above kings. In Indonesian histories they were often their rivals for power.

CALIPHS AND SULTANS

Muhammad's successors took the title caliph, which means "deputy" and signified deputy for Muhammad and God. Very soon rival dynasties of caliphs ruled and fought each other. By the eleventh century, rulers calling themselves sultan (meaning "power," "authority") challenged the caliph's claim to supreme authority. When Indonesian rulers converted, they joined an Islamic world community divided politically into numerous states. Archipelago rulers took the title of both sultan and caliph to emphasize that they, and not their ulamas, were the supreme authority in all matters civil and religious.

MOSQUE

Mosque is the English form of the Arabic (and Indonesian) word *mesjid.* It is a public place where the Muslim community gathers for communal prayer on Friday. Until recent times in Indonesia the Muslim community gathered in public worship was a male congregation.

Mosque architecture reflects the many cultures in which Islam has become known, but common to all mosques is a place for ritual washing prior to prayer and the *kiblat.* The kiblat binds Muslims to Mecca by indicating the direction in which a congregation should turn as a group to pray. Architectural elements of Middle Eastern mosques such as the dome, separate minaret, arched windows, and columns of pillars became usual elements of Indonesian mosque architecture only in the twentieth century. Such features were introduced into archipelago societies late in the nineteenth century by pilgrims returning from Arab lands, and by European architects who created Indo-Moorish styles.

Neighborhood prayer houses were the product of local labor and donations, but great mosques were erected at the expense of public figures. In addition to being a place of community prayer, the mosque is part of government as the site of the court of justice and place of assembly for society's adult males. Rulers diverted part of their income to the upkeep of mosques and the personnel running them. They appointed the weekly preacher. Provision of funds and control of the mosque message are political acts, and often the focus of conflict and power struggles. Mosques also provided meeting space and lodging for scholars, students, pilgrims, and businessmen. Mosques tied the landscape together, possessed it as Muslim territory, and enabled passage through it of people and ideas.

SUFISM: MYSTICISM WITHIN ISLAM

Mystics have a long tradition in Islamic civilization. They have often been persecuted by Muslim leaders who focus their piety on the sharia. Particularly offensive to enforcers of sharia is the doctrine of the Perfect Man who perceives the unity of the self with God. The concept of union between the individual and God is a submersion of the human within the supreme. Javanese thinkers carried this concept over to their understanding of the relationship between subject and monarch as union of servant and lord. This notion reinforced the Islamic teaching that subjects must submit to a Muslim king.

Mystics were called *Sufis.* Unlike regular mosque practice, music, dance, song, and intense meditation helped Sufis to bridge the gap between the individual and God. Sufism evolved from individual mystical experience into social movements formed around charismatic leaders.

Sufism provided for local spiritual needs in forms that matched and reflected local cultures. At the same time, the common elements of practice—devotion to spiritual leader, visits to holy sites, meditation, scrutiny of the Koran's inner or hidden meanings—are widespread throughout the Islamic world. Sufism is both esoteric philosophy and popular religion.

PILGRIMAGE

Pilgrimage to Mecca is one of the five requirements of Islam. In the era before steamship and airplane, the journey to Mecca was an immense undertaking for people from Indonesia's islands. Wealthy men set out with slaves and trade goods to sell at ports along their route to finance successive stages in the journey. In the twentieth century, as travel became cheaper and intellectual horizons widened, women joined male pilgrims making the journey to Mecca (only if accompanied by the male guardians sanctioned by religion, that is, father or husband).

Indonesians have been undertaking the pilgrimage since the 1500s. Most numerous must have been subjects of Javanese kings, for in Mecca until the twentieth century the term for all pilgrims from Southeast Asia was *Jawi* (people from the island of Java). The pilgrimage revealed to merchants the variety of goods sold in different ports, items in demand, and broadened their geographical knowledge. For those who stayed to study, pilgrimage offered the means to make copies of religious books which they brought back to add to the small stock of books circulating in the archipelago. Pilgrimage conferred the title *haji* on returning pilgrims and was a source of prestige for the commoner in societies dominated by kings and aristocrats.

Arabs from the southern Arabian Peninsula had a long history as seafarers. Northern Arabs were a continental people of stockbreeders (the nomadic tribes) and pastoralists (the sedentary tribes around oases). In the era of Islamic conquests, northern Arabs rapidly adapted to seafaring as shipbuilders, navigators, sailors, and sea traders. They developed war fleets through which they won control of the Mediterranean and became the major sea power in the Indian Ocean. Islamic civilization evolved following Arab conquests that brought a vast area from Spain to Persia under Muslim rule.

The Indonesian archipelago makes its appearance in Arabic texts from the tenth century. In a text compiled around 916, the geographer, Abu Zayd Hasan, included an account of Sribuza (Srivijaya), which had been written by an Arab merchant in 851. Sumatra is also recorded in the history of Ibn Khaldun (1332–1406). Archipelago rulers who adopted Islam between the thirteenth and seventeenth centuries became participants in an imported culture that was not the product of the Arab desert, but of cities with their traditions of literacy, commerce, monarchy, legalism, and learning. They joined the Islamic community when its world incorporated Spanish, North Africans, Turks, Yunnanese, Chinese, Persians, and Indians, and at a stage in Islam's history of the development of folk religion. Islam of the Hadramaut, Persia, and

India was characterized by veneration of saints, pilgrimages to the burial places of holy men, and reverence for genealogy. Indonesian Islam similarly developed in a culture of saints, feats of magic, seeking blessing at grave-sites and from holy men. Indonesian forms of Islam promoted travel to sites of learning in the Arabian Peninsula and attached great prestige to men returning to transmit their knowledge in archipelago mosques. Islamic rulers of Indonesian states honored traveling Arab scholars, appointed them as chief Islamic official at their courts, offered admission to royal families through marriage with a daughter, and provided funds for copying Islamic texts and building schools and mosques.

When Indonesian societies were converting, Islam was a seaborne civilization, adaptable to archipelago conditions. In the scholarly literature, much has been made of the connection between trade and conversion to Islam in the archipelago, to the extent of explaining conversion by the eagerness of archipelago rulers for greater profits from trade. Such emphasis degrades the religious appeal of Islam for the individual and overlooks the practical explanation. Missionaries, scholars, artisans, and adventurers (tourists) traveled on the same ships as merchants because these were the only vessels available and because all men financed the journey by bringing goods to sell. Archipelago rulers whose ports were on trade routes could draw on the services of foreign experts who were Muslim, become familiar with the Muslim network, and in time choose to insert themselves into that network through conversion.

Islam came to Indonesian rulers also through geography. The regions to the north and west of the Islamic heartland were inhabited by Christians and great kingdoms had to be conquered for Islam to expand. The regions to Arabia's east and south did not present such formidable obstacles. Islamic scholars regarded these regions as populated by teachable unbelievers. The way to the Indonesian archipelago was open, its populations accessible.

Historians of Indonesia often refer to the Islamic concept of equality of believers as a powerful reason inducing conversion in the four hundred years of Islamization of the archipelago. They contrast Islam's equality of believers before God with Hindu and Buddhist beliefs in a hierarchy of souls. But the argument is not tenable for three main reasons. First, it is based on the presumption that individuals in those centuries had a concept of equality of humanity within society and yearned for it. Second, it goes against Koranic teachings that accord a higher status to Muslims over nonbelievers, men over women, and owners over slaves. Third, the argument ignores the history of Islam in which fatwahs (binding rulings) proclaim submission of subject to a Muslim ruler as a religious duty.

The first rulers in the Indonesian archipelago known to have declared themselves Muslim headed small settlements in north Sumatra, Lamreh and Pasai. All the ingredients were present. They were coastal communities whose inhabitants lived on shore and at sea. Their small craft gathered Indonesian sea and jungle products from collection centers on the west and east coasts of Sumatra, and through regional trade networks they exchanged Indonesian produce for foreign manufactured goods. Lamreh and Pasai were conveniently situated on the Indian Ocean, at the head of the Straits of Melaka, for ships coming from India and Arabia. Foreign merchants who were Muslim established settlements at harbor towns on these Sumatran coasts. The ports provided services for Muslim ships carrying spices from the Hadramaut and cloth from Gujerat (northwest India), and dealt in these and Indonesian products with Chinese buyers and shippers. Since around 1000 C.E. there was also a Chinese trading community in Pasai.

The rulers of Lamreh and Pasai announced their Islamic credentials to men operating the Muslim sea network by taking the title sultan and replacing their native names with the Arabic Sulaiman bin Abdullah bin al-Basir (d. 1211) and Malik al-Saleh (d. 1297), respectively. Their graves are another indication of adoption of Islamic culture. In place of cremation, stone masons constructed the curved head and foot markers characteristic of Muslim graves, inscribed them in Arabic letters, and recorded the time of their death in the Islamic calendar. Ibn Battuta (1304–1369) visited Pasai around its fiftieth year as a sultanate. He was qualified to assess its Islamic features as a Muslim from Islam's Moroccan fringe, who had studied in Islam's heartland of Mecca and then been chief judge in the Delhi sultanate in India. Ibn Battuta wrote an account of Pasai on his return to Morocco in 1354. In it he recorded that the current sultan fulfilled the duties of a Muslim ruler: he supported visiting Islamic scholars, he promoted conversion to Islam through carrying war into non-Muslim districts, and he levied extra taxes on non-Muslims. Pasai's sultan made Friday prayer in the mosque an advertisement for his twin roles as religious and secular ruler. He went to the mosque on foot, dressed in the plain clothes of the Islamic scholar. Following prayers, he changed into royal robes and returned to his palace riding an elephant.

The right mix of conditions that occurred at ports such as Lamreh, Pasai, Aceh, and Fansur-Barus—location, products, increasing numbers of Arab and Chinese traders, growing familiarity with Muslims over time, and access to knowledge of Islam as a religion and a civilization—occurred also at Melaka. Melaka was the port of call for all the Zheng He fleets of the fifteenth century. Its third ruler made sure to secure its favored trading status with China by going in person three times to pay homage at the imperial court. He was officially designated a vassal king to the emperor, and the territory of Melaka was incorporated into the redrawn map of China. On his return in 1436 from his third mission to China, Melaka's ruler advertised along the Muslim sea network that his port was offering favorable conditions to Muslim merchants interested in the China business. He did so by proclaiming himself Sultan Muhammad Shah.

Melaka today is a district of the Federation of Malaysia, but it belongs to the histories of Indonesia as well as of Malaysia. When its founder established a state on the Malay Peninsula, he claimed to be a descendant of Buddhist kings of Srivijaya in Sumatra. Melaka's fifth ruler, Sultan Mansur Syah (r. 1459–1477), reconnected himself to Indonesian histories by marrying into the royal house of Java's Majapahit. Pasai and Melaka are important in Indonesian histories: Pasai is the home base of men who spread Islam across the archipelago, while Melaka's court, its style of living, its religious learning, and its literary language became standards for later sultanates.

The past that permeates Indonesian life is Islamic, but that Islamic past does not lie in excavated objects or in old records of population figures, income tax, and bureaucratic rulings. Indonesia's Islamic past is a heritage of stories, legends, and traditions: of miracles explaining how kings converted, of Muslim holy men whose feats of magic eclipsed the powers of Hindu and Buddhist priests, of heroes of Islamic literature and also of local heroes who embarked on journeys across Indonesian oceans and through Indonesian forests in quest of self-knowledge and a kingdom they would rule as sultan and caliph. This Islamic past infuses stories chanted in Malay, Buginese, and Javanese; it informs puppet theater; it permeates holy sites where Indonesia's Muslim saints are buried. Before conversion, things happened in a pre-Islamic era of chaos and darkness, or at a time when gods still walked the earth and married humans.

Conversion stories from all over the archipelago are uniform in attributing to the local king the honor of becoming the first Muslim. The introduction of Islam among the general population and upholding of Islamic law are also attributed to royalty, not to mosque preachers. Conversion stories tell of reigning monarchs who become Muslim as the result of a dream, a vision, or the visit of a foreign missionary. Royal conversion is sudden and unexpected; it is not the result of previous study, but a magical transformation.

The conversion of Pasai's ruler was the consequence of a dream. Muhammad appeared to Merah Silau, spat into his mouth, and transmitted to him knowledge of Islam. When Merah Silau woke up, he found he was circumcised, could recite in Arabic the credo of faith, and read the Koran. A ship then arrived, sent by the caliph of Mecca. Its captain installed Merah Silau as Sultan Malik al-Saleh and gave him state regalia and robes from Mecca. He taught the new sultan's subjects core Islamic beliefs and methods of praying and left a holy man from India to guide the new congregation.

After Pasai and Melaka, the right mix of conditions for the emergence of Islamic states occurred at good harbors along Java's north coast in the second half of the fifteenth century and in the sixteenth. There were well-established settlements of Chinese traders and artisans in the market for Indonesian products and providing port services. Their business activities multiplied the opportunities for traders operating in the Muslim sea network. Expanding Muslim quarters in ports meant, for Javanese, continual access to Islam; increasing familiarity with Muslim people, beliefs, business practices, and habits; a greater opportunity to gauge international trends; and an increased facility to think of the world in Islamic patterns and vocabulary. Port residents most in contact with Muslims converted: wives, their extended families, children, and people who perceived Islam as denoting prosperity, divorce from manual labor, and urban status. In these environments the management class of port cities became Muslim.

In Javanese histories ports were the sites of miracles worked by *walis.* Wali means "saint" and refers to the nine bringers of Islam and founders of priestly principalities in the empty spaces along Java's north coast. They are knit into local and regional histories, appearing with different names and life stories in oral and written traditions. Some are understood as having come from Egypt, while others were men of Pasai. In Javanese literature they are leaders of men as heads of their own kingdoms, or were relatives, teachers, and employees of Java's kings. All are honored with the title Sunan, which was later taken over by rulers of the Islamic kingdom of Mataram and its successor kingdom of Surakarta to signify that Javanese royalty had supplanted holy men as leaders in religion as in government.

The walis are important in the personal piety of individual Javanese, and their tombs attract pilgrims who make overnight vigils to pray for guidance, success, or a cure. The walis were targets of abuse by some Javanese thinkers of the late nineteenth century who attempted to explain how it was that Java had come under Dutch colonial rule. The *Babad Kudus* (Kudus Chronicle), composed in 1873, and the *Serat Dermagandul,* composed in 1879, denounced the walis as scheming, meddlesome vagabonds and hypocrites who had imposed a foreign religion on the Javanese, turned son against father, made Java vulnerable to Dutch conquest, and obliterated the pre-Islamic past by burning old books and inaugurating new histories that gave primacy to Islam. These texts had a limited impact in their time, and although many modern Muslims scorn

Saints of Javanese Islam. The saint, Sunan Kalijaga, is regarded as creator of Java's shadow (*wayang*) puppet theater. The saints are used in puppet plays telling of the arrival and spread of Islam in Java. Photo courtesy of Archipelago Press, Singapore.

veneration of saints, the walis are still revered in popular Islam. A portrait of the walis hangs alongside other heroes of Java in the museum honoring President Sukarno in Blitar.

According to oral and written literature from Java, the walis founded new states along Java's north coast in Demak, Cirebon, Banten, and Gresik. They made converts of the Javanese through acts of magic or of war. The most famous wali, Sunan Kalijaga, cleared the way for the Islamization of Java by defeating the Hindu kingdom of Majapahit and founding the Muslim state of Demak. He then acted as spiritual guide to the early kings of Mataram. Sunan Kalijaga's career is connected with events that, in historical time, stretched over two hundred years. He is understood as creating the Islamic culture of Java, which includes royal ceremonies, *wayang* (puppet theatre), and the *slametan* (ritual meal). By some accounts, Sunan Kalijaga studied with Seh Maulana, an Arabian saint and prince, son of the "king of Mecca," who had been sent to Java to convert the population. In other accounts, Sunan Kalijaga was a prince of Majapahit who, under the command of Sunan Bonang, transformed himself into a Muslim through a form of yogic meditation by a river. (The name Kalijaga means "watcher or keeper at the river.") After many years, Kalijaga emerged from trance able to speak Arabic and to fly through the air.

Sunan Gunung Jati is called the first king of Cirebon, and the multiplier of Islamic states in Java because he appointed a son, Hasanuddin, as governor and later as independent sultan of Banten. In some accounts, Sunan Gunung

Jati is a native of Egypt; in others, he is from Pasai and made the pilgrimage to Mecca and Medina. Another version says this sunan was descended on his mother's side from Prince Siliwangi of the Hindu kingdom of Pajajaran, while his father was descended from an Egyptian king named Molana Sultan Mahmud who was, in turn, a descendant of Muhammad.

In another version, it is Sunan Gunung Jati's son-in-law, not his son, who was installed as ruler of Banten. Faletehan was a stranger who put his military skills and leadership at the service of a Muslim king. He was the son of Makhdar Ibrahim, a Muslim scholar from India, who married an unnamed woman in Pasai. Falatehan presented himself to the new sultan of Demak, and was commissioned to lead the Demak fleet to attack Pajajaran's port. His successes were rewarded with marriage to a daughter of Sunan Gunung Jati. Faletehan then acted as representative for the wali in Banten, and then ruled in his own right as sultan.

The origins of Sunan Giri of Gresik show a different combination of the elements of conversion stories. A foreign holy man arrived in the east Javanese kingdom of Balambangan and promised its Hindu king to cure his daughter in the expectation that the king would then yield to the Islamic religion. The princess was cured and given as wife to the foreign holy man in appreciation, but king and court refused to convert. The holy man abandoned his pregnant wife and left the offending Hindu society. A son was born to the princess. Balambangan's Hindus placed him in a chest and threw it into the sea. In time the baby was rescued, raised by Muslims, and became the lord of the port city of Gresik. By some accounts, Sunan Giri ruled Java for forty days after the fall of Hindu Majapahit to purify the land of all non-Islamic traces.

Western scholars such as Ricklefs, Drewes, and Johns argue that Islam came indirectly to Indonesian societies, that is, not from Arabia, but from Islamized places on the fringe of the Islamic heartland such as Gujerat in India or Persia or Yunnan. Javanese traditions place their Islamic origins on paths that lead back to the homeland of Islam. All the walis are said to be related to a descendant of Muhammad called Shaikh Jumadil Kubra. This name is a Javanese form of Najmuddin al-Kubra, founder, in Islamic history, of the Kubrawiyya mystical sect.

Another meandering path that links introducers of Islam to its founder is stories of Sunan Ngempeldenta. One of these stories puts the source of Javanese Islam in Champa, a kingdom on the coast of Vietnam, whose ruling elites (as in Java's history) had been devotees of Hindu cults. Champa was an important trading center for Chinese and Japanese merchants and host to Arab trading communities. In this story, the Hindu King Brawijaya of Majapahit married a princess from Champa. This princess had a sister who was married to an Arab missionary for Islam named Ibrahim Makdum Asmara. The Cham princess brought her sister's sons to Java, and one of them, Prince Rahmat, received land from King Brawijaya and the income of villages in the Surabaya region. There he converted his laborers and dependents to Islam, and they called him Sunan Ngempeldenta. He married a Majapahit princess, and the son of this marriage became the wali Sunan Bonang. Sunan Bonang was the teacher of Sunan Kalijaga, who defeated King Brawijaya. Following defeat by Muslims, King Brawijaya vanished. His Cham queen converted to Islam and raised all of Brawijaya's children and grandchildren as Muslims. In this she was obedient to the instructions of Brawijaya who, although a Hindu, knew the divine path led to Islam.

A common character in Islamic conversion stories from around the archipelago is the stranger or missionary from overseas. The stranger often arrives

SUNAN NGEMPELDENTA: LOCAL TRADITION AND "CORRECT" FACTS

In the Sunan Ngempeldenta stories about the origins of Islam in the Surabaya area, local traditions conflict with official versions. One tradition has it that Sunan Ngempeldenta was not the son of Cham and Arab, but a Chinese Muslim. In 1964 M. O. Parlindungan published a manuscript that established a Yunnan Chinese connection in the Islamization of Java. The text was the subject of intensive scrutiny by the Dutch scholars H. J. de Graaf and Th. C. Pigeaud, who believed it to be an authentic document. It was the object of scorn in a campaign of denunciation by Javanese Muslims. The campaign resulted in a decree from Indonesia's ministry of religion condemning as false all historical evidence that Chinese Muslims introduced Islam to Java. All copies of the text were withdrawn from sale and its further publication was banned. The official version was generated at a time of domestic ethnic conflict and in an international context which made it desirable to link Indonesian Islam to the Arab heartland.

on a ship laden with cargo; he is always a man; he has superior powers which he demonstrates by such acts of magic as flying, moving mountains, and unexplainable cures for illness. The stranger is not an ascetic. He marries the daughter of the local king. By giving the foreign Muslim local in-laws, the native woman enables him to join Indonesian society, to belong. Wives and mothers of holy men have no names in these conversion stories; their function is to enter the foreigner into the local kingdom's royal family.

Conversion traditions link widely scattered parts of the archipelago. For instance, the first ruler of Ternate to adopt Islam for his personal and state religion supposedly did so after traveling from the far east of the archipelago to the Melaka sultanate at the archipelago's far west in 1460. He then returned by way of Java where he married a noblewoman and brought her back to Ternate as his queen. The *Hikayat Tanah Hitu* (History of Hitu, Ambon) tells of a sultan of Pasai personally traveling to Aceh to spread Islam, and then his grandson continuing this same role by converting the rulers of Jailolo, Tidore, and Ternate. Residents of Bima believe that they acquired their first knowledge of Islam from Minangkabau missionaries. Sunan Giri of Gresik fostered the spread of Islam to Lombok, Makasar, Kutai, and Pasir (southeast Kalimantan). Bugis and Makasar traditions ascribe the conversion of Sulawesi rulers in 1605 to miracles performed by three missionaries from Minangkabau. Pasemah conversion tradition links south Sumatra to Java and adds the aspect of the civilizing impact of Islam: religious scholars came from the Mataram kingdom and taught the Paṣemah's ancestors who were still a tribe wandering in the forest. Upon conversion they settled in permanent villages and became rice farmers.

Conversion stories also outline the process by which one convert became many. Conversion was by royal order, and by royal patronage of an Islamic establishment of mosque officials, judges, scholars, and holy men. Kings promoted conversion when they appointed only men who converted to Islam to lucrative, high-status jobs, such as harbormaster, controller of the market, and labor supervisor. Kings promoted conversion by appointing Muslims to open up new land for rice agriculture, and by sending armies to attack kings who were not Muslim.

The new Muslim king commanded his wives, children, court, and subjects to convert to his religion. The earliest example of the Malay language written in the Arabic alphabet (dated either 1303 or 1387) carries the declaration of the ruler of Trengganu that he has become Muslim and orders all his subjects to become Muslim too. Trengganu, which is on the east coast of the Malay Peninsula, today lies outside the nation-state of Indonesia, but was a part of the Malay culture zone of the western archipelago. The chiseled stone, which testifies that

Trengganu's ruler saw himself as promoter of Islam and implementer of sharia, commemorates the royal deed and moneys spent on the promotion of Islam.

The Jaka Tingkir stories from Java are more specific about the actual process of conversion. They begin with Demak. Once the king and his court had converted and had installed Muslims as the state's religious leaders, the next step was to require all hierarchies of subordinates to convert. Accordingly, the king summoned vassal princes and men who controlled the income and labor of villages to pay him homage by presenting themselves at court as Muslims. Muslim professionals replaced royal priests at court. They targeted holy men at large—mountain and forest hermits, ascetics, and their disciples. The king ordered all Buddhist books to be burned. Court favorites were given royal license to open up forest land and settle workers on cleared fields as farmers. They were to extend Muslim rule into these pioneer settlements by building a mosque and requiring farmers to perform the same public devotions as conducted in the city. Indonesian populations also became Muslim through the process of warfare.

JIHAD: HOLY WAR

In Islamic thinking, the world is divided into two regions, Muslim lands and Dar al-Harb, which means "house of war." It is the duty of Muslims to expand the borders of Muslim territory, and to do so by conquest. Such warfare is termed "holy war" (*jihad* in Arabic).The object of jihad is to remove all obstacles to conversion by creating an Islamic landscape of mosques, schools, and law courts. The individual living under Muslim rule who then fails to convert is subject to penalties (taxes, low-status occupations, identifying costume, and restrictions on religious observance) intended to convey to believers in other religions the supremacy and personal superiority of Muslims.

Jihad sometimes means an inner struggle between reason and passion. The vocabulary of jihad has been revived in several eras of Indonesian history. In 1999, fighting between Muslims and Christians for control of political power, economic resources, and religious space in Ambon was declared a jihad by national Muslim leaders.

Indonesian archipelago communities began converting to Islam from the thirteenth century, that is, after the great expansion by Arab speakers and Muslim princes west and east out of Arabia had ceased. Conversion of Indonesians was not through conquest by Arab armies and installation of Arab princes but rather by Indonesian raiding parties attacking non-Muslim cities and villages from sea and land. Warfare in the name of Islam occurred in Java, Sumatra, and Sulawesi.

Around the mid-sixteenth century, a Muslim army from the Cirebon sultanate on Java's northwest coast attacked and defeated troops of the Hindu Pajajaran kingdom. Banten was established as a vassal state to Cirebon. Banten's rulers continued the extension of Muslim-ruled territory, and their army pushed inland, capturing Pajajaran's capital and its villages in 1579. Armies of the sultanate of Banten also crossed the Sunda Straits into south Sumatra, campaigning as far north as the Palembang region. Banten's third king, Molana Muhammad, died in battle in Sumatra in 1596 fighting to extend Muslim government. To administer their newly conquered territories, Banten's rulers appointed as vassals only men who converted to Islam. In the east, the Hindu kingdom of Majapahit was defeated in battle by troops commanded by the Muslim ruler of Demak around 1478. In Sulawesi in 1605 the newly converted rulers of the joint kingdom of Gowa-Tallo' led attacks on surrounding kingdoms. Mandar was defeated in 1608, Sidenreng and Soppeng in 1609, and Bone in 1611. Defeated rulers who converted to Islam were reinstated as Gowa's vassals.

Scholars such as Van Leur, Wertheim, and Geertz were struck by practices of Indonesian folk Islam, such as the night vigils in sacred places and veneration of learned men. They compared twentieth-century Indonesian practice with seventh-century prescriptions for tribal Arabs and concluded that Indonesian Islam was a "veneer" or a "thin, flaking glaze" overlaying indigenous cultures. As in any religion, there is much variety within the daily observance and practice of Islam, and great diversity over time. Diversity in practice is also linked to an individual's social class, formal schooling, occupation, gender, marital status, age, and place of residence. In archipelago communities that entered the process of conversion five hundred years ago, Islam was experienced differently by each level of society, but all classes experienced change in their daily lives when their rulers became Muslim.

Conversion altered the way the believer understood the world. It replaced beliefs in the transmigration of souls and of rebirth with an understanding that life consists of a single existence on earth to be followed by paradise or hell.

Many passages in the Koran evoke for the male believer a conception of paradise born out of hot, dusty landscapes:

As to the Righteous
(They will be) in
A position of Security,
Among Gardens and Springs;
Dressed in fine silk
And in rich brocade,
They will face each other;
So; and We shall
Join them to Companions
With beautiful, big
And lustrous eyes.
There can they call
For every kind of fruit
In peace and security;
Nor will they there
Taste Death, except the first
Death; and He will preserve
Them from the Penalty
Of the Blazing Fire. (surah 44, verses 51–56)

Formal gardens with water, fruit trees, and pleasure buildings were signs of Islamic royalty in Indonesian sultanates. These gardens recreated the Koranic vision of heaven on earth and reserved it for the private enjoyment of kings, taken in company with women. Gardeners, builders, and servants were hired to create and maintain the Islamic vision of paradise in Indonesian settings for their bosses. Their daily labor introduced them to key promises of the Koran.

Conversion entailed a change in public behaviors. The rituals surrounding birth, marriage, and burial had to be aligned with the requirements of Islam. For instance, the Indian-derived practice of cremation of the dead and elaborate, long drawn-out ceremonies for the upper classes had to be replaced by simple, brief ceremonies for king and commoner alike of ritual washing and immediate burial in a shroud, with the deceased placed lying on the right side facing Mecca. Instead of the labor required to build cremation towers and pyres, and to construct funerary temples, labor was redirected to the cutting and carving of stone tombs. The tombstones were grouped together in fenced cemeteries to keep out animals and to mark the place as holy. Guardians of grave sites created and kept alive stories of Muslim heroes, presided over ceremonial cleansing, explained the significance of the symbols to pilgrims, supervised vigils, and sold mementos.

Men who joined in public prayer had to conduct themselves in the mosque in ways regulated by mosque officials. Among the oldest Islamic texts from the archipelago are manuals detailing the correct performance of prayers (words, body movements). Men who formed families had to learn Islamic regulations regarding registration of marriage and payment of dowries. They had to consult and pay specialists for advice on Islamic law and custom, such as procedures for the circumcision of their sons. If the Muslim ruler took his duties seriously, and implemented Islamic prohibitions on pork, alcohol, and gambling, his tradespeople were directly affected. Pig breeders and producers and sellers of palm wines had to find new occupations or specialize in selling only to non-Muslims; butchers had to learn new techniques for slaughtering animals.

PIGS AND PORK

Consumption of the pig was banned in Islamic diet in the seventh century. Although wild pigs did not thrive in the semi-arid conditions of the Islamic heartland, they did in Indonesia's rain forests. They especially adapted to forests inhabited by nomadic cultivators, uprooting their crops and eating tubers, fruits, and nuts.

Pigs were raised and presented as taxation in Hindu Majapahit; their flesh was consumed at feasts. There are references to pigs and dogs—another animal unclean in Muslim tradition—being brought to the capital by happy taxpayers. Majapahit texts tell that kings hunted wild pigs for sport, while commoners hunted them for food. For Muslims, the taboo on eating pork was a boundary marker between converts to the new religion and others. The taboo redirected cookery in the kitchens of palace, town, and village and brought Islam into the female domain of food selection and preparation.

In all Islamized regions of Indonesia pork has disappeared from local diets. In the twentieth century, the numbers of wild pigs declined as their jungle habitats shrank owing to agriculture and population growth. Pig breeding and hunting remain important economic activities only in Bali, Papua, and Manado.

There were consequences for alleged criminals when a ruler converted to Islam. Islamic punishments of flogging and amputation of limbs were gradually substituted for Indonesian judicial practices where the accused underwent trial by ordeals such as immersion in boiling oil and the condemned were executed by burial alive or combat against elephants and tigers. For public entertainments, Muslim rulers sponsored recitations of the Koran and made Islamic festivals into great public spectacles. They organized the public and private lives of their subjects into the Islamic calendar, changing the rhythms of daily life for everyone.

Muslims are enjoined to model themselves on Muhammad. One practical consequence of this injunction was alteration of the convert's outward appearance as a signal of inner change. In many areas of the archipelago body coverings were made from bark cloth. In Java laborers wrapped a length of cotton dyed in indigo around their waist. Fine cottons painted and dyed, and silks worked with gold, were costumes of the wealthy. Uncut cloth and cloth without stitches represented holiness in Hindu and Buddhist traditions, as did uncut hair for men and women. Upon conversion, the wealthy man added a tailored jacket or robe that covered the upper torso. Royals added tailored trousers in silk or fine cotton beneath the wrap of uncut cloth.

For men, a badge of their conversion was adoption of a head covering. A saying attributed to Muhammad was that the turban is a sign of reverence before God and a barrier between belief in Islam and unbelief. Throughout Indonesia's islands local variations on head wrappers for men proliferated. Their characteristic, in common with the turban, was the absence of brims or peaks which might interrupt the male worshipper as he bent his forehead to the floor in ritual prayer. In many areas men continued to wear their hair long, but concealed by the head wrapper. Cut hair was associated with the pious and cutting the hair was sometimes a public act before embarking on the pilgrimage. Muslim religious leaders rejected batik and other indigenous patterned cloth because their motifs derived from Hindu symbols or local religious traditions. They favored plain colors and plaids.

On Java, women's costume consisted of cloth covering the legs to the knees or ankles, a breast wrapper that left arms and shoulders bare, and a length of material used as a belt or carrying cloth, or as a head cover. Women in Islamic households signified their status by adding a tailored blouse covering shoulders and arms. Bare shoulders and arms became associated with ceremonial and performance costume.

The degree to which the contours of the female body should be concealed from view, and whether the hair, face, neck, hands, and feet should be covered, continue to be contested in Muslim countries. The requirements to cover the female body and to remove women from the gaze of men are laid down in the Koran:

And say to the believing women
That they should lower
Their gaze and guard
Their modesty; that they
Should not display their
Beauty and ornaments except
What (must ordinarily) appear
Thereof; that they should
Draw their veils over
Their bosoms and not display
Their beauty except
To their husbands, their fathers.

There follows a long list that includes father-in-law, sons, nephews, women, male and female slaves,

and that they
Should not strike their feet
In order to draw attention
To their hidden ornaments. (surah 24, verse 31)

Muhammad's wives and daughters and believing women are told they should "cast / Their outer garments over / Their persons (when abroad)" (surah 33, verse 59). The wives of Muhammad are singled out as being unlike other women: they should stay quietly in their houses and not make a dazzling display (surah 33, verses 28–34). Muslim men are enjoined to lower their gaze when women are present and guard their modesty (surah 24, verse 30).

Costume change is more than symbol and polite behavior. Islamic clothing required more articles and kinds of garments, more use of cloth, and therefore was the costume of the prosperous, a symbol of higher status and of upward mobility. It said that the wearer was not a porter, rower, field hand, or slave. It involved tailors, seamstresses, and sandal makers and stimulated the textile industry in all its many branches of growers of cotton, weavers, dyers, embroiderers, sellers, and importers.

In Ternate, where ruling families began converting to Islam in the late fifteenth century, the model for religious behavior was the Malay standard of Melaka, not Arabia. Ternate rulers adopted Malay costume upon conversion. The great variations in Islamic costume worn by women and men in Indonesia today reflect influences from many parts of the Islamic world, and a concerted effort by clothes designers and mass manufacturers to match Indonesian tastes with stricter attention to Koranic rules and Arab customs concerning covering the body.

Conversion to Islam, therefore, meant far more than appreciation of fine points of theology. Conversion affected sellers, suppliers, and buyers in the market. It changed the way people earned their living, what they ate, how they dressed, how they amused themselves, what images and symbols stimulated their imaginations, what they had to dread. Adoption of Islamic conventions went furthest with those who could afford it, least with laborers in fields and on construction sites. Where conversion spurred ambitious men to conduct raids against their non-Muslim neighbors, it affected commoners. They became victims of marauders, their fields trampled; they were conscripted as soldiers or as porters in the baggage trains of armies, or forced to row in war fleets.

Because of the uneven pace and place of Islamization, these changes occurred sporadically, piecemeal, as part of a long process. At first changes were confined to certain classes and locations. Over time Islamic states encircled and infused non-Muslim states with new modes of elegance, new symbols of wealth, new political models. They represented the latest in fashions, in government, in intellectual fads. Over time pockets of Muslims and Muslim minorities within Hindu and Buddhist states grew in numbers and importance, until most of the archipelago's kings presented themselves as Islamic rulers. Then they set about creating an Islamic landscape into which their subjects should fit their lives. It was not a linear movement toward an inevitable goal. Majapahit, Java's greatest Hindu-Buddhist kingdom, was founded in the same century as the sultanate of Pasai, and reached its greatest extent when the map was filling up with Islamic states at harbor mouths. It was knitted into every local history of conversion to Islam as provider of princesses and guarantor of status for would-be rulers.

4

MONARCHS, MENTORS, AND MOBILE MEN

Embedding Islam in Indonesian Histories

Two events of great importance for Indonesian histories occurred in the closing years of the thirteenth century. In northeast Sumatra a ruler, Merah Silau, employed Muslim professionals to inaugurate Islamic government in Pasai, and took the reign name of Sultan Malik al-Saleh (r. ?–1297). In east Java Prince Wijaya employed professionals who were Hindu and Buddhist to administer the state he founded, Majapahit, and took the reign name of Sri Maharaja Kertarajasa (r. 1294–1309). At opposite ends of the archipelago, then, and at the same time, Islamic and Hindu-Buddhist monarchies embarked on separate civilizing programs. In Indonesian histories, Pasai is remembered as source and vanguard for Islam in the archipelago; it offered local royals the glamour of belonging to the international set of men who called themselves sultan. Majapahit is remembered as setting archipelago benchmarks for polished manners, court ceremonies, and the arts. The kingdom bestowed on Indonesian sultans a status rooted in their own archipelago world by inserting Majapahit princes and princesses into their founding families.

Pasai looked toward the Indian Ocean and the China Sea. Majapahit looked toward the Java Sea and to Indonesian communities encircling its shores. Pasai's economy was geared to supplying western archipelago products to larger sea networks leading to China and India. Majapahit's economy was geared to collecting eastern archipelago products for the same networks. It also exported to archipelago ports, such as Pasai, the basic food supplies that enabled them to concentrate on wholesaling and distributing. Ports had a large percentage of seasonal inhabitants (Arabs, Indians, Chinese, Malays) who followed itineraries set by monsoon winds. Relations of port populations with peoples of their mountainous hinterlands were set within frameworks of periodic exchange and raids. Majapahit's far larger population had a port segment with international semimigrant workers too, but most of its subjects were settled in villages where farming was the chief way of earning a living. Craftspeople who worked in Majapahit's villages were integrated into the agricultural cycle and their jobs adjusted to the demands of court and port for specialized products.

Pasai is known from texts in Arabic and Malay. Majapahit is known through texts in Sanskrit and Old Javanese, and also through texts in Malay. Majapahit's twin legacies lie in the invention of history for Hindu Bali and in the invention of history for Muslim Java. In Balinese histories, Majapahit culture was re-created in Bali when its nobles, warriors, priests, and writers fled from east Java ahead of Islamic armies. In Javanese histories, Majapahit's kings prophesy and prepare the way for the Islamization of Java.

King Kertarajasa established his royal capital at a location midway between the modern cities of Kediri and Surabaya in 1294. The archaeologist Miksic, drawing on fourteenth-century evidence of dense human settlement, a money economy, and luxury items, concluded that Trawulan was the probable site of Majapahit's capital. Excavations have uncovered brick floors of former permanent houses and vestiges of a city water system in storage pots, water troughs, and clay pipes. Other finds include Chinese copper coins, gold jewelry, and small terra-cotta images of gods, people, animals, and buildings. Many stone and copper-plate inscriptions have been discovered in the vicinity of Trawulan, as well as remains of temples, tombs, and bathing places.

Majapahit was located along the course of the same Brantas River that had been such a vital waterway for earlier kingdoms. Like its predecessors, Majapahit harnessed peasant labor to sustain an export economy of shipbuilders, sailors, rice exporters, and traders specializing in east Indonesian spices and sea produce. Majapahit also harnessed peasant labor to sustain an administrative elite based in the capital and religious elites distributed among temple centers with their attendant market towns. These religious-economic centers were scattered along inland routes; they controlled outlying population clusters for the royal center.

Majapahit's villagers and the itinerants passing through its ports also provided manpower for the kingdom's armies on land and sea. In the 1300s, Majapahit navies patrolled the east coast of Sumatra, imposing a monopoly on the tribute trade of Sumatran ports with China. In the 1380s and 1390s its armed men attacked port cities such as Palembang and Melayu. In the late 1300s adventurers in the mountainous center of Sumatra reinvented Majapahit on a miniature scale to rule the Minangkabau. Majapahit navies sailed into the eastern archipelago, raiding coastal settlements as a preliminary step to setting up exchange of trade items. In 1343 a Majapahit army invaded Bali, from which point Balinese tradition begins Bali's history. In the 1400s, Majapahit navies patrolled the sea-lanes that were bringing the Muslim circle into being. Its traders sailed between the sultanates of Melaka and Ternate.

An account of Majapahit, written in 1365, about seventy years after its founding, and a chronicle of the kings of east Java, compiled around 1613, have been preserved by Balinese copyists. These two literary works support archaeological evidence for Majapahit having been an important center, deriving revenue from international trade and from its farmers to sustain a wealthy elite and its devotional cults to Hindu and Buddhist deities. The eyewitness account is of King Rajasanagara's tour of his domains, written by the palace superintendent of Buddhist Affairs, Mpu Prapanca. It was composed about the same time as Ibn Battuta was recording the Islamic pieties of Pasai's Sultan al-Malik az-Zahir. The chronicle, known as the *Pararaton* (The Book of Kings), was drawn up after Majapahit had been destroyed by Muslim armies as a record of a lost past in Java and a living present in Bali.

It was important to its author to create a distinguished pedigree for the king who was his employer and to connect Majapahit to an older past in east Java's history. Accordingly, the *Pararaton* opens with a very long description of the origins and antecedents of the founder of the preceding kingdom of Singhasari. The Hindu god Siva fathered him, and the Hindu god Brahma adopted him. When he founded Singhasari in 1222, after killing the king of Kediri, he took the title Ken Angrok, which means "lord of the mountain." He selected Ken Dhedhes, widow of the murdered ruler, to be his queen. The *Pararaton* then traces Ken Angrok's descendants, naming his wives and the children born to each mother, into descending generations. The author assigns to each royal personage dates, the name of their kingdom, and the name of their burial temple. There is no description of the extent of kingdoms, crops grown, or population. What is striking about the *Pararaton* is its testimony that east Java's kingdoms were perpetually at war with each other. Occasionally, the numbers of troops in a squad are given and conversations between military officers reproduced. Some local detail exists, such as the wife of an *adipati* (lord) offering refreshments to the king. Kings are commanders in the field; their opponents are often their near relatives.

The second part of the chronicle tells the story of Raden Wijaya, a prince of Singhasari who fulfils the prophecy concerning Ken Dhedhes. He is descended from her union with Ken Angrok and becomes, by victory over another king, the founder of Majapahit. The third part of the chronicle describes Majapahit at the peak of its riches, power, and influence in the reign of King Rajasanagara (also known by the name Hayam Wuruk). The final part of the *Pararaton* is a list of Rajasanagara's successors.

The *Pararaton* survived by being recopied on lontar leaves by generations of scribes employed in palaces in Bali and in the Balinese colony of western Lombok. On Bali, copying the register of Java's pre-Islamic rulers justified the claims of a whole new set of men governing the Balinese. Muslim kings on Java, however, perceived no reason to preserve or add to the *Pararaton.*

The Majapahit king whom the *Pararaton* particularly dwells on is King Rajasanagara (r. 1350–1389). He was the employer of Mpu Prapanca, author of the other literary text to have survived from Majapahit, again because of the labor of scribes in Bali and Lombok. In place of the *Pararaton*'s list of names and dates and its tales of heroes, Prapanca's narrative supplies an account of daily life in the middle years of the fourteenth century.

Prapanca accompanied his king on a lengthy tour of his domains in 1364. He completed his account of this exercise in advertising the royal presence the following year. Prapanca called his narrative *Desawarnana,* which means "Description of the Districts." The most recent translator of this Old Javanese text uses Prapanca's title; previous scholarly editions called it the *Nagarakertagama* (Realm Rich in Virtue). The royal route followed the commercial and pilgrim circuit of religious foundations and shrines that were scattered throughout Majapahit. Prapanca's task was to note the state of repair of Buddhist temples and monasteries; he also had to check on their income from donations and from the villages assigned for their support. Accompanying Rajasanagara on this tour was a huge suite of princes, princesses, officials, army officers, troops, and servants, plus their elephants, oxcarts, horses, grooms, and porters.

Majapahit kings' brand of religion was promoted in district towns by temples to Siva and Buddha. In the intervals between royal visits, rural populations were reminded of their king's pretensions by other temples to his ancestors, who were represented as gods. Prapanca says that Rajasanagara restored all the royal sanctuaries built by his forebears and that his officials followed his example by filling the landscape with memorial shrines, tower-temples, and linggas. Rajasanagara performed rites at all these temples. He also visited shrines that were located in magically charged places and consulted the hermits who tended them. Prapanca praises Rajasanagara and the royal relatives for their virtues. He says that, when royalty showed itself to the common people, it was as if the gods made themselves visible. The automatic consequence was prosperity of the land and welfare of its people.

It is clear from many cantos in the *Desawarnana* that the royal tour had more specific aims. The tour provided the king the opportunity to buy the loyalty of his local officials by distributing gifts of clothing, food, and gold, conferring titles, and admitting them to royal banquets. The tour allowed the king to address his district chiefs and remind them that their most important duties were to collect taxes and keep villagers busy farming their fields. To prevent tax evasion he ordered the chiefs to count the number of hearths in their districts at the end of every month. The king also used the tour to collect his taxes, which Prapanca dignifies by the term "gifts." Majapahit taxes were paid in the form of pigs, dogs, and fowl in such numbers that the porters struggled to carry them in baskets.

In writing of revenue, Prapanca distinguished between income from the royal domains in east Java and income from the revenue-generating territories on the shores of Sumatra, the Malay Peninsula, Kalimantan, the islands to Java's east as far as Timor and West New Guinea, and northeast to the Maluku islands. In the language of Prapanca, the rulers of these places "sought the protection" of Majapahit. They sent "tribute" each month to Majapahit in products that could be extracted from their subjects. Any countries disobeying the king were "attacked and wiped out completely / By the squadrons of the various meritorious naval officers" (Prapanca, 1995, canto 16, verse 5). The tax goods generated for Majapahit by these procedures made its ports attractive to foreign merchants. Prapanca calls them "friends" and says they came from kingdoms of the Tai, Khmer, Chams, and Vietnamese.

In east Java the royal domains were administered by the king's relatives and officials. Lands further west were ruled by vassals. These subrulers were required to present themselves at court at regular intervals. The source of wealth for the ruling house was the rice agriculture of farmers who were under the command of village and district chiefs. Population was concentrated in pockets of this landscape. Uncultivated land was plentiful, hence the efforts to ensure that villagers stayed put, cultivating farmlands within the boundaries of villages marked out by royal officials.

Royal wealth bought the support of distant vassals and of a class of men—and a few women—who were priests, hermits, nuns, copyists, poets, abbots of monastic communities, and scholars. Religious foundations, as places of learning, attracted students from other regions, and shrines were popular pilgrimage sites for "wanderers," a fourteenth-century form of tourist. Because of the number of experts in sacred texts and the proliferation of temples, Prapanca says Java was renowned for its purifying power. He praises King Rajasanagara for providing rest houses for the many monks and priests who journeyed from overseas to Java's holy places. Prapanca also shows how religious foundations supported monarchy: they staged regular ceremonies of prayer, rituals, and offerings on behalf of the king and his gods, and they staged spectacles, such as boxing, dancing, and theater. Vendors of all kinds set up stalls around religious foundations for the wanderers and the great crowds of court officials, district heads, and commoners who attended.

The *Desawarnana* presents an idealized picture of Majapahit: rulers of peerless virtue, mighty warriors, happy taxpayers, adoring fans of royalty. But, alongside the god-kings, the *Desawarnana* presents credible information on the state of Javanese society in the fourteenth century in details such as the use of copper and gold currencies. The flattery of Rajasanagara as a heavenly being did not prevent him from focusing on the earthly issue of taxes. Nor did this flattery blind Prapanca to Rajasanagara's very real problems of holding a state together. He shows his king trying to prevent villagers from fleeing demands by the state on their time and property.

It is apparent from the *Desawarnana* that jobs were the consequence of royal appointment and favoritism. An official derived his income from his percentage or "take" from peasant taxes and from royal gifts. When royal favor was lost, the job was withdrawn and the income dried up. Royal visits must have been ruinous for official and commoner alike, for they entailed huge expenditures of time and produce to host the enormous numbers of royals, attendants, and hangers-on. There were few guarantees for the commoner; royal edicts issued commands, not assurances. Having a daughter catch the eye of the king was the ordinary family's surety of a gift or protection where there was no body of written law or legal system to appeal to. Skilled craftsmen, such as metalworkers, and members of specialized occupations, such as ferrymen and porters, banded together in guilds to regulate their business, maintain a monopoly of skills within their group, provide mutual aid, and secure a mechanism for mediating with royal agents.

Much has been written on the conception of power in Javanese society, suggesting that it was unique, but Java's rulers had much in common with states throughout the archipelago. Indonesian states were organized as monarchies whose rulers claimed to share qualities of the divine. It was the job of court poets, sculptors, architects, musicians, and dancers to represent this claim in written and visual images, in recitation of court chronicles, and in theatrical performances. Such boasts by royalty can be found in inscriptions of the Sumatran rulers of seventh-century Srivijaya, in the genealogies of fifteenth-century Bugis kings (who traced their descent from the god Batara Guru), and in the statue portraits of Java's kings as Siva or the Buddha. Indonesian kings did not give up this claim when they converted to Islam. Then they announced themselves to be the Shadow of Allah. Furthermore, Java shared with all other archipelago political units the concept that maleness was an essential attribute of rulers. Women played a variety of roles in elaborating these concepts of monarchy. In the kingdoms of east Java women of all social classes were visible and active in public in relation to the king.

An attribute of royalty, in Indonesian conceptions, was generosity to sub-

WOMEN, PUBLIC LIFE, AND POWER

In the *Desawarnana* Prapanca's king is described as attractive to women. When he passed by in royal procession, the narrator says some village women rushed so fast to see the king that their breast-cloths fell off; others climbed trees to get a better view. Even pretty young nuns in forest hermitages imagined King Rajasanagara to themselves as the incarnation of the god of love and were left, on his departure, pining to be seduced.

The king himself was attracted to women. Prapanca records that King Rajasanagara enjoyed womanizing at the end of a hunt or a day of temple ritual. When his troops crushed Bali, its queen was brought to his palace; and women he particularly liked during encounters on his travels were taken into the palace. Women as other men's wives also had a role to play in demonstrating kingship. Each time Rajasanagara showed himself at ceremonies and on tours, the wives of his officials were in the royal entourage. On royal tours queens showed their faces to the crowds. Prapanca says that commoners derived blessing from the act of gazing on the faces of their royals, male and female.

Grandmothers, mothers, aunts, sisters, and wives of kings held special importance in east Java's kingdoms too. Rajasanagara's female relatives appeared in public at state ceremonies, they accompanied the king on tours of the realm in carriages with their own insignia, they were formally consulted on affairs of state, and they organized public ceremonies. The *Desawarnana* does not speak of women as mothers of royal children, or describe the king as a father. Commoner women are temporary entertainments; royal women are consorts, intercessors with the Buddha, and advisers. When Majapahit's chief administrator, Gajah Mada, died in office in 1364, those advising the king who should be chosen as his successor included the king's mother, aunt, and two younger sisters.

Queen Suhita is recorded in inscriptions from 1429 to 1447 as the ruler of Majapahit, not as the ruler's wife. She succeeded her father, reigning ahead of a younger brother. There were no children from Queen Suhita's marriage. Royal prerogatives were kept in the family: a sister of the queen's husband married Suhita's younger brother, and he succeeded as King Kertawijaya (r. 1447–1451). Rule by women was the exception in Java as elsewhere in the archipelago. Heads of political units from villages to kingdoms were men.

ordinates. Exchange with other royals was also a sign of status. Majapahit kings made gifts to rulers they chose as vassals in the business of extracting a region's wealth. Inscriptions record the royal network of givers and receivers. The last king of Singhasari, for instance, sent the Sumatran king of Melayu a statue of a Buddhist deity inscribed with the name of the deity, sender, and recipient.

Throughout the archipelago, metal objects such as swords, krises, receptacles, and jewelry became items of regalia. Carried before a ruler in processions, they signaled the right of an individual to reign. Krises and lances even received personal names and titles because they were thought to embody the essence of rulers who had owned them and to bring success in battle. In this aspect of royalty, too, Prapanca's king acted according to archipelago standards.

Mpu Prapanca was not the only court poet whose work survived the overthrow of Majapahit. Texts of the fifteenth-century court poet Mpu Tanakun

Section of wall carving from Panataran Temple, East Java. Visitors who walked around the temple could see models of correct behavior in the body language of gods and humans, men and women. Photographic Archive, Royal Institute of Linguistics and Anthropology, Leiden, No. 37981. Photo courtesy of the KITLV.

The Princess of Jengala in Java's forest. The forest is shown as a place of danger as well as of beauty. From Serat Panji Jayakusuma, manuscript, c. 1840, National Library of Indonesia, KBG 139. Photo courtesy of the Lontar Foundation.

were among treasures taken to Bali when Majapahit's aristocrats were dislodged from power by converts to Islam. Taken together, the record on lontar, stone, and copperplate provides information about daily life that could not be known or surmised from earlier stages in Java's history. We learn that ordinary people were organized in villages. Java had large tracts of territory only lightly populated. All kinds of itinerants moved along Java's roads, forest tracks, and rivers. Peddlers, porters, and roving bands plundered or hired themselves out as soldiers. There were holy men, scholars, medicine men, frauds, and adventurers. The stories of nuns in hermitages and princesses lost or popping up to prophesy suggest that there were women on the move too. Like the men, such women were detached from home and village obligations by poverty, adventure, temporary removal to a king's bed, or intellectual quest.

There were also villagers on the move, fleeing epidemics, trying to escape heavy tax demands, or going to jobs in town or capital. Some were avoiding conscription, whereas others sought their fortune by hiring themselves out for war. In many parts of Java, farmers cultivated the same piece of ground for several years, then moved to clear another plot after the soil was depleted or weeds overcrowded the cultivated crop. People also moved within the year. Farmers, for instance, often built small huts on their rice lands, slept at their work place during the growing season, and returned to their home village after the harvest. Men went on trading trips and fishing expeditions; girls entered households of aristocrats or princes. In addition, men were sent to capital or district town to work on the administration's building projects. Another form of mobile population within a loosely defined territorial unit was the sea people, who lived along waterways, harvested the sea, and paid their taxes to land-based rulers. There were men on the move out of Java, seeking a living, experiencing the world, attending a school beyond the Java Sea. Kings were on the move touring their districts, leading war raids, and relocating the capital when they proclaimed a new kingdom. Foreigners moved through Java's landscape too, carrying with them unfamiliar items such as cash, books, silks, and specialized knowledge.

Java's landscape presented barriers of nature: jungle, mountains, and dangerous animals. Passage through that landscape was also obstructed by toll-gates and sentinel posts. It was not marked out by border posts or walls. The furthest reaches of kingdoms vanished in forests or blended into the outlying districts of neighboring states. The king controlled a core area, had a personal army, and administered his area through royal relatives and favorites. Kings supported an industry of priests, poets, architects, astrologers, scribes, sculptors, and performers to broadcast their rule. At times kings could force vassals to attend court regularly, pay taxes, and produce laborers for public works and the army. At other times their ability to coerce or persuade was reduced by palace wars over succession, by disease, or by poor harvests. At such times vassals tried to set themselves up as independent rulers, or they came into the orbit of a competing ruler. In some cases, vassals sent payments to more than one king. Kings understood their territory in terms of numbers of taxpayers, rather than numbers of hectares. The titles they took—"Nail of the Universe," "Compassionate Buddha," "Defender of (Islamic) Religion"—did not include locality. They did not call themselves King of East Java, for example. Kings marked possession of territory by place-names and the construction of temples.

In all the spaces not yet peopled by human beings, Java's mountains, forests, rivers, and seas were believed to be filled with spirits, demons, gods, and goddesses. They interfered in the affairs of humans: evil spirits brought epidemics, spirit armies chose sides in warfare, and messengers from the gods lurked to announce the future to passing heroes. Benevolent spirits took up residence in villages. Their usual lodging place was in a banyan tree, a characteristic of Javanese villages at least since the fifteenth century.

Over a four-hundred-year period, villages are frequently mentioned in inscriptions. They were not little republics isolated from the high and mighty in bucolic harmony. Rather, there was a hierarchy within each village by which descendants of the original families who had cleared the land outranked the descendants of later arrivals. Residents included farmers and crafts families of sculptors, mask makers, and potters. Villages were broken down into clusters of households, and specific officials were granted the right in royal charters to collect taxes. Fourteenth-century inscriptions require traders and artisans in villages to use copper cash. Villages were the site of feasts, ceremonial reception of state dignitaries, and staged entertainments. Sometimes they were the site of pilgrimages because they were near holy grottoes or springs or the home of a man renowned for his magical and spiritual powers.

The late fifteenth-century Majapahit poet Mpu Tanakun described east Java as a site of villages, shrines, and gardens. The poem includes the important information that meeting hall and banyan tree were part of village life. The hunter, Lubdhaka, travels through this landscape in search of wild animals and ends up finding the path to enlightenment:

> *His journey took him to the northeast, where the ravines were lovely to look down into;*
> *The gardens, ring-communities, sanctuaries, retreats and hermitages aroused his wonder.*
> *There lay large fields at the foot of the mountains, with crops of many kinds growing along the slopes;*
> *A large river descended from the hills, its stream irrigating the crops.*
> *Now there was a village which he also viewed from above, lying below in a valley between the ridges.*
> *Its buildings were fine to behold, while the lalan roofs of the pavilions were veiled in the drizzling rain.*
> *Wisps of dark smoke stretched far, trailing away in the sky,*
> *And in the shelter of a banyan tree stood the hall, roofed with rushes, always the scene of many deliberations.*
> *To the west of this were mountain ridges covered with rice-fields, their dikes running sharp and clear.*
> *The gardens were close together and laid out in rows, and the many coconut palms were all shaded by mist. . . .* (Siwaratrikalpa, *canto 2, stanzas 4–9, Teeuw, 1969)*

The village, then, was a cluster of families ranked unequally. Villages were surrounded by rain-fed fields where farmers raised one rice crop in a year and grew vegetables and soybeans between rice cycles. Village elites deliberated in public pavilions; they elected one of their own as head. Villages were linked to a higher level of government by their headmen and by tax agents. They were linked to other villages and to markets by itinerant men who were traders, artisans, moneylenders, religious teachers, and students. A village could incorporate newcomers if they connected themselves to established residents through work or marriage, or if they showed signs of unusual powers. Coins of gold, silver, and copper linked village to capital and to men from overseas.

COINS AND JOURNEYS

In Indonesia's islands metal bars and coins existed alongside other forms of money such as textiles, spices, iron axes, and slaves. Precious cloths in a palace represented a form of wealth to be used as gifts, as payment for other goods, and as savings, in addition to their uses as wall hangings, material for clothing, and as objects of conspicuous display or ritual significance.

A metal currency is a symbolic method that requires a government authority to fix standards of weight and quality of manufacture; therefore the history of coins in archipelago communities is related to the growth of strong governments. That history also includes early Indonesia's contacts with states producing coins, the coins in international circulation, as well as the history of metals, their geographic location, and their manufacture. Coins cross boundaries of region, language, and religion; they are an information system. Coins also give evidence of which writing systems were employed by governments, when they carry inscriptions giving the names of kings and their titles.

Coins make journeys through time and place. For instance, when rice farmers were required to pay taxes in cash, they had to find a buyer who had a supply of cash, obtained as a loan from a broker or patron. Coins flowed into a ruler's treasury and out again as agents of the ruler paid soldiers, made donations to religious foundations, and purchased imported consumer goods.

For about five hundred years (eighth to thirteenth centuries) the temple-building kingdoms of central and east Java used gold and silver coins.

Their currencies, called sandalwood currency from the flower stamped on each coin, have turned up in coin finds in Bali, Sumatra, southern Thailand, and the Philippines. Gold coins were often cube-shaped. Round silver coins date from the 770s; these had the flower image on one side and a character in the Indian Nagari script on the other. From early in the ninth century coins manufactured in Java have inscriptions in Old Javanese, replacing the Sanskrit of the earlier coins. The finds of low denomination coins in ports establish Java's trading connections and show that Java's traders operated in a world where value was computed in metal. In the fourteenth century copper coins of Chinese manufacture were imported by Majapahit.

Chinese coins were designed for portability and ease of calculation, being small, light, and bundled together in units by a string passed through a square hole in the center of each coin. So many were purchased by traders in Javanese networks that they became a regular means of payment in Majapahit. Copies of Chinese coins were also made in Java. An inscription from 1350 refers to the use of copper cash in place of the silver coins used in the past. Charters issued by Majapahit kings reckoned fines, fees, and taxes in copper coins. Government made calculations of taxes levied on villages and individuals in numbers of coins. Cash was used by some members of the community to pay for services such as ferry crossing. Majapahit charters record payment of taxes in copper cash by boatmen and tradespeople.

A key function of Pasai and Majapahit in Indonesian histories is that they draw distinct territories and separate pasts into the one history. For example, Majapahit functions in the history of the Sundanese of west Java to link them to the mainstream. Sundanese literary heritage provides an explanation for the name Majapahit and stakes a claim to west Java origins for the kingdom's founder in the story of Raden Susuruh, a prince of Pajajaran. He meets a female hermit named Cemara Tunggal in his travels across the island. She tells him to search for the *maja* tree, which has *pahit* (bitter) fruit and to establish his kingdom at that place. The hermit also prophesies that Raden Susuruh will rule all of Java. She then reveals herself to be Ratu Loro Kidul, Queen of the Southern Ocean, commander of spirit forces. She promises to marry and serve all the kings of Java and to support them with her magic powers.

The Pasemah people of south Sumatra establish their beginnings in Majapahit. In a foundation legend, Atong Bungsu and his sister Putri Sendang Biduk arrived with their followers from Majapahit. Putri Sendang Biduk settled at Palembang and became a mighty princess of the southeast, while her brother journeyed into the hilly interior to where the Pasemah and Lematang Rivers meet and founded the village of Benua Kling. There the Majapahit man had four sons who became the founders of the four ancestral families of the Pasemah. Kings of Butung also claimed links with Majapahit. Its court traditions tell that Butung's first ruler was a woman who acquired a Majapahit prince as her consort. Their son later visited the east Javanese court and returned with royal gifts to inaugurate male rule of Butung. Rulers of Pasai, Melaka, and Banjarmasin obtained wives from Majapahit and sent princesses into its royal household.

Majapahit also owes its status as a major kingdom of the Indonesian archipelago to the labors of European philologists and to the Javanese scholars whom they trained. Between 1902 and 1916 publication of the *Desawarnana* and of the *Pararaton* created detailed knowledge of this kingdom to substitute for the vague assertions of past glory in popular belief.

MAJAPAHIT: SYMBOL OF NATIONAL UNITY OR OF JAVANESE IMPERIALISM?

All copies of texts by Prapanca and Tanakun disappeared from Java, lost in its many wars or burned by zealous Muslims, or disintegrated over time. Scribes in Bali continued to copy some Majapahit texts for their nobles who claimed descent from Majapahit's aristocracy. In 1894, when Dutch troops defeated the Balinese dynasty that ruled Lombok, they found in the royal library among other manuscripts a copy of the *Desawarnana.* It was, in 1916, translated into Dutch and reported in Holland and in Indonesia.

Knowledge of Prapanca's claim that Majapahit had ruled one hundred foreign countries became widely known among the new middle classes of Indonesia's cities. Javanese now had the Dutch conception of Majapahit as a mighty empire to replace their own version of Majapahit as a kingdom defeated, its culture wiped out to make way for Islam. Twentieth-century nationalists such as Yamin found in the Dutch interpretation evidence for an archipelago-wide political and cultural unity existing for centuries prior to colonial rule. They took Majapahit as an inspiration in their campaign for independence and a justification for imagining the new country as the successor state to Majapahit.

A kingdom of Javanese ruling non-Javanese was not a vision that appealed to all Indonesians. Many rejected Majapahit as feudal and imperialistic, having nothing to offer a modern country. Others who objected to a Hindu-Buddhist kingdom as the symbol of unity for Muslims championed Majapahit's successor state, Demak. Demak stood for the Islamizing of Java and so could represent the major intellectual transformation that had taken place in nearly all Indonesian societies.

According to Prapanca, Majapahit's ruling class excluded from the palace three groups of people classified as low-born: merchants, foreigners, and the impure. A century later, its kings were less fastidious, or they had shed such narrow views, for some Majapahit court officials and some population clusters were Muslims. Pasai tradition says that it was conquered by a Majapahit army in the middle of the fourteenth century. Pasai's important men and a princess were taken as prisoners of war to the Javanese capital, where they formed the nucleus of a Muslim community. Tombstones constructed according to Islamic forms and with inscriptions in Arabic are among the few objects to have survived from this Hindu kingdom. They date to the fifteenth century.

Majapahit is important in Indonesian literary traditions. In Javanese culture it signified a glorious kingdom of superhuman rulers, wise officials, refined arts, and universal recognition. Although knowledge of other Indonesian kingdoms, such as the fifth-century Tarumanegara, was lost until recovered by the Western science of archaeology in the nineteenth century, folk memories of Majapahit survived because knowledge of Majapahit was preserved in written form. The texts supplied stories for the puppet theatre and dance drama staged in villages, towns, and palaces in Java and in Bali. In Islamic literature composed on Java, Majapahit's Hindu gods and kings were fitted into a new, Islamic chronology where they were precursors of Islam.

Elsewhere in the archipelago, folk memories of Majapahit were created in sultanates founded after Majapahit had been conquered by Demak. In the new Muslim states of the sixteenth and seventeenth centuries, histories written to explain their origins often included a link to Majapahit. The Muslim circle of sultanates incorporated Majapahit, making it known from an Islamic perspective. These popular histories were composed in rhythmical verse and chanted aloud to an audience. Written in Malay in Arabic letters, they were a product of Malay culture of the western archipelago.

ANIMISM

Hinduism, Buddhism, Islam, and Christianity developed alongside local religions in Indonesian communities. Over time these traditions absorbed local beliefs and practices and supplanted local religious specialists in public importance. Like indigenous belief systems, the new religions were concerned with connections between this world and other worlds, with rites of passage (birth, death, marriage), and with defining correct behavior. Where they differed was in the claim to being valid for all people in all places and all periods of time. Indigenous belief systems (often called animism) were specific to a region or a community. They honored spirits believed to inhabit a specific locality or natural phenomenon, such as a sacred tree or rock. Those who lived within the orbit of spirits made no claims for the powers or relevance of their spirits beyond their own locality. In Indonesian contexts, universal religions, which were not contained by political boundaries, geography, or culture, provided a constant belief system for people whose mobility often took them away from the spirits of home.

ARABIC AS A LANGUAGE OF ISLAMIC CONQUEST

Islam and the Arabic language and script are inextricably intertwined. The expansion of Islam by wars of conquest and settlement in the decades following Muhammad's death led to the triumph of the Arabic language over the languages of many non-Arab peoples, including the Egyptians, Syrians, and Iraqis. As Islamic conquest expanded east into Persia, however, conversion became detached from adopting Arabic as the language of daily life. Persians retained their own language, but they replaced their writing system with the Arabic one. Similarly, the Turks, who became rulers of the core Muslim lands (Arabia, Egypt, Syria, and Iraq), retained their own language, but wrote it in Arabic script. (In the early twentieth century Kemal Ataturk ordered that modern Turkish be written in the Roman alphabet.)

Archipelago inhabitants began converting to Islam after the great expansion of Arabs had ceased, hence Arabic was a sacred language and a language of religious scholarship, but never an imperial language in Indonesia. Malay oral and written traditions associate being Malay with Islamic belief. These traditions survive in today's idiom *masuk Melayu,* which translates as "to convert to Islam." Literally the words mean to enter Malay identity.

The earliest Indonesian Muslims were coastal Malays. Following their conversion to Islam, they continued to use the Malay language, which was widely spoken in the western archipelago and was a trade language in the archipelago's ports. Malay acquired prestige as the language of Muslims. It became a Muslim language in the sense that it incorporated a large body of Arabic vocabulary, and its scribes gave up Indic scripts to write Malay exclusively in Arabic letters. Arabic script was slightly modified to handle the different vowel sounds of Malay. This writing style, called *Jawi,* became the medium throughout the archipelago for writing on Islamic topics.

Approximately 15 percent of Malay vocabulary is of Arabic derivation. Some words were present in the languages of non-Arab peoples with whom Malays came into contact through trade, and these were adopted through personal interaction. Most words entered Malay permanently through direct borrowings from literature written in Arabic. The nomadic quality of Malay culture promoted the rapid spread of many aspects of Islam. Muslim traders, teachers, and preachers introduced words of Arabic origin into the languages of many Indonesian peoples. Professional writers and performers fanned out to jobs opening up in new sultanates where they introduced the Jawi writing system.

An example of the powerful impact of Malay can be seen in Bima. Mbojo is the native language, but when the ruling class converted to Islam, Malay, not Mbojo, was used for all literary purposes. This development is attributed to the island's second Muslim king, who in 1645 ordered that texts were to be written in Arabic script because it was the writing system prescribed by God. Since the seventeenth century both compositions original to Bima and books imported into Bima have been in Malay in Arabic script. Malay created a web of stories, ideas, language, and moral reference that drew archipelago communities into a common Indonesian Islamic culture.

Malay extended this web of culture as the language of composition for legal texts, theological essays, and histories. It was the language of leaflets or single sheets explaining to the reader the meaning of signs and omens, how to determine auspicious times and days for actions and rituals, and how to interpret dreams. The earliest known Muslim writings in Malay date from the late sixteenth century. In seventeenth-century Aceh, Malay written in the Arabic script was being used for passports, laws, contracts, letters, and seals of authority.

Malay-language narratives written in Jawi, called *hikayat,* were composed in palaces by men versed in the literary heritages of Islam and in the folk traditions of archipelago societies. The *Hikayat Amir Hamzah* (Story of Amir Hamzah), for instance, tells folk tales from Arabic and Persian literature about an uncle of Muhammad and the battles he waged for Islam. Through Malay translation, speakers of other archipelago languages were introduced to a vast body of Islamic literature from Arabia and Persia. Hikayats also translated into Malay stories from other Indonesian languages and so circulated around the archipelago tales of local Muslim saints, the Hindu Rama stories, and adventures of homegrown heroes. The roaming ancestral heroes of the hikayats named the landscape through which they passed, and these stories are cited today to support claims to territory and stake boundaries between different dialect groups.

Hikayats also included histories, often called *sejarah.* The writing of history began in many archipelago societies after conversion of the ruling class to Islam. Central to these histories was the explanation of how that society became Muslim. The history of non-Muslims was of no importance, unless it explained the adoption of Islam as the community's religion. Pre-Islamic pasts were presented as a time of chaos. Former Hindu rulers were persons to be pitied because they did not know Islam or were placed within a chronology leading to Islam.

Historians of new sultanates took as their model the *Sejarah Melayu* (History of the Malays), written around 1612. It places the origins of the Melaka sultanate in Srivijaya and follows the adventures of a Srivijaya prince and his descendants in a chain of royalty leading to Melaka's first sultan. *History of the Malays* also connected its royal family to the region's most important royalty, the rulers of Majapahit. It says that Sultan Mansur Syah (r. 1459–1477) married a princess of Majapahit.

The *Hikayat Banjar* (History of Banjar) creates a history for the sultanate of Banjarmasin, where the ruling class of coastal Malays had converted around the 1520s. This history allocates to Pasai the honor of planting the seeds of Islam inside Majapahit territory, and into the extended royal family itself. It narrates the marriage of a princess of Pasai to the king of Majapahit, and says that the princess's brother who accompanied the bride to Majapahit was given permission by the king to settle at Ampel-Gading and to convert the local inhabitants to Islam.

Founding histories of sultanates follow the narrative of the first royal conversion with description of the first court and its ceremonies in order to establish the pedigree of the royal house. Bugis genealogies, which were constructed to show the descent of the ruling class from local gods, were rewritten to fit the gods into an Islamic scheme leading to Muhammad's revelations. Local histories often have a didactic character, too, explaining how a king should rule. Many give elaborate descriptions of the splendor of the court, of banquets, and of the wealth built on trade. Some were written as histories of the world. Nuruddin al-Raniri's history of Aceh, composed around 1640, began with creation and traced a divinely ordained path that set Aceh in an evolution from Egypt of the pharaohs through Arabia, Pahang (on the Malay Peninsula), and Melaka.

Hikayats existed alongside oral folklore. Literary Malay diverged from the way Malay was spoken in market towns across the archipelago. Although manuscripts incorporated local words, the literary language and the formation of letters remained uniform over vast distances and centuries. Courtiers and professional scribes at sultanates around the archipelago told the same stories with differences of fact, detail, and interpretation. Their narratives all had fixed features: they were composed in metrical, rhymed verse and their stories were placed within an Islamic frame of reference. Networks of professional writers extended from Melaka to Aceh, Pasai, Brunei, Sambas, Banjarmasin, Siak, and Bima, keeping in touch with each other, reading each other's works, studying to reproduce a standardized form of language and letter formation.

The professional scribal class learned the arts of writing and decorating essays, poems, histories, genealogies, treaties, and diplomatic correspondence from teachers and reference works. Manuals for the correct practice of letter writing were compiled for scribes who conducted the written business of kings, court officials, and the directors of commerce. These manuals were in the Malay language written in Jawi. The manuals also outlined procedures for envoys in charge of the ceremonial delivery and reading aloud of letters. There were manuals on the composition of letters between paired inferior-superior: subject to the king, commoner to a courtier, child to the mother. Styles for address between lovers and between Malays and Chinese were also set down in writing. Manuals provide evidence of how individuals perceived their relationships and position within hierarchies.

Archipelago sultans sent letters in Malay in Arabic script decorated with flowers and abstract designs and borders. The sending of such letters was a sign of royalty, not a private or intimate act. Rebel princes and claimants to royal ancestry circulated letters as a sign of their authority, an act of kingship. Men who could not read or write set aside funds for the support of men who monopolized such knowledge. The language of royal letters situated men within a cultural world of Islam. Such manuals illustrate how specific features were incorporated and possessed by literati and became a part of local intellectual life and practice.

PAPER, ISLAM, CULTURE, AND COMMERCE

The undulating Arabic script was not well suited to being written on lontar leaf, bamboo strips, and stone that had provided mediums for Malay when it was written in Indic scripts. Conversion to Islam promoted the use of paper in Indonesia as the medium for writing and also the binding of pages in book form. Professional writers who made copies of the Koran in the archipelago introduced a characteristic feature of Islamic civilization and demonstrated their acquaintance with the practice of schools in the Islamic core countries.

Paper had been used in Buddhist religious centers in the archipelago. In 689 the Chinese scholar I Ching requested fresh supplies of paper and ink to be sent from China to him in Srivijaya. Paper reached the Muslim world in the eighth century when a group of Chinese papermakers was enslaved and brought to Samarkand (in modern Uzbekistan) in 751. From there paper-making spread in Muslim lands, where it was used for books, for government records, and commercial transactions. Writing down contracts was also prescribed in the Koran.

The systematic use of paper and the production of paper for handwritten books and records facilitated a closer administration and promoted business relationships. They stimulated literacy and gave Indonesian landscapes an Islamic "look": The turbaned man carrying a book marked himself as a Muslim.

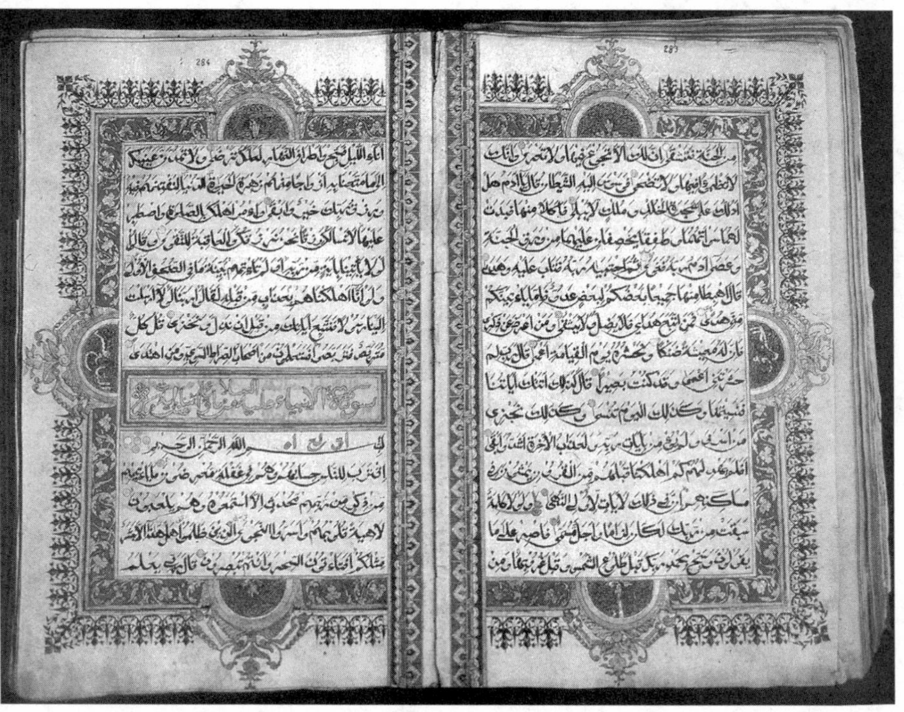

A Koran, with richly embellished text, copied at the Surakarta Palace by Ki Atmaparwita, 1797–1798. Koran, Widya Budaya Collection of the Palace of Yogyakarta, No. 1 131. Photo courtesy of the Lontar Foundation.

The religious duty of pilgrimage built into Islamic civilization the expectation and desire for mobility. Manuals written for the guidance of Islamic kings stressed generosity and patronage as manifestations of royalty. Pasai and the other sultanates were remote from the Islamic heartland, but the sea-lanes of the archipelago were crisscrossed by men who frequented regional centers of Islam and made study trips to Mecca. The custom of hospitality and generosity toward travelers, especially men with reputations for learnedness and piety, facilitated their travels and ensured their welcome in Indonesian societies. Manners, costume, books, language, and mosques gave daily life an Islamic look and feel.

NURUDDIN AL-RANIRI

An Indian from the Muslim city of Gujerat, Nuruddin al-Raniri (?–1666) studied in Mecca and then traveled in the Islamic world From 1637 to 1644 he was the most senior scholar in Aceh, where he labored to form his royal patron, Sultan Iskandar Thani (r. 1637–1641), into an Islamic king. He wrote for him the *Bustan al-Salatin* (Garden of Kings) as a guide to Islamic monarchy and compiled instructional materials in Malay on Islamic law, fasting, Muslim dietary laws, the duty of alms-giving, pilgrimage, and jihad for his Acehnese students. He wrote tracts against Jews and Christians, arguing that the Torah and the Bible were forgeries, and he campaigned against local practices of Islam that he considered wrong. He conducted public burnings of books and execution of men he branded as heretics.

Al-Raniri lost his preeminence following the death of his patron. Iskandar Thani's successor was his widow. She adopted for her reign title the female form of sultan to establish her status as independent ruler, implementer, and maintainer of Islam. As Sultanah Safiatuddin (r. 1641–1675), she tolerated Acehnese forms of Islam and al-Raniri had to look elsewhere in the Islamic world for patronage and employment. Aceh had three more female rulers before the religious establishment restored male rule. Today one of Aceh's universities is named not for Aceh's queens, but in honor of al-Raniri, upholder of orthodoxy.

In Java, Malay was a skill for religion school, Javanese for the palace. Java's royal libraries contained Malay translations of Arabic and Persian texts, but Java's royals neither admired nor understood the Malay language. Javanese, written in Arabic script, was the preferred language for devotional and mystical literature. Javanese, written in the Javanese script, continued to be employed for historical chronicles and documents; court lore; manuals of magic and practical arts, such as horsemanship; wayang plays; love poems; and didactic poems for princes. Malay in Jawi preserved knowledge of Majapahit in the hikayat. Javanese language and script preserved knowledge of Majapahit through the *babad* (chronicle).

Babads, written to be sung, were made up of stanzas that followed a prescribed number of syllables. Within each text were indications of the singing style. The opening stanzas usually stated when the babad was composed, using all the dating systems known to the author—Javanese, Islamic, and often also Christian. These stanzas usually also gave clues to the author. Reading was sung performance. In addition to the patrons, those attending a public performance could include cooks, janitors, tailors, and messengers who left their employer's workplace at the end of the day to return to their families, carrying a knowledge of "high culture" far beyond the residences of the wealthy. Traveling performers took babads to markets and village centers. The babad could be understood on many levels, as a tale of adventure, romance, and heroism, and as a conundrum of wordplays and hidden meanings.

Babads were written on paper or on palm-leaf. Some babads were prepared as scrolls, which could be slowly unrolled to reveal to the audience both the text and illustrations. Many babads were written on sheets bound into a book, the portable form of writing which Islamic texts had introduced to the archipelago. The pages of babads glow in gold and colored inks. Scenes from the narrative accompany the written word, and the whole is set in frames of foliage and patterns. Book and scroll differed strikingly from literary productions in Malay. Scribes working in Jawi took the Koran as their standard. Hikayats were composed as plain text with no images of kings, animals, birds, or buildings. Scribes who produced copies of the Koran sometimes enlivened the black lines of writing with red ink for the name of Allah, or set pages within frames of abstract patterns, but the text itself was the focus in production of Koran and hikayat. On Java, copying the Koran followed the same strict rules, but for histories and epic tales, Muslim Javanese culture produced a manuscript tradition of shimmering color. Pages were adorned with wild tigers and boars in forests, princes represented in the profile of wayang puppets, armies marching, flowers, birds, and princesses in gardens.

Paper and lontar leaf are perishable materials. Their preservation is the result of recopying by specialists. The oldest manuscripts surviving in Java, which date from the eighteenth century, cover events in the fifteenth, sixteenth, and seventeenth centuries and are products of Muslim Java. Babads from the pre-Islamic era have been preserved by copying only outside Java, in Bali and in Lombok. Babad texts were not understood as complete in themselves, and every generation's copyists added new material and rearranged the core stories of gods and rulers. Manuscripts with the same titles were not the same. Stories, sequences, characters, and locales of action differed in each reproduction.

The babad is not a historical source in the sense of giving a history of Majapahit through its royal edicts, treaties, and dates. Often human actions are explained by the intervention of gods. But babads do document that Islamic civilization produced a profound revolution within Javanese culture. Once Majapahit had been explained away in long passages devoted to gods, kings, prophecies, and warfare, the core of the babad turned to the understanding and practice of Islam by Java's learned men. These men came from two distinct groups: they were either the monarch's men and or they were roamers. The monarch's men enjoyed royal patronage and were judges in Islamic courts, heads of the mosque, and teachers. They explained sharia to the king, who enforced it. They expounded the doctrine that disobedience or revolt against a Muslim king was an act against Allah; the king paid their salaries and gave them gifts and public honors.

Roamers were holy men, Java's variant on a key figure of Islamic history. They chose Java's forest streams and mountaintops as places to meditate; they abstained from food, sleep, and sex to gain supernatural powers and the ability to perform acts of magic. Then they passed through Java collecting followers, who comprised a tightly knit band of initiates into their secret knowledge and a much larger crowd of hangers-on. The followers lived outside the norms and demands of the establishment of kings and kings' religious appointees. They shunned palace and mosque. Mobile holy men had the gift of prophecy. They were no friends to monarchs.

The climax to babad stories was the heresy trial, conducted by the king's religious men. The itinerant man debated theology with his accusers and judges. Sometimes he taunted them. Wandering men were executed; the king's men lived. Sometimes the wanderer eluded the king's men and vanished into heaven, or his mutilated body magically reconstituted itself before vanishing. The arguments presented in these trials show that Javanese thinkers were thoroughly informed on theological debates and controversies within the wider world of Islam. Geographic distance did not reflect intellectual distance. Becoming Muslim allowed some groups to seize power and public prominence, while others had to recede. From Aceh to Java, books and men perished in fire. Everywhere there was a struggle for the monopoly of knowledge and access to it.

Babads reflect the concerns of Muslim Java, which was the evolving product of Islam within a society that had been Hindu and Buddhist. Babads portray Java's kings in ways that connect them to god-kings of the east Java world as well as to sultans of the Islamic world. Attributes of kings shared by Hindu, Buddhist, and Muslim texts are divine essence; royal descent; victory in battle over neighboring kings; personal beauty; and patronage of religious institutions and scholars. The babads contain a message about monarchy that can be understood by reference to both Islamic and Javanese heritages: kings should preserve royal prerogatives; they should pursue occupations and habits suitable for royalty; they should foster religious observance that supports monarchy; they should cultivate meditation for the acquisition of spiritual knowledge and magical power; and they should curb cultivation of magical powers by other men.

In their distinctive ways, Malay and Javanese Muslim cultures spread out from coast to hinterland, from city to village, from king to commoner. They were not separated or sealed off from each other, for these were cultures of movement. There was nomadism built into Islam. Islamic trading networks provided highways for scholars; Islamic rulers and the pious were expected to provide for the traveling scholar; pilgrimage created a desire for and an expectation of travel. These features of Islam were nourished in Indonesian settings. Archipelago sea highways carried scholars to and from the Islamic heartland; ships carried the message of Islam made portable in book form; veneration of holy men made pilgrimages to sites inside Indonesia a feature of local Islam; rulers were bred in a world of self-advertising through promoting brands of religion. The habit of easy contact developed by centuries of sailing ensured that Indonesians were in touch with trends from overseas and with each other. Patterning relations in terms of inferior and superior created new vocabularies for explaining self to God and self to king. Local sources of pride, such as connections to Java's royal families, formed links between Indonesian communities.

Majapahit was born into an archipelago just beginning to connect itself to world Islam. It came to an end when Islamic states encircled it from outside and clusters of its subjects from within rejected the devotional cults of its rulers. Demak, then Pajang followed as small, Islamic successor states in Java, with the Hindu kingdoms of Pajajaran and Balambangan for neighbors on either side. In Javanese histories, Demak and Pajang make possible the establishment around 1600 of the most important kingdom of them all, the Islamic kingdom of Mataram. Mataram evolved in an archipelago whose sea-lanes included European ships and shippers alongside Muslims and Chinese. Mataram's kings built up their power by hiring as mercenaries men from Christian Europe as well as men from Muslim Sulawesi and Hindu Bali. Hindu Majapahit established itself in an archipelago that was becoming the site of Muslim states. Muslim Mataram established itself in an archipelago where ports ruled by Christian Europeans were scattered among the sultanates.

5

NEWCOMERS IN THE MUSLIM CIRCLE

Europeans Enter Indonesian Histories

Indonesian ships and shippers had a history of long journeys. They perfected the techniques of sailing within hours or days of land, and specialized in interisland routes. Shippers used knowledge of winds, currents, stars, and landmarks on coasts to navigate through reefs, shoals, along coastlines, and inner waters such as the Java Sea. Journeys between ports took days or weeks to accomplish. Archipelago sailors did not develop oceangoing navigation skills to carry them on journeys of many months across vast expanses of open water, and so they did not reach Europe. They did not establish Indonesian trading communities in European coastal cities.

European ships hugged coastlines too, but around the twelfth century European shippers embarked on experiments with navigation by instruments that would allow them to sail across oceans far out of sight of promontories and landmarks. European navigation skills developed as the product of both practical experience and book learning. Sea captains applied the compass and water clock and developments in trigonometry to plotting location. By the fifteenth century they were also using the quadrant and astrolabe to determine position and direction of sailing. Changes in design of ships also assisted transocean sailing. After three centuries of experimenting in sailing seas off northern Europe and along the west coast of Africa, European ships crossed the Atlantic to the Americas or rounded the southern tip of Africa and sailed across the Indian Ocean to India.

The European ships that first reached Asian waters in the 1490s were far smaller in size, number, and crew than those of the Zheng He fleets that had sailed from China to Aden in the 1430s but were larger than contemporary Asian ships. (By the 1490s China's government had banned construction of ships with more than two masts, and archipelago ships were adapted to short journeys and river travel.) Like the Chinese, European shippers were able to expand their routes into Asia by purchasing Arab navigation knowledge and skills. In 1498 Portuguese ships berthed in Calicut in India, and in 1505 they entered the sea highway to the Indonesian islands. They put in at archipelago ports, injecting a new set of men among the buyers and sellers. At the same time, ships sailing from Spanish ports in the Americas experimented traveling the long Pacific Ocean route. In 1565 Spanish traders established their headquarters in the sultanate of Manila, where the largest settlement of Chinese was established.

Two networks, operated by rival Christian Europeans, inserted themselves into established trade routes and ports of call. Spanish investors and their Chinese business partners linked Spanish settlements in the Americas to the Philippine Islands and China, and to ports in the Sulu islands, northern Borneo, northern Sulawesi, and Ternate. Portuguese investors and their Hindu business partners linked Portuguese settlements in India, Ceylon (now called Sri Lanka), China and Japan, Melaka, Banten, Makasar, Ternate, Ambon, Flores, and Timor.

All this took place in the era of the formation of the Muslim circle. In 1505, when the Portuguese sailed into the Straits of Melaka, Pasai had had an Islamic government for two hundred years. In 1511, when Portuguese ships anchored off Ternate, an Islamic government had been in control there for about thirty years. During the sixteenth century, Muslim governments established themselves in Aceh, Banjarmasin, and Butung, and along Java's north coast at Banten, Jayakarta, Cirebon, Gresik, Tuban, and Japara, all ports where the Portuguese did business. By the time Islamic government was introduced into southern Sulawesi early in the seventeenth century, a sizable Portuguese community already existed in Makasar alongside its Muslim merchants.

Portuguese communities prospered under archipelago rulers at various ports in the archipelago, but Portuguese authorities were determined to seize power over Melaka, for it controlled shipping traveling the sea highway between China and India. Like kora-koras, Portuguese ships could raid as well as trade. Cannon and armed assaults directed against Melaka in 1511 resulted in

DE BRITO'S INDONESIAN JOURNEYS

It is possible to get a vivid idea of the Indonesian island world five hundred years ago from the Portuguese Miguel Roxo de Brito's account of his fifteen-month voyage of trading and raiding in the eastern archipelago. In May 1581 de Brito joined a party of Malay traders on the clove-producing island of Bacan off the southwest coast of Halmahera. The kora-kora on which he was a passenger carried two hundred rowers and passengers. The ships put in for water at both inhabited and uninhabited islands dotting the seas. Wherever possible, they also took on food, additional rowers, and trade goods.

Their route took them to Wetar, Alor, Solor, and Flores islands, then to Java, and east to Bali and Bima to purchase gold and cloth. The ships then traveled to southern Sulawesi where the traders exchanged the gold and textiles for iron machetes. The machetes were transported to the northwestern tip of the New Guinea coast to exchange for massoy bark. The traders also picked up New Guinea slaves which they sold in Seram for sago loaves. De Brito's companions sold the loaves in Javanese ports to traders who needed a stock of this staple food to exchange in Banda for nutmeg and mace. At the end of the voyage, the final cargo consisted of New Guinea slaves, gold bars, and jewelry, aromatic and medicinal barks, and pearl shell.

The villages de Brito observed in the eastern end of the archipelago, where they stopped for supplies of fish, vegetables, and sago, paid homage to the visitors as lords and described their exchange of goods as gift and tribute. De Brito noted that the commoner populations of east Indonesian villages were scantily clad, while their ruling classes wore elaborate cloths with gold thread, acquired from the foreign traders who came seeking the products of the villagers' labor. On Banda, Seram, and the Raja Ampat islands De Brito saw villages surrounded by stone walls with watch towers and small guns, the effects of warships which captured people to sell or to put to work as rowers.

the Malay royal family abandoning its seat and relocating to other parts of the Malay Peninsula and western archipelago. A Portuguese ruling class then took over administering Melaka's markets and taxing its trade, and Portuguese ships patrolled the straits. The Portuguese continued Melaka's function as the principal place where buyers from China could meet sellers from India and remote parts of Indonesia.

To ensure continued stocks of archipelago products in Melaka's market, Portuguese envoys applied to sultans of the pepper ports of Aceh and Banten and to the Ternate sultan who controlled the spice ports for permission to do business. Portuguese envoys also sought authorization for their agents to work in north Java ports, which were collection centers for east Indonesian spices. They negotiated deals with rulers who were not yet part of the Muslim circle. From rulers in Flores and Timor the Portuguese applied to buy sandalwood, and from rulers of the southern Sulawesi kingdoms they negotiated rights to purchase rice, coconuts, and sea produce.

As a result of agreements with harbor authorities, the Portuguese were able to establish a trading network parallel to those of Indians, Arabs, Chinese, Malays, Javanese, and other Indonesians in the archipelago. They rented lodgings and warehouse space in the ports, employed local agents and laborers, and built churches. Like the other networks, the Portuguese network engaged in local trade and trade between major Asian ports. The Portuguese network also carried a small quantity of its Asian produce to markets in Europe. In the sixteenth century, around twenty-four hundred men left Portugal every year to work overseas in the Americas, in Portuguese settlements along the coasts of Africa, in Macau (China), and in Hirado (Japan). A handful of them made the Indonesian archipelago their workplace as servants of the Portuguese administration or of the Roman Catholic church, as private traders and as skilled artisans.

Melaka anchored the archipelago network. In the Portuguese hierarchy of settlements, Melaka was subordinate to the Portuguese-ruled city of Goa on India's west coast. From Goa Melaka received policy directions from higher levels of government and the church, as well as staff, supplies, ships, and specialized services. St. Paul's College offered European and Asian male students instruction in Latin, Portuguese, and the Greek and Roman classics. In Goa the municipal council tested and registered men seeking work in Asia as masons, carpenters, sculptors, metalworkers, and cannoneers. The printing press published holy texts, prayers, essays, and studies of Asian languages and the natural environment. From Goa the church's wandering holy men (priests, brothers) fanned out to Asian kingdoms, and there church standards were enforced. Men and books burned in Goa.

Portuguese traders, scribes, skilled craftsmen, adventurers, sailors, and soldiers were men. Like the Asian traders, they came without women, and they rented temporary wives from slave dealers in the ports where they worked. Those whose business bound them to a place for longer than a few months married local women. Within archipelago cities there developed little Roman Catholic communities of immigrants, their wives, in-laws, children, and servants, supporting a parish priest and church, or looking to the network to bring them occasional visits from traveling friars. Many Portuguese men on archipelago seaways did not come directly from Portugal, but from older communities of Portuguese overseas, such as Goa. These men were often the sons of Portuguese men who had married in Asia, or they were Asian converts to Christianity who spoke Portuguese.

The Portuguese injected a new look and sound into archipelago ports. Portuguese men covered the body with shirts, jackets, and trousers, and they wore shoes and hats. They fostered cultivation of tobacco and the habit of smoking it. A number of Portuguese words entered Malay and other archipelago languages, and Portuguese became a trade language used by buyers and sellers alongside Malay. The Portuguese introduced a new writing system, the Roman or Latin alphabet, along with a new means of producing writing in the mechanical press. They circulated printed books in Catholic neighborhoods. Portuguese envoys and priests made gifts of books to archipelago rulers who had not joined the Muslim circle. They discussed Christianity and debated Islamic beliefs with the non-Muslim rulers of the small kingdoms of south Sulawesi. They introduced Sulawesi rulers to European discoveries in medicine, astronomy, and map-making. Portuguese priests baptized the rulers of Suppa and Siang in 1544 and the following year baptized lords in other small states. They took the sons of a few Sulawesi princes to Goa for formal schooling.

Archipelago Muslims converted to Islam in a period of its history when Islam had lost its earlier receptivity to the knowledge of other civilizations. European intellectual, technical, mechanical, and scientific developments of the fifteenth and sixteenth centuries made little impact on intellectuals and theologians in Islamic lands. The books carried to the archipelago from Islamic countries remained handwritten in the era of printing, and they did not include great developments of the age, such as the discovery of the Americas. Because Muslims understood their religion as perfect knowledge, information originating in Christian Europe was sometimes considered irrelevant or useless. This attitude influenced reactions of archipelago rulers, scholars, religious thinkers, and writers to Europeans who were becoming a part of their societies in the sixteenth century.

Indonesian thinkers who were Muslim placed the Portuguese in the category of *kafir*. The word, which had entered Indonesian languages from Arabic, means a person who has no belief (rather than a person who believes in another religion) and has a pejorative connotation. Kafir hatred was encouraged among certain groups, particularly young men, in order to create conditions necessary for jihad. The sense of non-Muslims as polluting or as distracting Muslims from an observant life had a concrete result in the design of Muslim cities. In Banten and Jayakarta, for instance, Chinese and Europeans were not allowed to live inside the walled city unless they converted to Islam. As non-Muslims they were assigned living space outside the walls. In eighteenth-century Palembang non-Muslim Chinese were not even allowed to live on land. They were assigned to rafts moored on the river.

Christians carried their own strong impressions of Muslims formed in religion school and also from Portugal's and Spain's historical experience as vassal Muslim states on the western fringe of the Islamic world. From 921 to 1031 there was a caliphate in Spain. Voyages into Muslim Asia followed soon after Portuguese and Spanish armies had pushed the last Muslim rulers off their thrones at home and expelled Muslims who did not convert to Christianity.

The Portuguese were unwelcome to some Muslim rulers. Aceh's sultan, for instance, barred Portuguese from establishing a trading settlement in his port. Foreign Muslim merchants traveling to the archipelago were reluctant to enter it through the Straits of Melaka because they had to submit to Portuguese-imposed charges in Melaka and buy travel licenses there. They started sailing down Sumatra's west coast instead to enter the archipelago through the Sunda Straits that separate Sumatra from Java. This diversion of sea traffic brought an increase of business to west Java ports.

By the middle of the sixteenth century the mix of conditions that generated Islamic administrations in the archipelago were right in Banten: product, location, and Chinese settlement. The product was pepper. Banten's location at the entrance to the Java Sea offered the Arab network an alternative route to Indonesian markets and lower fees. Banten's sizable Chinese settlement attracted Chinese merchants and provided the urban services necessary to create a major port of call. One consequence of the installation of a Portuguese ruling class in Melaka was the rise to international prominence of Islamic monarchy in the Sundanese-speaking region of west Java.

Sundanese speakers form today the second largest ethnic group of Indonesia. The Sunda homeland combines a narrow strip of coast along the Java

Sea and the high Priangen mountains. It is a landscape of volcanic mountains, steep terrain, dense forest, mountain rivers, fertile soil, and natural sea harbors. In this western end of Java is evidence of an ancient stone ax industry that linked land and sea trades and brought Sundanese chiefs into communication with regional trends. This distant past of kingdoms named Tarumanagara and Galuh has left few physical traces, but writing on stone, copper plate, and lontar leaf shows first the influence of the international Sanskrit culture and then of Javanese culture. In the fifth century Taruma scribes composed the king's commands in Sanskrit; masons chiseled them on to stone in the south Indian Pallava script. By the eleventh century, Galuh's scribes were writing the king's commands in the spoken language (now called Old Sundanese) using the kawi script developed in east Java.

Old Sundanese was also the vehicle for works of religious devotion and instruction composed and copied in Hindu and Buddhist religious centers. This writing tradition on lontar leaf persisted into the eighteenth century. Professional writers still had patrons who wished to have family genealogies constructed establishing their descent from Hindu gods. Patrons wanted manuals for calculating auspicious times for journeys or marrying, and compilations of customs, myths, and magical sayings. Professional writers were also still producing lontar histories of Sundanese kings. These were the last vestiges of Pajajaran. From the mid-sixteenth century Javanese-speaking Islamic kings were extending their control over Sundanese-speakers. They patronized writers of Arabic who celebrated the lives of Muslim heroes and copied their stories on paper bound in book form. From the sixteenth century Islamic kings were in the business of spreading a Javanese Muslim culture into Sunda and west into Sumatran territories across the Sunda Straits.

Sundanese literary tradition ascribes the basis of royal wealth in west Java to a Javanese prince. In 1156 Raden Panca subdued a group of Sundanese and ordered them to clear trees for rice fields and to gather wild pepper in the surrounding forest. Under Pajajaran's rulers, the palace-capital and its web of monastic communities held the kingdom's territories. Forest-dwelling, semi-nomadic farmers were required to pay their taxes in pepper. Pajajaran's rulers put supplies into the international pepper market through Chinese and west Asian merchants who called at Pajajaran's port of Sunda Kelapa. Foreign traders settled further west in the delta of the Cibanten River. They supplied Pajajaran's rulers with rice for the royal table, pack horses for transport, and slaves.

With their inland connections and royal devotional cults focused on Hindu gods, Pajajaran's elite was not well placed to respond to changes taking place in the western archipelago in the sixteenth century. They could not acquire supplies of pepper sufficient to meet market demand from farmers whose farm sites kept changing and who only periodically gathered pepper from forest vines. Royal income could not support a navy capable of defending Sunda Kelapa. The port was captured by forces under the control of the Muslim ruler of Cirebon, Sunan Gunung Jati, in 1527.

To become a major power, Pajajaran's ruling class had to transform its subjects from part-time gatherers of a product growing in the wild to cultivators of pepper vines raised in permanent fields. Settled farmers could be controlled by government and its agents. In the sixteenth century, Chinese, Arab, and Portuguese buyers were seeking markets where pepper was regularly available in sufficient quantity and where the area administration enforced predictable standards in weighing and pricing of goods, policing, and security.

The traders who displaced Pajajaran's Hindu elite in the control of west Java's trade originated in the urban merchant communities of Java's north coast. They were Muslim, participants in a culture geared to commerce, settled in residential neighborhoods around mosque and market, and supporters of scholars from the Arab world and archipelago centers of Islamic learning. Sunan Gunung Jati installed his son, Hasanuddin, at the head of the Cibanten delta merchant community. In 1552 Hasanuddin declared himself ruler of the port, independent of Cirebon and of Pajajaran. He named it Banten.

The town was built in a delta formed by two branches of the Cibanten River, which had its source in mountains about thirty kilometers to the south. Banten had a deep harbor protected by many small islands from the open sea. Hasanuddin and his successors promoted the port's advantages by turning Banten into a royal city, a site of pilgrimage, a center of Islamic learning, an attractive market, and a place for repairing and provisioning ships. They used warfare to expand their access to pepper and control its sale. They recruited Chinese to turn their port and production into profitable ventures. By these means Banten's rulers created their personal wealth and the foundations that made Banten an important Indonesian sultanate of the seventeenth century.

To get the look right, Hasanuddin had his capital laid out in the style of a Javanese royal city. His palace was built as a series of structures within a walled compound. In front of it was the public square planted with banyan trees. Around the square were mosque, market, and rice storage buildings. The city itself was designed as a square, walled, with roads connecting the center to gates set at the compass points. Hasanuddin, who had a reputation as a student of Islamic sciences and of meditation, enhanced the prestige of the new royal capital by developing Banten as a pilgrimage site. He had deliberately chosen a place sacred to Hindus for his capital. The site owed its magical power to a luminous rock, which had been the meditation place of a Hindu holy man named Betara Guru Jampang. According to the palace chronicle, *Sejarah Banten* (History of Banten), after Hasanuddin had defeated armies of the region's Hindu prince, Betara Guru Jampang converted to Islam and instantly vanished. The rock on which he had been meditating was appropriated by Hasanuddin as a throne for himself and his successors. Within the new city's walls were soon numerous tombs of Muslim holy men. Banten's kings appointed men who could recite legends about these saints to be custodians of the graves. As their fame spread, the tombs became places of pilgrimage and meditation, attracting wandering scholars and many of the visitors to Banten's markets.

Banten's rulers also cultivated a reputation for generosity and hospitality to scholars traveling the Islamic world. They appointed foreign ulamas to head mosques and act as judges, and supported their studies. Banten's kings advertised the importance and renown of Islamic scholars by marrying their daughters to them. Men from Arabia and other Islamic lands became members of the extended royal family of Banten. These early acts of patronage produced their reward. In 1638, envoys from Mecca conferred the title of sultan on Banten's fourth ruler. He reigned as Sultan Abdulmafakir Mahmud Abdulkadir until 1651.

To increase their control of pepper-growing territories, Banten's rulers launched a series of wars. Hasanuddin first raided in Pajajaran lands to the south of his city. He described his soldiers' assaults on the Hindu kingdom as a jihad, and he ordered his newly conquered subjects to convert to Islam. Hasanuddin's son, Molana Yusuf (r. 1570–1580), continued the southern expansion of Banten by capturing Pajajaran's capital and the rice lands under its control in 1579. Molana Yusuf's son and successor, Molana Muhammad, carried war across the water to southern Sumatra. Defeated Sumatran rulers who converted to Islam and acknowledged Banten's kings as their overlord were allowed to continue as heads of their territories, now with the status of vassal and tribute payer to Banten. Molana Muhammad died in battle in 1596, fighting to extend Banten's rule in Sumatra.

Banten's rulers also sought to expand their influence by choosing their queens from the families of sultans who controlled important markets. For instance, one of Hasanuddin's wives was a daughter of the sultan of Indrapura, a port of call on Sumatra's west coast. In its orbit were the ports of Silebar and Bengkulu, both of which were acquiring new importance from their location on the "Muslim sea highway" that entered the archipelago by way of Banten.

The new Banten elite brought changes that affected the everyday life of their Sundanese subjects. Banten's rulers did not move their capital upriver to Batang Girang once they had conquered the Pajajaran capital. They remained planted in the delta, oriented to the archipelago trade and ideas networks. Javanese replaced Sundanese as the language of government, correspondence, decrees, and reports. Javanese also became the language of instruction in the Islamic religious schools that supplanted Pajajaran's web of rural Hindu and Buddhist religious foundations. Knowledge of writing Sundanese in kawi almost disappeared because the scribes now hired were those who could write in Arabic. Sundanese became detached from intellectual discourse; it lost status because it was now just the language spoken by the subject population.

There were immediate consequences, too, for the farming families who lived along the Cibanten River. The river was the water highway for Pajajaran's capital, the route that brought rice and forest products to the delta port. Farmers planted rice along its banks so that their fields could be watered by the periodic flooding of the river. Banten's second king ordered farmers to construct canals to carry river water to new fields laid out beyond its flood plain and to build holding dams. New villages and rice fields were established in forest clearings. In return for the right to grow their food, farming families had to plant pepper vines and ginger along the edges of their fields and surrender the produce to tax agents of the king.

Everywhere Banten's rulers extended their authority by holy war they required their new subjects to grow pepper. In the middle of the seventeenth century Sultan Abdullah Abdul Fattah Agung (also known as Sultan Ageng Tirtajasa, r. 1651–1682) required all males aged sixteen and over in his core territories to tend five hundred vines. In 1663 he extended this requirement to all men in his Sumatran territories. Pepper cultivation altered the lives of ordinary men and women by turning them into producers for overseas markets. It brought them under supervision of government agents, and it altered the ways a household shared tasks and how members spent their time. It also was the means of introducing new consumer goods from the coast into their houses and work sites.

Banten had location, product, and buyers. Its rulers were willing to force changes in the ways their subjects used their time and labor to increase supplies of products in demand overseas. Export to regions distant from ports required a mechanism for getting pepper to market. Indonesian populations were scat-

PEPPER AND LIFESTYLE

Pepper was introduced to Sumatra and Java from south India around 600 B.C.E. Black pepper is the result of picking unripened fruits and drying them in the sun, while white pepper comes from larger fruits left on the vine until ripe. The outer skin must then be peeled off and the fruit dried. Pepper could be fitted into farming because the vines were raised on the edges of fields planted with other crops.

In the sixteenth and seventeenth centuries archipelago suppliers felt increased pressures for pepper. Numbers of Chinese buyers in the archipelago increased. Arab and European traders also became regular visitors to pepper ports searching for supplies to sell to the Chinese and for additional sources to divert to Middle Eastern and European markets. The profits to be made from pepper convinced archipelago suppliers to produce more pepper for sale and in regular amounts.

One way to boost production in southeast Sumatra was by changing the way farming families allocated jobs among members and the amount of time spent on them. Farm women, when offered cloth in exchange for pepper, substituted the time-consuming chore of weaving cotton and directed that freed time to planting more vines and cultivating pepper. In northern Sumatra, Aceh's kings financed the laying out of pepper plantations from their taxes on trade. Their armed men raided villages in the non-Muslim interior of north Sumatra and their navy raided villages on the west coast of the Malay Peninsula for males of working age, and sent them to pepper farms that spread along the north coast of Sumatra. In Banten territories, pepper cultivation brought forced production for overseas markets and an increase in consumer goods; in Aceh, pepper brought slave production on commercial plantations.

tered, few in number, and mobile on land and on water. That is why armies raided villages for slaves, and why seafaring Indonesians operating from bases along the coasts of Kalimantan, Sulawesi, Sumatra, and in the Riau islands specialized in slaving. They raided villages for people to row in their fleets; they transported people by boat to sell in archipelago ports as agricultural laborers, porters, builders, craftspeople, and domestics. But Sulu, Bajau, Mandar, and Buginese slavers ran small-scale enterprises; they produced scores of slaves when hundreds of workers were needed.

Rulers of Indonesian port cities who drew their revenues from market stall rents, taxes on trade, and gifts from foreign merchants did not invest in local industry. They used their wealth to create political power: they bought luxury imports to advertise their royalty, and they purchased labor. Their wealth financed fleets to keep sea approaches to their ports free of robbers, and raiding armies to extend territory or acquire captives. Rulers were willing to accommodate foreign entrepreneurs who had international contacts, financing and organization skills, and networks of skilled and unskilled workers.

Arab and European entrepreneurs had the requisite skills in financing, management, and pre-industrial crafts, but their home bases were too distant, their populations too small, and the expense too costly for them to provide large numbers of laborers on land as well as ships. Chinese financiers operating out of southern China could supply export agents, wholesalers, clerks, carpenters, metalworkers, vegetable growers, peddlers, and porters. Agents could draw on men in numbers sufficient to supply Indonesian, Arab and also European enterprises in the archipelago. Chinese agents could provide an archipelago ruler with city services to attract foreign merchants; they could send chains of men into the hinterlands collecting produce for export; they could finance provision of goods for sale and exchange; and they could establish agricultural and mining industries that provisioned ports and provided taxable exports.

Unlike Arabia and Europe, South China and Southeast Asia form a region. When Chinese agents forged connections with Indonesian kings, the archipelago became a site of off-shore production for South China, stimulating an increase in the foreign communities resident in the territories of Indonesian rulers. Chinese businesses made possible the operations of other foreigners, particularly of Europeans, as well as fostering in Indonesian sultanates a dependence on imported products. Archipelago rulers amassed wealth and supported holy men and religious institutions, rather than fostering among their own subjects the skills which foreigners possessed.

When an archipelago ruler opened his port to Chinese traders, he then rented to other Chinese allotments of land on which to raise vegetables and fruits to feed the growing population of the port. He leased more land to men organizing the growing and processing of sugar cane. He allowed skilled craftsmen to establish workplaces. The port ruler licensed shopkeepers and operators of opium, gambling, and sex establishments. He appointed Chinese men as brokers, weighers, and harbormasters, writers, and tax collectors. Port rulers also authorized their Chinese trading agents to import labor to staff their businesses.

Chinese entrepreneurs did not turn to local sources or the slave market for laborers. The supply of slaves was unpredictable, and the habits and languages of slaves unknown to Chinese foremen. Rather, entrepreneurs shipped laborers from south China to the ports where they did business. They supplied Chinese traders with Chinese manufactured goods. Chinese peddlers trekked to villages where they exchanged the goods for pepper and other forest products and brought them to collection points for export to China. Indonesian populations far distant from archipelago ports were able to participate in production for international markets and acquire foreign goods, but they did not prosper because they were dependent on one, Chinese, source for sale of their goods and the prices they received.

Settlements of Chinese laborers sprang up in underpopulated spaces in the archipelago. In the seventeenth and eighteenth centuries Chinese communities mined gold in Kalimantan and tin in Bangka; they grew pepper and gambier in Riau and sugar in Banten. These self-contained settlements produced a single product for export at nearby ports by Chinese merchants, on whom the workers depended for food, clothing, tools, and opium. The laborers were connected to each other and their bosses by shared dialect and region of origin in China, by ritual oaths of brotherhood, and as profit-sharers. While they were residents of territory claimed by an archipelago ruler, they were only tied to him by the commercial connection through the king's Chinese agent. Chinese mining and agricultural communities often outnumbered the local ruler's rural population.

Chinese also filled jobs in the pre-modern administration of society, principally as collectors of tax. Indonesian kings sold the right to collect taxes on market stalls, the tax on the slaughter of animals, tolls to cross rivers, and tariffs on goods exported and imported. The Chinese tax collector hired Chinese as agents, police, and record keepers to recoup the amount paid to the ruler, cover costs, and make a profit.

KINGS AND CHINESE IN INDONESIAN HISTORIES

The oldest identifiable permanent Chinese settlement in Indonesia was situated in Pasai in northeast Sumatra and dates from the late eleventh century. The success of Chinese in archipelago states is often explained by poverty in China, and by the willingness of Chinese to work hard in difficult conditions. Chinese success must also be understood by reference to their origins. In addition to manual laborers, Chinese emigrants included skilled artisans who were products of China's long traditions of manufacturing and processing. There were also farmers with specialised skills in raising export crops and men with mathematical skills and commercial experience. Most important for their value to archipelago rulers, Chinese working in Indonesian communities had a wide knowledge of market conditions in many regions. They were mobile men with specific skills that could be applied in the regions to China's south where climate, topography, and natural resources were most similar.

Until the twentieth century, Chinese migrant workers in Indonesia were men. Those whose business kept them in a port for a few months rented women. Those who settled married women in the ports, leading to communities labeled Chinese that were made up of immigrant men, local women, their children, Indonesian in-laws, and the constant addition of new arrivals from China. Such communities had links to China and Indonesian societies of the archipelago. They emerged as a new social category that remains distinctive among Indonesia's many ethnic groups.

This history produced among indigenous members of the archipelago's widely scattered societies a common set of attitudes towards residents of Chinese descent. Locals saw Chinese as successful outsiders, arousing degrees of jealousy. Their access to cash in the era before banks meant that Chinese were moneylenders and made it difficult for a local entrepreneur to compete. Chinese were needed by Indonesians, courted and hated. To them, the foreignness made Chinese businesses seem secretive. The habit of employing members of the extended family meant that Chinese businesses were closed, rather than a source of employment and expansion of skills among locals. Because Chinese were part of an international network they appeared conspiratorial.

Their foreignness made the Chinese completely dependent on political elites from kings down to village heads. Their connections gave them opportunities to grow wealthy. By serving as record-keepers, harbormasters, brokers, tax collectors, and other agents of authority, the Chinese enhanced the power and wealth of ruling elites at the expense of the taxpaying population. Used by kings to extract wealth from the population, the Chinese, rather than the rulers, were seen as oppressors of the native majority.

In Banten one could find Chinese merchants, peddlers, artisans, manual laborers, and professionals, such as writers, accountants, brokers, interpreters, and weighers. Teams of Chinese laborers constructed public buildings, walls, bridges, and houses in wood and stone. Chinese designed and built the principal mosque, which was unique in Java's mosque architecture because of its five-tiered roof with Chinese-style curving tiles and stone prayer tower. In Banten's hinterland Chinese contractors leased land from Banten's kings to grow and process sugar for export. Their laborers built irrigation works to bring Cibanten River waters to the sugar fields. Teams of Chinese porters under contract to Chinese, Banten, Arab, and European merchants carried goods to village markets and returned with forest products. The numbers of Chinese in Banten continued to grow, especially under the seventeenth-century Sultan Ageng. During his reign Chinese were appointed to the key positions of harbormaster and head of customs and weighing.

Chinese influence varied depending on locality. As non-Muslims, the Chinese lived on the western side of the city, outside the walls enclosing the Muslim community. The international market was also on the western tributary of the Cibanten River, and there Chinese conducted their businesses with each other and with merchants and crews from other parts of Indonesia and from China, India, Arabia, and Europe. In this international market area or Chinatown were Buddhist and Taoist temples, and the stone houses of the prosperous. Flimsy wooden barracks housed most Chinese. The authorities considered children born in families of Chinese and port women to be Chinese. In Banten rural territories, the Chinese lived in self-contained bachelor communities on sugar plantations, or they passed through Banten villages as transients, bearers of goods, and holders and lenders of cash. Sundanese and Javanese became addicted to the services and goods the Chinese provided, but their worlds were parallel, separate, and distinct. The Banten royal city and Sundanese villages had no Chinese residents.

Chinese skills made Indonesian ports and export industries work. Their success attracted foreign merchants and kept them returning, so that the Chinese opened Indonesian societies to outside information and intellectual trends. Of crucial importance to Indonesian histories, the Chinese exposed Indonesian societies to Muslim knowledge, rather than to Chinese knowledge. In Chinese civilization the merchant was accorded the lowest rung in the social hierarchy. Overseas trade and travel were prohibited by imperial decree. Chinese emigrants were outcastes. Confucian scholars did not travel to teach. Official travelers were envoys of the imperial court whose task was to collect information on foreigners and their ways, not to transform them into Chinese. In Chinese settlements in archipelago communities the scholar class was absent. Chinese hierarchies were reversed, for the most senior and respected member of Chinatown was the merchant, not the specialist in Chinese literature, history, poetry, and painting. The Chinese network exposed Indonesian societies to the Islamic network. That network included men of learning as well as merchants, because Islam valued both study and commerce.

Indonesian elites who converted to Islam were not conditioned to admire the achievements of non-Muslims in arts and sciences. They did not wish to learn from them. Chinese people fitted into their category of kafir, alongside the Portuguese, to be pitied or scorned because they were not Muslim. Chinese were kept at a physical distance. They were not brought into royal families, although they often had the duty of donating girls from Chinese families to royal harems. In order to approach Indonesian elites Chinese had to remove signs of their foreignness. Men who held high positions in the sultan's service became Muslims as a condition of their appointment and as a sign of loyalty. Conversion allowed Chinese men to enter the presence of royalty and to be appointed to positions supervising Muslims.

The Portuguese who shopped at Banten used Chinese services. They hired Chinese carpenters to build houses and warehouses in the non-Muslim quarter. They purchased foods from Chinese market stalls, rented women from Chinese brothels, and contracted with Chinese porters to get them pepper supplies. They sold pepper to the China market through their settlement in Macau and also shipped pepper to Europe where it was in demand as a pre-industrial method of preserving and flavoring foods. The Portuguese were also in the market for other Indonesian tree products that were used in food preparation and storage in European kitchens. They could purchase cloves, nutmeg, and mace in Melaka or any of Java's ports. The price reflected the number of transactions that had brought the spices from their point of origin. Portuguese shippers therefore had an interest in buying spices at ports closer to the point of production, such as Makasar, or in the spice-producing territories themselves.

THE SPICE ISLANDS: INDONESIAN OR EUROPEAN HISTORY?

Older histories start the story of Indonesia with the arrival of Spanish, Portuguese, and Dutch ships in the sixteenth and seventeenth centuries in search of the home markets for cloves, nutmeg, and mace. These histories relate products native to Indonesia almost solely to Europe's history. In this version, the crusaders developed a taste for the luxuries of the East from their brief history as princes of feudal states in Jerusalem, Tripoli, and Antioch. Rotting meats back home in Europe needed spices found in Muslim markets. Hatred of Islam led Europeans to seek a sea route to the East in order to defeat Arabic-speaking merchants in commerce. According to this history, the "discovery" of the spice islands was followed by imposition of European monopolies on the production and sale of spices and devastation of local economies. In the industrial age Europe no longer needed spices, and the spice islands sank into oblivion.

An Indonesia-centered account of the spice islands covers a quite different set of topics: Indonesian uses of spices; forms of labor control; the evolution of hereditary monarchs; conversion of the ruling classes to Islam; the development of Ternate war fleets; and shifts in cultivation sites and sailing patterns to defeat European monopolies. An Indonesia-centered account integrates the eastern archipelago, including northwestern New Guinea, into Indonesian histories. The spice islands have an independent history, one that intersects with Europe but is not submerged by it.

About one thousand islands and island clusters are scattered across the eastern archipelago. They are linked by ocean currents and monsoon winds that ensure a boat propelled by sail and rowers could journey widely from home base and return. The spice islands (known to Indonesians as Maluku, the Moluccas in English) include Ternate, Tidore, Motir, Makian, and Bacan, which form an arc off the west coast of Halmahera. Cloves are native to them, while nutmeg and mace are native to the Banda island cluster. Europeans included Seram and Ambon in the term spice islands, because the Dutch transplanted spice-bearing trees there in the seventeenth century.

Islanders adapted to a physical environment of densely forested volcanic peaks and high rainfall by gathering tubers and fruits, and by fishing. The tree most important to their survival was the sago palm, which produces a flour that was baked into loaves, forming the staple food of commoners and the elite. Edible species of sago palm grow most plentifully in the swamp forests of Halmahera, Seram, Buru, Aru, and Bacan, and also on the western peninsula of New Guinea. Inhabitants of the very small spice islands increased their own supplies of sago by exchanging coconuts, fish, shells, and spices. People living in the remote Banda islands, which produce very little foodstuffs, solved the problem of survival by becoming builders of boats that were distinctive in having storage sections. They alone of the Maluku peoples became sea carriers of spices.

The crucial items in this exchange of products were spices and sago. The root crops that grow in the rain forests of the eastern archipelago are perishable; but sago loaves have a very long life. Sago loaves were not only a survival food on board ship, but also a food desired in many parts of the eastern archipelago, and they were a form of currency with which traders could purchase other goods. The female industry of processing palm starch into loaves was therefore closely linked to the male industries of harvesting the sea for fish and mother-of-pearl and of long-distance trading.

Nutmeg, mace, and cloves were easily transportable trade goods. Nutmeg and mace are two distinct spices produced by the one tree that thrived in the light volcanic soil of the Banda islands among the shade of taller trees in constant rain. Its fruit was harvested between June and December when there are intervals of sunshine. The nut at the center was removed, and its black coating was peeled off and dried to become mace. The nut could also be dried, then shelled, to produce nutmeg. Cloves were gathered in the tiny islands off Halmahera during the same period of the year. Twigs and leaves with unopened flower buds were picked by men, and then the family together separated the cloves, which are the unopened flower buds, and dried them on trays in the sun. Spice production required family teams of laborers, simple tools, and basic processing techniques.

Spices gathered and prepared from trees growing in the wild produced quantities sufficient for families to purchase food and pay their taxes to village leaders. Taxes levied in spices gave headmen a product they could exchange for items traveling along archipelago trade networks such as iron axes, krises, cotton cloth, copper, and silver. Spices could also buy for village elites Indian silk textiles, Javanese gongs, and Chinese coins. Exotic items became necessities over time. Workers became accustomed to the superiority of metal tools; elites enlarged their social distance from commoners by the possession of fine goods.

A very ancient, small-scale exchange of products for survival in a remote area joined wider sailing circuits and markets. Javanese and Malay sailors traveled to eastern Indonesia in search of spices, which were ultimately sold in China, the Islamic world and Europe. They created a demand for spices in many regions of the archipelago too. Indonesian peoples incorporated spices into their religious life, their cookery, medicines, and arts. Since the nineteenth century, spices have been superseded by food processing and refrigeration, by chemical dyes, imported medicines, and by cash, but Indonesians still use cloves in the manufacture of cigarettes.

The market demanded greater amounts of spices but also supplied the means for producing them. Women responded to the opportunity by giving up making bark cloth at home and turning their efforts to harvesting and preparing spices to exchange for cotton cloth. Village headmen organized spice plantations to reduce time locating trees in forests and to increase yields. Sago producers on Seram imported slaves from New Guinea to increase the numbers of agricultural laborers at their command. They developed sago plantations in order to provision more sea journeys and purchase more consumer goods. By the fourteenth century Banda sailors were traveling in a wide arc between Ternate, Seram, Kai, Aru, West New Guinea, Java, and Melaka putting east Indonesian products into international markets and importing foreign manufactured goods.

Sailors brought to eastern archipelago communities trends in the islands to their west. Foreign merchants who transacted their business with local men of importance paid them trading taxes, license fees, and the respect due leaders in other archipelago ports. They used the language for royalty. Most small island communities were ruled by village headmen in a hierarchy reaching up to powerful families. These headmen controlled village governance, taxing, inter-island relations, and trade through owning ships or goods sent on ships. In Ternate, Tidore, Makian, Bacan, and Jailolo (west Halmahera) leadership came to be centralized in one man and inherited on his death by one of his male relatives. These rulers were understood in Majapahit court circles as vassals to Javanese kings. In the 1480s and 1490s the ruling families of Ternate and Tidore converted to Islam. Within a few years the ruling families of Jailolo and Bacan had also converted and taken the title of sultan.

The east Indonesian archipelago forms an intermediate zone between Java and New Guinea. The languages spoken on Ternate, Tidore, Makian, and Halmahera belong to the Papuan family of languages spoken by peoples of northwest New Guinea and by some ethnic groups of Timor. Bacan people speak an Austronesian language which may be related to a Malay dialect of northeast Kalimantan. Bacan may have been the first point of call for Malay traders. Possibly Bacan's inhabitants adopted this language of the trade routes and, in their remote island, it developed distinctively.

Origin myths in east Indonesian societies show a long history of contact, wide geographic knowledge, and receptivity to cultural messages traveling along the trade routes. For instance, a Bacan chronicle tells of a king who assumed the international Sanskrit title Sri Maharaja. He had seven children who were scattered across the sea by a wild storm. They ended up as rulers of Waigeo and Misool Islands, Banggai and Loloda (northeast Halmahera), Seram, and Seki, while one succeeded their father in Bacan. Another origin story that shows an expanding knowledge of the world told of a foreigner from the Middle East named Jafar Sadek who married Nur Sifa, one of seven nymphs. Three sons and one daughter were born of this marriage between foreign Muslim and Indonesian celestial spirit. The children became the rulers of Ternate, Tidore, Bacan, and Jailolo.

By the sixteenth century Buginese sailors were regular customers in east Indonesian markets. Chinese ships never sailed into the region and Chinese manuals did not carry instructions for sailing east of Sulawesi. Ternate and Tidore responded to the opportunities for enrichment from trade by expanding the territories under their command. Spice sales financed the buildup of war fleets. The king of a water-based empire used his navy to make raids on distant territories, and installed there a vassal ruler or conferred on the local ruler titles and marks of honor such as royal letters, flags, and clothing. There was an exchange of women between the households of king and vassal. At times Ternate intervened in local conflicts or overturned local rulers in order to install as vassals men who were Muslim. Through sea power Ternate extracted taxes from seventy-two tributaries, including western Halmahera, coastal regions of east Sulawesi, Mindanao to the north, Solor, Banda, parts of Seram, and Ambon. Tidore's main vassals and revenue-providers were the northeast coast of Seram, the islands between Seram and New Guinea, and northern coastal districts of New Guinea.

The Portuguese who sailed from Melaka for the spice islands found a world of tiny islands, water-based kingdoms, and communities linked by sea circuits, positioned at the very end of a receiving zone for Muslim traders and teachers. The Portuguese were at first welcomed as new customers. They offered entrance into a network encompassing the Indonesian islands of Timor, Flores, and Sulawesi, sites in Banten and Melaka, and further afield China, Japan, Ceylon, ports in India and Africa, South America, and Europe. Given permission to establish businesses with local agents and build accommodations, the Portuguese added to royal collections such items as clocks, mirrors, and maps; they sold guns and cannon that could expand naval empires; they introduced maize and sweet potato; and they promoted Christian culture. Traveling with the Portuguese were priests, printed books, a writing system, a world view that paralleled Islam in offering a philosophy, a religious tradition, forms for government, art, architecture, literature, and commerce.

Portuguese Christianity valued royalty too. The Portuguese seemed to offer an alternative system to Islam; they were a competitor, with similar advantages in a part of the world that was just in the process of taking up the Islamic offer. Some rulers wavered; a few decided to try out Christianity and so forge links to commercial and intellectual centers in Asia and Europe controlled by the Portuguese. For example, the king reigning in Bacan in 1557 converted in that year to Roman Catholicism and took as his new name João and the title *Dom* (lord). He had his son baptized Dom Henrique. But the Portuguese network was too slight in Indonesian waters. There were not enough priests to supply demands from rulers in southern Sulawesi and the remote corners of the eastern archipelago. Most rulers who tried out Christianity reverted to Islam or were pushed off their thrones by stronger kings who were already part of the Islamic local and international network. Dom João was killed in battle by forces led by Sultan Baabullah of Ternate in 1577. Only in some settlements in northern Sulawesi, Ambon, Flores, Roti, and Timor did conversion outlast European colonialism in Indonesia. Descendants of local rulers and their followers today battle for Christian space and rights inside Muslim Indonesia.

The Portuguese were recorders of Indonesian histories. Envoys, priests, and travelers kept journals and composed memoirs that preserved their impressions, introduced the Indonesian archipelago to intellectual circles in Europe, and documented moments in Indonesian lives that have no other record. In these accounts, Indonesian men, women, and children from small communities, far removed from important states, live on. One such example is Nyacili Boki Raja, who attempted to rule as a Muslim queen in Ternate in the 1530s and to preserve royal prerogatives for her male children.

NYACILI BOKI RAJA: WOULD-BE MUSLIM QUEEN AND CHRISTIAN CONVERT

Nyacili Boki Raja enters history as Niachile Pokaraga in Portuguese documents. *Nyacili* is the female form of the title *kaicili* used by royals in the spice regions. Born the daughter of a ruler of Tidore, she allied the competing states of Tidore and Ternate in 1512 when she married the sultan of Ternate. Her royal husband had taken the name Abulais to mark his conversion earlier to Islam. As principal wife, Nyacili Boki added three sons and a daughter to Abulais's many children.

Sultan Abulais augmented his sources of revenue by allowing agents of the Portuguese to settle in Ternate. The chief Portuguese agent convinced him to overturn the custom of royal succession passing to an uncle, nephew, or favorite son. Abulais left his throne to his eldest son by Nyacili Boki, Abu Hayat, who was about eight when Abulais died in 1521. Nyacili Boki took over as Abu Hayat's regent and sought to protect her children from other contenders by placing them under the care of the Portuguese in the stone fort they had constructed in 1522.

In 1526 Nyacili Boki's father, the sultan of Tidore, died. She now turned to Ternate's council of elders, made up of the heads of descent groups, for support. By 1530 she was using Islam to defend her right to rule and to protect her children's interests against rivals for the throne. She declared jihad against non-Muslims and called for neighboring and vassal states to blockade the Portuguese, who still held her sons in protective custody or as hostages. During the war, Abu Hayat was poisoned, and one of his surviving brothers fled to Tidore. Nyacili Boki then married the most powerful man in Ternate, Pati Serang, and he attempted to rule as regent in the name of the youngest surviving son, Tabarija. In the continuing warfare the new head of Portuguese affairs captured Ternate's ruling clique in 1534 and sent the queen mother, Tabarija, Pati Serang, and other officials in chains to Goa.

Tabarija had been raised by Portuguese in Ternate. In Goa, the deposed ruler acknowledged Portugal's king as his suzerain by the Indonesian method of conversion to his suzerain's religion and became Dom Manuel.

In 1542 when Tabarija–Dom Manuel was about twenty-one, he returned with his party by orders of Goa's governor to rule Ternate. The new king was soon poisoned. When he died, the local Portuguese community acknowledged Nyacili Boki as queen of Ternate and vassal of Portugal. A son of Abulais by a different mother led an army to depose her and confiscated all her properties. She fled to the Portuguese community on Ternate, where Francis Xavier baptized her in 1547. As Doña Isabel, she became a royal pensioner receiving allowances from Goa. The Muslim queen who launched jihad against the Portuguese before converting to Christianity is expunged from Ternate historical traditions. Her career illustrates alliances royals made with local and regional powers, the use of marriages and conversions, and the role of the outsider as recorder. Her life demonstrates the many possibilities available to royals and would-be rulers of Indonesian communities.

In older books, the Portuguese were considered principally in terms of European history: the motives in Europe generating journeys to Asia; the creation of a Portuguese empire; competition with other European traders; their displacement in Indonesian histories by the Dutch. In such texts Indonesians fade into the background as passive observers, victims, or converts. The Portuguese must be considered in terms of Indonesian histories too, for there were important consequences from Portuguese voyages and evangelizing. In the eastern archipelago, for instance, the Portuguese, together with other foreign traders, built up demand for spices, and rulers forced Indonesian laborers to change the way they farmed, work harder, pay more taxes, and want more things. Clove and nutmeg cultivation expanded into new areas and demand for food supplies increased. Seram landowners imported more slave labor from New Guinea to boost their production of sago loaves to sell to landowners who concentrated on spices. More New Guinea chiefs began to prize iron axes and cloth and put more of their subjects on to Indonesian slave markets to increase their imports. Additional supplies increased the activities of Indonesian traders. Ambon became favored as a watering place for boats sailing between Java and Maluku. Ambon had a settlement of Portuguese traders, but it was also where the Muslim settlement of Hitu developed as a political and market center in the Indonesian clove trade.

The Portuguese sold their share of Asian manufactured goods (pottery, cloth, iron goods) to spice producers, and helped make imports necessities. They also added supplies of European manufactured goods into archipelago markets. Mechanical clocks and printed books introduced some Indonesians to a new knowledge system. Firearms, ammunition, and cannon were useful to some Indonesian rulers in equipping fleets and extending taxpaying territories under their command.

Only Indonesians resident in ports and working at sea knew of the Portuguese. Even on the sea highways Portuguese were always the minority. In the sixteenth century, Bandanese carried most of the local, interisland trade at the eastern end of the archipelago; Javanese and Malays carried most of the long-distance trade. In the western archipelago, to avoid Portuguese taxes, Muslim businessmen shifted their operations to Banten and so helped secure the economy for its new Muslim elite. The expansion of Muslim rule around the archipelago's shores, and the growing networks of Chinese businesses around ports, on overland routes, and in production were the major developments for sixteenth-century Indonesia. The Portuguese are most important in their role as recorders of that century.

Dutch ships sailed into Indonesian pepper ports for the first time in 1595. To obtain permission to land, work, and build, Dutch envoys had to deal with Indonesian officials of port and palace. Sailing Indonesian waters made Dutch captains acquainted with Indonesian technology, navigation knowledge, and places. Buying and selling introduced them to port inhabitants of many different ethnicities. Like the Portuguese, the Dutch recorded Indonesian lives, and the record of their various experiences was printed, distributed, and preserved in Europe. Alongside Indonesian inscriptions of kings, their tax decrees, narrative epics, and the religious productions of Indonesian thinkers are Dutch records of everyday life. In the last years of the sixteenth century the pepper ports of Banten and Aceh come alive through Dutch drawing and dialogue.

The Portuguese de Brito described sailing Indonesian seas with Indonesian crews and explained how goods moved through interlocking circuits of sea routes. Dutch men described the royal port cities with their sultans, officials, foreign traders, local sellers, and slaves. For example, a Dutch drawing of Banten's international market as it operated in 1598 explains how goods were presented and what each ethnic group sold. The painting also makes it possible to understand the differing scope of operations of male and female traders. The market is outside the walls of the Muslim city, located on the riverbank so that small boats could pull in and their male crew could sell directly to customers. Women are shown selling melons, beans, cucumbers, and textiles from tubular baskets in the open or under trees. From open stands male traders sell sugar, honey, bamboo, meats, fish, vegetables, rice, spices, pepper, and weapons. Men labeled by the artist as Gujeratis and Bengalis sell iron and tools, while Chinese merchants operate on the largest scale from covered stalls. Another Dutch sketch of the market from this time places Islamic commercial and cultural life in an Indonesian context. The merchant is a Muslim man in turban, body fully covered in a robe, with shoes. The slaves he has acquired in the port carry his goods. Male and female, they are scantily clad, without a head covering, their feet bare.

Another Dutchman, Frederik de Houtman, who reached Aceh in 1599, wrote of his experiences. From his account it is clear that Muslim ruling classes classified all foreigners by religion, which determined a visitor's place of residence, opportunities, and fate. De Houtman and his crew, on being captured, were offered death, or freedom and residence rights in Aceh if they converted to Islam. Five of the group changed religions, were given wives, and they disappeared into the mixed population of the port. Sultan Alau'ddin Ri'ayat Syah al-Mukammil (r. 1589–1604) offered de Houtman the post of king's agent in dealing with all Dutch traders, if he confirmed his loyalty to his employer by conversion. The sultan wanted an agent who could deal directly with these new Europeans, instead of relying on interpreters at his court who were fluent in Portuguese. De Houtman refused and spent eighteen months in jail.

De Houtman put his imprisonment to good use, improving his working knowledge of Malay with his guards. He preserved what they taught him by compiling a lengthy list of Malay words and usage with their Dutch translation and by writing up twelve conversations between men. In the first, a Dutch captain arrives with his crew, sends a letter to the sultan by elephant, presents himself to the sultan, and answers questions about gifts, his cargo, and the sale of weapons. A second conversation covers all the requirements for stating where a foreign ship has come from, its cargo, its itinerary, and the captain's need for fresh food and water. Other dialogues cover bargaining in the market, arranging care on land for sick crew members, asking directions for an inland journey, recovering debts, cheating practices, market prices, and general dinner conversation. The dialogues establish the direct involvement in trade of rulers, the reliance on foreign visitors for news and information of the outside world, and the Islamic atmosphere of court and port circles. For example, Acehnese begin and end all conversations with Arabic greetings, which are given their Dutch-language equivalents. De Houtman's dialogues and word list were published in Holland in 1603.

The Dutch sailed into Indonesian histories a hundred years after the Portuguese, who had begun laying down their network in an archipelago that was becoming Muslim. The Dutch arrived as Muslim governments were maturing. Their first port of call, Aceh, had almost one hundred years of developing Islamic institutions, values, and outlook; Banten, their second, had been Muslim for fifty years. At the eastern end of the archipelago Muslim rulers were established in the spice-producing regions, and at major stops along the way from Melaka. The Dutch wanted to negotiate rights to do business in the archipelago with Indonesian rulers and to push European rivals out of inter-Asian trade. They began laying down a Dutch network on top of the Portuguese in a chain of settlements along the routes to the spice islands. In 1605, they defeated the Portuguese at Ambon and took over their fort and settlement.

In that same year, kings in Luwu and Makasar converted to Islam and began launching jihads that resulted in Muslim rulers in all the southern Sulawesi states and in Bima, Butung, and Selayar. Around 1600 a Muslim ruling class took control of rice-producing villages in central Java and called the state Mataram. In the years the Dutch were learning to sail the Java Sea, Mataram rulers sent raiding parties to expand the territories under their control. Their armies then launched attacks on the port cities on Java's north coast. Over fifteen years they engulfed the north coast sultanates, overturned rulers, installed vassals and, in 1628 and 1629, carried war into west Java to subdue Banten and enclaves of Dutch merchants.

Throughout the seventeenth and eighteenth centuries, the Dutch operated on the fringes of powerful sultanates. They became one of Indonesia's sea peoples, sailing the archipelago's highways, trading, raiding, and placing their armies and navies at the disposal of Indonesian kings to defeat rivals. They aimed to control segments of the international trade in Indonesian sea and forest products through alliances with archipelago rulers, by negotiation or conquest. The Dutch fitted into large-volume Asian trading. They depended on Asian shippers and traders to supply goods for transport in Dutch ships and to break down Dutch imports into small consignments for resale in village markets of the archipelago.

Dutch men in the archipelago were traders, bookkeepers, inspectors, artisans, scientists, ministers of religion, painters, envoys, and soldiers. They were partners and husbands to Asian women, and they were fathers to children born in Indonesia. They represented Christian Europe to Muslim kings. To Indonesian military commanders, sailors, artisans, and farmers, the Dutch were bearers of innovations in firepower, boat design, mapping, metalwork, and agriculture. The Dutch used Malay in preference to their own language or Portuguese to communicate with Indonesians in the market, in palace negotiations, in workplaces, in religious service, and books. Their professional writers placed the Roman script as an alphabet at the service of Malay in competition with the Arabic writing system. In the seventeenth and eighteenth centuries the Dutch were ally and kafir, friend and foe, in Indonesian worlds.

6

INSIDE INDONESIAN SULTANATES

Dutch Vassals, Allies, Recorders, Foes, and Kafirs

In the seventeenth century Indonesian sultans sought to expand their power. Rulers of international ports extended their authority inland by attack and by installation of vassals. They saw conversion to Islam as a means to shape their subjects' thoughts and to solidify bonds between ruler and ruled, and so promoted Islamic institutions in town and countryside. Fringe scholars traveling the highways of the Islamic network were welcome in their capitals. Sultans controlled their subjects' time by requiring them to pay taxes through free labor and produce, and in so doing stimulated the flow of goods to markets where they taxed exports and imports. Rulers augmented their incomes by selling to the heads of Chinese networks the license to mine, to farm, and to collect taxes. Sultans extended their power by the tried methods of slavery, raids, and marriage alliances, and they added a new method: they employed and allied with the Dutch.

Ternate's and Tidore's sultans signed exclusive agreements with the Dutch for the sale of spices and used their augmented incomes to build up their war fleets and expand their tax-generating territories into the coastal regions of neighboring islands. In south Sulawesi, Arung Palakka, a Muslim prince, entered an agreement with the Dutch for firepower and fighting men that resulted in his becoming suzerain over all the kingdoms in the peninsula and the Dutch replacing his chief rival as head of the port of Makasar. In Java,

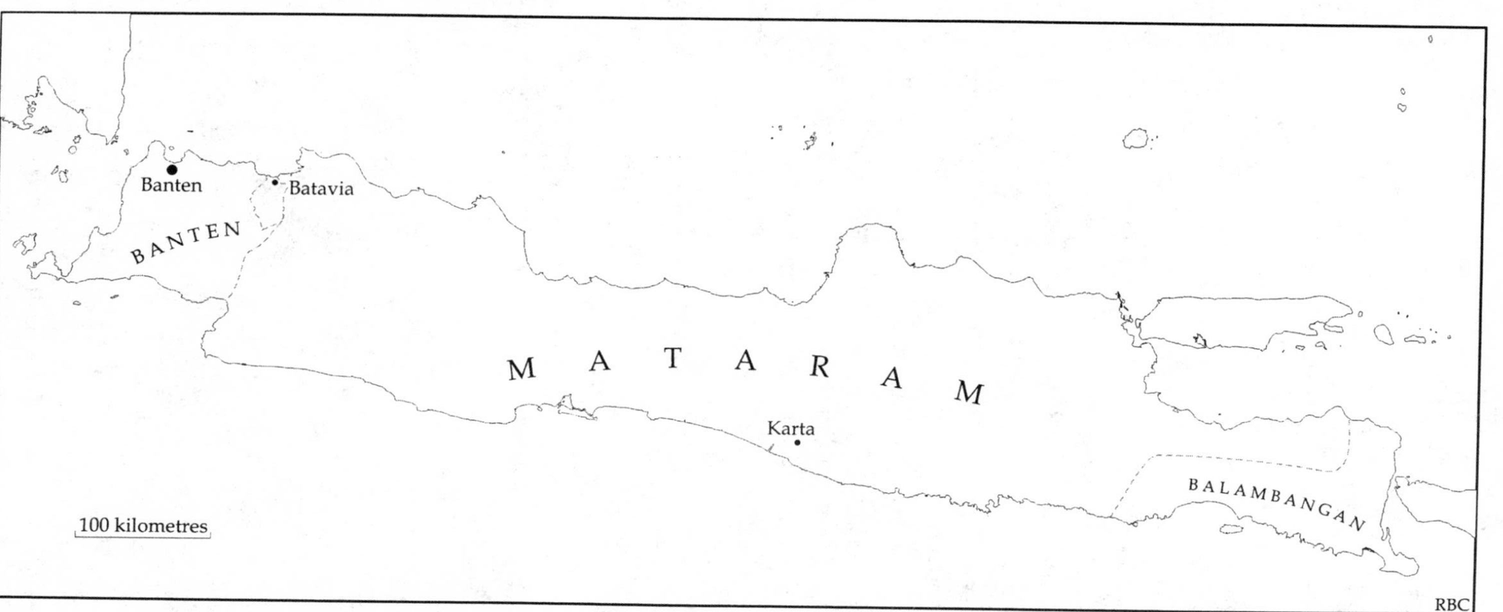

Java, Early Seventeenth Century

Mataram's kings hired Dutch soldiers to preserve their throne against rivals. Amangkurat I closed Java's ports, banned Javanese shipwrights from building large, oceangoing vessels, and licensed the Dutch as his seafarers. Butung's rulers signed agreements with the Dutch that released them from the dominance of Makasar sultans. In the 1680s vassals to Mataram kings turned to the Dutch, attracted by the promise of uninterrupted tenure in their districts and profits from Dutch experiments in growing new crops.

In Banten and Mataram kings accepted Dutch gifts and addressed the chief Dutch administrator as "elder brother." When the Dutch vassals became too strong and demanding, Indonesian royals turned to other mercenaries. They patronized Muslim preachers who declared the Dutch to be kafirs and called for jihads against them. Sultans left to their underlings and rivals the acquisition of Dutch weapons and manufacturing techniques. Their professional writers and thinkers wrote little about the Dutch and had little curiosity about their ways, whereas the Dutch made extensive inquiries into Indonesian methods of government, social customs, and languages. The Dutch used that knowledge to reverse the political situation. By the nineteenth century they were suzerains and Indonesian sultans were the vassals.

In imperial histories and histories by Indonesians, the arrival of five small Dutch ships in 1595 launches 350 years of Dutch rule in Indonesia. Imperial histories foreground the Dutch. In histories written by Indonesians the Dutch remain at the center of the narrative; princes, preachers, and commoners resist until the Dutch are expelled through the unified struggle for independence during the years 1945 to 1949. This mode of writing history answers and satisfies the demands of imperialism and nationalism but obliterates the histories of Indonesian societies. Through the nationalist perspective Indonesian kings are presented as glorious but ill-fated resisters of the Dutch, rather than men who set out to enrich themselves and preserve their privileges through hiring foreigners and excluding their subjects from new knowledge and roles in society. The nationalist perspective casts Indonesian people as victims of foreigners (the Dutch) rather than of ruling classes (Indonesian and Dutch). The imperialist perspective treats Indonesians as primitive in their economy, and either passive subjects or fanatic, obdurate resisters. Both perspectives neglect the histories of ordinary farmers and workers who seized advantage of new situations, learned new skills, and took on the challenges of modernity from train travel to formal schooling and political engagement.

The nationalist perspective omits the history of cultural and intellectual exchange. For instance, history books for Indonesian primary school children show Indonesian men armed with lance and kris fighting Dutch soldiers. The illustrations emphasize heroism, rather than the readiness of Indonesian war commanders to use European muskets and cannon, or record that they encouraged metalworkers to produce copies of European imports in their forges and purchased ammunition from Chinese and European traders.

The Dutch played many roles in Indonesian histories in the seventeenth and eighteenth centuries. Overall, they touched the lives of some classes and some regions significantly, in other places lightly or barely at all. As allies and foes they lived, worked, and married in Indonesian contexts where the main players were Indonesian.

In the archipelago sea peoples such as the Bajau, Buginese, Butung, and Malays, specialized in providing links to the outside world for communities in forested highlands such as Dayaks, Bataks, Minangkabau, Torajans, Timorese, and Balinese. Sea peoples brought the region's news and goods; often they imposed the political will of more powerful states. Indonesian sea peoples had a sense of themselves as members of a linguistic or ethnic group with a home base along a specific coast. They raided in many places for rowers on their ships. They sailed the archipelago. Their work habits and work sites were determined by knowledge of Indonesian seas, skies, and winds, by their knowledge of archipelago resources, and by client relationships with sultans and their agents. The scale of their operations was determined by the amount of goods a shipowner had to sell.

In the seventeenth century Indonesian sea peoples met with a competitor in the Dutch. From their own history of rule by Spain and struggle for religious freedom and autonomy, the Dutch had acquired a national and religious identity that overrode differences of home province and village. Their lives were governed not by kings, but by the merchants who controlled the administration of Dutch cities. Dutch ships sailed in the northern seas, the Atlantic, and, from the end of the sixteenth century, in the Indian Ocean, the China Sea, and Indonesian waters. Dutch work habits and work sites were determined by governing boards of commercial companies located in Holland's seaboard towns. In 1602 these companies merged into the United East Indies Company, or VOC (from the initials of its Dutch name, Vereenigde Oost-Indische Compagnie). In the seventeenth and eighteenth centuries the VOC was the largest single employer of European and Asian men in the Indonesian archipelago. In Indonesia's islands the Dutch were more like the Chinese than they were like Buginese or Bajau in their international perspective and global operations. They had substantial capital and large-scale management skills.

In their first years Dutch ships put in at Indonesian pepper and spice centers. Their envoys made gifts to harbor officials and the local ruler and sought permission to do business. Muslim rulers allocated them quarters outside the walls of their cities, alongside the Chinese. The Dutch presented themselves to Indonesian rulers as foes of other European traders and jostled for the largest share of the pepper and spice sales. They offered immediate payment in silver and other desired goods, such as Indian textiles, if other Europeans were excluded from the markets. In places where local authority was weak, the Dutch attacked and expelled rival Europeans. Where the local ruler was strong, the Dutch contended with unpredictable taxes, payments, and continuance of the right to do business. They soon decided to found their own headquarters to coordinate shipping, sales, and diplomacy, to stockpile goods, to repair ships, and to concentrate land and sea forces. That headquarters needed to be in a port under Dutch command, independent of Indonesian sultans.

The site that became the VOC's headquarters was a small port called Jayakarta. Its Sundanese and Chinese population numbered around 2,000 in 1600, and its ruler, a vassal of Banten, called himself sultan and used Javanese as the language of government. In 1618 Banten's Sultan Abdulmafakir sent armed parties to destroy the Dutch compound outside Jayakarta's walls. Its occupants held off their attackers for five months until VOC ships arrived to disperse Banten's men and lift the siege in May 1619. Dutch forces then deposed Jayakarta's sultan and burned down his palace and mosque. A European Christian administration replaced Javanese Muslim rule and renamed the port Batavia. The new government promoted the Dutch Reformed Church as the religion of Batavia's ruling class, replaced the Muslim calendar with the Christian, and set up schools, churches, and courts to promote a Christian culture.

NAMING AS A FORM OF POSSESSION

Sunda Kelapa was the original name of the site favored by the Dutch for their archipelago headquarters. It had been a port serving Pajajaran until 1527, when armed bands sponsored by the sultan of Cirebon conquered Sunda Kelapa and renamed it Jayakarta, meaning "great victory." Dutch scribes attempting to render the name in Roman script wrote it as Jacatra. In May 1619 VOC forces captured Jayakarta and gave it the name Batavia to honor the Germanic tribe from whom the Dutch considered themselves descended. Batavia then became the head of a sea network that in time linked the Indonesian archipelago to ports in Japan, Taiwan, Malaya, and southern Africa. To rulers of Indonesian states Batavia was the chief Dutch settlement in the archipelago and its governor-general was perceived as its king.

For decades Batavia was the smallest state in Java. It remained the Dutch administrative capital after the VOC was dissolved in 1800 and the Dutch monarchy took over the VOC's Indonesian ports. Between 1850 and 1940 Dutch power engulfed the entire archipelago, and Batavia became the capital of this Dutch colony, the Netherlands East Indies.

In 1942 the Japanese conquered the Netherlands East Indies and split it into three separately ruled regions. Japan's Sixteenth Army made Batavia its headquarters and named it Djakarta. Djakarta ceased to be the capital of an archipelago-wide state; it became simply the principal city of Java.

Sukarno proclaimed the independence of the people of Indonesia in Djakarta on August 17, 1945, two days after Japan's surrender to the Allies. Dutch troops retook the city in 1946 and revived the name Batavia. In December 1949, when Indonesia's independence was recognized internationally, the capital of the new federal Republic of Indonesia was declared to be Djakarta. The city has remained the capital, but since 1972, following revision of Indonesian spelling, it has been known as Jakarta. The name signifies the spread of Javanese Muslim culture which has displaced both colonial and older Sundanese pasts in the history of Indonesia as a new nation.

Dutch administrators imitated Indonesian rulers' policies for developing Batavia into an international market. They extended Batavia's control over the hinterland; they encouraged Chinese traders to put in at Batavia and Chinese artisans to settle there; they licensed Chinese to raise export crops, and to trade in the outlying villages; and they sold to Chinese the license to collect taxes.

Batavia's administration also coordinated Dutch shipping in Asian waters, sent delegations to Indonesian kings, and stockpiled cargo for distribution in Asian markets. Each year Batavia's rulers received ships from Holland, assigning personnel and cargo to various branches of the Dutch network in Asia. Each year they also assembled a fleet to make the long journey back to Europe carrying cargo from Asia, specimens of Asian plants, written records of business and discoveries, and the occasional Asian scholar and student.

Indonesians who worked the sea routes and lived in coastal towns were the first to encounter the Dutch. They formed their first impressions from Dutch ships, which were huge in comparison with Indonesian ships. The average Dutch ship journeying between Europe and Asia was 55 meters long and had three masts, several decks, and a crew of one hundred. They were usually armed with twenty-eight cannon, eight swivel guns, and many rifles. (Dutch ships built for sailing in the archipelago were smaller, 28 to 37 meters long with two masts and one or two decks.) By contrast, ships captained by Javanese, Chinese, Malays, and Buginese from the same period averaged between 7 and 11 meters, had crews of five to eight men, and were armed with two cannon, muskets, and gunpowder.

Because Dutch ships were large, they had to anchor in deeper water offshore. From the beginning, Indonesian and Dutch lives were entwined. Local ships, owned and crewed by archipelago peoples, sailed out to Dutch ships. Local sailors made first contact with the foreigners when they brought them food and fresh water, and ferried passengers and cargo into and from port. Local traders bought small amounts of VOC cargo for neighborhood markets.

Collecting local goods and loading a Dutch ship could take up to four months. Such a large enterprise required the services of many Indonesians to stow Asian goods in the holds of VOC ships and feed and entertain crews of two hundred and more. Port residents sold the Dutch chickens, salted fish, lemons, eggs, and oil for ships' lamps. Local entrepreneurs ferried VOC crews to brothels on shore. Local navigators came aboard VOC ships to pilot them through the numerous small islands, shoals, and sandbars that protected river mouths. Indonesians living in archipelago ports got an inkling of a huge industrial complex that marshaled men and goods for Asian destinations and drew on the latest knowledge in navigation, science, and manufacturing.

VOC ships were built in the company's shipyards in Amsterdam by Dutch convict and free labor. Ropes, sails, barrels, anchors, and nails were all made on-site in standardized sizes specified by the VOC. At the company's head-

VOC: THE COMPANY

The United East Indies Company's charter from the Dutch States-General designated it the sole agency to handle Dutch trading in Asia. All Dutch entrepreneurs there had to be affiliated with one of its six companies; only company employees could work in VOC businesses in Asia; all company cargo and personnel had to travel on company ships. The company's seventeen directors met in Amsterdam, where they appointed the governor-general and senior officials, merchants, clerks, artisans, scholars, and clergy, and authorized the fitting out of ships and the hiring of crews and soldiers. The VOC directors placed orders with Dutch agents for building ships and for assembling cargo. They also operated auctions for Asian imports, set standards for pilots, promoted new inventions, and financed research and publications in Holland and in Asia.

VOC directors ran their operation by written instructions, preserved in the company's voluminous archives. This paper record sometimes obscures the fact that VOC employees filled small niches in Asian societies; they did not overwhelm them. Although the Dutch organization is far better known, Chinese, Arab, and Indian networks, continued their operations after the arrival of the Dutch.

quarters there were abattoirs for the slaughter of cows and pigs and smokehouses for preserving meats. Live animals were also taken on board to supply fresh meat during the long sea journey.

VOC ships carried the latest in navigation instruments. Captains received maps, compasses, dividers for marking position on charts, a plane scale to calculate distances, instruments to work out astronomical positions, and sounding leads for sampling sea beds and estimating the depth of the ocean. Navigation manuals were written by men on the company's payroll. The VOC also had its own hydrographic department which produced charts and itineraries for captains. The company promoted inventions in firefighting equipment for ships and exported the new fire engines to Asian cities. VOC surgeons took on board saws, tongs, needles, syringes, and drills, and medicine chests containing herbs, honey, laxatives, syrups, powders, plasters, lotions, and chemicals.

The navigation skills that allowed the Dutch to become dominant in Indonesian waters combined practical experience, instruments, and literacy. First and second mate on VOC ships had to be able to read and write, and from the seventeenth century they had to demonstrate their practical and theoretical knowledge to special examiners employed by the VOC. Ships' captains were required to maintain written records of their journeys and submit them for inspection. In the eighteenth century the VOC established training schools for officers in Rotterdam and Amsterdam, and, in the years 1743 to 1755, experimented with a marine academy in Batavia to train local boys.

Between 1602 and 1795, five thousand ships sailed from Holland to Asia, carrying one million people. This huge exodus could not be generated by Holland alone, with its population of one and a half to two million. Other European towns and states supplied most of the soldiers on VOC ships. Dutch men sailed the ships and they staffed the civilian positions of the Company. Only one man in three returned to Holland; the great majority worked and died in Asia. Hardly any emigrants were women, so that Dutch men who formed families in Indonesian ports did so with Asian partners.

The VOC drew on the skills of Asian artisans for storage jars, baskets, and matting; it hired Javanese and Chinese shipwrights to build small boats able to sail up the archipelago's rivers. The VOC spread among archipelago shipbuilders European principles of design and navigation, especially in masts and rigging, iron nails, anchors, and the use of cotton and linen for sails. Archipelago sailors did not adopt European navigational instruments, but they did arm their boats with cannon and swivel guns and equip crews with muskets as well as pikes. Europeans learned about local shorelines, wind patterns, stars, and currents from archipelago sailors. They incorporated and preserved Indonesian knowledge in maps, charts, and atlases.

VOC ships introduced Indonesian sea peoples and port workers to Dutch inventions, products, and work style. Ports under Dutch control—Ambon (1605), Batavia (1619), Banda (1621), Kai and Aru (1623), Melaka (1641), Tanimbar (1646), Tidore and Kupang (1657), Makasar (1669), Minahasa (1679), and, after 1680, Tegal, Semarang, Japara, Rembang, and Surabaya—introduced Indonesian land dwellers to Dutch urban design, municipal administration, and lifestyle.

INDONESIAN KNOWLEDGE AND EUROPEAN MAPS

The Malay Peninsula appeared in maps drawn by Ptolemy (87–150 C.E.), who tried to make sense in Alexandria of travelers' tales of eastern lands, but no archipelago geographers are known. Instead, European cartographers preserved the knowledge of Indonesian sailors, captains, traders, pilgrims, and adventurers in maps drawn, with increasing degrees of accuracy, in the sixteenth and seventeenth centuries. For example, a portfolio of twenty-six maps drawn by the Portuguese cartographer Francisco Rodrigues was based in part on a voyage he made in 1511 from Melaka to Java, Bali, Sumbawa, Timor, Banda, Seram, and Flores. The maps also include Brunei and the spice islands, which Rodrigues did not visit but knew of from Indonesian seafarers.

Many European creators of maps did not themselves ever see the lands whose shapes they attempted to define. Captains, merchants, naturalists, explorers, and missionaries came to them, and philosophers and scientists met at their workshops in Venice, Antwerp, and Amsterdam to analyze the information, sort fact from fiction, and fill in blank spaces in their conception of the world. At first mapmakers confused the islands of Sri Lanka and Sumatra, the relative sizes of Java and the Maluku islands, and the relationship of New Guinea to the Australian continent. By the 1550s map-making began to catch up with the pace of voyages of exploration, but there was always a time lag between discoveries and publication.

The VOC employed Europe's best mapmakers. Seventeenth-century Dutch sea and land atlases show the steady accumulation of knowledge of the world far distant from Holland. Map-making followed, and enabled possession of, distant places by Europeans. Maps summed up the particular knowledge of places of many men, Asian and European. Maps generated a new way of thinking about the world; map-makers allowed individuals to see themselves within geographic and political relationships.

Batavia, always the principal Dutch city in the archipelago, was oriented toward the sea, to the fleets of Dutch ships, and to the waterways linking Batavia to Asia and to Europe. On the water's edge, Batavia Castle was designed to protect the harbor, ships at anchor, and the settlement. It housed offices and residential quarters for the chief representatives and merchants of the Company, clerks, accountants, warehouse keepers, ministers of religion, artists, surgeons, judges, and soldiers. Within the castle were warehouses, a church, and a meeting hall. In the early years, all VOC employees were to be in the castle and the drawbridge raised by nightfall. A barrier was stretched across the mouth of the Ciliwung River beneath the castle's guns. There trading vessels had to pay tariffs before ferrying goods to the town's markets and storehouses.

The walled town that grew around the castle resembled archipelago ports in assigning each ethnic group its own quarters and headman who represented it to the VOC. The European quarter had distinctive Dutch features in its town hall, square and church. European men filled posts as municipal councilors and overseers of charitable institutions such as Batavia's poorhouse, orphanage, and hospital. They were organized in militias for the town's defense and as honor guards for public ceremonies.

Contemporary Indonesian towns were clusters of villages surrounding an aristocrat's residence; houses were scattered among trees, and travel was by footpath and river. By contrast, the Dutch cut down trees, laid houses in squares, and traffic traveled along roads and canals. Contemporary paintings of Batavia's drawbridges, shuttered houses, wheeled transport, and narrow streets recall Dutch towns such as Leiden.

Batavia's administrators resembled archipelago kings in their view of religion as a statement of loyalty to the ruling class. Men aspiring to high positions in the company's Asian towns had to be Dutch and members of the Reformed Church. Any Portuguese, Eurasian, and Asian immigrants to VOC-controlled towns who were Roman Catholic had to convert to Protestant Christianity. Not until the 1740s were other branches of the Christian church permitted public worship and religious instruction in Batavia.

Dutch regulations regarding conversion did not apply to residents who were Muslims, Hindus, Buddhists, or followers of indigenous religions. This exemption did not spring from respect for beliefs the Dutch termed "Moorish," "pagan," or "heathen" but was the product of Dutch historical experience that had aligned nationality with religion. To the Dutch, Europeans were Christian; Asians had their own religions. Thus, the VOC permitted the construction of mosques and temples in Batavia, appointed and paid mosque officials, and accepted oaths sworn on the Koran. This VOC attitude was crucial for Indonesian histories. Most communities of the archipelago continued to be caught up in the religion promoted by their immediate rulers; most missionaries in the archipelago continued to be Islamic. As a result, Muslim populations lived in and surrounded Dutch-ruled towns where only a tiny core of Dutch personnel, their wives, children, and close associates were Christian.

Land surrounding Batavia's walls was permanently cleared for vegetable gardens, rice, and sugar. The VOC leased land to Chinese entrepreneurs who imported laborers from their home bases in China. These agricultural businesses were pushed progressively farther from the walls as the town expanded. The suburbs were home to immigrants who set up small businesses in rice dealing, crafts, and taverns. Most were former residents of Portuguese towns in India and the archipelago; they were usually part Asian, Portuguese-speaking, and former Roman Catholics. Other residents were past VOC employees who had chosen to settle permanently in Asia after fulfilling their contract with the company. In the eighteenth century, Batavia's principal Dutch inhabitants had houses inside the town and they built villas outside the walls set amid orchards and rice fields worked by local Sundanese or by slaves imported from Bali.

When VOC troops conquered Jayakarta in 1619, the strip of coastal land between the sultanates of Banten and Cirebon was declared to be Dutch, and Sundanese and Javanese officeholders in this area now owed allegiance to the Dutch. Coconuts, cardamom, and pepper now flowed to Batavia, whose Dutch rulers, not the sultans, now received the revenue from market and export taxes on these goods. The districts that formed Batavia's hinterland were, in the VOC administrative structure, under the oversight of a board of sheriffs. The daily life of the villagers was regulated in a variety of ways. Some lands were sold to Dutch and Chinese men, who ruled them as private fiefs, some were assigned to Javanese and Balinese men who were commanders in VOC armies, and some were controlled by Sundanese aristocrats.

Batavia was a small town under the VOC; in 1624 it had a population of 8,000. But by 1670 Batavia had a population of 130,000, making it larger than Aceh at mid-century (48,000) and comparable to Semarang (100,000 in 1654), Japara (100,000 in 1654), and Banten (125,000 in 1696). Batavia resembled those towns in the ethnic variety of its inhabitants and in the division between free and slave. The Dutch, who did not employ slave labor in Europe, adapted to their Indonesian context by becoming owners and users of slaves. Until a Dutch administration abolished slavery in 1819, most of Batavia's inhabitants were slaves.

Batavia also resembled archipelago ports in having a growing Chinese community that provided urban services to international traders and funnelled trade goods to its market. The VOC attempted to control the Chinese by issuing passes that restricted Chinese operations to two hours' walking distance from Dutch-controlled towns. But Chinese merchants were the face of Dutch interests in dealing with villagers and traders. They advanced credit, supplied goods, and collected taxes in villages that no Dutch man ever entered. Chinese shopkeepers, toll collectors, and porters knit the working lives of Indonesians into the profits of the Dutch East Indies Company.

For the Chinese, Batavia was a center in southern China's offshore zone of production for sugar, forest and sea products. The port was a hub for Chinese networks that were spreading throughout the region, investing Chinese workers in gold and tin mines and pepper and gambier farming.

Although Batavia was a Chinese town to the Chinese, and headquarters of a global enterprise to the Dutch, it existed within the archipelago world of ports. Batavia was a small town on the fringes of Java's largest state, the sultanate of Mataram. It was drawn into Javanese history at a time when Mataram's king was attempting to extend his control over the entire island of Java.

Mataram was an old name for lands in south-central Java that persisted long after the temple-building dynasties of the eighth and ninth centuries and the region had become a backwater in the days of Majapahit. The name returned to prominence in the last years of the sixteenth century. According to Javanese historical tradition, Majapahit was defeated by the Muslim state of Demak in 1478. Demak established Islam as the religion of the coast. A successor state, called Pajang, introduced Islam into country to Demak's south. In 1581 the ruler of Pajang rewarded one of his military commanders by assigning villages to him in the old Mataram lands. The new lord took the name of his fief in his title Ki Ageng Mataram (Glorious One of Mataram).

No contemporary inscriptions survive to document Demak and Pajang. In historical memory and in babads they link the documented dynasties of Majapahit and Mataram. Descendants of Majapahit's Hindu kings were said to rule Demak and Pajang and to pass on their royal blood to Mataram's kings. Centuries later, in the recounting of Mataram's origins, rulers of Demak and Pajang were accorded the title sultan, although there is no evidence that any ever used this title. The two states fade from Javanese record after fulfilling their mission of advancing the Islamization of Java.

Mataram's second ruler, Panembahan Senopati Ingalaga (r. 1587–1601), added territories and resources to the royal domain through military campaigns. Senopati's place is fixed in folk memory and babads by the honor attributed to him of drawing Java's many pasts into a Muslim culture. Tradition names him a holy man who gained control of powerful magical forces in Java's landscape. Senopati did not conquer or obliterate Hindu gods and Java's nature spirits, but endowed them with a special place in a Muslim framework. As the descendant of Hindu princes and as a warrior king, he fulfils the prophecy made at the fall of Majapahit by Ratu Loro Kidul, queen of the southern seas, that the royal man who journeyed beneath the ocean to her palace to spend a wedding night with her would be the rightful ruler of an Islamic Java. In return, Loro Kidul placed at Senopati's disposal the spirit forces under her command, and promised them to all his descendants who would perform the annual rite of visiting her. Today the royal houses and Muslim nobility of central Java regard themselves as descendants of Senopati. Each year the reigning sultan of Yogyakarta goes formally to Parang Tretes on the southern coast to commune with his spirit bride. Senopati's burial ground in his capital of Kota Gede is venerated as a holy site.

Mataram's fourth ruler, Agung (r. 1613–1646), is also revered as a holy king. His reign was bound up with the proliferation of Islamic symbols and with feats of magic that relocated Islam's holy places into Java's landscape. Agung was said to possess his Hindu forebears' ability to fly. Every Friday he flew to Mecca for communal prayer; he meditated at Muhammad's grave; then each time he scooped up a little soil to carry back to Java for his own burial ground. Jerusalem was recreated in Java as Kudus (from the Arabic form al-Quds). In 1633 Agung visited Tembayat, a religious school formed at another holy site, the burial place of the wali Sunan Bayat. There he received instruction in magical knowledge from the Muslim missionary's spirit. He dignified the saint's tomb by having a split gateway erected, where he inscribed his decision to abandon the Javanese solar calendar and to order Java's affairs within Islamic time and calendar. Agung installed religious courts and judges and ordered all men in his territories to be circumcised as a sign of their conversion to Islam or face execution. He set aside villages and rice lands for the support of religious teachers. By inaugurating the custom of having mosque leaders read the Koran and prayers in the palace every night preceding Friday prayers he presented Islam as the religion of royals.

In 1624 Agung had taken the title sunan, which equated him with the saints who had brought Islam to Java. In 1641 he announced that Mecca had conferred on him the title of sultan, by which he is known in Javanese tradition. Descendants used his titles of *panembahan* (honored lord) and sunan, a tradition continued by the royal house of Surakarta. No other Mataram king called himself sultan until the title was revived by the founder of the royal house of Yogyakarta in 1749. Yogyakarta's royals are buried around Sultan Agung at Imogiri. The site retains its reputation as a holy place, but its custodians have yielded to modern understandings of Islam and no longer claim that visiting Imogiri is the equivalent of pilgrimage to Mecca.

Today, pilgrims step outside the modern world to honor Java's holy kings. They must remove the watches that track secular time, set aside cameras, and replace Muslim or Western dress with the costume of Javanese *abdi dalem* (palace retainers, literally: slaves of the inner palace) to enter the burial grounds of Senopati and Agung. There Islamic prayers accompany offerings of flowers and pilgrims prostrate at the graves in dim, incense-filled air.

Sultan Agung is the production of popular piety, folk Islam, and tourism. The king the Dutch first encountered was barely in his twenties and had succeeded to Mataram just six years before the founding of Batavia. It was not his pious works that impressed the Dutch, but his military campaigns against Java's ports on the sea highway to the spice islands. Mataram's wealth rested on control of the Solo River and the road to Semarang and on the capacity of its rulers to make subjects produce agricultural goods for export. Rice, sugar, and teak wood were transported down river and by porters to the north coast ports for export. Ambition to add port taxes to royal revenue and to control north coast industries, such as the metalworks in Gresik where Chinese manufactured guns and cannon, propelled Agung to raise armies and launch them against the ports. Javanese sources record armies of eighty thousand.

Agung began his campaigns by attacking the teak and sugar centers of Lasem and Pasuruan in 1616. In 1619 he conquered Tuban. His navy established his suzerainty over Sukadana (southwest Kalimantan) in 1622 and over Madura in 1624. Some places he took easily, but Surabaya withstood a five-year siege before its ruler submitted in 1625. Gresik had to be destroyed. Even after places were subdued, rebellions broke out, so Agung's military commanders were constantly at war. By 1636 Agung's soldiers had torn down the walls of all the old independent sultanates. Their rulers, now vassals to Mataram, had to journey to Agung's palace at Karta in central Java each year. The process of orienting the north coast populations away from the sea had begun.

As well as using military assaults to add resources to the royal treasury, Agung captured skilled artisans to work in his capital. The Kalang, a group which long maintained a separate identity in Yogyakarta, were descendants of war captives brought from Balambangan after Agung's campaign against invading Balinese in 1635. They were employed as metalworkers, leather workers, carpenters, broom makers, and porters. The Pinggir were also descendants of Balinese slaves imported by Agung. Pinggir men were porters, grooms, and animal attendants for armies; Pinggir women were wet nurses and cleaners in the palace.

In the course of these campaigns, Agung turned west. Cirebon's royal family secured its tenure as vassals, leaving only Batavia and Banten independent of Mataram. In 1628 Agung sent an army against Batavia, then in its ninth year. Advance parties of soldiers constructed rice fields to augment supplies for the forces that took four months to cross the five hundred kilometers of river, mountain, and forest. Peasant-porters damned the Ciliwung and sealed Batavia off from its surrounding lands, food supplies, and trade goods. But the Dutch, like archipelago sea peoples, lived on sea as well as on land. Dutch ships maintained control of the sea approaches to Batavia, and the few hundreds of Dutch besieged in Batavia could hold out until disease and desertion depleted the Mataram forces. Agung ordered his generals executed at the site of their disgrace. When he sent another army over land the following year, VOC ships destroyed stockpiles of rice and transport boats at Tegal and Cirebon; other boats in the royal navy were lost at sea in storms. Cut off from supplies, the land forces withdrew.

While Batavia and Banten were freed from the threat of armies from central Java, they were not immune from the spread of Javanese culture. Some army captains, who chose not to return to Mataram to face humiliation or another campaign, set themselves up as heads of their own domains in west Java with bands of followers who were dependent on them for survival. Many followers were farmers who applied to Sunda's rich soils the farming techniques of central Java and devoted their labor to the support of a captain and his armed men who provided them protection. Their lords presented themselves in Pajajaran lands as bearers of the Muslim court culture of central Java. They married into the region's families and acquired local girls to distribute among their followers.

SIVA, ARIF MUHAMMAD, AND INDONESIA'S MINISTRY OF TOURISM

Near Garut in West Java, pilgrims follow a road through a village, cross a lake by raft, then climb a small hill that is in the middle of a ring of mountains. On its summit is Candi Cangkuan, a temple dedicated to Siva and attributed to the eighth-century kingdom of Galuh. Alongside the temple is a grave in the Islamic form with upright stones carved in arabesque shape at each end. The tomb bears no inscription, but a board carries the information, in Indonesian in the Roman alphabet, that the grave holds Eyang Embah Dalem Arif Muhammad. The Javanese titles link the bearer of the Islamic name to the Mataram palace. Pamphlets explain that Arif Muhammad was a warrior of Mataram who, after defeat at Batavia, came to the Garut area with his followers. Descendants of his seven children still live in a small compound several meters from the grave site.

The site is under care of the government's tourism ministry. Until 1966 Siva's temple was foundation and rubble only, its sculptures gone, its building blocks taken to construct the tombs of Arif Muhammad and the many individuals buried around him. In that year excavation began at the site under the direction of archaeologists, and the graves surrounding Arif Muhammad's were relocated to a cemetery further off. The cleared site was fenced and provided with a ticket booth, picnic tables, museum, and curator. A collection of seventeenth-century books in the museum comprises a Koran, a book of Islamic law, a grammar, and a book of exegesis, all penned in black ink in Arabic script.

Hindu god and Muslim warrior turned agricultural pioneer share a mountaintop. The site is on the tourist itinerary. Some of the visitors come to pray and hold night vigils at this site; some report cures of physical and mental illnesses. The government packaged a Muslim piety that retains an association of high places and Hindu remains with holiness, and is still in thrall to Javanese royalty, into a tourist outing following eradication of communism and communist men and women from Java. It is a managed representation of the past to citizens of a modern republic. This specifically Javanese Muslim culture is now being challenged by an Indonesian Islamic consciousness inspired, not by Java's past, but by today's Iran, Egypt, and Afghanistan.

Agung's successor, Amangkurat I (r. 1646–1677), inherited a conglomeration of fiefs. Agung had thrown armies at independent rulers and then tried to ensure that distant territories would prove regular revenue providers by installing favorites as administrators and entangling them in marriage alliances. When Amangkurat surveyed his inheritance he saw obstacles of every kind to asserting his authority. There was Java's landscape of mountains and thick forest, its dispersed concentrations of population, its few roads and navigable rivers; the contradiction in wanting to increase revenues through agricultural production while drawing large numbers of men off the farm to support armies; productive regions and businesses the king could not touch, a consequence of his father's buying the support of religious teachers by giving them fertile tracts of land and laborers and exempting them from paying taxes; opposition to Amangkurat's succession within Agung's extended family; and competition for trade and markets from Batavia, which Agung had not managed to conquer.

Early in his reign Amangkurat signed a peace treaty with the Dutch and admitted VOC envoys to his capital. As a result, he is the first Javanese king to be the subject of a critical assessment rather than the extravagant praise required of Javanese authors. Dutch men wrote their assessments of archipelago kings for their employers, the directors of the VOC, who demanded detailed descriptions of archipelago states. From far-off Holland, they stipulated that written reports should contain information on a state's system of government, local economy, principal crops, and military capacity. Javanese chroniclers recorded genealogies, royal appointments, and palace politics; Dutch reports carried different kinds of information. One of the first Dutch men to provide an outsider's appraisal of Mataram was Rijklof van Goens (1609–1682), who headed VOC embassies to Mataram, making the journey from Batavia into central Java five times between 1648 and 1653.

RIJKLOF VAN GOENS: DUTCH MAN, ASIAN CAREER

Rijklof van Goens experienced Mataram's long 1629 siege on Batavia as a ten-year-old, having left Holland for Java with his parents the year before. Orphaned early, he was raised in the household of a

VOC official in India and prepared for his own career within the company. He gained a wide knowledge of Asia's palaces through his many postings, his fluency in Asian languages, and his family ties. He survived three wives, all of them women born to Dutch fathers and Asian mothers and raised in Asia. After his ninth year, van Goens spent only twelve months in Europe. He ended his working career in Batavia as the VOC's governor-general in the years 1678 to 1681.

Van Goens was curious about Asian societies and sensitive to the nuances around him. He responded to the beauty of Java's landscape, but this appreciation did not soften his assessment of sultanates as difficult places for Dutch men to work. He judged Javanese men as swift to take offense and unpredictable partners in business. He sided with those VOC officials in Java who were urging on the company's directors a policy of acquisition of land and direct control of agriculture and labor, instead of relying on the goodwill of Indonesian rulers to obtain trade goods. Despite living fifty-two of his sixty-three years in Asia, van Goens was a product of a seventeenth-century Dutch culture that rejected kings, reserved reverence for God, and introduced the handshake as the appropriate mode of courtesy between men who perceived themselves as equals. This background shaped the narrative van Goens wrote for the VOC in 1655.

Personal observation and Javanese informants supplied van Goens with an understanding how Amangkurat imposed his will on his empire. Movement into and within Mataram territories was monitored at tollbooths, where tax agents investigated the contents of traders' baskets and armed guards questioned travelers about their origins and destinations. The king appointed officials to each district who reported directly to him and who were rotated each year. Appointees to head provinces were kept at court; subordinates were stationed in the provinces. The king also operated a network of spies, numbering at least four thousand, according to van Goens. Military commanders in the regions had to supply a written report on the number of men they conscripted for warfare and their stocks of weapons. The nobility had to live at court and maintain expensive suites of wives, servants, followers, and horses. Every week they joined Amangkurat in the public square for jousting and to watch contests between wild animals or condemned men who were sent, unarmed, to fight tigers. In the evening, nobles had to give lavish parties with dancing girls.

At his court Amangkurat practiced royal display and distance. In his public appearances he was always surrounded by bodyguards. Twenty thousand men armed with pikes and some muskets formed a square around jousting and animal combat when the king attended; his inner bodyguard was female. The king ate with princes of the royal family and older military commanders and invited other palace men by turns to attend. Palace etiquette required elaborate courtesies to the king that struck van Goens as "slavish." Amangkurat also used polygamy as a tool of political control. Through the distribution of women he spread over society a web of relationships and obligations. The circulation of women between village, town, and royal city served to bind their male relatives to the reigning king and to intertwine palace and countryside.

POLYGAMY AND POLITICS: FEMALE PAWNS AND TOO MANY SONS

The Koran requires a written contract of marriage and dowry for a wife, sets the number of wives at four, prescribes equality of status between the wives and their equal treatment by the common husband. Islam does not limit a man in the number of slave girls he may have in his household. The Koran describes attendance by many virgins as a man's reward in paradise. Indonesia's Muslim kings reproduced this vision by maintaining households filled with women. European travelers record huge numbers of women in the households of seventeenth-century archipelago kings: three thousand women in the palace of Sultan Iskandar Muda of Aceh, twelve hundred in the Banten palace, four hundred owned by a king of Tidore, ten thousand in the palace of Amangkurat I of Mataram.

Java's kings exhibited no obedience to Islamic regulation where equality of wives was at issue. Principal wives were ranked as queens and official consorts, and could be demoted from rank in punishment or to make way for a more favored newcomer. Javanese terms for women below the rank of consort express the degrees of their servility. *Priyantun-dalem* were women residing at court who were married by the king during their pregnancy and divorced after birth, so that the child was legitimate and the number of legal wives at any one time never exceeded four. *Lelangen-dalem* translates as "royal playthings"; they were palace women such as dancers whom the king did not marry, but any children they had by the king were recognized and raised by him. *Lembu peteng,* which means "dark cows," was the term applied to girls whom the king sampled on tours. Children born from such brief encounters were neither recognized nor raised as royal.

The inner part of the palace was a city of women. In addition to wives and concubines, personal attendants and female officers were in charge of preparing and tasting the king's food and carrying his regalia. Four thousand women in Amangkurat I's palace were textile workers. Aceh's sultans had boys castrated and employed as palace eunuchs to guard their households of women. In Java's palaces women armed with pikes and muskets guarded the household and protected the king against assassination. When he ventured in public they formed a human wall around him. Guards often became temporary wives.

Royal polygamy was a mechanism by which a king acquired allies. He took into his household women who were daughters of all classes of men: princes, nobles, army commanders, vanquished princes, village heads, religious teachers, artisans. The daughters born from the king's liaisons could be distributed to other men. Princesses were married to vassals of royal descent and to military commanders; girls born to commoner mothers were bestowed on village heads or Chinese merchants. Men receiving a wife from the king could boast of enjoying royal favor.

There was always a web of tangled relationships in court and countryside. Men summoned to court to pay homage were in the presence of the many women reserved for the king. Women used their powers to secure the king's attention, to detach him from other women and their kin, to form cliques of supporters. They competed to further the fortunes of their sons and relatives.

An immediate consequence of royal polygamy was to create many claimants to the throne among sons and brothers of the king. Polygamy introduced a multigenerational dimension to the royal family, for a ruler who lived to old age could be surrounded by sons who were themselves already fathers and even grandfathers, as well as sons who were still infants. A king's adult sons might be very close in age, born within weeks of each other to different mothers. Succession did not automatically pass from father to oldest son, but to the son who could demonstrate highest status through his mother. Where a king had no son by a queen, the highest status claimant could be a brother, uncle, or nephew. Adult men passed over for succession by a boy were likely leaders of revolt.

Men whose origins were a mystery readily claimed a royal for a father. Babad literature contains episodes of young men appearing at court to lay claim on the king. Their unruly behavior and their inability to conform to the norms for men raised by abandoned women were held as proofs of royal paternity.

In scholarly literature on power, Java's royals are presented as preoccupied with inner quietude and spiritual power. The reality was that half-brothers could never accept the elevation of one of their number as king. For eighty years, royals raised armies to compete for the throne of Mataram. They recruited Bugis, Balinese, and Dutch mercenaries to shore up their throne or attack a rival. Java's kings were rarely able to win loyalty or affection from their subjects, so they were exposed to challenge from siblings. Royal polygamy weakened Mataram and created conditions in which the Dutch became the rulers of Java.

Van Goens described Amangkurat's policy of arbitrary appointments and dismissals as a royal strategy for maintaining authority. Amangkurat imposed the death penalty for all offenses; the accused were burned in oil or brought before the king, who personally stabbed them. According to van Goens, Amangkurat had learned how to conceal his feelings while waiting to succeed

Agung. Where Agung had begun his reign by warfare and consolidated his power by patronizing Islam, Amangkurat inaugurated his reign with terror directed against his father's most trusted advisers, his royal half-brothers, and political ulamas in the religious foundations. In 1646 the king executed a half-brother, a senior military commander, and around two thousand religious teachers. He rid himself of potential avengers by assembling the wives, children, and followers of his victims and having them publicly massacred. By 1647 at least six thousand were dead. With his enemies eradicated and a culture of fear established, Amangkurat applied his system of palace hostages, spies, and polygamy politics to maintain his rule.

Wealth buys power. Amangkurat sought to increase royal revenues by expanding rice agriculture. He appointed men to pioneer new agricultural settlements on the western borders of his kingdom. Royal charters record that eleven hundred people were sent, under Wira Prabangsa, to clear land of jungle and lay out rice fields in the region known today as Krawang; six hundred were sent under Wira Sabo to Tanjung Pura and two hundred under Wira Tanu to Cianjur. (*Wira* is a title meaning foreman or overseer.) The men so charged had to collect the surplus rice harvest and send it to Amangkurat's capital at Plered. The long-term effect of these appointments was to plant Javanese speakers in Sundanese territory and Javanese Muslim culture in the Hindu lands of Pajajaran. Sundanese tradition ascribes permanent rice fields to the Javanese. The sultanate of Mataram came to consist of a central core and pockets of taxpayers scattered among people who were subjects of Banten or Batavia.

The north coast region Agung had conquered was a fertile plain where thousands of peasants grew rice and surrendered tiny surpluses to their district head to fulfill their tax obligation. Little rice found its way to open markets. Realizing that district heads and port administrators had a source of wealth that could be turned to building up an army and detaching themselves from Mataram's overlordship, Amangkurat moved to bring all export trade under royal monopoly. In 1651 he tried to end private interisland trade by prohibiting Javanese from leaving Java and banning Javanese entrepreneurs and carpenters from building large trading ships. In 1652 he banned the export of rice and wood, and from 1655 to 1661 he closed ports on the north coast to VOC traders.

Monopoly of the flow of goods and their sale was a key goal of Indonesian kings and the Dutch East Indies Company alike. This commercial orientation of royals and company ensured that they would do business together. VOC agents approached sultans with requests for the exclusive right to purchase a product such as pepper or tin. Sultans agreed to exclude all private traders, Asian or Dutch, from a share in the item under monopoly. In return, the Indonesian ruler secured a regular purchaser for his stocks at a price negotiated in advance and guaranteed in silver. He also limited the ability of his subjects to grow rich in specific branches of trade. The VOC was in the business of wholesaling and long-distance trading. It aimed at cutting out all competitors by seizing control of the sea highways and imposing a system of licensing and passes on Asian sea captains. It pressured archipelago rulers to sign exclusive contracts with it for bulk exports and used its armed power against weak or uncooperative governments. The VOC carried this policy to extreme and brutal extent in the tiny cluster of islands making up the Banda archipelago.

BANDA: MONOPOLY WITHOUT KINGS

Ten small islands forming the Banda group lie remote in the Banda Sea, but they were the object of sailors on account of the nutmeg trees which grew only on the islands of Lontor, Neira, Ai, Run, and Rosengain. When the Dutch first visited the Banda islands, they estimated a total indigenous population of around fifteen thousand and fifteen hundred traders from Java and Melaka. Monarchy had not evolved in this mini-archipelago. The Dutch borrowed from international traders the term *orang kaya* (rich people) for the heads of leading families, who had become rich through the nutmeg trade. Dutch agents acting for the VOC established a trading post on Neira. To survive the intense competition for the nutmeg trade, they fortified it. Nassau Castle, built in 1609, was the first Dutch fort in Indonesia.

Banda was unable to control foreign traders as it lacked a central authority and its ships were adapted for trade, not naval warfare. VOC policymakers determined to seize control of nutmeg production and limit the number of trees in order to keep prices high. After ten years of warfare, Jan Pieterszoon Coen injected a new fleet into the eastern archipelago made up of European soldiers and Javanese and Japanese mercenaries. They again attacked Banda villages, expelled foreign traders, exiled Banda's leading families, and this time enslaved surviving commoners. The VOC then leased nutmeg groves to Dutch men who imported their work force from Java, Irian, Tanimbar, Bali, south Sulawesi, and Butung. Ambonese foremen supervised the plantation laborers.

The Dutch monopoly on production of nutmeg and mace, which continued until 1824, brought about the complete transformation of Banda. Multiethnic slave labor raised a single crop; inhabitants became dependent on Dutch suppliers for all outside goods; new ruling classes of Dutch and Ambonese controlled workers' lives. Eventually Banda slipped into insignificance in the colonial economy because its plantation crop was geared to pre-industrial uses.

In many history texts, the monopoly system is discussed solely in relation to European trading companies, while the Asian partners and trade networks are ignored. VOC ships did push Asian ships out of inter-island shipping, but they still accounted for only 40 percent of archipelago sea trade. Shipping registers maintained by Dutch port officials remind us that the majority of all trade was conducted by Asians on Asian-owned and operated ships. The term "monopoly" obscures the fact that the VOC depended on Asian partners to conduct its Asian trade, and that the monopoly system was applied to only some of the many items for sale in Asian ports. The lucrative trades in salt and birds' nests, for instance, were never VOC monopolies.

The historian Reinout Vos has coined the terms "state trade" in place of monopoly and "parallel trade" to refer to trade in items not covered in monopoly agreements. Sultans and the VOC licensed private traders in areas under their jurisdiction. The VOC called private traders who were European "burghers." They never numbered more than a few hundreds in contrast to the thousands of Javanese, Chinese, Malays, and Buginese working in archipelago ports and markets. In VOC terminology, unlicensed European traders were smugglers, and unlicensed Asian traders were pirates.

Overall, the lasting impact of the VOC on archipelago production and trade was to secure the largest share of profits to itself. VOC ships were bigger, so they could carry more goods. The VOC had more capital, so it could finance operations simultaneously in more markets. Trade was complementary, but Asian shippers and businessmen were concentrated in the small-scale end. They were pushed into buying up goods in small ports and carrying them to stapling ports for sale to VOC merchants. VOC ships carried timber, metals, rice, textiles, and spices for sale in Asia and in Europe; archipelago ships carried coconuts, tamarind, fruits, and rice for sale in local ports. Indonesian entrepreneurs could not compete with the Chinese networks to become large-scale suppliers to the VOC. Indonesian rulers were often unable to refuse VOC terms. While Dutch territories in the archipelago were small, scattered, and isolated, Dutch entrepreneurs working from them made profits from peasant producers. Through military support the Dutch kept Indonesian ruling classes in power because those classes were the mechanism that kept Indonesian laborers working.

Arung Palakka was a Buginese prince of the Bone kingdom who engaged Dutch military forces to relaunch his career in south Sulawesi. In the first decade of the seventeenth century heads of the kingdoms of Luwu and Gowa-Tallo' had converted to Islam and launched attacks on neighboring states to install Islamic governments. Arung Palakka was around eleven when Bone was reduced to vassal status. His family was forcibly brought to the Gowa capital of Makasar as hostages. On reaching adulthood Palakka led a group of followers in an unsuccessful revolt against Sultan Hasanuddin (r. 1653–1669). He then took up the wandering, unruly life of the prince in exile. With his militia and a fleet of ships, Palakka tried setting up on Butung, then he involved his militia in the affairs of Bima, Sumba, Bali, and Bantaeng. In 1663 he arrived with his men in Batavia. At first the VOC attempted to handle this potentially dangerous addition to Batavia's society by settling Arung Palakka and his followers on rice land. They proved themselves useful as mercenaries, fighting in their own company alongside Dutch troops in assaults on VOC trade competitors in Sumatra's east coast sultanates.

In 1666 VOC forces joined Arung Palakka and his men in a joint attack on Makasar. Makasar was the capital of Palakka's enemy and a thriving port supplying rice, east Indonesian spices, and slaves to foreign traders. Javanese traders had moved there when Amangkurat restricted trade and shipbuilding in Java's ports. For the VOC, Makasar was an important link in controlling the sea-lanes and the movement of spices, and it was ruled by a sultan who had refused all VOC requests for monopoly agreements. The outcome of three years of fighting was to transform Arung Palakka into supreme territorial chief of south Sulawesi. He installed his relatives in all the kingdoms of the peninsula. Makasar became VOC territory, and from 1669 its entrepot trade was under VOC direction and monopoly stipulations.

MAKASAR AND ANTI-MACASSAR

Another name for Makasar is Ujung Pandang, which means Pandanus Cape, and derives from the profusion of pandanus palms growing there. In Makasar language it is Jumpandang, and was the name of the fort of the kings of Gowa. The Dutch renamed this fort Rotterdam Castle after their victories in 1669 against Sultan Hasanuddin, and they called the city around it Makasar. Jumpandang remained the name of the town for speakers of Makasar, and it became the official name of the city, in its Indonesian form, in 1972 as a symbol of decolonization. Makasar lived briefly in English vocabulary in the anti-macassar, which was a cloth protecting armchairs from hair products made from south Sulawesi palm oils.

Arung Palakka remained the head of an army. He regularly sent soldiers to fight alongside VOC troops. Like kings of Java and the VOC governor-general, he was the head of a band of fighting men, using diplomatic alliance and warfare to achieve his political goals. In hiring VOC soldiers he was acquiring European and Indonesian professional fighters armed with muskets and swords, backed up by fortresses and by major supplies brought by sea.

In Makasar folklore the Bone prince has been transformed into a Makasar prince forced into exile by his father, the king of Gowa. Arung Palakka fulfills his destiny by defeating the father and seizing his rightful place as ruler of southern Sulawesi. His grave is a holy site that still draws pilgrims. In official Indonesian history all the documented cases of Indonesian rulers fighting alongside the Dutch against other archipelago rulers have been collapsed into Arung Palakka. He is presented as villain, rather than as representative of a ruling class that hired foreigners to achieve its political ends.

Raden Haji was another archipelago prince who saw an opportunity in Batavia's armed men. A son of Sultan Abdulmafakir of Banten, he bore the title haji because his father's successor, Sultan Ageng, had removed him from palace politics by sending him twice to Mecca. Raden Haji was absent from Banten in the years 1669 to 1671 and again from 1674 to 1676. In 1680, Raden Haji, now crown prince, launched an attack on the reigning monarch.

By 1682 his forces included VOC regulars and mercenaries. VOC officials were initially willing to back Raden Haji's bid for power provided he rid Banten of its professional gangs of robbers, denied refuge to Batavia's criminals and runaway slaves, renounced Banten's claims over Cirebon, and ceased politicking in Mataram.

Sultan Ageng fled to the south coast with princes who remained loyal to him. He was captured by VOC troops in 1683 and died in exile in Batavia. By 1684 Raden Haji's mercenaries had changed sides or deserted him. Now Sultan Haji (r. 1682–1687), he was dependent on Dutch goodwill. Previously, Sultan Ageng had acted as an independent king in an archipelago world of many states and rulers. But Banten's palace politics allowed an aggressive neighbor state to secure its advantage. The ingredients that had put Banten on the map—pepper, an open market, a Chinese settlement—were reassembled in Batavia. The treaty Sultan Haji signed with the VOC in 1684 closed his pepper market to all save VOC agents. The bulk of the Chinese community transferred its operations to Batavia. Pepper traders funneled supplies more to the VOC state. Banten's ability to advertise itself as an important Islamic center was also diminished when VOC troops captured and exiled Sultan Ageng's most important Muslim leader, Shaikh Yusuf, in 1663. The sultanate of Banten became Batavia's weakened neighbor.

SHAIKH YUSUF, DENOUNCER OF THE OCCIDENTAL OTHER

Shaikh Yusuf (c. 1624–1699) was a member of the Gowa royal family who was sent, in 1645, to study in Aceh. From there he moved to Yemen and then Mecca in a study career that stretched to thirty-three years. In 1678 he reentered Makasar with the Arabic title *shaikh,* which means leader. Makasar was a changed place. Sultan Hasanuddin's Jumpandang fort was now Rotterdam Castle; Dutch men controlled Makasar's trade; and Yusuf found much to condemn in the Islamic community. Cock fighting, gambling, and smoking opium were public entertainments; the sultan and religious judges tolerated the continuation of rites and offerings in places that had been sacred in the pre-Islamic world of the Makasarese. Unable to establish a leadership position for himself, Shaikh Yusuf looked for a more receptive place in the archipelago's Muslim circle. He found it in Banten. Sultan Ageng respected his learning, installed him as his spiritual adviser, and honored him by giving Yusuf one of his daughters as a wife.

The shaikh's reputation for learning and holiness became a powerful weapon in Banten politics. He denounced non-Muslim government in the archipelago. In 1683 he put himself at the head of two thousand men and launched a jihad against the Dutch. Shaikh Yusuf was captured by VOC troops and exiled, first to Ceylon, and then to South Africa, where he died in 1699. In 1705, Sultan Abdul Jalil of Gowa asked the VOC to return the shaikh's body to Makasar for burial befitting a royal relative. The VOC complied, and Yusuf's tomb in Makasar became a pilgrimage site.

Shaikh Yusuf is enshrined in other historical memories too. To today's Capetown Malay Muslim community Shaikh Yusuf is the wali who brought Islam to convicts and exiles transported there from the VOC's Indonesian territories. In his place of exile a burial ground is associated with the shaikh and considered holy. President Suharto made a pilgrimage to this site during a state visit to South Africa in 1995. Shaikh Yusuf's name remained illustrious in many Indonesian communities. Ulamas in Madura claim descent from him.

Shaikh Yusuf's patron, Sultan Ageng, became the hero of a Dutch babad. In 1763 a rhymed historical tragedy, composed in French, based loosely on Sultan Ageng and the rebel prince, was published in Holland. "Sultan Agon" is presented as a model king, pious, wise, preparing to retire and divide his kingdom between two sons. At his court is Fatimah, daughter of a king of Makasar and Bone driven out sixteen years previously by the VOC's governor-general, Cornelis Speelman. She is promised to the younger brother and united with him in opposition to "the Christians." The older brother enters a secret alliance with Batavia through a European renegade in Banten, and the play climaxes in a battle that leaves all the principals dead, following a noble speech by Agon.

There is no record of *Agon, Sultan of Bantan* ever being performed on stage. Its importance lies in the attempt by some Dutch men to consider events from Indonesian perspectives, to see in Indonesians a range of human behavior, and to a make a critical assessment of VOC actions in the archipelago.

The play's European plotter, the renegade Jean-Luc de Stenvic, draws attention to the fact that Dutch men lived, worked, married, and worshipped in Indonesian sultanates. The VOC was a restrictive employer. Its wages were low, its demands high, and it regulated every detail of a man's life. Neither company employees nor self-employed residents of Batavia could marry without permission or change the terms of their employment. Nor could they legally make money in unlicensed trading ventures, because the VOC regarded that as smuggling and punishable by imprisonment or deportation. In the archipelago, however, the VOC was but one possible employer for Europeans. All around were archipelago kings who were adding to their staffs coachmen, grooms, and men skilled in languages, commerce, crafts, music, warfare, and management of markets. Muslim rulers would not promote adherents of other religions to positions offering access to the ruler and supervision of Muslim workers. To foreigners of ability they offered high positions on condition they converted. At Sultan Ageng's court were Chinese men who had converted to Islam, bore Sundanese names and titles, and held important posts. Among Ageng's group of Muslim foreigners was a Pangeran Wiraguna, who had begun life as a Dutch boy in Holland.

HENDRIK LUKASZOON CARDEEL, A.K.A. PANGERAN WIRAGUNA

Hendrik Lukaszoon Cardeel was born in Holland, raised as a Christian, employed by the VOC as a stonemason, and posted to Batavia around 1670. By 1675 Cardeel was a Muslim and employee of Sultan Ageng of Banten in charge of constructing a new fortified palace following the latest European design. His conversion to Islam was signaled by circumcision, Indonesian name, and Muslim marriage. Cardeel became Raden (later Pangeran) Wiraguna, husband to Nila Wati, one of Ageng's palace concubines.

European men entered Indonesian histories when they found an Indonesian employer for their skills. They established families with local women and usually disappeared from VOC records. Wiraguna distinguished himself from such men, however, because in 1682, when VOC forces were fighting in Banten, he sought to return to Christianity and a new life in Batavia, Ceylon, or Holland. A VOC investigation conducted in 1684 described Cardeel as "completely Javanese," unemployed, and husband to a "shrewd" woman. Eventually the VOC permitted Wiraguna to reestablish himself among the Dutch as Cardeel. He appears in VOC records in 1695 as a self-employed resident of Batavia, a landowner and operator of a saw mill with a contract to supply the VOC with timber. In 1697 he divorced Nila Wati. Four years later he named as his heir a boy born to the slave woman Magdalena of Batavia. In 1704, the Banten palace demanded that Cardeel make restitution for the eight male and female slaves who had been given him as a wedding gift by Sultan Ageng. In that year VOC records show Cardeel remarried, this time by Christian rite, with an Anna Stratingh. The last reference to Cardeel in VOC records is in 1706, when he was a supplier of charcoal to the company.

Cardeel's history in Java represents the Dutch freelancer or entrepreneur who adjusted himself to meet the demands of his employer. European men, like Chinese men, lifted themselves out of circles their origins seemed to dictate and became part of Indonesian histories.

Shaikh Yusuf voiced what was objectionable about the Dutch: they were the Occidental Other, outsiders, non-Muslims, and (in some places) rulers of Muslims. He established a perspective on Westerners that remains to this day. It is easiest to treat the Dutch as assaulting Indonesian societies. Putting the spotlight on archipelago princes who made alliances with the VOC brings the Dutch inside Indonesian histories. A few Dutch men made the ultimate journey and became Indonesian. Most Dutch men did not, but, in Indonesian settings, they became more like Indonesians in their control of labor, methods of taxation, and domestic relations. Sultans and governors-general provoked great upheavals by their alliances and rivalries. Their actions caused the redistribution of peoples around the archipelago as mercenary bands, migrants, and settlers. Sultans and their Dutch allies created the conditions that allowed prophets, visionaries, and militia thugs to insert their voices into the affairs of archipelago states and to launch their followers into rebellions that destroyed kingdoms and created new ones.

7

NEW AND OLD STATES
Freelancers, Prophets, and Militias at Large

Alliances and rivalries between sultans and the Dutch set archipelago peoples on the move. Men displaced by the new ruling classes regrouped under charismatic leaders as militias for hire. Buginese, Balinese, Madurese, Chinese, and Dutch mercenaries jostled with roving bands of land and sea robbers for a share in battles and the spoils. Ambitious men hired them to launch challenges to established kings. Monopoly agreements between sultans and the VOC produced a class of traders who operated off-limits, without licenses or passes. The cargo they shipped into small bays and up rivers—firearms, ammunition, opium, and slaves—fueled political changes and introduced havoc into villages. Ordinary people, severed from their home bases, fled or were captured and exiled to foreign cities and new work sites. Merchants, squeezed out of business in their home port by the policies of sultans or the VOC, transferred their operations and their families to other centers in the archipelago. Whole families attached themselves to leaders and followed them to new regions in the island world and into other communities. Their leaders involved themselves in the affairs of local ruling families through marriage alliances, administrative positions, and warfare.

Chinese bands became another wild element in societies in motion. Entrepreneurs in southern China expanded the range and number of their operations in the archipelago. Large communities of Chinese men without women operated alongside local groups, made accommodation with them or competed for control of resources. Their numbers overwhelmed local authority—Indonesian, Dutch, and Chinese.

Upheaval created opportunities for freelancers (anyone not employed by the VOC or a sultan). Prophets and thugs emerged from obscurity, from physical or spiritual journeys. They appeared suddenly in palaces and capitals to denounce sultans, the Chinese or the Dutch, to prophesy chaos and promise a path to a golden age. The movement of peoples on land and across seas that characterizes the seventeenth and eighteenth centuries brought more communities into historical view. The modern state of Indonesia may be considered heir to a single state constructed in the nineteenth century by the forces of Dutch military, economic, and administrative colonialism. Those forces engulfed regions both Javanese and Dutch perceived as outer islands. Colonial rule connected distant societies to Java and packaged the result into one state. Groups from Aceh to Papua now campaign to undo that state, to separate communities and destinies, to deny histories of interconnectedness. Seventeenth- and eighteenth-century freelancers pushed people into areas once the sole domain of distinct ethnic groups and bound archipelago histories together.

Indonesia's islands were thinly populated. Rapid and easy communication was difficult in mountains, ravines, and forests, and this terrain allowed freelancers to evade central government, to gather followers, and to strike out on their own. Java's landscapes were dominated by forests. They bordered villages, market towns, religious foundations, ports, royal cities and rice fields, and were living space for semi-nomadic farmers and communities that formed around shrines. Kings' agents and spies, peddlers and porters, professional students and holy men passed through this forested landscape. No professional forces existed to protect the public. Their place was supplied by roving bands of armed men operating from forest bases under leaders called *jagos.*

JAGO: PREDATOR OR LOCAL HERO

The Javanese word *jago* means fighting cock, but also designates the leader of a band of men. A jago was a man who depended on a forceful personality, who was not confined by domesticity, and who lived on the fringes of society spying, selling information, and hiring out his men as vigilantes. Jagos were distinguished by their wild manners and appearance. They wore their long hair loose, instead of bound under a head cloth; they were careless of polite norms; and they claimed knowledge of the occult. They used amulets and oaths to bind men to their service. They were the terror of rural communities, stealing buffaloes and destroying houses, or they were local heroes who assaulted and robbed tax collectors and moneylenders. They sold their services to kings and rebels. During battles they frequently changed sides. Chinese bosses employed jagos to patrol the opium business; Javanese and Dutch officials hired them as informants and to control workers.

In twentieth-century urban contexts, jagos were small political bosses who delivered workers to factories, kept industrial order, controlled brothels and gambling, put protesters on the street for politicians, or organized arson and looting. They were freelancers of Indonesia's struggle for national independence. In East Timor jagos launched massacre, plunder, and arson in retaliation against the Timorese movement to withdraw from Indonesia. Using the vocabulary of jihad, jagos today assemble militias to extend Muslim space and to undermine national government.

Jagos strut through babad literature and the reports of Dutch administrators. Babads celebrated the perpetrators of lawlessness, random violence, and challenges to local authority that worried district officials as emergent royalty. Wild men erupting from forest strongholds were attributed a personal beauty and magnetism that attracted men and women followers. Obscure or mysterious origins were proof of royal ancestry. Success in battle was owing to magical weapons in the jago's possession or his ability to make himself invisible and to fly. Such men found scope for their talents and an array of potential patrons in a Java that contained the sultanates of Banten, Cirebon, and Mataram, and the VOC republic of Batavia. A few found in palace turmoil opportunities to determine royal succession and policy; some saw Java's thinly populated regions as the place to set up on their own as kings. Such jagos drew on the spiritual and human resources of another semi-autonomous institution in the Java landscape, the *pesantren.*

Pesantrens were Islamic schools. A man with a reputation for book learning and esoteric knowledge attracted followers, called *santri* (religious scholars), who revered him as spiritual advisor, considered themselves blessed by his presence, and kissed his hand as a token of their deference. Villagers sent their boys to the pesantren to learn to recite a few prayers and portions of the Koran. Professional students accumulated knowledge by traveling between pesantrens, seeking the specialist knowledge of different teachers. When they had learned all a pesantren head had to impart, they received a testimonial naming their teacher, and a chain of teachers that stretched back to a wali or to Muhammad himself.

Pesantrens originated in two traditions: the Islamic *madrasah* (school) and the Javanese village whose taxes were made over to a religious foundation. Pesantren communities did not shut out the world for religious contemplation. They ran businesses that flourished through their tax-free status. Students paid for their tuition by farming their teacher's rice fields or working in his businesses. Pesantrens were not celibate or monastic communities. Scholars of religion, their followers and villagers lived family lives. The pesantren head extended his personal influence through marriage ties. He designated his heir from his sons or sons-in-law. His religious aura safeguarded him from challenge.

Pesantrens were connected to the archipelago Islamic tradition. Java's scholars wrote religious commentaries in Malay in Arabic script. They also kept alive Java's poetic tradition, composing moral tracts and romances in Javanese. All the great palace poets had a pesantren education; court literature grew out of rural centers of Islamic learning.

Pesantrens had an ambiguous relationship to Java's royals. They were the recipients of royal favors, and were often linked to Java's royal houses through marriage. They upheld royalty when they taught as Islamic doctrine that a Muslim king was the deputy of Muhammad, and that opposition to royalty was treason against God. At the same time, because pesantrens were like ministates or autonomous districts within a kingdom, they were potential threats to royal authority. They provided a sanctuary for disappointed and unwanted royals. A pesantren head, whose visions guided him to denounce the king, could lend powerful support to a rebel prince. He could levy men from the villages under his command for military duty. In Java's history, pesantren heads expanded their political influence beyond the religious community by attaching themselves as spiritual advisers to jagos. They aided jagos' causes by advertising prophecies, by supplying magical amulets to a jago's fighters, and by leading their own men into campaigns they declared to be jihads.

The turmoil of Amangkurat I's rule opened up opportunities for the well-connected jago. All kinds of men harbored hatred for this king. Conquest and royal favoritism had displaced local dynasties. VOC merchants and Chinese businessmen were favored over Javanese merchants. Royal appointees seldom held their positions for more than three years. Men with records of service were summoned to court and murdered. Hundreds of religious scholars had been massacred in 1646. Whole families were wiped out when their male heads offended royalty. Amangkurat's spies created anxiety and uncertainty everywhere. Trunajaya (c. 1649–1680) enters Javanese history in 1670 backing the crown prince in a bid to depose Amangkurat I. In Trunajaya the twin centers of opposition flowed together: he was the jago with mysterious royal background, magnetic personality, and magical gifts; and he had connections into the pesantren mini-states as son-in-law to the head of the Kajoran religious community.

Trunajaya's royal background was rooted in Madura. Indonesian histories often treat Madura as a fringe area of Java, and characterize its people (Indonesia's third largest ethnic group) as a tougher, coarser version of the Javanese. Madura rulers were vassals of Java's kings and intermarried with Java's royal houses. The island's lack of natural resources, its aridity, and the reputation of its men as murderous preserved it from colonization by Javanese rice farmers. Instead, Madura families crossed the narrow strait to Java seeking farmland. Madura harbored rebels from Java's courts, and exported mercenaries to mainland kingdoms.

Trunajaya's Islamic connection came from Kajoran, an important religious foundation in central Java, controlling farming and craft villages and a network of scholars. Its head, Raden Kajoran, was a descendant of Sunan Bayat. Trunajaya claimed to be a prince of Madura and through it a descendant of Majapahit's kings. He led a band of armed men into Java, and married a daughter of Kajoran's head. The father-in-law added his men to Trunajaya's band and obligingly circulated the prophecy that Mataram would fall.

Trunajaya also turned to Java's other rulers for help. From Banten, traditionally a foe of Mataram, Sultan Ageng sent Trunajaya two holy cloths. Trunajaya was unsuccessful in gaining help from Batavia. The Dutch, though republicans, sided with monarchy in Indonesia. So the VOC rejected Trunajaya's application for a loan to purchase small arms, artillery, and ammunition. It sided with the reigning king and took advantage of Trunajaya's rebellion to strengthen its own position: VOC soldiers would fight to keep Amangkurat on his throne in return for free consignments of rice and teak wood.

Trunajaya tried to attract the widest possible array of followers. He denounced Amangkurat I as failing to uphold Islamic law, and he covered himself in Islamic authority by asserting approval from Mecca for a jihad.

Susuhunan Amangkurat II stabs Trunajaya. This important painting shows in stylized form a historical monarch. It also shows the power base of Mataram kings by the late seventeenth century to be courtiers, tame religious officials, and Dutch military men. Watercolor by an unknown Javanese artist, c. 1680. Photographic Archive, Royal Institute of Linguistics and Anthropology, Leiden, No. 1029. Photo courtesy of the KITLV.

Trunajaya also claimed glorious ancestry as a descendant of Majapahit's royal house and situated himself within magical traditions associated with warrior heroes. He was also a man open to new technology. When, in 1677, he claimed to have made himself invisible and flown to a VOC ship commanded by the Dutch admiral, Cornelis Speelman, it was for the very modern purpose of stealing forty barrels of gunpowder and one hundred cannonballs.

Fourteen thousand men responded. Javanese, Madurese, Buginese, and Balinese welcomed Trunajaya's vision of a reconstituted Majapahit. In 1677 Trunajaya attacked the Mataram capital and destroyed the palace. Amangkurat I and a diminished band of wives, children, retainers, and armed men fled. The king died seeking refuge on the north coast. Trunajaya urged the crown prince, now Amangkurat II, to establish his capital at the site of Majapahit, and to avoid dealings with non-Muslims, especially the Dutch. Amangkurat II (r. 1677–1703) showed a fine political sense for picking and choosing among potential vassals and allies. As crown prince he used Trunajaya, the jago, to push his father off the throne; as king he chose the VOC as his ally and went after Trunajaya.

Trunajaya made off with the wealth of the Mataram palace and set up his own capital at Kediri, the ancient site of east Java kingdoms, assuming the title sultan. Around 1680 he was captured by his former patron's men and executed.

Surapati is another jago to whom babads attribute royal origins. They pronounce him a descendant of Majapahit princes and a member of Bali's nobility. He enters the VOC official record in 1678 as a Balinese heading a band of armed men for hire. In that year he took an oath of loyalty committing his men to fight as a company within the VOC army. His origins appear to derive from the chaos of raiding and slavery. Balinese princes sold subjects to Indonesian and Dutch slavers to finance wars between kingdoms in Bali and military campaigns in east Java. In Batavia, Balinese slaves became detached from the caste world and belief system of Balinese Hinduism. They took on the religion of their Christian owners or they joined the city's Muslim population. Balinese remained a distinct segment of Batavia's Muslims, with their own mosque and neighborhood. Surapati emerges from this community of Balinese Muslims. When he swore loyalty to the VOC, the clerk recorded that he did so in the presence of an Islamic official who raised a Koran above his head for the oath.

Surapati's men were part of the VOC contingent engaged by Raden Haji in his bid to overthrow Sultan Ageng of Banten. In 1684 Surapati deserted. For some time he, his men, and the women they had accumulated farmed in the Banten hills. When the VOC advertised a bounty for his capture, Surapati led his band into central Java. He entered Mataram's capital in 1685 with eighty soldiers, twenty sick and disabled men, sixty women and children, and some prisoners. Amangkurat II assigned them rice lands and women and made Surapati head of Mataram's Balinese community.

The Dutch had helped Amangkurat II capture Trunajaya and secure his throne. In return they received annual quotas of rice and teak for export and control of the north coast ports. Now Amangkurat II turned to Surapati to reduce the vassal that had grown too strong. In 1686 Surapati's forces attacked the VOC fort that guarded Mataram's palace, killing most of the Dutch. Survivors were given the choice of conversion to Islam or death. The king then pressured his Balinese mercenaries to leave. Surapati and his followers made their way into east Java, where he established fortified headquarters at Pasuruan and took the title Raden Arya Wiranegara. His followers were augmented by Balinese, Malays, Madurese, and Buginese. Surapati made them grants of rice lands in the fertile north coast plain.

At this time, east Java was thinly populated by Hindu farmers who were in the orbit of the kingdom of Balambangan, a client state of the Balinese kingdom of Buleleng. Within this Balinese zone of influence the Muslim Surapati set up his checkpoints to control the movement of villagers and tax trade. He levied taxes in birds' nests from villages on the southern coast in order to attract Chinese traders and buy firearms. He also used marriage diplomacy to protect his space by giving a daughter to Balambangan's Balinese ruler.

Babads celebrate Surapati as royal warrior. Dutch military commanders saw him as a formidable foe because he incorporated European methods of fighting into his battle plan. He bought European firearms, drilled his men, and had his laborers construct earthworks modeled on Dutch fortifications. Mataram's new king perceived Surapati as a troublesome jago who raided outlying villages and offered a haven to rival royals on the eastern fringes of his kingdom. In 1706 the king engaged VOC troops to join the attack on Pasuruan and eliminate Surapati's meddling in Mataram politics.

The new king of Mataram was Pakubuwono I (r. 1704–1719), a son of Amangkurat I and brother to Amangkurat II by a different mother. When Amangkurat II turned Surapati on the Dutch in 1686, his half-brother began his campaign to persuade the VOC to back him for the throne instead. Amangkurat II's son succeeded him as Amangkurat III in 1703, but his line had lost the VOC's support. With Dutch backing, his uncle proclaimed himself king of Mataram in 1704. In 1705 his forces ransacked Amangkurat III's palace and drove him out of the capital. Amangkurat III fled with his followers to Surapati. In 1706 Pakubuwono I and the VOC went after Surapati, who died of wounds in November 1706. Amangkurat III and Surapati's sons continued raids into Mataram until 1708, when the refugee king surrendered to the Dutch. The Dutch obliged Pakubuwono I by exiling him to Ceylon.

Surapati's descendants continued careers as jagos. They showed up as fighting units in the many battles between Mataram princes into the middle of the eighteenth century. Six sons by various mothers fought with rebels against Pakubuwono I. Men claiming descent from Surapati joined Chinese bands in attacks on VOC forts in 1741. They joined Prince Cakraningrat IV of Madura when his troops ransacked the capital of Pakubuwono II, and they backed Pangeran Singasari when he tried to topple his nephew, Pakubuwono III, from the throne in 1755.

Java, with its contending states and spheres of influence, provided the conditions for a Surapati to emerge. At different times he was employed by the VOC, by a Banten prince, and by two Mataram kings, Amangkurat I and II. Through marriage politics he was father-in-law to the king of Balambangan. His career took him from one end of Java to the other. In all kingdoms and in Batavia Surapati found the Dutch as traders, soldiers, diplomats, innovators, and husbands. (His patron-turned-enemy, Amangkurat II, was rumored to be the son of Cornelis Speelman.) Surapati's personal experience as a mercenary showed him that small numbers of VOC soldiers could defeat far larger armies of Indonesian kings. The payments kings made for VOC military services resulted in heavy tax burdens on Javanese workers and in diminished sovereignty for Java's kings. All this made Surapati voice consistent opposition to the Dutch in Java in language borrowed from the Koran and from contemporaries such as Trunajaya and Shaikh Yusuf, even as he accepted Hindu Balinese mercenaries in his forces. Surapati's opposition to the Dutch as the non-Muslim Other has earned him the official status of champion of Islam and hero of the Republic of Indonesia.

SURAPATI'S LEGACY: THE CONVERSION OF EAST JAVA

In 1743 Pakubuwono II (r. 1726–1749) rid himself of problems in Mataram's eastern provinces by transferring Surapati's former lands to the Dutch. Rebel bands used east Java as a place of retreat; Balinese princes still considered it as tributary territory to their kingdoms in Bali. The VOC could defeat Indonesian armies, but it could not directly administer territories distant from its Batavia headquarters. Its method was to use local officials and Chinese networks to get production and trade moving. When it became chief landlord of east Java, the company continued Surapati's system of administration. It appointed as officials only men who were Muslim, and ordered them to make conversion of the Hindu population a priority of office. The second strategy was encouraging immigration of Muslim farming families from Madura and central Java. In this way the VOC achieved Surapati's goals: Balinese influence was lessened, the forest refuges of rebel bands were reduced, and the landscape was permanently settled by farmers who raised crops for export. Over time Muslim immigrants became the majority population. East Java was detached from Bali's orbit and was integrated into the history of Muslim Java under the Christian overlordship of the Dutch.

Professional soldiers on Java were bodyguards to princes related through the tangled webs of royal polygamy, shifting factions, and court coalitions. From around 1500, soldiers had muskets and cannon, as well as pikes, spears, daggers, and battle axes. They fought on horseback, from elephants, and on foot. Soldiers wore protective jackets made from local vegetable fibers and shell disks, reinforced with thick bark or cotton wadding. Smiths copied European models to produce metal jackets and helmets in their forges. Soldiers also used spiritual means to survive battle. They bought amulets from holy men and marched beneath banners inscribed with verses from the Koran. Some meditated to acquire invulnerability or sought possession of a weapon that was believed to have magical powers.

All men had a kris. The kris was the product of a smith's metalworking and ritual knowledge and acquired a spirit in the fire of the forge. The finished object was named, and the number of its curves was linked to its special attributes. Hilt and sheath were embellished according to the wealth of the owner. Once a year a man ceremonially washed his kris and treated it with oil, perfume, and incense, while reciting prayers. The kris was knit into Islamic ritual; a youth received his first kris after undergoing his initiation of circumcision into Muslim manhood.

Javanese armies were huge. Trunajaya headed fourteen thousand men in his mission to overthrow Amangkurat I; Pakubuwono I sent ten thousand Javanese against Surapati. Most of these men did not fight; they were porters and servants drafted into service when kings sent their local lords into battle. Military commanders used cannon to frighten and scatter the sprawling armies of their opponents. Actual combat was the job of commanders and troops personally loyal to them. Mercenaries from Sulawesi, Bali, and Madura fought as separate squads under their own commanders and banners.

VOC armies consisted of European soldiers, auxiliary units of Batavian Asians, and mercenary squads of Javanese, Balinese, Madurese, Timorese, Ambonese, Buginese, and Malays. VOC forces accompanying Pakubuwono I's 10,000 Javanese troops were made up of 930 Dutch men and 2,500 Indonesians. The Europeans who fought in Java's wars, always few in comparison with the numbers of Javanese troops, were the product of the corporate power of the Dutch East Indies Company. The VOC, as the largest employer and purchaser in Holland, had standing orders for weapons. It outfitted each soldier with small arms and a sword, cartridges, carrying pouches, and belts, smoke bombs and grenades. The VOC installed swivel guns and cannon on its ships and exported artillery to defend Dutch settlements in Asia. Developments in European weaponry had produced cannon that could destroy fortifications. They were light enough to be dragged across fields, but they were not of much use in the mountainous terrain of Indonesia's islands. The Dutch used cannon to greatest effect from their ships, destroying coastal forts. On land the Dutch relied on training, firearms, and swords.

VOC soldiers were successful when they fought alongside large Indonesian armies. The peasant conscripts that formed the majority in Javanese armies built tunnels up to the walls of opponents' forts and undermined their foundations. European soldiers, trained to fight as a unit, positioned themselves in the center of the advancing line of a Javanese army. When they were in range of their opponents the front line of soldiers fired, then knelt to reload while the next line fired. White men could not flee battle, for they could not melt into Javanese villages. The only alternative to fighting was an uncertain future in deserting to the other side. Isolated forts were vulnerable; VOC soldiers could be cut off from supplies. Indonesian auxiliaries sometimes deserted them; mercenaries could change sides. VOC troops could be overrun in ambush, but in open battle VOC fighting squads were effective.

When they felt strong, Java's kings plotted to rid themselves of the VOC, but they could never give up their dependency on the Dutch. Despite the warnings of prophets and condemnation of ulamas, and despite the heavy price the VOC charged for its services, Java's kings always returned to the VOC to save their thrones. Between 1677 and 1749 VOC troops were engaged in all the dynastic battles princely half-brothers inflicted on Mataram's population. For example, VOC troops fought for Pakubuwono I when his kingdom fell apart in rebellions in 1717. They supported Pakubuwono's heir when this son succeeded as Amangkurat IV in 1710 and was challenged by two of his half-brothers. VOC troops supported Amangkurat IV's heir, Pakubuwono II, through five years of wars between 1740 and 1745. In the 1750s VOC troops protected Pakubuwono III's throne against three of his uncles.

The alliance made between Arung Palakka and the VOC in 1666 for the conquest of south Sulawesi had major repercussions across the archipelago. The combined Palakka-VOC victory in 1669 propelled an exodus of Buginese from Sulawesi. Buginese soldiers became professional mercenaries available for hire in Java, Sumatra, and the Malay Peninsula. Other Buginese fanned out across the archipelago, taking up rice land in "empty" regions and establishing small shopkeeping and manufacturing businesses in archipelago towns. Buginese princes married into Malay royal families. In 1718 Buginese extracted from the ruling dynasty of the Riau archipelago the exclusive right to hold the office of governor and pass it on to their descendants as a hereditary perquisite.

Buginese also established themselves as a major sea people, specializing in transporting weapons, sea produce, and slaves. Buginese mercenaries prolonged the dynastic wars that weakened Mataram. They fought with rebels against the reigning king and his Dutch allies; other Buginese fought within VOC armies against rebel princes.

What began for the Buginese as escape from VOC domination in the late seventeenth century ended up as a cultural pattern of continuous emigration. In the Republic of Indonesia Bugis emigration fostered the extension of government authority into the new territories of Irian and East Timor. Slaving is outlawed; Buginese shippers now specialize in transporting refugees and illegal emigrants from China and the Middle East to isolated coasts and islands between Indonesia and Australia.

ABORTED JOURNEY: FROM MAREGE' TO AUSTRALIA

Australia's northern shores formed the southern boundary of Indonesian waters for sailors from Sulawesi. They were hunting ground and worksite for Makasar and Bugis men, who fished for trepang which was in demand in Chinese markets. They secured use rights from Aboriginal communities by giving titles and flags to local chiefs and gifts of tobacco and metal axes. They named their work areas Kayu Putih (today's Kimberley) and Marege' (now Arnhem Land). In this history, which begins in the seventeenth century, trepang collectors were seasonal visitors. Because Aborigines did not gather or manufacture items salable on their sea routes, trepang collectors did not settle agents on Australian shores or establish permanent settlements. Nor did they hire locals as workers or raid their territories for slaves.

Australian shores were Sulawesi worksites in a period of European exploration and settlement. From the middle of the nineteenth century the northern coast was being pulled into an Australian history made in the south of the continent. By 1906 Australian authorities denied Indonesian trepang collectors fishing rights. Although Buginese and Makasar men were the first regular visitors to the coastal fringe of northern Australia, they did not put down roots, build permanent settlements, attract traveling ulamas, or reproduce their own civilization within Aboriginal societies. The named spaces of Australia never became a part of the Indonesian state.

The policies of sultans and VOC administrators also created opportunities for another set of freelancers. By the middle of the eighteenth century Chinese businesses had expanded into many corners of the archipelago, and Chinese immigrants were becoming another turbulent element in the spaces between many jurisdictions. In international ports such as Banten, Batavia, Semarang, Gresik, Surabaya, and Makasar well-established communities of Chinese concentrated in Chinese neighborhoods or specifically designated suburbs. Indonesian and VOC rulers appointed the richest merchants to represent the Chinese community. The Dutch gave them honorary military titles and ranks as majors, captains, and lieutenants; Indonesian rulers incorporated them into their own systems of naming and titling. Such Chinese representatives acted as ambassadors. They made gifts and public speeches to honor Indonesian and Dutch rulers on festival days and negotiated for contracts and licenses to be distributed within the Chinese community. City administrators left it to these men to set the standards for the Chinese community, to oversee marriage and inheritance issues, and to deal with criminal problems involving Chinese. They regarded wives and children in Chinese households as Chinese, even though wives were local women and the children were born locally. Chinese men who had converted to Islam and spoke Javanese with their wives and children took Javanese names. Their lives revolved around Chinese mosques; they were patrons of Javanese arts, admitted to the fringes of Javanese polite society. Temples, mosques, and graveyards in Chinese suburbs of Indonesia's cities show the degrees of Chinese assimilation and rootedness.

Batavia's Chinese majors and captains hired peddlers and coolies, henchmen, spies, thugs, and policemen from the constant inflow of Chinese immigrants. They were responsible to the VOC for Chinese both in the city and outlying districts, but their personal police forces became completely ineffectual outside Batavia's walls. Importers of labor dropped off new recruits along shores and inlets beyond the reach of Batavia's harbor authorities. These illegal workers were the kind of tough men who had lived in poverty in farms and

CHINESE TEMPLES, TOMBS, AND CEMETERIES

Chinese temples in Jakarta date from around 1650. Most are rectangular, multiroofed buildings set within a walled compound. Temples contain a main altar and image, and side annexes for subsidiary deities. Wall panels inscribed in Chinese characters preserve the name of the temple god, and the date and names of donors. Some temples were open to the entire Chinese community; others served members of a clan, migrants from a common locality in China, or occupational groups such as rice merchants and sailors. Temples honored Buddhist or Taoist deities; those dedicated to local spirits were built near places holy to the Javanese. Mosques for Chinese congregations were the focus of neighborhoods of Chinese Muslims, who were termed *Peranakan.*

In China the filial son erected a stone memorial to his father. He maintained the tombs of past generations, and made regular offerings. When Chinese men died outside China their sons carried on the tradition of public memorial. Old Chinese cemeteries in Indonesian cities record preservation of Chinese habits overseas and the prosperity some migrants attained. They also show that the skills of stonemason and inscriber of Chinese characters traveled beyond China.

Chinese communities no longer continue this tradition in contemporary Indonesia. Urban land is too expensive to purchase for burial grounds, while public displays of attachment to traditions of China are not acceptable to many Indonesians. Cremation, which often replaces burial, is also another sign of the long journey of assimilation by Chinese, for it is the burial form of Southeast Asian Buddhism.

Many holy grave sites in Java are attributed to Muslim men of Chinese origin, such as Pangeran Hadiri. According to local tradition, he was a captain shipwrecked off the north Java coast who married Ratu (Queen) Kalinyamat and founded the port city of Japara.

cities in China. On sugar estates in the Batavia region they were bound by clan bosses into associations for mutual protection and owed allegiance to no other authority. These men knew how to turn the iron machinery of a sugar mill into weapons. In October 1740 they reacted swiftly to the VOC's determination to reduce their numbers by deportation and to rumors that the real plan was to take deportees to sea and throw them overboard. Armed bands marched on Batavia. They easily eliminated VOC patrols and began storming the city with cannon.

The previous year VOC officials had attempted a population count. Within Batavia's walls was a free population of 7,233, consisting of 4,199 Chinese, 1,276 Europeans, 1,038 Mardijkers (former slaves and free persons of Indian origin), 421 Eurasians, and 299 categorized as Others. In the districts around Batavia were 35,000 Javanese and Balinese and 10,574 Chinese. In the city Chinese outnumbered the Dutch by three to one, while Chinese were the fastest-growing group in the immediate hinterland, where individual Dutch people owned villas. When Chinese militias made their surprise attack, Batavians panicked. Dutch and Javanese turned on Chinese inside the walls. For three days they hunted down and killed Chinese men, their (Indonesian) wives, and their children. VOC troops rallied after the initial assaults to scatter Chinese militias and subdue the city's outlying districts.

A Javanese chronicle's account of the Chinese assault on Batavia casts its leader as a jago. He is known by the Malay title and name of Cik Sepanjang (Mr. Tall). He is an expert in magic and the occult and cloaks his men with invulnerability. Cik Sepanjang, known in Dutch records under his Chinese name of Tan Sinko, was driven to revolt, according to the babad, by ill treatment from the VOC. It says 9,000 Chinese men were massacred, a figure double the census count for Chinese in Batavia. Dutch eyewitnesses gave figures for the massacre ranging from 1,000 to 10,000. Fear of the Chinese persisted, and survivors had to leave the walled city. But, without Chinese, Batavia became unworkable. The vegetable and meat markets were gone, trade badly damaged, the city's prosperity threatened. For a year Chinese were allowed inside the city during business hours only, then controls were relaxed and VOC officials encouraged renewed Chinese immigration.

Chinese bands that had attacked Batavia and witnessed the massacre retreated into the forest. By 1741 they were in Mataram territory, where they found society in upheaval because of years of treaties between Mataram's kings and the Dutch. VOC forts dominated coastal cities; VOC officials controlled trade and milked tariffs to the exclusion of Javanese officials.

Farmers' taxes steadily increased to meet the growing annual quotas of rice and lumber for the company. Independent rice traders could not compete with a corporation that received almost half of its rice export free of charge. Nor could they compete with a corporation that used its ships to block river mouths and harbors to other shipping until its own ships were full. Men who owed their tax to local officials in the form of their unpaid labor found themselves rented out to the VOC by their officials. They were set to work on VOC construction sites and docks but received little or no share of the monies the VOC paid to rent their labor. The VOC also recruited workers directly, angering Javanese officials because they were cut out of their squeeze and because the workers were released from their customary obligations to the nobility.

Mercenary bands of Buginese, Madurese, and Balinese crisscrossed Mataram's provinces looking for employment as soldiers, vigilantes, or police. Their commanders, who had been awarded villages and rice lands as payment for their services, conducted tax collections like plundering raids. Wandering holy men found discontented and unemployed men to listen to their condemnations of society and to take part in the solution offered, which was rebellion and murder of local authority, whether Javanese, Chinese, or Dutch. In Chinese quarters and enterprises angry men were indentured to their bosses. Rural Chinese artisans and their families fled to towns to escape bands of robbers roving the countryside. In the royal capital of Kartasura a VOC garrison protected the reigning monarch and billed the palace for its cost. Many courtiers were critical of the king for permitting Dutch merchants to infringe on Javanese sovereignty. The king, who knew he had Dutch military backing, did not feel the need to court support. He appointed, dismissed, or even killed his officials at will. The usual royal half-brothers plotted to overturn the succession, and, by 1741, the king looked for militias capable of trimming Dutch pretensions and powers.

Chinese bands from west Java seized their opportunity. They overran Chinese sugar and saw mills, murdered their owners and managers, and offered workers the choice of death or joining them. They joined forces with Javanese bands to attack Europeans living outside the walls of VOC garrisons, killing them and destroying their property. By the end of 1741 combined Chinese and Javanese forces attacked VOC forts. Some they overran, killing all occupants and massacring the wealthy of all races—Javanese, Chinese, and Dutch—in the port cities. VOC officials estimated that Semarang was attacked by three thousand Chinese and forty to fifty thousand Javanese. Fifty cannon were trained against the VOC fort in a long siege. The attackers were repulsed only when supplies and reinforcements arrived by sea from Batavia.

Pakubuwono II refused requests for armed assistance from besieged VOC forts. He demanded payment from the Dutch and attempted to lure Indonesian soldiers who fought under VOC commanders to defect and attack the Dutch. But Chinese and Javanese bands turned against the king of Java, too. In 1742 they overran the royal capital. Pakubuwono abandoned Kartasura with a small party and a VOC guard. The Chinese did not attempt to install a Chinese as king of Java; instead they supported a young grandson of Amangkurat III (whom Pakubuwono I and the VOC had toppled from the throne in 1704). Chinese and Javanese rebels hailed this boy as the Sunan Mas (Golden Sunan). With an armed escort of one thousand Chinese, one thousand Javanese, and three hundred Buginese, he made a publicized pilgrimage to the graves of the saints of Islam at Demak to gather spiritual and public support.

The fighting also provided opportunity for another army. Madurese soldiers led by Cakraningrat IV, the hereditary ruler of west Madura and vassal to Mataram, crossed the strait into central Java. Cakraningrat IV had a longstanding plan to rid himself of vassalage to Mataram. Since 1729 he had refused to appear in person at the Kartasura court to pay homage to Java's king. He had been unsuccessful in getting the VOC to accept him as a vassal and protect him from the obligation to pay taxes to Mataram. Now Cakraningrat led his troops against Pakubuwono II. Half-brothers of the king joined Cakraningrat with their private armies. In November 1742, Madurese, Javanese, and Chinese militias broke into Pakubuwono II's palace, ransacked it, and raped the women abandoned in the king's flight.

Javanese military commanders led unexpected strikes against the Dutch from hideouts in the forested hills. In this guerrilla war they had the advantage of surprise, of moving in terrain known to them, of being able to hide in Javanese villages. Because they looked different from Javanese men, Chinese militias could not hide among the civilian population. Their tactics were siege and assault. VOC military commanders used religious and occupation difference and local hatreds to divide the bands fighting them and guaranteed rewards to Javanese who turned against Chinese insurgents.

In the chaotic years 1741–1745 the Dutch became the supreme jagos of central Java. Many groups turned to them for protection. Pakubuwono II changed sides again and VOC troops saved his throne. Many Javanese officials requested that the VOC release them from Mataram's control and accept them as vassals. The Dutch offered them autonomous rule and hereditary succession

JAVA CAREERS: THE STORY OF SLAMET

Slamet's journey began in slavery. A Balinese slaver delivered him to Semarang where he became the employee of senior VOC merchant, Willem Dubbeldekop. In the port city world of north Java, the Hindu Balinese converted to Islam and took the Muslim Javanese name of Slamet. After Dubbeldekop emancipated him, Slamet set up in trade on his own. Using his VOC connections he was appointed representative for Malay merchants at Juwana. During the wars of the 1740s, Slamet trapped a Chinese rebel leader, killed him, and sent his head and amulet to the Dutch commander of Juwana's fort. As a reward the Dutch made Slamet head of a village of twenty-five Javanese households near Rembang and assigned to him sole right to levy taxes in goods and labor on its inhabitants.

in return for cooperation in extracting goods and services from the general population. Chinese merchants, artisans, tollgate operators, and laborers, who had been attacked by Javanese mobs during the general social uprising, fled to VOC-controlled centers. Their representatives urged the VOC to release them from their status as subjects of Java's princes and accept them as subjects of the company.

When VOC troops began having successes against militias, Java's princes temporarily dropped their challenge to the throne. They were not contesting political ideology or how to run the state, but control of men and resources. Some the Dutch exiled. Armies faded away. The Dutch signed a new treaty with Pakubuwono II which gave them control of a strip of coastland two kilometers deep along the north coast and the banks of all rivers flowing into the sea. They also received east Java and the right to veto all royal appointments. Pakubuwono II surrendered to the Dutch his rights to tax the Chinese and to sell the tollgates which had given him an annual cash payment and stipends for his relatives.

Pakubuwono II sought a new capital, as Chinese and Madurese troops had destroyed the sanctity of his palace. In 1746 a great procession, that included his Dutch jagos, accompanied Pakubuwono II to his new palace at

Surakarta. He took from Kartasura only the stone throne of the kings of early Mataram. He had lost territories, laborers, and vassals. District officials no longer journeyed to pay him homage at his court, which became a quiet place. Few needed to flatter him for favors; they flattered the Dutch governor-general instead. When Baron G. W. van Imhoff paid the first visit ever by a governor-general to the court of Mataram, Pakubuwono II recognized publicly he was no longer center of the universe by making the long journey to Semarang to greet van Imhoff and escort him to the capital. Many royal male relatives had already left court permanently, signaling that they no longer acknowledged loyalty to Pakubuwono or his heir.

Pakubuwono II was king of Java at a time when court politics and his own contempt for Chinese obscured his vision of the world beyond his palace. He had seen the VOC as a weak vassal. He had not grasped that a mammoth corporation backed the few dozen Dutch men in his kingdom. Astonished that the Chinese whom he despised could overrun VOC forts, he had plotted to rid himself of the Dutch. He ended up ruler of shrunken territories and wholly dependent on Dutch jagos for his survival. On his deathbed in 1749, Pakubuwono II willed Mataram to the VOC.

The Dutch official who received Pakubuwono II's cession of Mataram did not understand the transfer to mean that Mataram was to become a subject territory ruled by the governor-general from Batavia. To him cession meant that the Dutch now maneuvered among the factions at court to determine succession to Mataram's throne. The Dutch usually sided with the claim of eldest son of a high-ranking mother; they did not back half-brothers, uncles, or nephews. In 1749, therefore, the VOC supported a sixteen-year-old boy over the adult contenders, because he was the only surviving son born to a queen. Pakubuwono II's half-brothers fought against their nephew, who took the reign name Pakubuwono III, and against each other as well.

In 1754, one of the contenders turned to Java's myth and history for a solution, proposing that the kingdom of Mataram be split in two between nephew and uncle and that the VOC be retainer and ally to both royal houses. Under this deal, which the VOC brokered in 1755, Pakubuwono III became head of a kingdom named Surakarta; his uncle became ruler of a kingdom named Yogyakarta. The VOC retained control of the north coast, made cash payments to Pakubuwono III, and provided troops to support Yogyakarta's new ruler against contenders for his throne. In 1756 Yogyakarta's prince took the reign name Hamengkubuwono and the title of sultan.

The VOC's brokering of these arrangements, known as the Treaty of Gyanti, is often described as an imperialist act to dismember Java. At the time, the treaty was understood as a Javanese decision and a Javanese solution, borrowing from Java's past the precedent of dividing a kingdom between contending heirs. In this Javanese world the Dutch acted to secure the uninterrupted flow of trade goods to their ships. Javanese royals regarded the treaty as a temporary arrangement. In 1755, and for many years, Pakubuwono III had no son. Hamengkubuwono expected that he or his heir would succeed to Surakarta and unite it with Yogyakarta to re-create Mataram.

During his long life, Hamengkubuwono had more than thirty acknowledged children, including sixteen boys. He named his oldest son heir in 1756, but had him poisoned in 1758 and named his third son successor. Hamengkubuwono then began negotiations for the marriage of this new crown prince to a daughter of Pakubuwono III to seal his plans for reunification of the two kingdoms. But in the late 1760s Pakubuwono III fathered a boy by a village girl who had been provided for him during one of his trips outside the palace. She was raised to the status of king's consort and her son claimed the throne of Surakarta as Pakubuwono IV when his father died in 1788.

Hamengkubuwono's plans to reunite Surakarta and Yogyakarta were also thwarted by his half-brother, Mas Said. He fought on for recognition of his claims, rather than accepting the cozy arrangements of the Gyanti Treaty. The VOC ended the continual fighting in Java by forcing Pakubuwono III to allot four thousand families within Surakarta territory to Mas Said. Mas Said took the title Mangkunagara and called his conglomeration of taxpaying families Mangkunagaran. This was not a separate kingdom with its own territory; the prince's capital and entourage were in the Surakarta capital.

Mangkunagara upset the ambitions of his half-brother in Yogyakarta by marrying his own son to Pakubuwono III's daughter. After Pakubuwono III fathered a son, Mangkunagara politicked to ensure that his own boy would succeed him as Mangkunagara II. In 1792 the VOC backed these plans. The heads of Surakarta, Yogyakarta, and Mangkunagaran kept on plotting to take over each other's kingdom through marriage alliances and intrigues with religious officials. In public they ignored the existence of other royal centers. They persisted in regarding each other as the major enemy and the Dutch as ally. It was not until the twentieth century that the heads of Java's royal houses actually met each other.

The ideal ruler is described in the opening passages of Javanese wayang performances as male, of royal descent, a warrior, and one possessed of a powerful inner force which he must learn to control. A king's self-control, achieved through meditation, promotes justice and prosperity for his subjects, compels their service and absolute surrender. Court poets described their king as exuding a divine light. The reality of royal Java from the late seventeenth century was civil war, contraction of territory, increasing pressure to extract incomes from villages to support a large, non-productive upper class, and the sale of Java to foreigners. Internally, too, royal Java shrank when Mataram was split. The permanent division of Mataram demonstrated that the royal family was incapable of generating a political consensus.

For the common folk of Java these political arrangements had consequences. Their villages were now split between three ruling houses. Some villagers now paid taxes to Pakubuwono III of Surakarta, some to Hamengkubuwono I of Yogyakarta, while others paid taxes to Mas Said. Villages were even divided internally, their inhabitants owing taxes to Surakarta, Mangukanagaran or Yogyakarta. This peculiar situation meant that there were many conflicts over jurisdiction, and much movement by people between villages as they sought to evade their own king's tax agents and police. It also meant that the proliferating royal houses squeezed their subjects harder for taxes because the royals multiplied while the subject population remained the same.

Another major effect of the division of Mataram was the end of war. Javanese commoners were no longer summoned for support duties, and roads were safe for men and women wishing to carry goods to markets. In the last half of the eighteenth century they could grow, sell, and exchange their crops. Chinese continued to run businesses for Dutch and Javanese rulers and they extended their operations in villages and towns across Java. No sympathy ever developed among rulers or commoners for the people who made their economies work. It suited ruling classes to despise the possessors of skills that they needed and to keep Chinese communities distinct. In Indonesian settings Chinese were able to make great gains, but they were always targets of scorn and vulnerable to attack in times of crisis. Chinese and local gangs frequently fought for control of resources.

Java's monarchs sold the labor of ordinary people to Chinese, Eurasians, and Europeans, in exchange for cash to support lavish lifestyles. Nothing was done to regulate the living conditions of their subjects; poverty was widespread and with it hatred of foreigners. Laborers bound to Chinese and European enterprises had the protection of neither their king nor any Javanese institution. In such conditions religious leaders attracted followers, and prophecies of the imminent collapse of the monarchs or the vanquishing of Chinese and Dutch circulated and were warmly anticipated. These circumstances maintained the Dutch role as royalty's supreme jago.

Mataram's kings had destroyed individual wealth by their raids on Java's north coast ports, their bans on shipbuilding and interisland trade, and their concessions to the VOC. Dutch military commanders destroyed Makasar's trading community in wars between 1666 and 1669. Shipowners, shipbuilders, pilots, merchants, and entrepreneurs were deprived of their regular occupations. An exodus of men from Demak, Tegal, Japara, Gresik, Surabaya, and Makasar relocated to ports in the archipelago where there was still scope for their operations. The depredations of Mataram kings and the VOC resulted in the diffusion of skills around the archipelago, an increase in the number and importance of ports, the spread of urban Islamic culture, and the development of Javanese and Makasar communities outside their home regions. These communities became a magnet for further immigration. As the numbers of migrants increased businesses diversified to include small industries, rice farming, and raising crops for export. The influx of outsiders posed challenges to local ruling families and altered the makeup of indigenous communities.

Many uprooted Javanese transferred their headquarters to the sultanate of Banjarmasin, which lay across the Java Sea on the southern coast of Kalimantan. Banjarmasin and Java already had many connections: sailors based along Java's north coast and in Srivijaya's Sumatran ports had for centuries carried rice, salt, iron, and textiles to Kalimantan river towns to exchange for gold, diamonds, beeswax, and tree products. They introduced words of Sanskrit origin, concepts, and devotional objects of Hindu and Buddhist religions to Kalimantan peoples who lived on the fringes of the rain forest, along riverbanks, coasts, and the shores of inland lakes. Towns located at river mouths developed mixed populations that included Javanese and Malays as well as local ethnic groups. Navies and envoys from Majapahit put in periodically to levy tribute in forest products. Banjarmasin's ruling class modeled palace and court culture on the east Java kingdom.

Banjarmasin's historical tradition continues the link with Java in explaining the origins of its Muslim government. Envoys from Demak brought Islam to the port. Around 1530 the local culture hero, Pangeran Samudra (Warrior Prince of the Sea) converted to Islam and took the reign name Sultan Suriansyah. Java continued to exert political pressure on Banjarmasin's ruling class when Mataram succeeded as the most powerful state in the region. Banjarmasin had to send annual missions of homage and Kalimantan products to the

Mataram capital. Then, following Mataram's attacks on Java's north coast ports, Javanese merchants poured into Banjarmasin.

VOC monopoly policies gave Banjarmasin the way out of submission to Java's kings. In 1635 Banjarmasin's rulers agreed to sell their pepper exclusively to the VOC. By 1641 they felt able to give up sending the expensive tribute missions to Mataram. The VOC's conquest of Makasar produced another influx of traders, for the fluid networks of Asian shipping shifted to Banjarmasin. It became an important entrepot and center for shipbuilding and sale of ships. Pepper sales financed the ambitions of men vying to head Banjarmasin. Rival factions fought for control of the sultanate through coups and assassinations.

Conversion to Islam had brought a Malay style to Kalimantan coasts. In that setting, Malays, not Arabs, represented Islam. Kalimantan peoples who converted adopted Malay because they perceived it as the language of Muslims and of Muslim government. Converts adopted Malay forms of dress, diet, house style, and occupations associated with Malays. They exchanged hunting wild boar and tending domesticated pigs for fishing, trade, small industries, and government. Converts called themselves Malay to distinguish themselves from Kalimantan inhabitants who had not converted.

Immigrants from Java created Javanese Muslim neighborhoods within Malay towns. Immigrants also applied to the hinterland of Banjarmasin the farming techniques of central Java. They encroached on the habitat of Kalimantan peoples who lived in the rain forest; they set in motion migrations by indigenous peoples and new adaptations to Kalimantan's environment. The immigrants gained monopoly of government power and resources and reduced the indigenous population to the status of primitive inhabitants of the interior. In academic texts, the non-Muslim peoples of Kalimantan are called by the general name of Dayak.

DAYAK JOURNEYS

The term Dayak covers many distinct speech groups in Kalimantan. Today it has the meaning of people living away from the coast, and includes nomadic groups, shifting cultivators, and settled peoples. The term is associated with tribal warfare, male fertility cults, tattooing, head hunting, and long houses where several families live together. Dayak has a connotation of remoteness. It designates non-Muslim minorities in the Republic of Indonesia.

Kalimantan's thick rain forest was a formidable barrier to human settlement before the twentieth century. Archaeological evidence points to settlements along coasts and riverbeds. The nomadic lifestyle of hunting and temporary planting in forest clearings is an adaptation of the last four hundred years, made by Dayaks as they were pushed deeper into the forest by the growth of ports and the web of coastal Islamic culture. Dayak migrations through the interior of Kalimantan led to its eventual settlement. Dayak peoples supplied labor and raised food for Chinese mining communities; they paid their taxes to Malay river chiefs by raising pepper vines in forest clearings. Through these relationships they achieved intermittent communication with the outside world.

In the nineteenth century Dayaks were the object of Kalimantan explorers and ethnographers. Colonial administrations set up forts and sent regular patrols to wipe out tribal warfare and head hunting. Modern Indonesian administrations target Dayaks for "development," which means settlement in permanent single-family dwellings on small farms, wage labor, and the systematic eradication of Dayak forest landscapes by logging companies. Farming families from Java and Madura have been settled in "empty" Kalimantan territories to relieve overcrowding in their home regions. Their agricultural settlements are a tool of expanding government control and the mechanism for spreading Muslim culture and Javanese and Madurese peoples across the face of the archipelago.

As a consequence of contact with archipelago Muslims, Dayaks made two kinds of journeys. The spiritual journey led to Islam; Dayaks emerged from it as Malays. Others made a physical journey into the interior of Kalimantan. Their migrations have made possible the steady extraction of resources. Many of these Dayaks also made the spiritual journey to Christianity. In independent Indonesia Christian and Animist Dayaks see their space shrinking and the economic resources of their habitat being usurped by outsiders. In 1967 in West Kalimantan Dayaks drove Chinese farmers off their rice fields and from their homes. From 1997 Dayaks have made violent attacks on Madurese immigrants. Some attempt, since the fall of the New Order, to reverse a long process of absorption into Indonesia.

Butung's royal family also used the VOC to free it from the pressure of a more powerful Indonesian kingdom. Butung is a cluster of small islands off southeastern Sulawesi. It was a stopping-off place for sailors on the east Indonesia-Java circuit. The land itself did not produce much that was in demand. Farmers supported the royal and aristocratic establishment through taxes levied in onions, coconuts, chickens, bananas, sugar cane, and their unpaid labor. Entrepreneurs financed building ships and outfitted them for trade. They raided the sea-lanes and their own interior highlands for slaves, and they exported to eastern Indonesia heavy cutting knives and swords produced by local metal workers. They imported cloth, coins, guns, opium, sago, and tree bark.

Butung's royal family converted to Islam in 1540. Islam imposed male rule on a pre-Islamic past of queens who had connected themselves to Majapahit by taking wandering Javanese princes as husbands and sending their sons to Majapahit for training. Conversion brought with it vassal status to the most powerful regional Islamic sultanates of the day, first Ternate, then Makasar. Butung's rulers turned to the VOC in order to recover independent status. They maintained diplomatic relations with the VOC and relied on Dutch sea patrols to protect their coastal villages from armed fleets of Buginese and other east Indonesian slave-raiders.

The presence of VOC ships and merchants in archipelago ports was a constant temptation to archipelago princes. They saw in the VOC muscle and money they could use to achieve their ambitions in their own corner of Indonesia. For example, the tin of Bangka Island and an alliance with the VOC enabled a younger brother to usurp Palembang's throne in 1724. Pangeran Jayawikrama offered the VOC 400,000 rixdollars and eighty slaves in return for troops to help him overthrow Sultan Ratu Anom. The VOC obliged. Jayawikrama, who took the reign name Sultan Mahmud Badar al-Din (r. 1724–1757), authorized his Dutch ally to build a trading post in Palembang and negotiated a fixed price for an annual delivery of tin to Batavia.

Palembang's tin came from Bangka Island. The extraction of tin was a sideline of Bangka's farmers who washed riverbank soils in flat pans until the ore was separated from gravel and soil particles. They surrendered the residue to Palembang's rulers in payment of their taxes. Before the industrializing West found a use for tin in food storage and as a lightweight, flexible building material, tin was in demand in China for a quite different purpose. The tin was beaten into a thin foil and used as backing for sheets of paper that were burned in religious ceremonies. Around 1740 Sultan Mahmud decided to increase the quantity of tin coming into his market by replacing part-time Bangka panners with professional miners. He authorized Muslim Chinese at his court to import men from southern China and to run mining as an industry with a tightly controlled labor force and product.

Sultan Mahmud's other customers paid for Palembang's tin with cloth, gunpowder, weapons, opium, and ceramics. The VOC's price was lower than the sultan's agents could get in the open market, but the company paid in silver and promptly. A portion of the sultan's annual income was now predictable and guaranteed. VOC ships protected him against rivals, such as the neighboring sultanate of Jambi, and could disperse the large fleets of pirates that cruised the Straits. From Mahmud's point of view, he was an astute merchant prince. To the VOC and many historians, the Dutch forced on the sultan a contract to sell tin at below market rates.

Dutch men rattled around the archipelago in and out of company employment. Some found a place in Indonesian kingdoms for their skills as coachmen, musicians, and artillery men. Others found in Indonesia a workroom for their scientific interests. With Indonesian assistants they walked into forests to obtain specimens of plants and learn their names and properties; with Indonesian assistants they collected shells and sea creatures, minerals and rocks; through conversations with Indonesian colleagues they collected words from Indonesian languages and tried to understand the construction of Indonesian sentences. Some kept diaries of their travels and made sketches of people and places they visited. Some Dutch men collected archipelago folk tales, customs, legends, and histories.

Occasionally the name of an Asian specialist is preserved in Dutch records together with the knowledge transferred. The Batavian Chinese doctor, Chou Mei-Yeh, for example, numbered senior VOC officials and their families among his clients. In 1710 he accompanied the retiring governor-general, Joan van Hoorn, on his return journey to the Netherlands as his personal physician. During a short stay in Amsterdam Chou gave demonstrations of his diagnostic methods, lectured on the curative powers of ginseng, and deposited diagrams of the human body with his patrons. In most cases the names of Indonesian scholars and assistants are unknown. Their knowledge was preserved in written form through publication in Holland. Freelance Dutch men who operated portable printing presses contributed to the archipelago's stock of scientific information by publishing the results of Dutch researchers in Batavia. They experimented in setting Indonesian languages and scripts in metal type and in adding a new form of book alongside Indonesian handwritten texts.

PRINTING AND THINKING

Printing was an ancient invention of the Chinese. Europeans made the press a major tool of intellectual life with the advantages of a twenty-six-letter alphabet and a measure of freedom in some western European cities. Within four decades of printing the Gutenberg Bible in Mainz in 1455, printing was introduced into Islamic lands by Jews expelled from Spain in 1492. The Ottoman Turks banned setting Arabic into type, so the first Muslim press of the Arabic world was not set up until 1822. As a result, books from the Islamic heartland that found their way to the Indonesian archipelago before the middle of the nineteenth century were handwritten, few in number, and costly.

Printed books arrived in Indonesia through the Dutch. From 1617, presses in Holland published books and pamphlets in Dutch and Malay for communities in the Indonesian archipelago. Because Arabic had been printed in Europe since 1530, the Dutch were able to set Malay in Arabic script too. Devotional texts, such as the Bible, prayers, and catechism, were printed in Malay in both Roman and Arabic scripts and exported to VOC settlements in Asia. The first printing press was shipped from Holland in 1624.

Presses were portable. They consisted of a wooden frame and a tray for the type and were operated by turning handles. Draftsmen and supplies of paper, printer's ink, lye baths, and proof plates had to be sent from Holland. Regulations and notices were printed by the Batavia presses, while daily record keeping was handwritten. As in Europe, printers in Indonesia combined academic interests and artisan skills with commerce. Dutch men who ran presses employed Indonesian assistants, and they published books intended for Indonesian as well as Dutch readers. For instance, Lambertus Loderus held the license for government printer in Batavia in the first years of the eighteenth century. He printed official documents under contract and also published and sold books. He researched, wrote, and published a Dutch-Malay dictionary in 1707. Another publisher, Harmanus Mulder, brought out a Malay-language catechism in Arabic type in 1746.

The Indonesians for whom printed books had the greatest impact were Christians and men who worked in VOC offices as clerks and assistants. Most Indonesian scholars rejected the press until the mechanical production of books became acceptable in Islamic countries. Sumatran and Javanese printers borrowed techniques developed by Muslim publishing houses in India for typesetting Arabic to produce books that closely resembled manuscripts. From the middle of the nineteenth century Indonesian publishers printed books in Malay on Islamic topics for a clientele in religious schools and mosques and used the traveling scholar and catalogue as their publicity and distribution network. This different history of access to printed books meant that Christian Indonesians were exposed to sources of Western knowledge two hundred years before most Muslim Indonesians. All publishers, Dutch and Indonesian, worked under government surveillance.

Dutch men with scientific and literary interests gathered to form the Batavian Academy of Arts and Sciences in 1778. Most were high-ranking members of the VOC who met to pursue interests in the Asian world around them and to keep in touch with the latest scientific developments in Europe. Through the academy's printing press they circulated results of their research, and they pooled their private collections to form Indonesia's first museum. The academy also served as an exclusive club where members conversed in Dutch. Javanese did not fill the roles of caretakers and servants only; in the nineteenth century a few Javanese became members and contributors to the Academy's publications.

SMALLPOX AND SLAVERY: CAUSES OF A FREELANCE INTELLECTUAL

Willem van Hogendorp was a founding member of the academy, a senior VOC official, and a successful businessman. He spent the years 1774 to 1784 in Java. The academy gave him a reason for pursuing his intellectual interests and a means of disseminating them through its journal. He drew on Batavia's archives to write histories of the Muslim kingdom of Jayakarta and of the VOC in Java. Van Hogendorp was also exponent and publicist of scientific developments in Europe. He worked to create public support for vaccination against smallpox by publishing a play and an essay in 1779 and by establishing a cash prize for the best essay on vaccination.

Van Hogendorp's principles led him to be critical of slavery. He found the government-licensed printer, Lodewyk Dominicus, willing to publish his protest in the form of a play. *Harsh Blows, or Slavery* criticized the treatment of slaves by that segment of Batavia's population called "Portuguese," that is, Eurasians and Asian Christians. (It did not treat Dutch or Indonesian slaveowners.) In the play, the vicious treatment of domestic slaves by a Eurasian woman and her Indonesian overseer leads to murderous revolt by the household's victims.

The intellectual and commercial interests of other Dutch men turned to plants. Indonesian landscapes provided the settings and Indonesian laborers the means for experiments with imported plants, such as coffee.

In the eighteenth century the impact of Dutch freelancers on enterprises such as printing and agriculture was slight. Few Indonesians knew of the Dutch or had any personal experience of their activities. Perhaps a few hundred Indonesians read from a printed book; another few thousand raised coffee bushes on the edges of their rice fields or trekked into the Priangen hills for wage work on coffee plantations; none of them sipped a cup of coffee. The isolated activities of a few Dutch individuals in the eighteenth century were to have radical impacts on the lives and minds of millions of Indonesian workers in the nineteenth century.

A CUP OF JAVA: COFFEE AND CONSEQUENCES

The coffee plant, native to Ethiopia, was introduced to the mountainous southwestern region of the Arabian Peninsula around the fourteenth century. Coffee bushes and the habit of drinking coffee were not introduced into Indonesia by Arabs but by the VOC in 1696. Dutch men with personal interests in botany and agriculture and who owned private estates around Batavia had their local workforce experiment in raising and propagating the seedlings. VOC officials used their personal networks with Sundanese nobles to establish the coffee industry in the highlands of west Java. Plants were given to Sundanese district heads who directed farmers to deliver the harvested beans to fulfill their tax obligation. The first harvest was in 1718. The VOC paid the district heads in cash and textiles. It took over the coffee business at the warehouse where the beans were packed and stored until they could be transported to Europe.

At first the VOC paid high prices for coffee, giving local farmers an incentive to grow more coffee than their tax quota for sale to VOC agents. The opportunities attracted migrants into the area. By 1725 three million pounds were harvested and the district chiefs were becoming rich from their percentage of the profits. As supplies of coffee from Java added to coffee available from other production areas in Amsterdam's market, prices for the luxury product began to decline in Europe. The VOC's solution was not to expand the number of coffee drinkers but to reduce the amount of coffee grown by cutting the prices paid the west Javanese farmer, requiring some coffee bushes to be uprooted, and banning sales of coffee to private wholesalers. Such actions brought economic loss to communities just learning to enjoy a higher standard of living, marked by the increased numbers of Sundanese households able to own a buffalo.

This experiment in coffee production was undertaken by officials who argued for more direct VOC involvement in Indonesian societies. They wanted to bypass Indonesian kings and court factions to work directly with the provincial nobles who controlled networks of village heads and jagos.

Some Dutch men who worked in the archipelago put down roots as husbands and fathers in households where the daily language was Malay, Portuguese, or a mixture of both. They did not marry princesses or women of noble descent. Well-to-do Indonesian households accepted as sons-in-law only foreigners who converted to Islam. Dutch men purchased women on the slave market as brides; some married the Eurasian daughters of colleagues; others turned to the village and urban residential neighborhood. The same class of women that entertained Java's passing royals supplied partners and wives to Dutch men.

The households of many VOC men were migratory. A career that began in Melaka could have stops in Ambon, Makasar, and Palembang before climaxing in Batavia. The VOC careers of men made women mobile too. Slave girls from Bali could end up in European households in Batavia. Eurasian girls born in Batavia followed husbands to postings in Ceylon, Bengal, and Semarang. A few women from Holland also traveled the VOC network.

The Dutch household offered social mobility to some women from the fringes of Indonesian societies. If a slave girl were purchased as a marriage partner, under VOC regulations the prospective husband had to emancipate her and bring her to church for baptism with a Christian name. On the wedding day she was written, under her new name, into the register of European inhabitants of the town. Some women went from slave to female head of an establishment of many domestic servants. They gained a public role in the mixed Dutch societies in Indonesian ports where women's status was determined by husband's rank and fortune. Children born to European men outside marriage also made journeys. If acknowledged by the father, they too were baptized with Christian names and inscribed as European in VOC registers. If unacknowledged, children shared their mother's lot. If she were a slave, they inherited her status. If she were a free woman, they made their way in the Indonesian quarters of towns. The company periodically conducted sweeps of these neighborhoods, taking light-skinned children and consigning them to charitable institutions and workhouses.

The lives of female freelancers can be known only through the actions of male owners and relatives and from entries in VOC registers of births, marriages, and deaths. Women journeyed from social outcast into the predicaments of domesticity. Men's journeys crossed larger spaces and more documents record them. Pieter Erberveld's identity as a Christian Eurasian is preserved in the baptismal register of Batavia's synod; his character as a litigious landowner is established in VOC records of lawsuits; his passage to Muslim religious visionary in the entourage of a Javanese jago of reputed royal origins is predi-

SUSANNA, MAGDALENA, AND HELENA: FEMALE FREELANCERS OF THE VOC WORLD

The lives of a slave from Bengal, a woman from Holland, and a slave from Sulawesi intertwined in Batavia. The Bengal girl was born late in the seventeenth century and worked in the household of Marten Huysman, the VOC's officer in charge of its Bengal business. He called her Susanna and took her with him when he was transferred to Batavia. There he married Magdalena Chasteleyn who, with her brother, had taken the long sea voyage from Holland for a life in Java.

Huysman maintained parallel families and acknowledged the two children he had with Susanna. The son died in infancy, but the daughter, Lea, surpassed her mother by achieving the status of wife, female head of household, and first lady in her marriages to a VOC director in Bengal and then to the VOC governor of Banda. Huysman's wife, Magdalena, also had a son and a daughter. Both lived to adulthood and married into families holding important posts in the VOC. Magdalena's granddaughter, Catharina Huysman, married Governor-General Baron van Imhoff (r. 1743–1750).

This governor-general received a slave girl as a gift from a female ruler of the Bugis kingdom of Bone. Van Imhoff also had two sets of children. The boy from his marriage died in infancy. He acknowledged a son and two daughters by his Buginese slave, baptized them, and sent them to Holland. The part-Indonesian son inherited his title and married into Holland's nobility. In Batavia, van Imhoff emancipated the slave mother and had her baptized with the name Helena Pieters. Before his death he arranged her marriage to a VOC official in Batavia and left her an extensive estate.

cated on two sessions of torture, leading to his criminal trial and execution in April 1722 by the VOC.

Erberveld (spelled Elberveld in some sources) was a contemporary of Surapati and a resident of Batavia when the Balinese jago first signed on with the VOC. He had been born around 1660 in the Siamese kingdom of Ayuthya. His father was a German tanner of hides whose specialty made him a mobile man. In Siam the elder Erberveld established a household with a woman purchased from one of the brothels that were income producers for Siamese royalty. Around 1668 he moved his trade and household to Batavia. There Erberveld adjusted his domestic life to the standards of the city's Christian, European government: he had his wife and children baptized on November 4, 1671. Baptism, legal marriage, and European name transformed the former slave of Siam into the European lady Elisabeth Erberveld. The half-Siamese children were entered into Batavia's register of Europeans as Sara, Johannes, and Pieter. In Batavia the father prospered. His children grew up rich but excluded from high society that was based on birth in Holland and senior rank in the company. Batavia in the 1670s had few institutions for making a European scholar out of local boys. Senior VOC officials sent their sons to Holland for schooling. But Batavia's mosques and religious schools in the west Java countryside provided another path into knowledge.

In December 1721 Pieter Erberveld, dressed in the white robes of a Muslim teacher, was arrested in his Batavia house together with other Muslim teachers, Javanese aristocrats, wives, children, and slaves. At his trial Erberveld denied accusations that he had studied Islam, distributed amulets inscribed with Arabic words, and was the prophet for Javanese confederates and 17,000 armed men. He denied that he planned the overthrow of the VOC government and the extermination of all Christians. He denied ambitions to set himself up as king of Batavia and to transfer rule of Batavia's hinterland to the head of his army, Raden Kartadria. The facts died with the execution of Erberveld, Kartadria, three women, and fourteen male followers, and confiscation of their possessions. Erberveld's skull was placed on a spike and displayed at the site of his house; a plaque in Dutch, Latin, and Malay denounced him as a traitor. His skull can still be seen near the Gereja Sion (Zion Church).

VOC writers constructed their own babads of Pieter Erberveld. Features familiar from the Javanese genre are prominent: men of unverifiable origins emerge from obscurity to assert their right to rule; their spiritual leader denounces rule of Muslims by non-Muslims, prophesies the fall of the Dutch, and calls for the elimination of Christians from the holy land of Java. The spiritual leader circulates stories about the magical powers of his jago, and he distributes amulets among followers. In Javanese versions, Erberveld's Siamese mother is transformed into a "native"; through her the son becomes Muslim. Erberveld feels the injustice of VOC rule over his native land and he joins with Java's aristocrats who want to expel the Dutch from Java. This telling makes the case for an unbroken record of opposition to the Dutch by Muslims and the other "natural" leaders of the Javanese, their aristocrats. In a Malay-

Pieter Erberveld marker. Photographic Archive, Royal Institute of Linguistics and Anthropology, Leiden, No. 51475. Photo courtesy of the KITLV.

language version by a Chinese author, Erberveld is described as wicked, a fanatic ambitious for worldly power, with a blood lust to kill all Europeans and Christians in Java. His conversion to Islam is explained as the result of his hatred of Europeans, and he dies cursing Christians.

Some Dutch men on the fringes of VOC communities made journeys of the mind, journeys into politics, and journeys into nightmare. Across the archipelago individuals and communities made journeys, fleeing the actions of powerful kingdoms, starting out on new adventures, setting up new states. There were more individuals who did not fit established categories: more Eurasians, more Chinese Muslims and Chinese Indonesians. There was more spilling out of ethnic communities from their heartlands, a constant spread of Islamic culture in towns and a push into countrysides. Individuals seemed to burst into home communities from the obscurity of prolonged stays abroad or concealed pasts; other individuals were exiled. By the end of the eighteenth century Dutch men were traveling all the waterways of the archipelago; they were part of the world of movement, competition, rivalry, fighting, and chaos. They were rooted in a few spots around the archipelago.

Since the middle of the eighteenth century a few Dutch men had made journeys into the interior of Java; some had begun to transform Indonesian landscapes through clearing forest, through joining Indonesian societies as residents, workers, and relatives; others created miniature versions of Dutch cities. A handful of archipelago residents had made the reverse journey. They were absorbed into Holland's towns as the part-Asian children of Dutch men, or they made temporary stays as students of Leiden University. A few had made the journey into Christianity and European identities; some had an acquaintance with European books. Indonesian and Dutch worked side-by-side as envoys, traders, soldiers, sailors, and skilled laborers.

There was no idea yet of Indonesia as a political unit. Javanese and Dutch looked out on an archipelago of wild spaces inhabited by sea pirates, unruly Chinese, and migratory bands of mercenaries with families and holy men in their train. Archipelago sultanates looked to Java as source of the glory of their kings and as the source of politics that disrupted working lives and threatened to engulf subsidiary communities. The VOC enabled some archipelago kings to pry themselves loose of Java's grip, but Javanese Islamic culture spread into archipelago towns, and Javanese migrant rice farmers systematically pushed back forests and turned forest dwellers into people marked for the civilizing influences of the newcomers.

At the end of the eighteenth century, Indian soldiers led by British officers became a new element in the sea-lanes and wild spaces of the archipelago. By 1811 they had defeated VOC and Mangkunagaran soldiers on Java. These jagos of British imperialism withdrew by 1816, but they left a lasting mark on Indonesian histories. British and Dutch drew lines on the map defining their spheres in Asia. These spheres became the modern states of Malaysia and Indonesia. Dutch Christians and Javanese Muslims moved into the space Europeans demarcated as Dutch. Their combined actions created the basis of one state made up of interlinked communities around the Java Sea.

8

MAPS AND MENTALITY
European Borders Within Indonesian Worlds

The western archipelago of Sumatra, the Malay Peninsula, the Kalimantan coasts, and the Riau islands functioned as one world for its inhabitants. To outsiders this was a shifting world of sea peoples and river-mouth societies perched on the edge of mangrove swamps and mountain ranges, with no one great power keeping order. The importance of the western archipelago to outsiders was that it straddled the sea route connecting India, the Arab world, and Europe to the huge China market. Malays, Buginese, Chinese, Indians, Arabs, English, and Dutch crowded its sea-lanes and river markets, evading the decrees of sultans and governors-general, circulating textiles, guns, and opium. In the nineteenth century strong outsiders with fast steamboats imposed order in the region, while at the same time dismembering it. English and Dutch diplomats meeting in Europe divided the western archipelago into two areas of action, defined around themselves. To its inhabitants, the western archipelago remained a single thought world, united by Islam, Malay culture, seafaring, migrations, royal marriages, and historical links to Java.

The VOC was dissolved on January 1, 1800, by the States-General in Holland and its Asian territories were transferred to Holland's royal family. VOC men had belonged to Indonesian worlds of changing commercial partnerships and royal intrigue. They were rooted in VOC Asian enclaves by family ties and long-term residence. Individual officials grew rich while the company, overstretched and inadequately controlled, collapsed into bankruptcy. The VOC had been in the forefront of modernizing Europe. It was based in cities; it supported practical, technical, and scientific education; it had standardized industries and coordinated manufacturing; it used testing and inspection. The VOC was the agent for introducing objects, techniques, and corporate organization into Indonesian societies, but it had little impact on Indonesian thinkers anywhere. VOC officials, scholars, and employees lived in enclaves; Dutch people ranked low in Indonesian status systems. Few Indonesians were willing to admire products of the Christian West. Consequently, the VOC brought no intellectual revolution to archipelago societies. Instead, the VOC borrowed from the societies in which it worked the very values that were being renounced in Europe: autocratic rule, emphasis on hierarchy and etiquette, and hereditary rights. Governors-general acted like archipelago royals, rarely leaving their enclaves, never journeying to view the territories governed in their name by Indonesian officials. They competed for the control of Indonesian labor, but, just like Indonesian kings, they left it to the hereditary nobility and Chinese agents to extract the products of that labor.

Dismemberment of the region was the work of new men who had come of age in a Europe dominated by the French Revolution, Napoleon, and the Civil Code. They looked on Eurasians, slavery, and the old businesses of tree barks and spices with contempt. Their plans ran to controlling production, wage labor, and turning Indonesian kings into cogs to make European enterprises work. They thought of the archipelago as a bounded place, with a Java under Dutch domination controlling Indonesian destinies.

Sumatra derives its name from Samudra-Pasai. Early European travelers who first put in there applied the name Samudra to the whole island, as do modern Indonesians who inherit European perceptions. Its inhabitants gave no single name to Sumatra. Regional names reflected different historical experiences. In Sumatra's interior, names identified the dominant ethnic group farming mountain valleys or traveling through forest landscapes as shifting farmers. Along the coasts, peoples and regions were named by a king's capital. No kingdom ever formed Sumatra into a single political unit. Mountains, forests, rivers, and people could only be welded into a single state by the force of modern technology and ideology.

The northernmost region of Sumatra is the heartland of the Acehnese. Aceh formed around the port of Banda Aceh, where sea-lanes from the Malay Peninsula, Kalimantan, India, and Arabia met. The royal capital of Aceh Dar us-Salam controlled the river mouth. Pepper, Islam, and the Portuguese conquest of Melaka put Aceh on the map. Many of Melaka's traders moved their headquarters to Aceh in 1511. Aceh's rulers took the title of sultan early in the sixteenth century. Sultan Ali Mughayat Syah (r. 1514?–1530) began the formation of an Acehnese state by attacking Melaka and the sultanate of Johor and by imposing suzerainty over ports on both sides of the Straits. When he captured Pasai in 1524, Aceh became heir to one of Indonesia's oldest sultanates. Successors raided for population in the Malay Peninsula and Aceh's hinterland. Captured peoples were sent to farms specializing in the production of pepper for export or were used as manual laborers, market workers, and domestics in the capital.

By the early seventeenth century the palace was protected by stone walls, moats, and cannon and housed a huge establishment of staff, troops, palace women, and eunuchs. A chain of small forts controlled the marshy plains. The surrounding town had separate wards for the many international traders, markets, and artisan quarters. The capital attempted to control outlying districts by regular armed patrols. Kings appointed Muslim leaders to head village clusters and financed rural religious schools. They appointed Muslim vassals over conquered territories, and married into the royal houses of Pahang, Perak, and Johor on the Malay Peninsula and into the Sumatran states of Pariaman and Indrapura.

Through Islam, Aceh knitted itself into Indonesian histories of the western archipelago. Its armies extended Acehnese rule down the west and east coasts of Sumatra; its religious scholars traveled archipelago sea routes; its court held itself as a model of Islamic government. Arab and European visitors to Aceh commented on the Islamic cast of city government. Islamic judges and punishments controlled public space. Under Islamic law convicted thieves forfeited a hand or foot, and amputees were a daily sight. Public life centered around the Great Mosque, Bait ur-Rahman, built in 1614 by Sultan Iskandar Muda. Conversion was a requirement for royal favor and appointment. Kings periodically evicted non-Muslim Chinese traders and artisans from Acehnese territory. Portuguese and their Asian converts were persecuted. Acehnese navies regularly attacked Portuguese shipping and the Portuguese administration that had supplanted Muslim government in Melaka in 1511.

Aceh was never a taxpaying vassal to Java's kings, for Majapahit's navies had not sailed so far north. The people and storytellers of Aceh did not look to Java for symbols, royal ancestors or models of court culture. Javanese never became the language of the palace or a symbol of high status. The Acehnese language is related to the language spoken by the Cham people of mainland

Southeast Asia. Stone inscriptions of Cham language in an Indic script survive from the late fourth century C.E., but it is not known if Acehnese had a written form before conversion of the ruling class to Islam. Malay, written in Arabic letters, became the language of court and official documents, histories, poetry, romances, and religious works. Acehnese remained the language for everyday use and for a rhyming verse called *sanjak* that was accompanied by drums, flutes, and stringed instruments. Aceh was not entwined in royal Java histories or Javanese Muslim culture. Muslim culture was expressed through Malay symbols and sustained by contact with major religious schools in the Islamic world. It was to Arabia, not Java, that Acehnese religious scholars looked for guidance in internal conflicts, especially in defining the nature of royal rule.

FEMALE RULE, ISLAM, AND ACEH

From 1641 to 1699 Aceh's rulers were female. Sultan Iskandar Muda (r. 1607–1636) created an Acehnese empire in the western archipelago, and tradition holds that he inaugurated a golden age in literature, religious scholarship, and the arts. His successor, son-in-law Iskandar Thani, is remembered as patron of orthodox Islam, suppressing mystical texts and their authors from Aceh religious life. Female rule began when Iskandar Thani's chief wife (the oldest daughter of Iskandar Muda) succeeded him as Sultanah Taj ul-Alam Safiatuddin Syah in 1641.

It is usual, in Western histories, to explain the four women who ruled Aceh in the second half of the seventeenth century in terms of a power struggle between monarchy and families who controlled pepper districts and tax collection. Aceh monarchs were acquiring absolute power by shutting out of trade important families who had a say in determining royal succession. In this interpretation, the heads of pepper families backed female candidates because they expected women rulers to be weak. This was also the view recorded by Ibn Muhamad Ibrahim, a scribe accompanying the mission sent to Aceh and Siam by the shah of Persia in 1685.

Aceh's queens were challenged by heads of villages, military commanders, and religious teachers. The interval between the death of one queen and designation of her successor was a period for attacks on the capital. Opposition was phrased in Islamic terms. Manuals on monarchy from Arabia and Persia defined the essentials for rule as male gender, personal beauty, courage and skill in battle, integrity, generosity, and leadership of public prayers in the mosque on Friday. A ruler who failed to uphold Islamic law would be unable to attract traders to his kingdom, bringing a decline in the economy and collapse of public morals. Malay manuals on monarchy therefore allowed that if no suitable male candidate existed, a pious female could succeed to avoid the greater evil of rule by an impious man.

Female rulers could not occupy public space. Aceh palace rules dictated that the queen be concealed from direct communication with men by a curtain. Officials, merchants, military commanders, and envoys thus had to present their treaties and petitions to palace eunuchs; decisions were made known on paper bearing the royal seal. Like archipelago kings, Aceh queens maintained large households of women, because they gave the monarch links to powerful men in the kingdom. The queens appointed male representatives to lead public prayer and tried to purchase support from Islamic leaders through donations to Islamic institutions. They also tried to broaden their bases of support among the important foreign trading groups and non-Muslim minorities in Banda Aceh. Franciscan priests reported that harassment of Christians had been greatly reduced under female rule. Safiatuddin (r. 1641–1675) attempted to gain Dutch support, possibly through marriage to a senior VOC official. The Dutch merchant, Johan Nieuhof, who was the source of this story, claimed that Batavia's ruling council of the Indies vetoed the proposal.

Other queens sought support through political marriages. Aceh's last queen chose a Hadrami Arab as consort. He bore the title *sayyid,* meaning he claimed descent from Muhammad. By 1699 the religious faction was able to triumph over the pepper merchants backing female rule and forced the queen to abdicate in favor of her husband. When he took over as Sultan Badr al-Alam Sharif Hashim Jamal al-din Ba'Alawi al-Husaini, Aceh's religious faction realigned the sultanate with the Islamic heartland and its traditions of male rule. They turned Aceh away from archipelago visions of Islam and factions favoring alliance with the Dutch.

The conflict over the nature of Islamic monarchy showed two competing factions in Achenese society. One faction, led by the heads of religious schools, controlled networks of ulamas and was linked to the Islamic heartland; the other was led by prominent families who controlled the pepper business and allied with the dominant power of the day in the archipelago. For decades that power was Dutch. This split within Acehnese society continued when the Jakarta-based government of the Republic of Indonesia succeeded the Dutch. Today's Free Aceh Movement is characterized by an Islamic vocabulary of opposition, a union of religious and military leaders, a rejection of Javanese Muslim culture, and a preference for association with the world Islamic community over incorporation into Indonesia.

Unlike Aceh, most Indonesian regions developed within a context of links to Java. Sumatra's east coast settlements along the lower reaches of rivers at Jambi and Palembang were connected to Aceh's world of the Malay Peninsula, the Riau islands, and Kalimantan but also to Java. Jambi and Palembang courts took Majapahit as their model of civilization; Javanese was the language of high status. The formation of the Melaka sultanate across the straits had pulled Jambi and Palembang into a Malay Islamic culture. Their rulers married into Muslim dynasties of the western archipelago. Malay became the language of writing and Arabic the writing system. Intellectual and religious ties were with courts in Aceh, Johor, Makasar, Banten, and Cirebon, although Javanese continued to be spoken in the Palembang court. The politics of location dictated that Jambi and Palembang sultans acknowledged the overlordship of Mataram until the VOC presented itself as the more immediate local power in the mid-seventeenth century.

The interior of Sumatra was home to a great variety of peoples who spoke distinct dialects of Malay, and were linked loosely by family alliances and trade with the Malay speakers of the coastal plains. Some groups, such as the Minangkabau, lived in fortified villages in fertile valleys of the highlands. Others, such as Batak clans, cultivated forest clearings. Interior peoples of Sumatra were organized politically by kinship lineages. Each group's founding myths claimed descent from a distant ancestor who was of divine origin or a prince from Java; the ancestor's wanderings established the group's territory. Interior peoples exchanged rice and forest products with coastal peoples for salt, textiles, and iron. They raised pepper vines and mined gold for export too.

Highland valleys supported larger populations than those scattered on land and boats at river mouths. Highland peoples sent goods to markets by rantau, a Minangkabau word meaning to go on a journey away from the home village. Male traders traveled between market centers in the interior, acting as the distributors for a localized economy. Others hazarded travel down to the coast. Preparations for going on rantau included arming oneself with a talisman and making offerings and prayers. The trader who went as far as the coast or beyond needed to establish connections to allow him to do business and to provide him with lodging. The solution was marriage to a local woman, which established the relationship of in-laws and business partners between men who were previously strangers and furnished a residence with domestic labor. Polygamy enabled traders who regularly worked in several towns the opportunity of establishing multiple households and business partnerships. Some traders settled permanently in coastal cities and then acted as agents for others making the occasional journey from the highlands.

The Minangkabau belong to kin groups which trace their descent through the female line and typically placed the family house and kin lands under female control. Women farmed on family-owned land, alongside their brothers. They did not depend on their husbands for food or shelter. A man had visiting rights with his wife and children in the house owned by the woman's kin. Polygamous husbands rotated between households in the village and those they established in trading stations. Wives of the interior were responsible for agriculture and the sustenance of their families. They prepared goods the men obtained from the surrounding forest and remained in the interior, unless sent for by husbands who settled permanently downstream.

Rantau connected men of the interior with the world of the western archipelago and with the Islamic heartland. The rise in numbers of traders at Sumatran ports increased the number of men from the interior making journeys to markets and into other Indonesian histories. Rantau men brought back religious teachers. Some Minangkabau men left the interior to study at centers of Islamic learning in Banten, Aceh, and Johor. When they returned they supported religious teachers in applying new standards to their culture and customs of origin. In the name of Islam they opposed female custodianship of family homes and rice lands.

Coastal kings, trying to extend their authority into the hinterland to ensure a steady supply of goods for sale to foreign traders, established a kind of rantau in reverse. Kings licensed Chinese entrepreneurs to bring in peddler-porters. European traders also employed Chinese networks to get Minangkabau gold and pepper. Competing purchasers pushed up prices and made Sumatran kings wealthy. Princes and nobles used their funds to attract followers and purchase arms instead of investment. An important consequence for ordinary people was the increase in taxes and in the level of violence. Wealth allowed royals greater contact with archipelago societies, Mecca, and Batavia. Rulers imported European luxuries, and readily turned to the Dutch for weapons and assistance, while they hosted traveling religious scholars and cultivated the Malay concept of sacred Islamic kingship.

Rantau brought Minangkabau people into closer touch with Indonesian Islamic histories. Before the nineteenth century, Indonesian Islamic histories included the sultanate of Johor, whose capital was on the southern tip of the Malay Peninsula. Johor's royal family claimed leadership of Malay Islam because the last sultan of Melaka, Mahmud Syah, had reestablished his dynasty in Johor in 1518 after being driven from Melaka by the Portuguese. Its navy imposed Johor's claims on both coasts of the Straits of Melaka. For instance, Johor princes installed vassals in Siak, a river-mouth settlement on the Sumatran side of the straits and a source of timber, rattans, and resins. When the VOC wished to purchase timber for its ship masts from Siak, it sent agents to Johor. Treaties with Johor, dating from 1685, provided that Siak men, under the supervision of an agent from Johor, would cut trees for VOC purchasers. In this business, the VOC was the supplicant. There is not the slightest conception of "three and half centuries of Dutch rule" in the letter Johor's prince sent the VOC: "I want an end to the cruising of Dutch ships in Siak's waters. These ships will only be allowed to stop for water, wood, sirih, and pinang" (quoted in Andaya, 1975, p. 143).

Siak's leading families saw in the VOC a source of cash and trade goods and an ally with whom they could deal directly when Johor's power in the area weakened. Their opportunity came in the aftermath of the murder of Sultan Mahmud of Johor in 1699. In the absence of a male heir, the head of the opposition party at court proclaimed himself king and attempted to take over leadership of the Malay world. In 1718 a man claiming to be a son of the murdered sultan and using the title Raja Kecil ("young prince," "heir presumptive") emerged at the head of a personal army, recruited from Minangkabau men and sea people, and attacked Johor. When he failed to install himself as king, Raja Kecil sailed to Siak, where he pushed aside Johor's officials and set himself up as an independent ruler with the title sultan. He sought protection against Johor and its Buginese allies from the VOC, guaranteeing the Dutch regular timber supplies in return.

The Siak and Kampar river systems allowed agents from the coast to travel up into Minangkabau and Batak territories with goods to purchase pepper, gambier, coffee, and gold. Siak merchants sold these products to the VOC, to Chinese, Arab, Bugis, and Malay traders, and to British and Danes. Traders also put in at Siak for slaves. Slaves built ships for Siak merchants and were rowers; in Batu Bara they wove the silk that Siak traders exported all over Sumatra.

In the western archipelago alliances constantly shifted. Civil war broke out in the 1740s between two sons of Raja Kecil who were fighting for the right to succeed him. After one son led a massacre of VOC employees in their Siak post on Gontong Island, the Dutch helped the other brother seize the throne. When control of Siak shifted to the rival line in 1779, the VOC did business with the new sultan, whose troops joined company contingents attacking Buginese in the nearby Riau-Lingga islands. The VOC rewarded the head of its Siak army by making him ruler of Selangor on the Malay Peninsula. Siak did not develop an empire or client states on the Peninsula. Its princes were content to loot Selangor, and to cruise the straits, trading and attacking other shipping.

Johor's capital shifted between the southern Malay Peninsula and Riau, a cluster of small islands that includes Singapore. They lie off the southern tip of the Malay Peninsula across many sea routes. The *Sejarah Melayu* (History of the Malays) describes the area as a single world of Muslim princes, Malay adventurers, and seafarers. This hub of archipelago businesses operated outside the pass system of the VOC and accommodated Chinese offshore production. By the end of the eighteenth century ten thousand Chinese men were growing pepper and gambier vines there.

After 1669 the settled population of the Riau archipelago had an influx of Buginese from south Sulawesi. A dual administration developed; the sultan of Johor was always a member of a Malay royal family heading Malay retainers, while Riau's governor was a descendant of Buginese immigrants with his own Buginese staff. The distinctions were not sharp. The first generation of Buginese men married Malay women, and there were many Malay-Bugis alliances among the polygamous officials. Malay displaced Buginese as the language of Riau's Bugis population. Although a major literature in Buginese exists in Sulawesi, Buginese literature from Riau is written in Malay. This area saw itself as the promoter of Islam and of a Malay Islamic culture throughout the western archipelago.

The sultanate of Sambas was another Malay river-delta sultanate of the western archipelago. Its capital was on the Sambas Kecil River where it enters the coast of west Kalimantan, just below the present-day border of the Malaysian state of Sarawak. Its location made it a stopping-off place for traders from the Malay Peninsula, Sumatra, India, and China. Malay-speaking people have been in this area since the fourteenth century. By the seventeenth century the Malay ruling class of Sambas monopolized trade and shipping and extracted from local producers goods for their international trade. The producing class were Dayaks who lived in scattered villages in the capital's hinterland, where they grew root crops in forest clearings and paid their taxes to the rulers downstream in the form of forest products. Such goods financed the sultanate's imports of tobacco, opium, and salt.

In the middle of the eighteenth century, the reigning sultan, Umar Akhamuddin, recruited Chinese from Fujian and Guangdong provinces to mine for gold in the interior. The mining was organized by Chinese *kongsi* (clan or dialect associations, sometimes called secret societies). They financed the recruiting of male laborers from China and supplied foremen. Miners built trenches, channeled streams, washed the gold free, and sent it downriver to Chinese agents for sale. The sultans of Sambas profited from this arrangement as long as their navies controlled traffic on rivers leading to the sea; there was no direct Malay administration of the interior. Chinese mining groups were far beyond reach; sultans could not enforce bans forbidding the Chinese to farm and own guns. Chinese mining groups competed for lands rich in ores and for the services of Dayak villagers who raised food crops and provided labor at mine sites. Chinese men married Dayak women. They opened up more agricultural land and shipped Dayak products down rivers not under the control of Sambas naval patrols. They also evaded the sultans' tax agents as they shipped goods into Dayak communities.

Within the western archipelago the VOC acted as one of the many sea peoples—trading, sailing, and marauding. VOC functionaries made and broke alliances with princes; they corresponded with local powers in Malay written in Arabic script; they competed for the bulk trade. VOC-era Dutch men saw the western archipelago as a natural region of connected coasts and common language, religion, and lifestyle. They lived and worked more at sea than on land in this environment. Their land settlements were generally built on small islands in river deltas and bays. Spatial separation from mainland royal capitals marked the Dutch as non-Muslim. Apart from Melaka (after 1641), the Dutch controlled no city government. Nowhere did they create a mini-Holland. Dutch voices were not influential at courts where royal succession was being debated. Palembang's Golden Age for its chroniclers was precisely the period of closest cooperation between sultans and VOC officials. Time had made the VOC part of the scene.

International sea-lanes pass through Indonesia's islands, so the policies and actions of outsiders have always influenced Indonesian histories. The bringers of Islam in its Arab, Persian, Indian, Egyptian, and now Iranian and Afghan formulations have had the most profound and lasting impact. A major consequence was creation of a zone of mobile sultanates and mini-empires within the cultural unity of Malay Islam. In the nineteenth century British and Dutch outsiders pulled apart the mini-empires that straddled the Straits of Melaka and apportioned the region's sultanates into two political units that had no reference point in Malay Islam.

Such changes affected the entire archipelago. They had begun with naval battles between the English and the Dutch, the rise of Napoleon, his enmity toward Britain, his absorption of Holland into his empire in 1795, and his installation of his brother as king of Holland in 1806. When Napoleon went to war against Britain, Britain attacked Dutch overseas territories that had been incorporated into the French empire. In 1795 the British attacked and seized Padang on Sumatra's west coast and Melaka. In 1796 they took over Ambon. The old VOC network had included Cape Town and Ceylon, with their Indonesian communities formed from penal colonies and the followers of princes and prophets ejected from Java. These territories were taken over in 1806. In 1811 British troops landed on Java and defeated Dutch and Javanese forces there.

Following Britain's defeat of Napoleon, Holland regained its independence and entered negotiations with Britain to recover former territories in the name of the new Dutch monarchy. Decisions taken in London and The Hague in 1815 affected Indonesian communities permanently. From that time the space in which Indonesian histories would take place was determined. Britain did not return southern Africa or Ceylon to the Dutch, so that Indonesian communities in these territories have become part of African and Sri Lankan histories. Nor did Britain return Melaka. Its Indonesian residents also entered a history charted by Britain. British administrations withdrew from sites along Sumatra's east coast, Batavia, Semarang, Makasar, and former Dutch settlements in the eastern archipelago. In 1824 a treaty between Britain and Holland demarcated separate spheres in the western archipelago for their rival commercial and political interests. The Malay Peninsula, Singapore, and the northern coast of Borneo were declared a British sphere of influence, Sumatra a Dutch sphere. This treaty guaranteed the sultanate of Aceh an existence independent of the two European powers. In 1871 the Treaty of Sumatra confirmed these divisions but assigned Aceh to the Dutch.

These policies of outsiders ultimately engendered two colonies and two labels to describe the inhabitants of each: Malay and Native. Britain had purchased Penang Island, at the northern entrance to the straits, from the sultan of Kedah in 1786. In 1819 Britain leased Singapore from the sultan of Johor. Between 1874 and 1896, through negotiation, Britain brought the sultanates of Perak, Selangor, Pahang, and Negri Sembilan into a federation that officially confirmed the royal Malay families in office while transferring real power of policy and taxation to British officials. In 1909 Britain negotiated with the king of Siam for the cession of four Malay sultanates within the Siamese empire: Kedah, Kelanten, Trengganu, and Perlis. By 1914, with the inclusion of the sultanate of Johor, British Malaya had reached its final form.

From 1816 all Holland's Asian territories were located within the Indonesian archipelago. Dutch men now operated along the coasts of Sumatra, on the west, south, and east coasts of Kalimantan, on the coasts of Sulawesi, in Java, and on a few islands in the eastern archipelago. The Dutch incorporated sultanates into their colony by negotiation, commercial expansion, and warfare. By 1914 the boundaries of the Netherlands East Indies were established.

As a result, British Malaya, headed by the Christian kings and queens of Britain, included Aceh's former tributary states on the Malay Peninsula, as well as the sultanate of Johor, which had claimed moral leadership over all sultanates in the western archipelago. The Dutch East Indies, headed by Holland's Christian royals, incorporated Johor's tributary states in Sumatra. It removed from Johor's leadership the Malay river-mouth sultanates of Sumatra, Kalimantan, and Sulawesi and attached them to Java. The Dutch revived the Java connection for territories that once had been tribute payers to Java's kings. The Dutch colonial government, based in Java, linked the communities of Javanese in archipelago ports back to the Javanese core, and it promoted the continued migration of Javanese throughout the archipelago. Dutch colonial policy promoted the dominance of Javanese Islam over the Malay tradition.

The governments of the modern nations of Malaysia and Indonesia have preserved the divisions of the western archipelago and added refinements. Only Brunei and Singapore today exist outside them. Brunei is the sole independent state still constituted as a sultanate. Singapore, once the seat of sultans of Johor, is now a republic dominated by descendants of southern China's offshore workers.

These changes appear dramatic, clear cut, and decisive. But words on paper, agreed to in negotiating sessions in European capitals, did not automatically make archipelago communities into colonial subjects looking to London or The Hague for guidance and inspiration. For decades after the agreements of 1815 and 1824, inhabitants of the western archipelago were unaffected. For instance, the Dutch treaties with sultans on the west and south coasts of Kalimantan were notices of possible future Dutch interest posted to warn off other Europeans. For Kalimantan Malays they meant small-scale, sporadic trade, but nothing that altered their thought world or way of life.

On paper, the sultanate of Siak was cut off from the Malay Peninsula, yet Siak remained a Malay Muslim kingdom. Its economy and the daily occupations of its people remained oriented toward the straits and its sea traffic. Its religious leaders and students still studied in Islamic centers in the western archipelago and in the Middle East. Siak's royal family still held on to its political and economic privileges. It did not officially enter vassal status to the Dutch colonial state until 1858, when the reigning sultan signed a contract with Batavia ceding control of Siak's foreign relations and responsibility for its defense to the Netherlands East Indies. Siak lost its economic importance to the Dutch in the nineteenth century. The Dutch did not revive the VOC's monopoly of Siak's timber exports, as its shipbuilding was turning to iron and steel. Siak's royal family continued to derive its riches from the export of its timber through Chinese firms. In the second half of the nineteenth century Siak's rulers established plantations for rubber, coconuts, coffee, tobacco, and nutmeg and exported the products to Penang and Singapore.

Siak royals made trips to Batavia to hobnob with the high and mighty of the colony—other visiting sultans and senior Dutch officials. They drew their salaries from the colonial government and traveled through landscapes remade by colonial road and rail networks, migrant labor, and taxation in cash. The grids of colonial rule that transformed Sumatra to Siak's north did not penetrate Siak. Siak people remained bound by tradition, habit, command, and taxes paid by their labor to their hereditary royal family until the great shaking of society caused by the Indonesian revolution in the 1940s.

On Java Napoleon's appointee as governor-general, Marshal W. H. Daendels (r. 1808–1811), had proclaimed a new era of liberation by tearing down the Batavia castle and its walls and by advocating the dignity of free labor. He quickly adjusted to local realities. All along the north coast Javanese families were rented out by their district chiefs to build Daendels's post road linking Batavia to Surabaya. The tollgates and rest houses constructed along the highway served old purposes of control of movement and taxation. Java's workers, using machetes, picks, and shovels, cut through jungle, toiled up mountain slopes and in the heat of coastal plains to improve the foreigners' communications and enable government to move soldiers to points where British troops were expected to land. For the road workers, Daendels was a man of cruelty rather than enlightenment. Reports to Europe on their hardships contributed to the early removal of Daendels from Java.

Daendels's successor, J. W. Janssens, followed VOC military practice. Mangkunagaran soldiers from central Java fought alongside Dutch forces against the British. To Indonesians, British armies must have looked like a VOC force because fully half were Indian. Four thousand men recruited from Bengal fought under their own officers in five volunteer battalions.

Europeans most immediately felt change during the short period of British administration from Batavia of 1811–1816. The British, under Lieutenant Governor Thomas Stamford Raffles (1781–1826), presented their administration as a radical change, as indicated by a term for the period, the British Interregnum. Raffles and his group did not admire the ways in which Dutch people had adapted to Indonesian settings. They disdained the female costume, which was a variant of Javanese wear; they were astonished at how little Dutch Europeans spoke and at their greater use of Malay; the British also deplored the few schools teaching a Western syllabus. They closed down Batavia's slave market, founded an anti-slavery association, opened a theater to perform English plays, and established a newspaper that contained reviews, poetry, and personals columns as well as government news and regulations. They revived the Batavian Academy of Arts and Sciences and energetically began to collect and catalogue information on the distant past of Java and Sumatra. They went on expeditions into the Java countryside to measure landholdings of farmers and calculate a new tax system that would be based on payment in coins instead of in crops and labor. They explored Hindu and Buddhist temple sites and organized teams of local villagers to rip away their jungle cover.

Raffles collected specialists in Javanese arts to expound on their knowledge, gather manuscripts, copy inscriptions, and assemble samples of Javanese crafts. He and others in his entourage drew together their sources in vast, illustrated compendiums on Java and Sumatra. In addition to the great histories of Java, the "Indian Archipelago," and Sumatra compiled by Raffles, Crawfurd, and Marsden, individuals employed by the British administration produced many records of everyday life at the beginning of the nineteenth century in their paintings, letters, diaries, and systematic studies. The British had little access to Muslim Indonesia; ulamas did not rush to discuss language, poetry, and mosque architecture with English men. No British parties ventured to Muslim sacred sites, so few English texts discussed the living Islamic traditions of archipelago communities.

INDONESIAN LIVES DURING THE BRITISH INTERREGNUM

John Newman (c. 1795–1818), born in India of British and Indian parents, accompanied the British army to Java as a draftsman with the job of preparing maps and surveys. During his posting to Java from 1811 to 1813 he made many paintings of everyday life. From his paintings, we know that Javanese pike men wore batik cloth sewn into trousers, that women sold items in the market, and men tended food stalls and carried portable food stands through neighborhoods. Traders used teams of pack ponies with large carrying baskets to transport goods, and men were involved in the care of small children. One of Newman's watercolors shows a Javanese farmer with two bullocks harnessed to a wooden cart whose wheels are solid, without spokes.

As British officers took charge of Dutch fortresses and city administrations, they called for reports on local conditions, numbers of inhabitants, and data on daily occupations. A Dutchman, Johan Knops, contributed a word picture of Semarang in 1812. Knops's report illustrates the great diversity of the city. Semarang's inhabitants included individuals born in Europe and people of mixed Asian and European descent, Chinese immigrants married to Hindu Balinese women, Muslim Chinese married to Javanese women, and Christians descended from Portuguese men and Indian women. There were Buginese, Moors (Indian Muslims), Arabs, and Malays. Among the nineteen hundred Malays, thirty were recorded as both traders and ulamas, and nine men ran schools out of the prayer houses. One hundred boys attended the religion schools.

The British of Raffles's entourage were different from the Dutch mainly in the rapidity of changes introduced and advertised enthusiasms. Dutch amateurs and specialists had always worked with Indonesians to explore the archipelago's natural landscapes, languages, and medical knowledge. There were always a few Dutch men who objected to slavery and tyrannical rule, and who judged Dutch practices critically. Raffles projected a public image of English reform, in contrast to Eurasian backwardness, and it suited Dutch men who took over from the British in 1816 to contrast themselves as new men against VOC types. Dutch historians attacked the British claim to total revamping of the tax system in the short space of four years, but they conceded the British administration did introduce change.

Closing slave markets and campaigning against slavery affected Indonesian lives. Slaves and those who made their business dealing in slaves had to find new means of employment. But change was more dramatic than actual. Some men in Raffles's entourage owned slaves, and neither the British nor their Dutch successors had the resources to impose their new preference for free labor on Indonesian employers and slavers. The Dutch ended slavery only in the towns they controlled and switched to the use of contract labor (a different form of coercion) on plantations for new industrial crops such as rubber. In 1860, when Dutch military power began expanding out of Java into the territories of the sultans, the Dutch ordered their new Indonesian subjects to end slaving and slavery. By the 1890s Dutch naval patrols had mostly stopped slave raids and transport of slaves to archipelago markets and work sites. By that time colonial authorities perceived a larger problem in creating sufficient jobs to sustain a rapidly rising population trained, at colonial work sites, to want wage-paying employment.

The most vivid example of change that immediately affected ordinary Javanese and their royals was Raffles's refusal to act the part of vassal to Java's kings. Like his Dutch predecessors, Raffles involved his administration and his forces in Javanese palace politics, but to a new degree. He did what no VOC official had ever done: in 1812 he directed European soldiers to attack the palace of a Javanese king. Javanese regarded the palaces of their kings as sacred space. Storming the palace of Sultan Hamengkubuwono II of Yogyakarta meant polluting it. British forces were made up of twelve hundred Indians, seven English officers, and four hundred Javanese from the Mangkunagaran substate within Surakarta. One of Hamengkubuwono II's half-brothers commanded other Javanese troops. Raffles rewarded this half-brother by conferring on him the title Pakualam and assigning to him four thousand of the households that had previously paid taxes to Yogyakarta's ruler. In this way a substate, called Pakualaman, was created within Yogyakarta to satisfy a prince too powerful to be accommodated by the Javanese system of succession.

After British guns had leveled the palace walls, crown prince and king were captured. Raffles deposed Hamengkubuwono II and installed in his place a half brother who took the reign name Hamengkubuwono III (r. 1812–1814). In the public ceremony of installation, Raffles underlined the new position of Europeans in Java. After members of the court had performed the ceremony of kissing the new sultan's foot, they were directed to make the same statement of submission to Raffles's local European representative.

THE KISS IN PUBLIC

Javanese rules of courtesy required juniors to approach their superiors on their knees and to make the *sembah* before and after speech. (The sembah is a gesture of joining the hands together, bowing the head and slightly inhaling.) In ceremonies to mark respect and submission and request blessing, children and bridal couples kneel to kiss the knee or foot of their parents; a wife kisses her husband's feet after washing them in the traditional wedding ceremony; courtiers kiss the knee or foot of their sultan. The Islamic custom of kissing the hand of a man revered for his piety and religious learning is practiced throughout Indonesia.

Such public marks of respect were limited to specific pairs of inferior-superior and performed at set points in the year. Paying such honor to people outside the prescribed hierarchies caused consternation, anger, and resentment. Javanese felt that their codes of respect and blessing were violated when they were expected to kiss the foot of a European. Indonesians were shocked when television and newspapers relayed pictures of Vice President Habibie kissing the hand of President Suharto early in 1998. Honoring Suharto, who by then was widely denigrated as despotic and corrupt, with a gesture attesting holiness was considered, at the time, one more sign of moral disorder in Indonesian public life. Indonesians who kissed the hand of President Abdurrachman Wahid (r. 1999–2001) chose to emphasize their perception of him as revered religious leader, rather than his secular status as elected head of all Indonesians, Muslim and non-Muslim.

A Javanese account of the British assault on the Yogyakarta palace is in the diary of Pangeran Arya Panular (c. 1772–1826), one of the many sons of Yogyakarta's first sultan. Panular began his diary when the palace was under bombardment. He recorded how, in the terror of the attack, princes, officers, and men abandoned the king and crown prince to seek safety in the countryside. Wives, concubines, and servants also fled, taking babies, jewelry, and portable possessions. Left behind were small children, their nurses, the female palace guard, the sultan, and his heir. Panular, fourteen of his retainers, and his daughter, who was a minor wife of the crown prince, stayed with him through the assault and were also taken prisoner. In Panular's observation, British and Indian troops were disciplined, brave, and unafraid of death; they seemed to him to have a light that showed divine favor. By contrast, Javanese, with their antique weapons, low pay, and lack of training, were poor artillery men. Panular says their commanders were unreliable cowards and blames religious leaders and the princes for their failure to set examples of loyalty and courage.

Panular called his text *Babad Bedhah ing Ngayogyakarta* (History of the Assault on Yogyakarta). His babad records, in the metrical verse of Javanese tradition, a modern occurrence: the beginning of colonial rule. The attack on the palace made Panular a new man in some respects, for he analyzes royal behavior critically in his account and omits the traditional passages of glorification of kings. This record is still the work of a man of the palace, one who was son, uncle, cousin, and father-in-law to Yogyakarta's kings. One sees the palace man's pride in serving his prince and the offense when loyalty is not returned. Panular sought his daughter's promotion within the royal harem's ranks of wives and consorts as a reward for her loyalty to the crown prince. The babad records the world of the past as it narrates a founding event in Indonesia's history.

Little information on palace women enter the historical record beyond their titles, ranks, and children, but we know something of Panular's mother and daughter from his diary from 1812 to 1814. His mother came from Balambangan and may have been the means of procuring a reward for her male relatives when she was taken as an unofficial wife by the VOC official Nicolaus Hartingh. He was the VOC's governor of the north coast of Java from 1754 to 1761 and was active in negotiations that divided Mataram in two. The future Sultan Hamengkubuwono I expressed his personal gratitude to Hartingh by giving him a woman from his own household. Hartingh returned the compliment with his partner from Balambangan, who was taken into the new Yogyakarta palace under the name Mas Ayu Tondhasari. About twenty-three years later Tondhasari gave birth to Panular. The royal father transferred care of this son to Bendoro Raden Ayu Srenggana, one of his official wives.

Tondhasari disappears from her son's narrative as his future is secured among the royal schemers of the palace, far from her lowly relatives. After Hamengkubuwono I died in 1792, the son who succeeded him promoted half-brother Panular to the rank of prince and assigned him villagers from whom he could levy taxes and services. Panular, like all Javanese princes, resided in his own establishment within the palace compound and never visited the areas that produced wealth for him. In his babad he shows little interest in his villagers, apart from wanting to know if they farmed fertile land. There is no sense of pride in a maternal ancestry that led to the village and common people. The village enters the palace world only to provide taxes and girls.

The European assault on Yogyakarta forced Java's Muslim princes to make choices. They could interest themselves in European learning and culture, they could turn to Islamic culture and to Islamic leaders for inspiration and resources to challenge European ideas and technologies, or they could reattach themselves to their Javanese heritage in order to steady themselves in a world shattered by European guns and presumptions. Panular's diary documents such strategies in descriptions of his male relatives. One of his half-brothers chose the West and became Raffles's man as Pakualam I. He and his sons wore European clothes, imitated European manners, drilled their troops in European style, talked of history, literature, and language with Raffles, and owed their rank and fortune to their usefulness to the British. One of Panular's full brothers had learned Dutch. A nephew adopted Turkish costume as his battle dress, saw himself as a Javanese Muslim, and refused to speak Malay or any European language in favor of Javanese. He forced Europeans captured in battle to become retainers in the Javanese mode.

The British interregnum challenged Javanese identities in another way too. The presence of Indians kindled an almost illicit interest in Java's older past. Java's Muslim princes claimed descent from Hindu gods. Many of the junior and non-commissioned officers of the British army were high-caste Hindus from wealthy land-owning families. To Indian officers, the Javanese were a recognizable relic of a Hindu past. Admitted to the residences of princes in Surakarta and Yogyakarta, these Indian officers revived an interest in Hindu philosophy and traditions, and obligingly staged Hindu rituals. Pakubuwono IV of Surakarta attended them, both publicly with the palace crowd and incognito.

This new interest in Java's pre-Islamic past was also nourished and glamorized by the British, who were busy excavating and sketching Hindu temples and collecting Javanese versions of Indian epics. British amateurs argued that

Indianized Java was the authentic culture of the Javanese, and considered it in danger of being extinguished by the foreign religion of Islam. Nineteenth-century Dutch scholars also focused on Java's Indian past. European fascination with Java's Hindu-Buddhist past encouraged in some elite Javanese circles a disdain for everyday expressions of Islamic piety. The authentic past as imagined by Europeans supported these Javanese in their claims to social distinction and political power.

Ordinary Javanese felt the Indian impact too. Some were engaged to uncover ancient sacred sites. As they stripped away mounds of dirt, vines, and trees, they introduced into their nineteenth-century world temples, sculptures, old altars, and ancient magical symbols. When they dug around the base of temples they brought into view friezes that told stories of the pre-Islamic world of gods and demons. Places that had retained a vague association with holiness and the past now obtruded their difference in a Muslim countryside. In addition, princes fleeing the attack on the palace sought refuge in villages where their mothers had been born and where they now claimed relatives. There were rumors of a plot between Indian officers and Pakubuwono IV of Surakarta to drive Europeans out of Java. Seventeen Indians were executed and fifty-three were sent in chains back to India. Indian deserters found refuge in villages where they married local girls. Some Indians stayed behind after the withdrawal of British troops; they offered specialized skills as elephant keepers and bodyguards to the kings of Java. Some officers married into elite families. Indians who settled in Kedu established a dairy business to cater to Indian dietary requirements. One hundred Bengal lancers remained to work as a mounted constabulary for the returning Dutch. Professional soldiers offered their services wherever there were clients. In 1825, when Prince Diponegoro marched against his nephew, Sultan Hamengkubuwono V, and his nephew's Dutch backers, he had Indian mercenaries on his payroll, as well as a physician and herbalist from Bengal.

Powerful outsiders created local opportunities. Dutch and English drew lines on the map to serve their own purposes, but their actions took place within local contexts. The treaties written in London and The Hague were intended to keep out European rivals, but in the archipelago world of small and large states treaty arrangements could provide an Indonesian prince with a European ally who would back him when he ignored demands of a neighboring Indonesian king for homage and tribute. In numerous Indonesian palaces the arrival of British forces and takeover of Dutch towns and fortresses had presented the opportunity to recalculate relations with the Dutch, the latitude to make new alliances, to break royalty's addiction to Dutch aid, and to rid Muslim territories of Dutch Christians. When Napoleon was defeated in Europe, it was natural to the Dutch that they should negotiate with the British for the return of forts and ports in the archipelago. It was not equally apparent to Indonesian ruling classes that the Dutch should return to former roles. In Ambon, south Sulawesi, and Palembang local princes led attacks on returning Dutch administrators and troops, or shelled Dutch ships sailing back to resume old privileges in trade and political influence.

Javanese were not passive observers of European rivalries either. Their world had been profoundly shaken by British actions. During the five years the British were in Java, four sultans had occupied the throne of Yogyakarta. In all of the accessions and depositions Europeans and the European-backed faction at court had the power of decision. Disgruntled princes sought in these upheavals the opportunity to reinsert themselves as the kingmakers of Java. They armed their followers and joined a conglomeration of private armies responding to letters from Prince Diponegoro in which he called for the elimination of non-Muslims from Java and claimed the title of sultan for himself.

Diponegoro (1785–1855) was a grandson of Yogyakarta's first sultan, who had owed his position and kingdom to Dutch military and diplomatic intervention. Diponegoro was a nephew of Hamengkubuwono II, whom Daendels pushed aside in 1810 and whom Raffles forced to abdicate in 1812. He was the eldest son of the prince Raffles chose to be Hamengkubuwono III (r. 1812–1814). Diponegoro was also half-brother to the ten-year-old boy Raffles subsequently installed as Hamengkubuwono IV (r. 1814–1822). The Dutch put Diponegoro's five-year-old nephew on the throne in 1822 and appointed Diponegoro as one of three advisers to this fifth Hamengkubuwono. In 1826 the Dutch brought back Diponegoro's uncle from exile, but in 1828 Hamengkubuwono II was deposed for the final time. Hamengkubuwono V resumed his reign and continued as sultan until his death in 1855. Diponegoro's desire to become sultan was thwarted by Europeans.

Diponegoro's ambition was also frustrated by Javanese norms of succession. His claim to succeed was based on his father and grandfather, but there was no supporting royal ancestry or rank on his mother's side. She had been only a minor, temporary wife of Hamengkubuwono III. Diponegoro passed into the care of a queen who lost her importance in the palace when Hamengkubuwono I died. She took Diponegoro with her when she was permitted to leave the palace for the pesantren of Tegalreja, a pilgrimage site and center for the study of Javanese Islamic literature.

Diponegoro grew up as a prince with income from his own tax lands but outside the palace. His perspective on the royal capital and understanding of its politics were formed in an Islamic mini-state, a thriving environment of artisan workshops, trade, and rice lands where there were no royal tollgates and no Chinese leaseholders collecting the king's taxes. His early years were a period of growing prosperity for Yogyakarta's farmers. No royal surveys were made of cultivated land between 1755 and 1812, leaving many farmers free to raise rice, tobacco, indigo, peanuts, and cotton for sale without paying taxes. Diponegoro became familiar with the problems and perspectives of farmers because, unlike his royal relatives who never left the capital, he visited his territories. He also built up a following in the pesantrens and through his pilgrimages to holy sites in central Java.

Diponegoro's travels allowed him to learn of changing political and economic conditions and how commoners perceived them. He witnessed the harmful effects of his uncle's reign, the heavy exactions on farmers and artisans for his building projects, his increased taxes in 1812, and his extensive dealings with Chinese entrepreneurs. Diponegoro saw the proliferation of tollgates between 1816 and 1824 and the increase in marauding gangs. Yogyakarta's kings leased land and laborers to Chinese and Europeans who organized their workers for growing export crops. He saw the seat of Java's sacred kings controlled by non-Muslims. He saw the reduction of royal territories as British and then Dutch officials took direct control of large slices of Java. A reduced base of taxpayers had to support an increasing number of royal retainers, officials, favorites, and relatives. By the 1820s a prosperous farming society was being reduced to poverty.

The pesantren prince saw impropriety and pollution everywhere. When Hamengkubuwono IV was placed on the throne by Raffles and set up his household, he chose as partners four women who had been concubines of his father, uncle, and grandfather. The royal choice upset the women's relatives, religious leaders, and factions in the palace. Javanese custom frowned on circulation of women between kin and generations as likely to bring ill-fortune to the reign, while marriage with a father's wives was expressly prohibited in the Koran. Another proof for Diponegoro of the moral contagion in the palace was the wedding ceremony of Hamengkubuwono IV to one of his queens. The royal bridegroom entered the mosque on the arm of Britain's representative to the Yogyakarta court, the non-Muslim John Crawfurd. Attending them, and condoning this intrusion into Muslim space, were royal male relatives, the chief mosque official and his staff, ulamas, and pilgrims returned from Mecca.

In Diponegoro's eyes, Yogyakarta's sultans favored too many Chinese and lifted them to prominence and positions of power over the Javanese. He particularly despised the man who was head of Yogyakarta's Chinese community over the years 1803 to 1813. He was born Tan Jin Seng (?–1831), a native of central Java, and a man operating in several worlds as speaker of Javanese, Malay, and the Hokkien dialect of Chinese. He had attracted the notice of Javanese court officials as chief representative of the Chinese community in Kedu from 1793 to 1803. In Yogyakarta Tan made himself useful to princes and the British as a moneylender and rice merchant. Hamengkubuwono III rewarded Tan with appointment as a district head, allocated to him the income of one thousand households in Bagelen, and conferred Javanese titles and name on him. The new Raden Tumenggung Secadiningrat celebrated his elevation by converting to Islam. He submerged his public Chinese identity in that of the Javanese Muslim nobleman by cutting his pigtail, adopting Javanese costume, and seeking a palace woman as his official wife.

RADEN AYU MURTININGRAT: TROPHY BRIDE

She enters the historical record as commander of the female bodyguard of Sultan Hamengkubuwono II of Yogyakarta and occasional wife. The palace women of a former ruler were normally retired from their status of wife and dismissed from royal service, or they were kept on in the palace for other duties, such as teacher of young girls. Hamengkubuwono III, however, selected his half-brother's former bodyguard to be one of his wives and bestowed on her the title Raden Ayu and personal name of Murtiningrat. She bore him a daughter. Hamengkubuwono IV later took Murtiningrat as a wife, and they also had a daughter.

The new Raden Tumenggung Secadiningrat (Tan Jin Seng) applied for the raden ayu to be his chief wife. His reach did not extend so far: a Chinese convert was not to be given the temporary wife of kings of Java. In September 1816 Hamengkubuwono IV allowed Murtiningrat to accompany ex-Sultan Hamengkubuwono II, her first royal husband, when the Dutch exiled him to Ambon. Murtiningrat did not follow the ex-king as far as Ambon. She disappears from the historical record in 1817.

Diponegoro was forty years old in 1825 when he burst out of his private lands in rebellion against Hamengkubuwono V and his Javanese and Dutch backers. The rebel prince's language of opposition appealed to the newly poor, to religiously committed, and to royal factions. Farmers faced droughts and harvest failures from 1821 to 1825. Carriers of goods saw royal taxes consuming their profits. Diponegoro promised righteous rule and justice in taxation. To religious circles he denounced the submission of Muslims to non-Muslim tax collectors, landlords, and agents of government. He derided the palace faction that allowed non-Muslims to depose and install Java's sultans. He preached hatred of European and Chinese for their refusal to embrace Islam, their prosperity from taxing and selling opium to Muslims, and their foreign clothes, diet, and habits. To the religious he promised that Java would be exclusively a land of Muslims; to disaffected palace staff he offered himself as sultan. Diponegoro was no revolutionary, however. He stood for monarchy and inherited privilege. He had no intellectual interest in ideas outside the traditions of Javanese Islamic mysticism.

Fifteen of the twenty-nine princes in Yogyakarta and forty-one of eighty-eight senior palace officials initially joined Diponegoro. They brought armed bodyguards and retainers with them. The religious hierarchy of the palace and residents of tax-free villages and religious schools in the Mataram and Pajang areas also rallied. A band of one hundred and eight kiais, thirty-one hajis, fifteen ulamas, twelve religious officials, and four teachers brought men armed with pikes, spears, and krises. As businessmen they, too, were suffering from tolls and the effect of droughts, and they calculated that, by siding with Diponegoro, they would increase their own political power as advisers and appointees of a new sultan. The uprising was centered in Diponegoro's home region of south-central Java, and related uprisings occurred in territories stretching from Tegal, Rembang, and Madiun to Pacitan.

Diponegoro's strategy against Hamengkubuwono V was to make the collection of income from the countryside impossible. Armed gangs who joined his cause attacked the residences and workplaces of Europeans and Chinese, not the royal capital. Massacres with axes, knives, and lances sent survivors fleeing the countryside for towns and cities. Diponegoro attempted to cut the capital city off from its revenue and its food supply as well: he pressured farmers to refuse to sell their produce in Yogyakarta. He and his advisors stayed mostly in the old Mataram heartland, communicating with the heads of other rebel groups in central and north Java by letter. The war was a series of provincial uprisings loosely coordinated and controlled by Diponegoro. Men joined and deserted, depending on the tide of battle and on Diponegoro's personal leadership.

Diponegoro stressed the Muslim character of his ambitions by calling his war a jihad. He looked beyond the archipelago's sultanates to the Ottoman emperor, as head of the Islamic world, for support. He rode into battle dressed in what was thought of in Java as Turkish costume: trousers, jacket, and turban. In areas controlled by his vassals Diponegoro attempted to install an Islamic administration. Agents were instructed to collect taxes in accordance with sharia; booty of goods and people was to be distributed according to Koranic injunctions. Prisoners of war were presented with the choice of conversion or death. Those prisoners who chose conversion were obliged to dress, speak, and live as Javanese so that no traces of foreign manners and custom would remain in Java.

Like all Javanese kings, Diponegoro assumed a string of reign titles, including the Islamic royal epithets First Among Believers, Lord of the Faith, Regulator of the Faith in Java, Sultan, and Caliph of the Prophet of God. He was a product of the palace and inheritor of royal Java. He had no time for Muslim scholars who opposed monarchy itself and argued that Islamic communities should be governed by judges and teachers of Islamic law, not kings. Like Trunajaya and Surapati, Diponegoro advertised his visions and periods of meditation in mountain forest retreats. He circulated news of his communion with Ratu Loro Kidul, the spirit bride of Java's kings. Like his predecessors, Diponegoro also adopted older titles such as Erucakra, which means "Emergent Buddha."

In the first two years of rebellion Diponegoro's armies had successes. He used the landless and the itinerant as troops, porters, and guards of mountain strongholds; he could incite farmers to attack passing columns of Dutch and Javanese troops. By 1827, however, his men began losing battles. Chinese suppliers refused to sell ammunition to the rebels after Diponegoro's followers massacred families of Chinese, including Chinese Muslims, in towns across central Java. The Dutch adapted their tactics to Diponegoro's guerrillas, building forts across the countryside and sending out mobile columns of troops to patrol villages and rice lands. Farmers went back to their fields; markets opened around the forts; traders returned to safe market centers. Lack of ammunition and declining rural support diminished the effectiveness of Diponegoro's battle strategies and fighters. A major setback to recruiting men and winning support from villagers came in 1827 when important Muslim leaders withdrew their endorsement of Diponegoro's cause. They disbanded their men and returned home, or went over to the Dutch with their fighters when Diponegoro declared himself imam, regulator of Islamic life, and set himself over Islamic scholars. In 1829 Diponegoro's chief religious adviser was captured. Princes quickly changed sides as the Dutch gained control of the countryside. By 1829 most of Diponegoro's military commanders had left him. In January 1830 his uncles and brothers asked to make public submission to Hamengkubuwono V and his Dutch backers. Diponegoro held out in the hills a little longer. When he was finally lured from his hideout and captured on March 28, 1830, his personal following was reduced to a few hundred retainers, slave women, minor wives, and servants.

Most Western accounts label the conflict of 1825–1830 the Java War and explain it as a war of Javanese against the Dutch. Official Indonesian histories call it the Diponegoro War and characterize it as one of many struggles to free Indonesians from colonial rule. But Diponegoro was fighting to unseat a Javanese king as well as to remove Dutch and Chinese influence over Java's political, economic, and cultural life. Not all Javanese wanted him to win. Some Javanese officials judged that their jobs and prospects were more secure under Dutch employers than under Java's royals. Madurese mercenaries swelled the Dutch forces that fought against Diponegoro. And not all Muslim leaders welcomed the idea of Diponegoro as sultan. Ulamas accompanied the Indonesian troops who fought under Dutch officers, and Arab sayyids represented the Dutch in negotiations with Diponegoro's representatives. The Surakarta court remained officially aloof from the conflict. Among its princes were supporters of the Dutch as well as supporters of Diponegoro.

Diponegoro is now revered as a hero of Java, of Islam, and of nationalist struggle. His portrait is displayed beside a photograph of Indonesia's first president in the Sukarno museum in Blitar. At the time, Java's ruling elite was more ambivalent in its estimation of Diponegoro. The *Babad Dipanagara,* which was written at the Surakarta court of Pakubuwono VI (r. 1823–1830), deplored the prince's pesantren entourage and outlook. The writer saw Diponegoro as a prince who absented himself from his natural setting, the palace, and who lowered himself in preferring the company of ulamas to royals. In a late nineteenth-century babad by a Yogyakarta writer, Diponegoro is just one of many princes who went into battle. In exile, Diponegoro constructed his own account. His rebellion is written into the history of making Java a Muslim land. The babad begins with the fall of Majapahit to Islamic armies, narrates the history of Mataram and division of the kingdom and then relays the circumstances of Diponegoro's life and the insults and injuries he endured as a result of the Dutch presence at court.

Dutch men at the time felt the arrest of Diponegoro to be an important event in their history in Java. General H. M. de Kock, who led Dutch forces and engineered the capture of Diponegoro, commissioned the artist Nicolaas

Pieneman (1809–1860) to preserve that lowest moment for Diponegoro in a large painting. Diponegoro had presented himself for negotiations with de Kock in Magelang as a prince of Islam, rather than as heir of royal Java. In the painting, Javanese men followers surround their imam and women kneel. Dutch soldiers issue from the house of Holland's representative; the Dutch flag flies over it. Lances surrendered by Diponegoro's retainers lie in the foreground. At the top of the steps stands de Kock pointing to the coach that is to drive Diponegoro away into exile.

Diponegoro's defeat did not immediately reconcile followers to the Dutch-imposed solution to palace rivalry or to the entrenched Dutch presence in Java. Some loyalists took their families into east Java, where they opened up rice fields. Some established schools of religious learning that became the nucleus of villages and industries. Some followed Diponegoro into exile in Sulawesi. He was held first in Manado, and then, from July 1833, in Makasar in rooms within Fort Rotterdam. His burial site remains a place of pilgrimage. His followers and those who attended other princes into exile created Javanese neighborhoods in Sulawesi settings. In Manado, descendants formed Islamic villages in territory that was becoming Christian in the second half of the nineteenth century.

Some Dutch circles were affected by the mystique that surrounded Diponegoro. Prince Henry, the sixteen-year-old son of the future William II of the Netherlands, visited him in his Fort Rotterdam prison in 1837. Henry wrote privately to his father to describe a man who, in miserable, hot quarters, spent his time copying the Koran and drawing and met him with a pretended cheerfulness. "He is very aloof, earlier he did not even wish to speak Malay," the prince recorded. "He has a pleasant appearance and one senses that he is still full of fire" (quoted in Wassing-Visser, 1995, p. 246). This first member of Holland's royal family to visit Indonesia saw the arrest of Java's hero as a stain on Dutch honor. Prince Henry warned his father that such treatment would drive all other Indonesian princes into the enemy camp in future conflicts. Neither Diponegoro's reputation as a holy man nor the impression he made on the young Prince Henry induced the real holders of power to release him from his small rooms or increase his comforts. Diponegoro remained in Fort Rotterdam until his death.

Diponegoro lived long enough to see Chinese regain control of trade and manufacturing in Java and to see the forging of a powerful alliance between Javanese aristocrats and the Dutch to tax Java's farmers. Javanese district officials who owed their jobs to the Dutch focused their energies on making their jobs heritable by their sons. They propagated the idea that they were the natural leaders of the Javanese, that sacred ties bound them to the people, and that only through them could the Dutch rule. To preserve their privileges they pushed their sons to learn what made the Dutch rich, powerful, and inventive. When Diponegoro died in Makasar in 1855, there were more non-Muslims in Java, and government by non-Muslims extended into more parts of the archipelago than ever before.

Princes, European landleasers, and contractors toasted their mutually rewarding relationship in freemason lodges and clubs in Yogyakarta and Surakarta, which sank to the status of small principalities within the Dutch colony. The chief Islamic officials in a district married into the families that ruled it for the Dutch. Lesser ulamas cultivated different careers. They traveled between pesantrens and holy sites, or they settled in villages where they took in male students as boarders. In their self-image they, not the cooperating nobility, were the natural leaders of the Javanese. Palace and colonial capital were equally irrelevant to them. When social conditions worsened, a few burst out of the Islamic community into the colonial world to denounce the government of Christians and their Indonesian allies and to lead their handful of followers, fortified by amulet and prayer, against the guns and swords of the colony's police force.

The Diponegoro War cost many Javanese lives from starvation and illness; few were direct casualties of battle. Farming families had meager resources to tide them through hard times when fields could not be planted, were ravaged by pests, dried up in drought, or were destroyed by soldiers. The Diponegoro War showed that commoners, as well as princes and ulamas, hated the foreigners who traveled through their landscapes and controlled their lives. For the farmer of Java, the lasting change was not so much the European boss behind the Javanese as the shrinking of space for shifting agriculture, the progression of settled farming, and the inescapable supervision of government officials. A multiplication of jobs took people off farms and subordinated their labor to supervisors who were Chinese, Eurasians, or Indonesians from other parts of the archipelago. The burden of taxes could no longer be evaded by flight from the home village. Empty land and territory without functioning government ceased to exist in nineteenth-century Java. The lives of ordinary Javanese became more bound up in a cash economy and dependent on world markets.

People living in the western and eastern ends of the archipelago felt the impact of the changes in Java that followed from the Diponegoro War later. The wealth that Java's farmers produced for the Dutch helped finance colonial expansion. The experience of ruling Java showed the Dutch how they could work around and through the indigenous elites. The Dutch saw the Indonesian workers' adaptability, readiness to take up new crops, willingness to learn new farming techniques and try new jobs. Victory nurtured in the Dutch the habit of command. The economic and political ambitions of other outsiders encouraged the Dutch to bind Indonesian histories into a single space, to go farther than Majapahit's navies, and to realize the dream of Java's kings in directing the entire archipelago's resources and taxes to Java.

9

MANY KINGDOMS, ONE COLONY
Bringing Indonesian Histories Together

During the nineteenth century Indonesian lives became fused in the Netherlands East Indies. Within the archipelago's many communities there developed an overlay of shared experience. More people than ever before became aware of Europeans living and working in the archipelago, and more came under Dutch political and military control. Greater numbers of Indonesians inhabited space influenced by men with foreign customs, new work machines, and new ways of organizing daily life. Towns multiplied. There were more Javanese on Java and across the archipelago. There were more Chinese and more Indonesians circulating. There were Chinese coolies in Sumatra, Buginese traders in Bali, Javanese soldiers in Aceh, and Batak clerks in Batavia. Railway lines, steamship connections, telegraph and post offices, schools, banks, clinics, research stations, and government offices across the archipelago introduced uniformity in many aspects of daily life. The sons of archipelago elites left royal cities for colonial ones. Ordinary men were attracted to cities and factories where they learned to drive steam engines, run and repair machinery, while ordinary women operated sewing machines and prepared rubber for processing. Sultans drew Dutch pensions, and mosque officials lived on government stipends.

The colony formed between 1850 and 1914 with its center of power on Java was never a single state. Many sultanates headed by Indonesian kings existed inside its boundaries, alongside territories headed by Dutch administrators. Differences were preserved. Dutch and Indonesian scholars explored difference and publicized it. They sought out old customs and revived oral traditions that emphasized the many variations between Indonesia's communities. Vernaculars were written down, and introduced to the classroom to enhance regional and ethnic pride. Dutch and Indonesian scholars joined in academic societies to study and preserve ethnic pasts and channel modern experience through ethnic particularity. Christian communities formed in territories where formerly Muslim coastal peoples had raided for slaves. Indonesians who conducted their work and study lives in the Dutch language formed a new class, separated from most of their fellows by language, culture, orientation, ambitions, and privilege. New Indonesian classes found power as voices of ethnic aspirations. When race entered calculations of difference, alongside religion, the sense of disparity also proliferated: Dutch and Indonesian competed in scorn for each other inside the one colony.

Colonial rule introduced the inventions of modern Europe into Indonesian communities. The machines that altered individual lives became a permanent part of the landscape. New crops and jobs introduced new forms of labor and supervision of labor. Wars defined and determined the careers of regional elites and destroyed the lives and homes of commoners. Wars introduced mechanized transport, inserted commercial plantations into conquered lands, and imposed Dutch solutions on internal conflicts. Dutch-engineered railroads, trams, and roadways complemented sea-lanes. Women travelers included sex workers, wives, and traders, as always, but now there were also itinerant female coolies and wage workers, and a few schoolgirls with ambitions to become professionals.

Indonesians quickly responded to electricity, fast travel, and mass-produced goods. Sometimes they accepted the Western invention only when it was mediated through the Islamic world: printed books were permissible when they came from Muslim publishing houses in India or Egypt; autopsies were acceptable when a fatwah determined how they could be lawful; Western-type schools with paid teachers and a set, graded curriculum became desirable when operated by private Muslim organizations. Other men welcomed Dutch inventions because they allowed fulfillment of Indonesian dreams: the Dutch steamship took them to Mecca in two weeks, and the Dutch passenger train brought women to markets beyond walking distance.

Military campaigns, commercial expansion, scholarly investigations, and high-minded clubs equipped the Dutch to think of the colony as "our Indies," inhabited by a huge variety of peoples fused into one as "Natives." Sultans and senior Indonesian administrators did not break habits of dependence and collaboration. Their colonial stipends financed the studies of their children in Dutch schools, but some in this privileged younger generation rejected the contemptuous homogenizing of Native. In the first years of the twentieth century they busied themselves with modern ideas of what it meant to be Javanese or Sumatran. They formed associations to debate how to live in a modern colony where European Christian notions influenced everything from marriage to respect for the dead, law, and taxation. The most visible individuals began a journey that transformed Native into Indonesian. More wanted to turn Native into Muslim under a Muslim government. Most thought in terms of Muslim government that was Indonesian. For a few, Islam came first; they saw in nationalism a European plot to smother Muslim identity. All Indonesian lives were forever transformed by the experience of one political unit of non-Muslim origin, and by its centering in Java.

Batavia was the strongest state on Java after the defeat of Prince Diponegoro in 1830. Its rulers turned to the task of rebuilding the economy after the devastation of the war. They devised a government-run cultivation system to stimulate Javanese farmers to grow more crops for export. Farmers had to pay their taxes in specified amounts of sugar, coffee, tea, tobacco, or indigo and to sell any surplus they raised to the government at fixed prices. Batavia's goals were cheap crops, profits from European sales, and an industrious and prosperous peasantry in Java. Starting in 1830, Javanese officials in territories under direct Dutch administration were given seedlings to distribute to farmers. Dutch inspectors were sent into the countryside to supervise planting, harvesting, and processing.

From the perspective of Java's history, the cultivation system was not an innovation but the prolonging of an outmoded system of taxation. Java's farmers had always had to pay their taxes in crops which were then exported through royal monopolies. The Dutch made the same method for getting profits from cheap labor more efficient. The cultivation system was run by the Javanese official class that now, after the Diponegoro War, owed appointment and tenure to the Batavian government. At its height, in 1860, no more than 190 Dutch men were involved in operating the cultivation system. Ninety Dutch crop inspectors and one hundred supervisors worked alongside Javanese officials directing two million laborers working about 5 percent of Java's land area.

The cultivation system proved a success for the Indies government, because the volume of exports rose continually throughout the nineteenth century. Profits were invested in the Netherlands. European science and Javanese labor achieved production increases. European researchers made advances in soil and plant science; European engineers improved factory equipment and processing methods; Javanese workers learned new skills and increased their working hours to generate profits for the Dutch.

As early as the 1840s the colonial government determined to get out of the business of running export agriculture and turn it over to European businessmen and companies. The government redirected its policies to creating an environment attractive to private investors through financing agricultural research, extending roads and steamship services, upgrading ports, and suppressing outbreaks by workers protesting conditions and wages. Between 1845 and 1864 the government withdrew from the tea, tobacco, and indigo industries; it continued to run the sugar industry until 1891 and coffee production until 1915. Even before the official end of government control, private entrepreneurs working under contract raised many crops. From 1850, all sugar mills were operated by private owners.

Javanese who raised more crops than their tax quota sold them to government agents for cash. Workers on plantations and workers who built the road and rail network serving the cultivation system were also paid in cash. Workers with cash bought the market products that they had previously made at home when not busy in their fields and vegetable plots. They bought tools, clothes, coconut and palm sugar, cooked foods, pots and utensils, mats and baskets. When they were doing well, they bought jewelry, decorated krises, and leather goods. They bought opium and items made by other Javanese, not goods manufactured in Europe. Holland was still an agricultural country in 1830 when the cultivation system was introduced; its industrialization occurred over the years 1890 to 1914. Javanese home industries produced for the Javanese worker; they were not overtaken by Dutch factory goods until the twentieth century. An important consequence of the cultivation system for Javanese was that some artisans and craftspeople moved from part-time to full-time production. Some farmers specialized in rice production to sell this basic food to other farmers specializing in soybeans, peanuts, and maize. The increase in the number of markets and market stalls in the nineteenth century was the result of workers focusing on particular areas of the economy.

The cultivation system itself required the services of many kinds of workers. Before 1830, across Java there were carpenters, cart builders and drivers, wheelwrights, boat builders, makers of tile and brick, operators of lime kilns, potters, and blacksmiths. Women dominated the garment industry as spinners, weavers, and decorators of cloth. All these individuals had operated from small workshops on a part-time basis. Commercial agriculture turned many into full-time workers building warehouses, factories, bridges, roads, and housing and transporting goods. Blacksmiths now repaired factory machinery, potters supplied the vessels for boiling sugar syrup, mat makers wove mats for drying tea leaves, and others made straw bags for transporting sugar.

Experience of the cultivation system differed for individual Javanese according to where they lived and which crop they had to raise. Families living in country above three hundred meters altitude had to raise coffee. Coffee was suited to small farms because it is a shrub that could be raised along with food crops; it can be harvested within four years and produces for six to seven years. Farmers sometimes sold the job of harvesting, preparing, and transporting the beans to men who headed teams of workers. In other cases, farming families performed all the tasks involved in coffee production. Farmers could continue growing their own food while raising coffee to pay their taxes and generate a cash income on the side.

Coffee was also grown on plantations. Coffee plantations in west Java were established in areas the government considered "empty" land, that is, on hillsides used periodically by shifting farmers to grow their food. Plantations created demand for a labor force to strip the hillsides of forest, and to plant, tend, pick, prepare, and transport the coffee. They attracted migrants from other areas of Java. Plantation laborers worked for wages; they spent their cash purchasing rice, vegetables, prepared foods, laundry, and sex from area farmers. Coffee cultivation diversified the population and increased the use of cash. Some families paid their taxes by working on coffee plantations, a burden when the work site was far from their villages. All plantation laborers experienced work in a new, regimented form under a specialist staff of managers, foremen, and team supervisors.

The cultivation system was different for the Javanese who grew sugar, because sugar grew best in flat, well-watered land, which was where farmers grew their rice. Sugar cane has a growing cycle of fifteen to eighteen months. In the first six months, the canes were grown in irrigated furrows which then had to be drained while the canes ripened. After harvesting, the canes had to be transported to the sugar factory and the root stocks dug up, collected, and burned. The sugar industry required large amounts of labor at specific points in the year. Under the cultivation system, rice-growing families had to work part-time in sugar fields or the sugar factory in order to pay their taxes. Women and children weeded and cleared cut cane; men prepared fields, harvested, and transported cane to the mills. Villages often could not supply enough part-time laborers, so sugar companies hired laborers who worked in gangs under a foreman and were paid in cash. Seasonal laborers created demands for accommodation and food, and so generated income-earning opportunities in villages. Reserves of female and child workers kept all wages low.

Because canes rapidly lose their sugar content after being cut, they have to be transported to the factory for immediate processing. Sugar factories were built near the site of production, so that, historically, there is a close connection between rural life and factory labor in some parts of Java. Early in the nineteenth century, canes were crushed by wooden or stone rollers to extract the sugary liquid. These rollers were turned by buffalo, windmills, or waterwheels. The juice squeezed from the cane was then mixed with lime to clarify it and then boiled in open kettles or vats to concentrate it. The resulting syrup was left in clay cones so that the molasses could drip out, leaving sugar behind. Sugar processing created jobs for buffalo cart owners and drivers, operators of lime kilns, and potters.

During the nineteenth century, Europeans replaced waterwheels and buffalo with steam engines and installed iron boilers in place of clay kettles. Indonesians were trained to operate the new machinery and to be laboratory technicians, labor supervisors, and pay clerks for European management. By 1930 sugar was the preeminent export crop grown along the northern coast of Java. The typical sugar factory took cane from one thousand hectares of land, employed twenty European technicians, three hundred full-time and four to five thousand part-time Javanese workers. Two hundred thousand hectares of Java were under cane, with ninety thousand permanent workers and about one million during the six-month season of harvesting and processing that began in May.

The sugar industry encroached on local water supplies and on land that an expanding population might have cleared for rice cultivation. More rice had to be raised from established fields than previously when there was abundant forested land to be cleared nearby. Rice yields could be increased only by more weeding and by more intense cultivation. Rice farmers hated the competing demands of factories, which drew away potential workers from their own fields. Into the busier work world of Javanese families came more social problems. Wage labor freed young men and some young women from parental supervision. It attracted the unemployed and detached as seasonal workers who were potential clients for the expanding gambling, opium, and sex industries. Sugar brought periods of prosperity for sugar workers, but it made them dependent on world sugar prices, which fell drastically after 1926 and collapsed during the Depression. Javanese farmers blamed sugar for all their problems. Sugar factories became a symbol of colonial rule and a target for attack.

Indigo was another plant that could be integrated into the rice farmer's work space and schedule. It requires hot, humid conditions and plentiful amounts of water. Leaves can be cut five months after planting and every three months thereafter. Indigo caused great resentment when the cultivation system obliged farmers to raise and process it, because processing was dirty work and, like cane growing, time consuming. The leaves had to be soaked in a fermentation tub for eight hours, then pounded to separate the dye from the water. The liquid dye then had to be cooked in kettles into a paste, pressed into cakes, and dried on racks. Indigo was widely used on Java for dyeing the locally grown coarse cotton that ordinary people used as clothing material. It was a part-time, home-based industry. Europeans introduced the water-powered mill to separate dye from water and increased production for export until indigo was replaced by synthetic dyes.

An individual's class affected experience of the cultivation system as much as crop and location. For instance, landholders who rented their land to the government or private companies for planting cane received a lump sum in cash. Some then rented land from fellow villagers at low prices in order subsequently to lease it out to a sugar company at a higher rate. Government and private companies also rented village common fields from the headman and core families controlling local communities. The cultivation system introduced surveyors and land assessors into villages and generated profits for landholders. Such farmers became moneylenders in the village and tightened their control on local government.

In 1850 the colonial government abolished tollgates and market taxes. These had been a major impediment to farmers who wanted to increase production and sell crops after they had met their tax quota. Markets were an average of five kilometers apart, open every fifth day in rotation, and subsidiary tollgates were often erected at the entrance to villages. Farmers swiftly found new buyers in district and regional markets who were purchasing to provision local and overseas consumers.

Village people who raised their living standards and income built houses of stone, sponsored performances of wayang, or made the pilgrimage to Mecca. Wealth and piety created status in their circles. Prosperity made a man a taxpayer. Like businessmen everywhere, prosperous farmers resented paying taxes. Religious leaders cast their objections in the language of Islam. Taxes were impositions of a government of nonbelievers and were in forms not sanctioned by the Koran. When there were tax revolts, most protesters were not the army of wage laborers, whose earnings were too low to make them taxpayers. Those obeying the call to Islamic revolt were small businessmen.

Rural manufacturers ran family businesses in their yard, staffed by family members and dependents. To grow into substantial businesses they needed capital. They could not obtain loans at fixed low rates of interest because the government did not create banks and credit unions for the small business operator until the twentieth century. The only source of cash was the unregulated loan from the local Javanese official, landowner, or Chinese shopkeeper. The small entrepreneur had no protection against high interest rates. Without cheap loans, Javanese merchants could not break into wholesaling and distribution, the lucrative part of trading which remained the monopoly of Chinese. Rural entrepreneurs could improve their living standards, but they could not make enough to generate savings or invest and expand their businesses.

When the cultivation system was first introduced, failed experiments, bad growing conditions, and inadequate supply networks caused famine. The hardest hit were the village poor in Cirebon. The system, which was geared to sales in European markets, was operated by Dutch and Javanese officials who paid themselves a percentage of the crops delivered by farmers. They set their own standards of honesty without check or outside review. Migrants who traveled the countryside seeking employment often found themselves out of work and out of food. Rice milling was commercialized. The government sold exclusive rights to build and operate rice mills to favorites, who then exercised their monopoly powers by buying peasant rice cheaply, and selling the milled product to other markets. Among the many political scandals in the operation of the cultivation system, relatives obtained contracts from senior government officials to produce for export; they cultivated Javanese officials so they could obtain "trouble-free" labor. Workers put in long hours for low wages in unregulated workplaces without mechanisms for redress of grievances.

Doubts about the propriety of the cultivation system arose in Holland as soon as the new, fast mail routes brought news from Java of harvest failures, famines, and arbitrary exactions. Dutch men at the time, and later Dutch historians such as Gonggrijp, Day, Colenbrander, and Stapel, denounced the cultivation system as exploitative and the cause of rural impoverishment. Critics argued that Javanese farmers were obliged to neglect their subsistence plots because of excessive demands on their labor; farmers bore the brunt of agricultural experiments; they had no protection against corrupt inspectors and officials; and they were victims of low prices. Critics also noted that farmers were brought under the oppressive rule of a centralized government that could enforce its decrees. Hostility toward the cultivation system created a colonial opposition in Holland, and established colonial policy as part of public debate.

The cultivation system has been much studied and almost universally condemned in the scholarly literature. In the 1980s, however, review of the evidence by Boomgaard, Elson, Fasseur, Fernando, Knight, and Van Niel concluded that arguments for the impoverishment of the peasantry were not based on actual data. Critics of the cultivation system had assumed the existence of a prosperous peasantry prior to 1830. They called payments that farmers made to Javanese officials "tribute," while they called the same payments to colonial officials "forced delivery," yet both were taxes. The current scholarly consensus is that the cultivation system was oppressive, but it multiplied the number and kinds of jobs available and offered some farmers the possibility of material prosperity. Instead of viewing Javanese as passive victims, this research emphasizes their dynamic response. Contemporary government reports of increases in the number of buffalo and agricultural tools owned by farming households, increased purchases, and rising numbers of farmers who took up full-time production of export crops or started brick-making and transport businesses support these conclusions.

The cultivation system had multiplying effects far beyond the hectares it covered in Java. Wherever Indonesian farmers saw an introduced crop bringing good profits, they learned how to raise and market it. The archipelago has many hillsides suitable for coffee, for example. Archipelago farmers needed only access to coffee seedlings and a network through which to sell their beans to add coffee bushes to the crops they raised. They did not wait for the extension of Dutch rule to become growers of coffee. Late in the nineteenth century the necessary conditions obtained in central Sulawesi where Torajans farmed in high valleys. Buginese and Arab traders journeyed up to the Torajan homelands with goods Torajan chiefs wanted. They exchanged guns and ammunition for coffee beans that had been grown by laborers subject to the chiefs. Buginese boatmen transported the coffee to ports where Dutch steamships called. There the coffee was sold to traders who boarded a steamer and sold it in a regional market or in Batavia.

The cultivation system rested on exporting crops produced in Java. The system imposed the questions of who owned the land and how could the Dutch control its use? As the Dutch understood it, Java's kings owned the land and allowed farmers to occupy it in return for taxes. Land meant soil plus people living from it. Kings did not sell land or give it away; they gave away or sold the right to use the labor of people in a specified area. When Batavian governments acquired land by treaty from Java's kings in payment for military services, they followed Javanese practice by leasing territories, with their occupants, to European and Chinese businessmen. Batavian governments perceived forests as empty or waste land, ignoring Indonesian peoples who passed through forests going from one temporary farming site to the next. Batavian governments sold parcels of "empty" land outright to Europeans and Chinese. Where the Dutch acquired land by conquest, such as in the environs of Batavia, they applied Dutch conceptions of ownership, marked boundaries, created titles, and sold off blocks.

In Java's history, permanently cultivated fields have formed an advancing frontier on forest. Java's kings expanded their domains by appointing officials to lead teams to open up rice lands. Laborers who cleared forested land were allocated plots for house, garden, and rice and were remembered as village founders. The Dutch discovered that men who took part in village government were considered descendants of the founders. They occupied large holdings and employed relatives and tenants to do the actual farming. In the course of a man's life, he might work on another's land and in time inherit the right to allow others to work it. Women farmed vegetable plots on house land; they worked in fields as planters, weeders, and harvesters. Their relation to the land was determined by the status of male relatives. Some individuals might inherit rights to use village land but live in another village because of marriage or employment. Men who moved to towns might retain rice fields in their birth village.

Farming was not an individual's sole occupation. A farmer might spend part of his year in paid labor, tending coffee bushes, working in a sugar mill, driving a cart. Another farmer might spend part of her year weaving mats or cloth for sale, carrying soil on construction sites, selling goods in the market, and making snacks for sale. In Java, the terms "peasant" and "farmer" mean male and female rural laborer and refer to a great variety of workers with a wide range of access to land.

Between 1830 and 1850, when the Indies government ran the cultivation system, it had to negotiate with an area's aristocrat and village headmen to get land set aside for export crops. A government bureaucracy could not negotiate with hundreds of families for the part-time use of their small shares of land. The colonial government promoted the concept of village land as owned equally by all village residents. The "village commune" notion promoted the rapid extension of commercial agriculture, whose profits flowed to the Netherlands, while hampering the emergence of a class of rich peasants with concentrated landholdings. Under the Agrarian Law of 1870, the Indies government declared that indigenous farmers had the right of possession of land they cultivated (native tenure). Foreigners could not own land. They could rent uncultivated land on long leases, but could lease cultivated land from villages for only three years. As a result, Indonesians of Chinese and European descent could not own rural land.

Following the defeat of Diponegoro in 1830, senior Dutch officials prevented disaffected Javanese princes waging more wars by shrinking royal Java to the core domains of the rulers of Surakarta and Yogyakarta and by taking direct control of all territories formerly allocated to princes and vassals. The cultivation system was put into the regions detached from the two kingdoms. To compensate their loss of territory and income, the Dutch government made annual payments to the susuhunan of Surakarta and the sultan of Yogyakarta. In 1831 the rate was 754,987 guilders for the susuhunan and 465,000 guilders for the sultan. Kings now had a guaranteed income, but it had to be distributed among royal relatives and officials, and grants of taxing rights to villages had to be parceled out from a much reduced territory. The cash attracted merchants eager to foster new habits of expense and dependence on luxuries in the two kingdoms. Extravagant living made kings, princes, and court officials always eager to increase their incomes.

The cultivation system stopped at the boundaries of the "independent" kingdoms, but there was no Dutch law prohibiting Europeans and Chinese from renting land from royals, and the kingdoms had a long tradition of leasing villages and tollgates to Chinese and Eurasians. Now, in the age of large-scale export agriculture, Europeans wanted vast acreages to raise a single crop by standard measures and calendar and to manage their business directly. Javanese methods of apportioning households to royal appointees meant that Europeans had to combine many leases to form one estate. Within that estate were households whose services had been sold to the one European businessman by twenty or thirty Javanese officials. These officials had never seen their lands or knew their farmers except as distant suppliers of wealth. The European who leased land, in contrast, aimed to travel throughout his territory, to know "his" people, and to organize their time and efforts to match a unified business plan.

Once a European had pieced together a large estate, he then had to deal with the farmers. If the crop to be grown required mountain slopes, he had to obtain laborers able to spend part of their working week away from home. If the crop had the same requirements of area and water as farmers' crops, then the European, with the villagers, had to design a system of rotating crops that bound all who cultivated the land. The European leaseholder usually conducted his arrangements with the principal men of the village. There were no controls put in place by Java's royals. They sold their subjects to foreigners who were not bound to any standard of justice in treatment and payment of workers. Hatred for foreigners grew as people saw themselves as nothing but work machines creating profits for non-Muslims.

J. DEZENTJE: EURASIAN PRINCE OF CENTRAL JAVA

J. Dezentje was one of the richest leaseholders in Java's royal domains. In 1836, 38,717 Javanese were producing coffee for him. He was a Eurasian whose Javanese language, manners, wealth, and usefulness to royalty procured him one of Pakubuwono VI's many daughters as a wife. Dezentje built her a house modeled on her father's palace. She was addressed as raden ayu, the title given the chief wife of Java's aristocrats. To the princes, Dezentje was a vassal who paid his rent twice a year at festivals marking Muhammad's birthday and the end of Ramadhan. They indulged in the pleasures of the wealthy together, hunting, exchanging women, gathering in clubs. Princes and Eurasian both viewed the Javanese laborer as someone who should be pressed harder to generate more income. They saw the Batavian government as a nuisance, to be manipulated by entangling its local representatives in their financial and sexual networks.

The cultivation system permanently altered Java's landscape. Lowland and mountain forests gave way to farms. Already in VOC times Java's teak forests had gone. Extensive cutting and clearing of land for crops put more soil into rivers. Rivers became too shallow for boats in the dry season, estuaries silted up, and sandbars formed in the harbors along Java's north coast. In 1777, the VOC prohibited villagers from entering forests in Rembang, Pajankungan, and Palo to cut trees for house building materials and fuel and limited the size of private boats in order to conserve forests. From the 1850s the Indies government began developing a forestry service of paid Dutch and Indonesian employees whose jobs included the mapping of forested areas, designating forest stands closed to use by villagers, guarding these forests, replanting deforested areas, and managing protected stands.

Forest conservation meant more government interference in the daily lives of villagers, who were deprived of everyday necessities for a Dutch notion of the common good. The villagers' anger sometimes led to attacks on forest officials and licensed woodcutters. In the past, the forest was a refuge from government, armies, taxes, and epidemics. The forest was a place for dissidents to have visions and for people who did not convert to the dominant Islam of the plains. It was where the leader of the opposition launched his march to power. As forests shrank, government power expanded.

Consolidation of estates for agriculture in Surakarta and Yogyakarta territories meant the disappearance of village boundaries and markers and loss of a local identity. In the areas of direct Dutch rule a gardened landscape expanded continually. Between 1890 and 1910 the Indies government financed the clearing of 1.5 million hectares of forested land for peasant farming, and private planters leased another 400,000 hectares for raising commercial crops. Java's farmers also cleared land on their own, as the new economy offered cash returns to those who raised peanuts, maize, palm oil, soybeans, and rice. In 1850 the Indies government hired European hydraulic engineers to design irrigation works for permanent fields. The Irrigation Service was established in 1885, and by 1940, 1.3 million hectares of rice land in Java were irrigated.

People moved through Java's opened landscape on the new network of roads and railways. Europe exported rail to its colonies between 1860 and 1914. Railways were immediately important to a region's economy, because they reduced porterage costs and transported goods and people swiftly to markets and ports. Their construction depended on bank financing, engineers, iron foundries, machine shops, acquisition of land, and a mobile labor force. In Java, where the first rails were laid in 1867, the rail system also brought technical education and apprenticeship programs for locomotive drivers, mechanics, and colliers; it created the new jobs of station manager, ticket clerk, guard, and porter.

Railway construction in Indonesia took place in the age of photography. The visual record tells us that labor teams were composed of men, women, and children. Female and child labor carried away the soil excavated by men. Families organized in labor teams followed the railway lines as they were laid. The Indonesian landscape of mountains, rivers, and gorges presented formidable and expensive problems to engineers. Building the railways was arduous work, but the wages were higher than those paid to farm workers. At its peak, railway construction employed around nine thousand workers a day. More workers were needed to shift earth, make wooden sleepers, and build the masonry walls of tunnels and the bridges. Private companies hired Chinese laborers to lay railways, and to dredge harbors and expand port facilities.

Both government and private companies built railways all over the archipelago until 1930. Railways connected industrial and agricultural enterprises to small towns, which developed into commercial centers. Trains brought mail, news, government officials, and soldiers. Locomotives traveling through rural landscapes confronted rural inhabitants with imported technology. Railways involved archipelago residents in other ways, too. Tracks linked sugar fields in east Java to factories. Men, not engines, pushed wheeled trucks laden with canes along the tracks to the mill. In Aceh, tandem bicycles were fitted to rail lines and sped Dutch, Javanese, and Ambonese soldiers on patrol in the 1890s.

RIDING THE TRAIN IN JAVA

Ordinary Javanese proved they were neither tradition-bound conservatives rejecting modern inventions nor passive observers of colonialism's building projects. In 1869, when there were only thirty-five kilometers of track in Java, 49,569 Javanese boarded the train. In 1876 nearly one million Javanese traveled by rail, most buying one-way tickets. For Javanese, the railway was the means of escape from the village to a new life and a job. Ticket sales show that opportunities were on average twenty-five kilometers away from home.

By the 1890s railway lines connected most big towns on Java. Trains carried Javanese to pilgrimage sites, as well as to the sugar mill and the textile factory. Through the train window ordinary people learned to think of their homeland as a site of modern enterprise and add this image to other images of Java as the home of ancient heroes or the place where Muslim saints once walked. Maps and diagrams posted in train stations helped produce these new conceptions and allowed people to see their home town in relation to the provincial capital. The seating in train carriages demonstrated the hierarchies of colonial rule: Europeans and Javanese aristocrats traveled in first-class carriages, Eurasians and Chinese in second class, and ordinary Indonesians in third class.

Clerk and policeman, agents of colonial rule. Photographic Archive, Royal Institute of Linguistics and Anthropology, Leiden, No. 4964. Photo courtesy of the KITLV.

Java's train travelers passed through landscapes that were becoming more thickly populated. In 1830, the year the cultivation system was introduced, Java was home to between 7 and 10 million. Its population was 16.2 million in 1870. In 1890 trains crisscrossed a countryside of 23.6 million. By the end of the nineteenth century nearly 30 million people lived in Java. Many reasons have been put forward by scholars to explain the rapid rise in Java's population in the nineteenth century. For Javanese, rising population meant a landscape filled by people instead of trees, more workers detached from landholding and from expectations of permanent settlement in one village, more mobility, weakening ties to aristocrats, and a younger population. Mobile people came into contact with people from other regions more frequently; they became more aware of individual Europeans and saw that the Dutch presence reached into many regions and controlled many aspects of public life.

WHY DID JAVA'S POPULATION GROW?

Population growth is generally explained by lower rates of child mortality and a longer individual life span, owing to elimination of diseases, provision of clean water and ample food supplies, and mass education. In Java these were important achievements of the twentieth century. They cannot explain the population growth that characterized the nineteenth century.

Ricklefs (1986) identifies districts along the north-central coast where Java's population spurt took off and fixes the time as the second half of the eighteenth century. All scholars agree that population rose steadily in the nineteenth century. Some identify the cause as colonial rule itself: the Dutch brought an end to civil war, increased the amount of land under rice cultivation, and introduced food plants, such as cassava and maize, that could sustain populations unable to afford rice. Others see the population increase as the lasting consequence of the cultivation system. They point to the burden of increased taxes on working families and the expansion of jobs. In this argument, working families perceived that more children increased the numbers of potential earners in a household, so couples had more children to pay taxes and buy consumer goods.

These explanations are sometimes placed in an ethnological context of kin patterns, job allocation, and the status of women in Javanese society. Scholars point to the absence of absolute preference for sons and the fact that Javanese rice agriculture draws on the labor of women and children of both sexes. Some scholars argue that the new earning power of children encouraged couples to want large families. Other scholars note that age at first marriage dropped during the nineteenth century. Again, the explanation is related to the cultivation system, which expanded the number of nonfarm jobs, so that couples with disposable income could afford to marry early. Girls marrying at twelve lengthened their childbearing years.

It is not possible to know what Javanese husbands and wives thought about family size 150 years ago. What can be established are the factors that rid Java of sustained famine in the second half of the nineteenth century: a network of roads and railways; trucks and trains that replaced buffalo carts; telegraph systems; and a commitment by the colonial government to move supplies to famine areas when information and transport systems made it possible to do so. The major famines of the nineteenth century occurred in the 1840s, before railway lines were laid or telegraph connected hinterland to capital. Major famines did not occur again until the years of Japanese rule, when Japanese policy dictated the creation of autonomous economic regions and forbade shipping rice to famine areas.

In 1803 the big news in Minangkabau villages was not coming out of capitals in Europe or Dutch-ruled towns in the archipelago, but Arabia. Returning Minangkabau pilgrims brought stories of religious reformers called Wahhabi who had seized control of Mecca and were imposing a strict application of the Koran to the conduct of Arab community and private life. In Minangkabau communities, teachers of religion who lived outside the official hierarchy of mosque, official appointment, and patronage were immediately receptive to the Wahhabi message. They taught village boys and took in advanced students as boarders. Their base was in villages and farms raising coffee, pepper, and gambier for export. Their connections were to other rural schools, to men traveling the land and sea routes of the Islamic world, and to Islamic centers in the heartland.

Minangkabau reformers began by denouncing specific male behaviors. Cock fights, opium, alcohol, and gambling were declared un-Islamic. Similarly condemned were Minangkabau customs surrounding dowry, marriage, and domestic residence. Reformers urged men to break with Minangkabau practice by establishing and ruling their own household, paying a dowry in accordance with Koranic rules, and bringing their bride to live in their own house. They urged their followers to adopt ascetic habits, to set an example of Islamic piety, and to advertise their presence in Minangkabau society by a distinctive appearance. Instead of wearing textiles woven with Minangkabau designs, decorated with gold and silver thread, men and women followers adopted plain white or blue costumes that concealed the body shape. Men wore a brimless head covering and grew beards; women had to cover themselves almost completely, exposing only eyes and nose.

Minangkabau reformers were called Padris. The term emphasized their connection to Mecca; Padri meant a man who had traveled through Pedir, the major embarkation port in Aceh for Arabia. The name also signaled that the source of their authority was outside Minangkabau society. Padris targeted Minangkabau power centers from which they were excluded. They denounced mosque officials who condoned un-Islamic practices, the men who held senior positions in kin lineages, and the men who controlled village government. They condemned men who ran gambling and opium businesses. Above all, they attacked Minangkabau monarchy, the claims of its kings to be God's shadow on earth, and the cult of royal divinity. The reformers found no justification for kings in Koran or early Muslim tradition and argued that Muslims should be ruled by Islamic law. They preached that the men qualified to interpret sharia and rule the community were religious scholars: themselves.

Within ten years the Padri movement advanced from establishing communities of "correct" Islamic practice and denouncing the centers of power in Minangkabau society to launching armed assaults on opponents. Religious scholars personally led armed bands. Their master was Tuanku Imam Bonjol (1772–1864), who carried war into Minangkabau communities from his fortified city of Bonjol. His strategy was to protect life and property if communities surrendered and agreed to observe his form of Islam. In territories subdued by conquest, prisoners and booty were taken. Imam Bonjol swept aside the rule of lineage chiefs for Islamic administrations, consisting of four officials in charge of religious law, teaching, observance, and collection of taxes. Supporters of the old order tended to cluster in the gold mining districts of the royal domain, with its Java pedigree of inherited privilege and entitlement. Men who made their living raising or exporting crops had no use for the legacy of a Hindu Buddhist past; they supported the Padris. In 1818, when the British representative T. S. Raffles toured Minangkabau districts where Padris were the dominant force, he was shocked to discover stones covered in Old Javanese inscriptions overturned, disregarded, or treated with scorn.

It is impossible to know how Minangkabau women perceived the civil war that engulfed their communities. Many men found the Padri message appealing, for it gave them a new status in society based on their own efforts, not female ancestors. Padri women living in their husband's house and reliant on husband's income perhaps felt the gratification of living a life more closely reflecting Muhammad's teaching. They relied on the continuation of village tradition to provide them with housing and rice land in the event of divorce.

In 1815 Padris murdered Minangkabau's royal family. Padris now competed with lineage heads for power. War had broken out during a period when the important regional power was Aceh. British-Dutch rivalries created opportunities for Sumatran states. Aceh's rulers were expanding south into the interior of Sumatra, imposing Islam on ethnic groups such as the Gayo and Alas. Padri leaders began turning their armies north, aiming at the non-Islamic mountain communities of Bataks. In 1819 the Dutch returned to Padang to resume their contacts with Minangkabau's royals and the village and lineage heads who had controlled exports of gold and pepper through this west coast port. In 1821 opponents of the Padris, who still controlled villages and clans and upheld Minangkabau's royal tradition, signed a treaty transferring sovereignty to the Dutch.

The few Dutch forces could not immediately defeat the Padris. The Minangkabau terrain of sheer mountains, forest, and narrow passes made columns of troops vulnerable to ambush; Padri fighters were lodged in fortified towns and rural schools. Dutch soldiers' muskets and gunpowder were unreliable in humid weather. During the 1830s the Dutch blockaded Minangkabau ports on both sides of Sumatra and broke the Padri grip on power in 1837. Fighting units dispersed after the Dutch arrested Imam Bonjol and exiled him. After 1837 clan and lineage chiefs ran Minangkabau communities for the Dutch.

The end of the Diponegoro War in Java had consequences for Indonesians everywhere. Dutch troops, ships, and supplies were now available for battle in other regions. Indonesian parties to civil war could hire these mobile forces. Professional fighters entered weak Indonesian states that seemed likely to be taken over by other European powers. In the 1840s the Dutch launched military expeditions into Bali and Flores; in the 1850s they sent troops into Jambi and Banjarmasin. In the 1860s Dutch commercial power began its attack on Sumatran jungles and introduced plantations into Malay and Batak areas. From the last years of the nineteenth century missionaries brought Christianity to remote mountain valleys; they stemmed the advance of Muslim missionaries into Toraja and Batak lands, planted Christian villages in northern Sulawesi in the heart of historic sultanates, and signaled the farthest reaches of Dutch power with the formation of Christian villages in Roti and New Guinea.

Government of all these places came under Dutch scrutiny and forms that were determined in Batavia. Java was where the Dutch learned how to be colonial rulers. There they turned Java's kings into decorative supporters of the arts. Through state pensions, the Dutch financed royal preoccupations with women, boys, and opium. Java's aristocrats became salaried officials heading the Native branch of the colonial civil service. There, too, the Dutch learned how to work with the Muslim hierarchy, how to isolate opponents as "religious fanatics," and how to transform men, women, and children into workers who financed Dutch expansion north, west, and east of Java.

The Dutch applied this model wherever colonial troops imposed an outsider's solution to internal feuds. They made large annual allowances to sultans who obligingly transferred lands and laborers to Dutch companies. The Dutch bestowed honors on sultans and financed their new palaces and prestige items such as racing horses. Intractable sultans were deposed, their sultanates extinguished, and the royal castoffs distributed around the archipelago to die in exile in west Java, Ambon, or Manado. Other royals were retained on colonial payrolls but colonial bureaucrats reduced their status to the equivalent of district heads of Java. Everywhere colonial officials identified indigenous chains of authority and turned clan, lineage, and village heads into the administering class. They did not recruit Dutch men for jobs below district government. Europeans did not readily settle in tropical climates; recruiting, training, and maintaining Dutch men in the Netherlands Indies was expensive. Indigenous officials were given a stake in the colonial enterprise. There were the obvious rewards of salary, job, a percentage of profits. A job in the colony's administration introduced Indonesian *datus* (chiefs), arungs (lords), and rajas to a world of colonial behaviors, schools, honors, language. What was prestigious was Western or admired by Westerners. This colonial world ran parallel to the indigenous worlds the datus and rajas governed, where they were objects of respect or scorn.

The Dutch abolished the sultanate of Palembang in 1823. In Banjarmasin, after wars involving colonial troops from 1859 to 1863, the Dutch abolished the sultanate and imposed direct rule. In the 1850s Dutch forces fought in Jambi; they allowed monarchy to survive until 1899. Colonial forces and colonial agreements spread to the islands east of Java. Treaties with Bali's rajas in the 1840s curtailed their sea rights. In 1843 the Balinese ruler of Lombok accepted Dutch sovereignty, while retaining his powers to tax the Muslim villages in his fief. In 1855 and 1856 representatives of the colonial state were installed in the Balinese kingdoms of Buleleng and Jembrana. All Bali's kingdoms were brought into the colonial state through military campaigns in the first years of the twentieth century. Leading royals in Badung and Klungkung killed themselves, their families, and their retainers rather than submit to colonial authority, but junior family members took over as rajas and ruled for the colonial state. Campaigns over 1838 to 1846 brought Flores into the Indies. In 1882 Aru and Tanimbar were added, as were Sumba and Sumbawa by 1907. During the first decade of the twentieth century Dutch control became established in southern Sulawesi too. In the other major push, west into Aceh (1873–1903), colonial forces abolished the sultanate in 1907 and relied on hereditary district governors, the *uleebalang,* to run the everyday lives of the colony's subjects.

In all these campaigns, arungs, datus, uleebalangs, and rajas became part of the colonial machinery from the point of view of the colonial state. Commoners paid their taxes through them and were funneled into construction projects, factories, and plantations of the colonial state by their "traditional" chiefs. Through their chiefs ordinary people became workers, subjects, and spectators of the colonial state. At the same time, rajas and uleebalangs continued to uphold their privileges as "traditional" heads in their own worlds. They painted themselves as the natural leaders of the people, bound by sacred bonds of heritage, and continued to demand unpaid labor from commoners in their houses and grounds.

Islamic officials also entered the encroaching colonial state. When the Dutch incorporated Indonesian states into the Netherlands Indies, they took over many of the obligations and customs of Muslim kings, including the patronage of Islam. For example, the Dutch appointed and paid the salaries of religious officials. The VOC had provided free passage as far as Ceylon for royal delegations going on pilgrimage. The colonial state brought pilgrimage within reach of far more people when it instituted regular steamship service between Batavia and Aden in the 1890s. The colonial government established the Clerics' Council in 1882 to settle issues and establish consensus in Muslim family

Bait ur-Rahman Mosque, Aceh, 1897. The mosque was designed by an Italian architect and constructed with colonial government funds to appease Acehnese over the destruction of their chief mosque during the Aceh War. Photographic Archive, Royal Institute of Linguistics and Anthropology, Leiden, No. 27024. Photo courtesy of the KITLV.

law. It paid government subsidies to schools run by Muslim religious teachers if their curriculum included secular subjects such as arithmetic and Malay language alongside Arabic and theology. Another obligation of Muslim kingship that the colonial government assumed was support of building mosques. In 1933, for example, it donated the cost of a new stone minaret to the principal mosque in Medan. The colonial government, recognizing the leadership of Islamic officials and the weight attached to their actions by the colony's subjects, engaged mosque officials in the business of the colonial state. For instance, they were trained as inoculators during smallpox epidemics and paid to supervise labor on government irrigation projects and plantations. The colonial government also protected Islam by banning Christian missionaries from teaching in Muslim communities or establishing schools and hospitals. This ban was maintained until 1912 in the sultanates of Surakarta and Yogyakarta. Christian missionaries were directed by the colonial government to areas where the local population had not adopted Islam, such as central Sulawesi, northern Sumatra, the interior of Kalimantan, and West New Guinea. Colonial officials also attempted to avoid situations that might give offense to Muslim officials. For instance, the Dutch did not impose unified time zones across the archipelago so as not to alter the prayer times which mark the Muslim day and which were set by mosque officials in thousands of prayer houses across Indonesia.

Non-Muslim government mediated with the leaders of Islam through the Office of Native and Religious Affairs. It issued exit permits to pilgrims, supervised licensed Muslim schools, and was sometimes asked by contending parties to adjudicate issues of Islamic practice. For example, in 1932 factions of the Hadrami community asked the colonial government to settle a dispute regarding the status of sayyids and use of the title. As descendants of Muhammad, sayyids claimed exclusive right to the title and public acknowledgment, such as the hand kiss. Other Hadramis argued that in the modern world sayyid was a title any respectable man could use and was the equivalent of the Malay *tuan* (Mister). Both sides drew on Koran and Hadith to support their arguments. Muslim officials, charged with the conduct of Islamic life in communities across the archipelago, shared a common experience of contact with colonial government. When Muslim leaders outside this system of patronage challenged the colonial government, they included cooperating Muslim officials in their denunciations, prophesied the elimination of "tame" religious officials along with the Christian state, and promised the creation of a true Islamic society that had neither kings nor governors-general nor collaborators.

FANATICS VERSUS FRIENDS OF GOVERNMENT

In Islamic societies, one group of learned religious tended to accept government service as paid officials in religious courts, mosques, schools, and foundations, while another, often regarded by the community as more pious, did not. The latter group lived from income they earned in commerce or land owning and from donations. In Indonesian histories independent ulamas have launched rebellions against sultans, colonial officials, and the Republic of Indonesia.

It is common in the literature on Indonesian Islam to suppose an opposition between Islamic leaders and the aristocracy, but intimate connections of marriage and business usually existed between the two. Daughters of prestigious ulama dynasties married Javanese princes; Buginese rulers appointed their relatives as judges of Islamic courts.

Another common supposition among Western scholars of Indonesia is opposition between *adat* (customary law) and sharia (Islamic law). Nineteenth-century Dutch researchers collected the oral lore of many ethnic groups and compared local traditions with sharia. They found differences, particularly in family matters relating to inheritance of property and residence of married couples. But adat is a word of Arabic origin that Indonesian ethnic groups applied to their traditions. They were placing local usage within a framework of Islam, not in opposition to it. Islamic teachers could be famous for their knowledge of both adat and sharia.

The colonial government drew political lessons from the research. When bringing Indonesian states into the Netherlands Indies, colonial officials appointed as administrators men who were considered experts in customary law. Colonial government declared itself the protector of native custom against the foreign intrusions of the West and of Islam. Colonial officials observed that rebellions against sultans and the Dutch were generally led, not by princes or the official religious hierarchy, but by ulamas who stood outside the patronage system. Colonial policy attempted to preserve division among ulamas. It rewarded cooperative ulamas with public deference, appointments, jobs for their sons, and gifts to their causes, and attempted to isolate independent ulamas by treating them as irrelevant or deriding them as fanatics, while keeping them under surveillance.

All governments of Indonesia have attempted to tame religious leaders. The Japanese army of occupation (1942–1945) brought rural ulamas to the big city, formed an association to contain them, and created "armies of God" for ulamas' youthful followers. The government of President Suharto also created official organizations for ulamas, distributed prefabricated mosque kits to city neighborhoods, incorporated ulamas' views into family legislation, paid for Islamic universities, and broadcast the commemoration of Islamic festivals on state television.

For Indonesians, the colonial state exerted its greatest effect in commerce and labor. The plantations established in sultanates along Sumatra's east coast in the second half of the nineteenth century extended Dutch political, commercial, and police power into the lives of coastal Malays. They altered the economy of Batak communities and stimulated the migration of Bataks to cities on the coast. Plantations introduced Chinese and Javanese into Sumatran space and generated, in the areas of Western enterprise, modern transport and communications systems that connected the region to Java and to Holland. Tobacco was the first plantation crop, followed by rubber, coffee, and sisal, but it remained preeminent in the plantation economy. Its importance exceeded the flow of profits to Holland, for tobacco became part of Indonesian lives and is today a major cause of death.

THE EVIL WEED

The tobacco plant is native to North America. Its introduction to the archipelago, along with the habit of smoking, was a consequence of Spanish and Portuguese sea voyagers who linked Europe, the Americas, Africa, and Asia in the sixteenth century. Indonesian men and women quickly developed a habit for tobacco, which became part of rituals of hospitality and was enjoyed as a mild narcotic and a refreshment for laborers. Women compressed it into wads and chewed it or shredded it finely and added it to betel wraps. Men rolled tobacco, dipped it into opium, and smoked it.

Tobacco also came to archipelago communities through the VOC. Some of the tobacco imported to Amsterdam from the Americas was re-exported to the Indonesian islands, where it was again sold. Tobacco was often among the gifts VOC agents presented to archipelago kings; the company distributed it to sailors, porters, and construction workers as part of their rations. The Dutch also spread the habit of pipe smoking, for the VOC purchased clay pipes from factories in Gouda and shipped them to island markets. Tobacco was also shipped in rolls. Rolling tobacco was a female industry in Holland. Women stripped the leaves, then laid them out on a table and passed them through a wheel which twisted the leaves into a roll.

Indonesians developed a distinctive cigarette, called *kretek,* that mixes cloves with the tobacco. Cigarette manufacture began as a cottage industry. It became a site of competition and conflict between entrepreneurs who characterized themselves as Muslim or indigenous and those they labeled Chinese or foreign. Since the 1950s the cigarette industry has been controlled by Chinese factory owners and distributors. Locally made cigarettes circulate without government health warnings; smokers smoke in public places; and nicotine has replaced cholera, smallpox, and dysentery as a major threat to health.

Tobacco requires hot, humid conditions to thrive. It quickly became part of a farmer's crops. Long before Dutch companies started plantations, Javanese farmers were raising tobacco, alongside food crops, in Kedu, Bagelen, and Banyumas for sale to local markets. In northeastern Sumatra, Batak farmers, who practiced mixed agriculture in forest clearings, raised tobacco together with maize, rice, pepper, and gambier. They gathered rattan from the surrounding forest and panned for gold along riverbeds. They exchanged their surpluses with coastal Malays for textiles, salt, opium, tools, and household implements. The possibilities prompted many Bataks to leave their hill homelands and migrate to the east coast ports, where by the 1820s Bataks were becoming the majority ethnic group. For example, Serdang had three thousand Malays and eight thousand Bataks; Langkat had a population of seven thousand Malays and thirteen thousand Bataks. Bataks who converted to Islam in the ports exchanged their Batak names for names taken from Arab history and tradition and identified themselves as Malays. In this way they escaped the discriminatory taxes sultans imposed on non-Muslims and the social opprobrium attached to the non-Muslim. They also gained the tools for literacy. Batak was written into Arabic script, and the sons of well-to-do converts discovered a world of ideas and inventions beyond the related hill tribes.

To increase tobacco exports, coastal sultans attempted to extend their authority into the Batak hills. To increase production they turned to the colonial state for capital, technical input, and organization. In 1860 the sultan of Labuan sent an envoy to Batavia in an attempt to interest Dutch trading houses in investing in tobacco. He licensed Jacobus Nienhuys to advance cash to Bataks to raise tobacco in their jungle clearings. The farmers were to sell exclusively to Nienhuys, who would export the processed tobacco only through ports under the sultan's control. Nienhuys could not tempt Batak farmers to reduce their other crops and raise only tobacco. He then leased land from the sultan and attempted to hire Malays and Bataks as wage laborers. When he was unable to recruit sufficient numbers of men, Nienhuys sent agents to Penang and hired 120 Chinese to work in teams under their own leaders. He allocated each leader a subdivision of his lease, distributed seedlings, and contracted with them for exclusive purchase of the harvest.

Although the initiative for joint business ventures came from Sumatran sultans, they were quickly swallowed into the colonial state of regulation, invention, and growth. European capital and European regulations engulfed the Batak farmer's export sideline and the private planter's business. Around 1870 the Chinese team leader became an overseer working under the direction of company managers, rather than an independent contractor putting a team of workers into the field. Now managers determined planting methods and weeding and harvesting schedules, submanagers transmitted orders to overseers, and workers were hired as individual laborers.

Europeans now dictated the way tobacco was to be integrated into east Sumatra. Tobacco, grown as a single crop, rapidly withdraws nutrients from the soil. One hundred and thirty years ago the solution was to plant a field to tobacco for one season only, and then allow the soil quality to rebuild over eight to ten years by the activity of other crops until the field was again suitable for growing tobacco. Tobacco plantations, therefore, required immense holdings. The European company leased land from the Malay sultan who claimed control of the hinterland. Imported laborers cleared vast tracts of land permanently of trees and dense vegetation using shovels, axes, and picks. Tobacco was planted in the cleared ground, and at harvest the entire plant was uprooted. The indigenous population was then allowed use of the land again to grow their rice, maize, and peanuts. When the land's fertility was restored, the Bataks were required by the plantation company to move to another former tobacco site to raise their food crops, and the imported labor force was brought back to plant tobacco again.

Under this system, laborers imported from China, Malaya, and Java lived in barracks on the plantation. They cleared land and raised tobacco, harvested it, transported it to drying sheds, and made it into cigar wrappers. Bataks who grew rice and maize on former tobacco clearings were forbidden to raise tobacco themselves, nor were they permitted to cut wood and rattan in the forest. Although not employees of the plantation company, Bataks lived under its authority. Plantation companies reduced Bataks from businessmen raising crops for sale to farmers raising crops for local consumption alone. Bataks also filled jobs related to the plantation as policemen and trackers of runaway workers. A bounty was paid for every returned employee, so that little sympathy developed among the Bataks for the imported laborers. From 1881 Batak chiefs received a share of the lease money planters paid the Malay sultans.

The sultans acquired large sums of cash in rent. They built European-style palaces, added to their female retainers, entertained Chinese and European businessmen lavishly, and made pleasure trips to the Malay Peninsula to spend their money at British racetracks. Before the period of profitable leases, sultans lived in modest wooden homes on piles. They were approachable mediators and brokers. Regular cash income turned them into grandees living on a level far removed from ordinary folk. In 1946, when angry mobs turned against the ruling classes all over Indonesia, the east coast sultans and their families were murdered and the sultanates abolished.

Tobacco was a profitable investment for Europeans. In 1873 there were thirteen tobacco plantations in east Sumatra. By 1876 there were forty, each employing around two hundred workers. The first plantations were run by a single planter, but very soon the lessors of land from Malay sultans were companies that were closely tied to banks and their concern for maximizing profits. Workers had no bargaining power against their bosses and no means to improve wages and conditions. In colonial legend, histories, and novels, the east coast of Sumatra was a new frontier, a remote, empty corner of the archipelago untouched by commerce, against which a tiny number of whites, barely controlling a mutinous work force, ripped out the jungle and tamed the land. The Sumatran experience can be seen more accurately as an example of shifting cultivation on an immense scale. Two hundred seventy thousand hectares were progressively cleared.

The first plantations were along riverways, so that the prepared tobacco could be transported to the coast and supplies of food brought in by boat. In 1873 Deli, the chief port of the east coast, was included in regular routes of the Royal Dutch Steamship Company. Workers began building the first railway line in 1886. Telephone and telegraph services connected the European plantation staffs to their managers in Deli and these to their directors in the Netherlands. A branch of the colonial post office was opened in Medan, the European city that developed around Deli, followed by branches of Batavia banks. The area was incorporated administratively into the Netherlands Indies in 1887 as the East Coast Residency with Medan as its capital. In 1908 the

Dutch guilder, the official currency of the Indies, displaced the British Straits dollar. The area's orientation to Penang was further reduced when the Indies government opened up Belawan as an international port to replace Singapore and Penang as outlets for plantation exports.

Rubber plantations followed tobacco and contributed to fusing Indonesian peoples into the colonial state. The pneumatic tire was invented in 1888. Rubber was suddenly in demand for bicycles and, after 1905, for the automobile industry. Rubber is the manufactured product of the sticky substance which oozes from a rubber tree when its bark is cut. The world's rubber came from trees that grew wild in South and Central America, in Malaya, and in equatorial Africa. Its use had long been known to Malays who extracted latex as a sideline to farming. The cultivation of rubber trees on plantations is the product of European research institutes that developed techniques of seed selection, spacing of trees, ground cover, tapping, and processing the latex into sheets of rubber.

European companies began planting rubber trees on freshly cut forest land along the east coast of Sumatra in the late 1880s. They imported Chinese and Javanese men to cut down the jungle and plant rubber trees in straight rows. They imported Javanese women to tap the trees and work in the rubber-processing factories. Rubber plantations brought with them gangs of laborers to construct roads and railway lines connecting factory to port and linking rubber territories to the world.

Rubber brought high prices. Sumatran farming families planted rubber trees along the borders of their fields. They had the labor and skills to tend and tap trees and process the latex. By the early twentieth century, Indonesian small holders produced much of the rubber exported from Sumatra, an example of Indonesian response to opportunities created within the colonial state. Indigenous cultivators quickly applied the findings of rubber research institutes, which were financed and directed by Europeans. They were neither conservative nor otherworldly peasants, but entrepreneurs who took from modern science and produced for modern markets.

Sumatran plantation workers were called coolies, a term with negative connotations. Although it conjures an image of a male laborer detached from home and female society, it also designates in Indonesian histories the female laborer. In 1905, five thousand of the sixty-two thousand Javanese coolies in the East Coast Residency were women. But plantation populations were predominantly male and adult. Only the surrounding Batak and Malay communities had normal proportions of women, children, and men. The Javanese coolie was not a person created by commercial agriculture and imperial capitalism; he or she was already detached from the land. Labor recruiters found workers searching for a day's pay carrying goods, working on a construction site, weeding, or selling sex; they could be found on the main roads, at river crossings, at markets, in ports, and at pilgrimage sites. These were mobile laborers who became immobile only when they signed a contract to work for a fixed number of years on a Sumatran plantation. Many ended up as permanent settlers in Sumatra. Those who returned landless to the Javanese village resumed the coolie's prior drifting in search of paid employment.

Coolies found the regime of work on the plantation new, for it entailed fixed hours (sunup to sundown), supervision by a foreman who was of another Indonesian ethnic group or Chinese, and ultimate subordination to the European manager. Some coolies provided personal services for Europeans: male coolies were servants and messengers; female coolies worked in European households as cooks, laundresses, and sex partners. Coolies were treated as unmarried, even though many married men and women were recruited. In the plantation barracks they were cut off from the moral order of domestic life. Male coolies' competition among themselves and with their bosses for the few women was the cause of most murders on plantations.

Employers justified a lower female wage by assuming women would make extra money selling sex and domestic services to men in the barracks. Women coolies could not afford not to work, and so few bore children on the plantation. Coolie work on Sumatran plantations differed from labor on sugar plantations and railway work teams on Java where workers were hired as family units, with specific tasks assigned to men, women, and children. The work load in Java fluctuated during the year, as many workers lived at home and maintained their own vegetable plots and other income-producing jobs.

Coolie labor in Sumatran history is also associated with a short period of recruiting Chinese men. From 1863, recruiters sought Chinese workmen in Penang and also went directly to villages in China. By 1900 there were one hundred thousand Chinese coolies on Sumatran tobacco plantations. Few men returned to China upon completion of their work contract. Some hired themselves to planters as recruiters or as free laborers and foremen. Others went into businesses that served the plantations: they bred pigs, raised vegetables, or ran shops, gambling, and opium centers. Others moved to new cities, such as Medan, to fill jobs as wage laborers and shopkeepers. Only in the first years, when tobacco cultivation was becoming a European business, were Chinese the majority of the labor force. Javanese workers were preferred by plantation managers because they were considered to be more docile workers than the Chinese.

Plantations were a closed society. Coolies were ruled by violence. Verbal abuse, blows, canings, poor food, overwork, and overcrowding were the lot of most coolies. The Coolie Ordinance of 1880 represented an attempt by the colonial government to define the rights and obligations of employer and employee, while serving the interests of plantation companies by maintaining a low-paid labor force in place. The central feature of the ordinance was a written contract, registered with local government, for every coolie. The contract specified a ten-hour work day for a three-year period. The contract required the employer to pay wages regularly, provide medical care, lodging, washing and drinking water. The employer had to return coolies to the place of recruitment, if they wished, upon completion of their contract. The Ordinance also determined punishment of coolies for running away, refusing to work, acting disorderly, and fighting. The colonial police force arrested runaway employees and returned them to their employer. A Labor Inspectorate was established in Medan in 1905 where coolies could register complaints about mistreatment, but it was ineffective because the employer could still bar workers from leaving the workplace.

Conditions on European plantations were so bad that China sent a mission in 1886 to interview Chinese community leaders, merchants, and coolies. The mission's findings led China to attempt to establish consulates in the Nanyang to protect men it had formerly regarded as refuse and traitors. The Indies government rejected China's efforts to represent Chinese working in the colony until 1912 when it authorized a consulate in Batavia.

Migration from China ended in 1931. The world depression had made itself felt in the plantation business. By then the plantation work force was almost wholly Javanese, and managers preferred to hire families over unattached men. In place of gambling and opium establishments and prostitution, plantations had family housing, clinics, and schools. A plantation schoolmaster in 1920 was Tan Malaka (1897–1949). He was also a paid employee of the Comintern, a writer and visionary, and an opponent of Indonesian "feudalism" and colonialism. During the struggle for independence Tan Malaka opposed the republican government's strategy of negotiation and compromise. In 1949, the friend of coolies was executed by the new National Army of Indonesia.

Christian missionaries also brought Indonesians into the colonial state. Mission fields were planted in the farthest corners of the territory thought of as Dutch by policymakers in Batavia. Attachment to the religion of the colony's rulers made Indonesian Christians conscious boundary markers, and the things they shared with the Dutch—education, training, orientation, sympathy—made them mobile within Indies space.

The first conversions on Roti dated to 1729, when some political leaders became Christian. Roti Island lies in the far southeast of the Indonesian archipelago. Its economy was based on the palm tree, vegetables, rice, fishing, and pig-rearing. Its natural sea network linked it into the histories of Ndao, Sawu, the Solor islands, Butung, southern Sulawesi, and the northern coast and islands off Australia. Roti's oral histories told of the origins of fire and house building, the domestication of plants and animals, and the genesis of the Roti people in the mating of heaven and earth. Elaborate genealogies linked people to ancestors and home districts. The Dutch found no one king with whom they could deal when they first sailed to Roti in the 1660s. They negotiated treaties with men who seemed prominent. Recognition by foreign (Dutch) merchants confirmed the status of these local leaders and formalized their power. The eighteen domains and powerful families with whom the Dutch negotiated in 1662 hardened into the political structure of the island. They lasted until the late 1960s when they were abolished by the Republic of Indonesia.

By the middle of the nineteenth century most of Roti's ruling families were Christian, and by the middle of the twentieth most ordinary Rotinese were too. At the time of contact, the Rotinese had not devised or borrowed a script to give permanent record to their language. Rotinese took from the Dutch the Roman alphabet and literacy. The first school on Roti was opened in 1735. Church and school positioned Roti people within the archipelago's broader history, for church and schools used the Malay language, rather than Rotinese or Dutch. Their Malay was written in the Roman alphabet, so that these most remote peoples were connected to Europe, not Mecca. Church and school brought Roti into an arc of Christian space enclosing the Dutch state and its center in Batavia. Dutch schools gave the Rotinese, ultimately, the language of citizenship in independent Indonesia.

Minahasa, on the northeastern peninsula of Sulawesi, was a fringe territory of the sultanate of Ternate. It realized an independent existence through links to the Dutch and conversion to Christianity. The region was home to a number of ethnic groups whose oral traditions linked their ancestors to loosely defined districts. Religious ritual honored ancestors. Men attained status by giving feasts and taking heads. The oldest treaty between tribal leaders and the Dutch, dating from 1679, defined land borders to west and east and freed the tribes from tax obligations to the sultan of Ternate. VOC interest in the area was its rice, which it shipped to the Maluku sago regions. In 1796 the VOC distributed coffee plants to chiefs and required them to supervise the growing of coffee on mountain slopes and delivery to VOC agents.

The company constructed a territory within which small ethnic groups could grow into the Minahasa people. The colonial government introduced Christianity, which created their sense of a common identity. The first Protestant mission arrived in 1831. Within fifteen years, eleven thousand of the population, which then numbered around ninety-three thousand, had converted; by 1880 three-quarters of the population had been baptized. State and church brought an end to tribal warfare and head-hunting. They offered men status through government jobs and leadership in church in place of the feast-giving that promised the living a future status as a sacred ancestor. State and church brought a Dutch sense of order to how people lived: adat was collected and assigned its geographic space; villages were rebuilt with roads and houses in straight lines. Husbands became head of the household, and the old understanding of marriage as an alliance of families was replaced with the Christian concept of union of two individuals. Mission schools taught in Malay. They amalgamated tribal myths into a common history and created a sense of Minahasa through the Dutch-drawn map in the classroom. An us-them mentality distinguished Christians from Muslims. Missionaries trained indigenous men to be preachers and teachers and by the end of the nineteenth century handed over control of their work to the independent Indies Reformed Church.

Minahasans were drawn into the colonial economy as producers and exporters of rice, coconuts, coffee, and cloves. The population doubled between 1850 and 1895. Two-thirds of the peninsula's forest gave way to permanently cultivated fields. When Batavia established a government school system that offered streams of education in Malay and Dutch, Minahasan parents enrolled sons and daughters. More than 10 percent of all government schools in the archipelago were located in the small territory of Minahasa. Minahasan men were equipped to venture into the rest of colonial space as soldiers, administrators, clerks, and professionals. They moved easily through hierarchies policing, teaching, and organizing the daily life of Muslims in the colonial state.

Sharing education, religion, and language with the colonial ruling class gave Minahasans the ability to see themselves as something more than village people or members of an adat community. They perceived themselves as *bangsa Minahasa* (Minahasans), developed, civilized. It was a view shared by the Dutch. Minahasans were the first to participate in ruling colonial territory. In 1919 adult males with a minimum annual income of three hundred guilders elected thirty-six members to the Minahasa Council, Indonesia's first elected assembly. Minahasans also elected delegates to the People's Council, which the Dutch established in 1916 to be an assembly of men, some elected and some appointed by government, from all regions and population classifications of the Indies, to debate colonial policies. Minahasans also took part in nationalists' discussions over how to turn Dutch colony into self-governing state. They championed regional autonomy within a federation of the states that had been bound into the Netherlands Indies.

Indonesian subjects of sultans entered the colonial state through the European steamship. Commercial steam-powered ships were sailing in European waters by the 1830s. From the 1860s they began regular operations within the archipelago. By the end of the nineteenth century, naval steamships had established Dutch authority over all the archipelago sea-lanes, intimidated local rulers, put down "pirates," provided security for licensed trading vessels, and helped end interisland slave raiding and trading.

The greater control the Dutch could now impose profoundly affected Dutch and Indonesian lives. Dutch residents of the archipelago could maintain personal and intellectual contacts with Europe when steamships brought letters, newspapers, magazines, opera companies, and travelers. Participation in Indonesian cultures became less important for Dutch residents as they mixed with the rapidly increasing number of Dutch officials, businessmen, adventurers, wives, and working women that the steamships brought every month to Batavia. As a result, European suburbs developed in archipelago cities. These enclaves became irritants to those excluded by color and religion. In this way the steamship contributed to the growth of movements for self-rule.

The first steamship built by Indonesian laboring men, constructed in Surabaya in 1825, was used to carry mail between Java and other islands. Steamship services in time connected all the islands within the Indonesian archipelago, bringing affordable transport with set freight charges and predictable arrival and departure times. Peoples' lives ceased to be controlled by wind patterns and distance from sea highways. Farming men and women could find new outlets for their produce; their sons could escape into new occupations by a period of schooling in a distant town or island. The path to Mecca or The Hague began on a feeder service to the port of call for the Royal Dutch Steamship Company. Expanding travel services helped generate identities no longer bounded by village and district town. Regular contact with peoples and products from other islands launched some people on the way to a conception of Indonesia as a political and cultural unit.

Ports on the steamship routes were transformed, for they needed large, permanent labor forces for shipyards, specialist services for seamen and other visitors, and staff for offices of customs inspections. Indonesian craft brought in cargo from ports too small to host steamships. Railway lines connected production centers to ports, and tram lines within cities transported people and mail to the ports. Because work was permanent and year-round, laborers settled in ports with their families, expanding the residential quarters of the working poor. Important dock workers' and railway workers' unions formed in the harsh environments of ports in the 1920s.

Steamships played a key role in the expansion of the colonial state. They transported troops as well as the mail, and the regular arrival of the steamship was a visible sign of an organizing center. Steamship routes directed people and the flow of information to Batavia. From 1866 to 1890, routes, ports, and schedules were developed by the Netherlands Indies Steamship Company. It was owned, financed, and operated by the British India Steam Navigation Company, which directed Indies mail, products, and passengers from the archipelago to the outside world through Singapore and a web of British connections. From 1891 all government business went to the Royal Dutch Steamship Company, a private company. Its job was to direct shipping to Batavia, so that export products, people, and mail began their journeys to Europe and Arabia from the Dutch Indies capital, not Singapore. In this way, a private company reinforced colonial borders and helped foster the idea of an archipelago union distinct from the British colony in the western end of the archipelago.

The steamship operated as part of an organization that had its headquarters in Holland, backed by international capital. With offices and agents throughout the archipelago, it managed ports and a labor force, coal and food supplies, and cargo distribution systems. Its Indonesian staff of skilled, semiskilled, and manual laborers came into intimate contact with the modern world. Some Indonesians were graduates of new machine shops and technical education. All were paid in cash and bought packaged foods and manufactured clothing, consumed urban services, and were potential clients for newspapers, schools, adult literacy programs, and labor unions.

The steamship altered the relationship of ordinary pious folk in the archipelago to Islam. Dutch steamship routes led to Arabia as well as to ports in the archipelago, Singapore, and Europe. The pilgrimage, now a two-week voyage, became possible for the ordinary man who had savings. By the 1920s, fifty thousand men undertook the journey each year. Mecca and Medina became real instead of imagined places in the thinking of Indonesians. They superseded journeys to Imogiri and other acts that ulamas had once said were the equivalent of going to Mecca, such as reading a holy text. The Dutch steamship forged a connection to another set of men and another kind of politics.

Archipelago kings were quick to recognize the implications of the steamship. The wealthy attempted to secure for themselves this latest invention. Sultan Alauddin Muhammad Daud Syah of Aceh sent agents to purchase a steamship from the British. This act supplied one of the reasons propelling the Indies government to invade his kingdom in 1873.

Colonial space was created by conquest. Over half a century, military expeditions were fitted out in Java and launched into the archipelago from Aceh to Bali. The modern gun developed for wars in Europe and America was quickly applied to warfare in Asia. Mass manufacture meant that the Dutch had supplies and spare parts; they had fast ships, telegraphic communications, and flat-bottomed gunboats that enabled them to sail up shallow rivers to resupply troops. But the colonial wars fought by the Dutch around the archipelago between 1890 and 1914 were not won by the latest Western weapons technology. Modern guns were designed for wars fought on plains. Indonesia's battlefields were mountains covered with dense undergrowth, inhabited by tigers, wild pigs, snakes, leeches, and biting insects. Dutch wars were largely fought and won by Indonesian troops. Javanese, Timorese, Ambonese, Buginese, and Minahasan soldiers, trained in Western drill, were equipped with swords as well as rifles. They operated in small mobile groups and brought districts under control by advancing a string of forts and patrolling the territory around them.

Archipelago armies ceased to be an obstacle to the Dutch in the 1890s. Colonial standing armies of Dutch and Indonesian troops confronted formidable opponents in Aceh fighters, who made lightning attacks from inaccessible mountain hideouts. Colonial troops could be overtaken when Buginese fast-sailing boats suddenly pulled out of a hidden bay, or Balinese, massed in groups, acted in unpredictable ways, such as launching suicide attacks. But local armies held together by enthusiasm, not by regular training or a supporting technical culture that could build and maintain seemingly limitless supplies of weapons. The Indonesian soldier in Dutch service was an unconquerable adversary, whereas the Indonesian soldier, conscripted by kings or lured to martyrdom in holy war by a charismatic leader, was a foe who could be defeated.

For people who passed through colonial landscapes enclosed in their own world, the state remade by the Dutch was simply irrelevant because of the central focus of their lives or their gender. Such people are reminders that the things that stand out so strongly in histories of the nineteenth century—colonial policy, railways, and plantations—did not dominate the thoughts of the

Dutch and Indonesian soldiers on patrol in Aceh, 1890s. Conquest introduced the latest in technology, here steel rails and bicycle-powered transport. Photographic Archive, Royal Institute of Linguistics and Anthropology, Leiden, No. 10,219. Photo courtesy of the KITLV.

majority of the population. While many Javanese may have been wage laborers in a sugar factory and purchasers of packaged food, their lives revolved around their religious leader, their kiai. They listened to his teaching, attended to his comforts, and drew near him in their leisure hours to feel the grace of his physical presence.

TRAVELERS THROUGH COLONIAL TIME: MAS RAHMAT AND ADRIANA DE STUERS–DE KOCK

The diary of a Javanese kiai gives a glimpse of another world within colonial space. Mas Rahmat, a trader, owned large lands in Banyumas that were under the management of his wife. He had an extensive pesantren education in Arabic texts and Javanese literature. Between 1883 and 1886 he wandered through central Java and Madura, visiting pesantrens, meditating in caves, telling fortunes, and preaching. He kept a record of who acknowledged his learning and mystical insights, judging by the hospitality he received, the gifts of food and clothing, the numbers who came to sit as he spoke, who kissed his hand. His journeys took him through a Java remade by deforestation, permanent fields, railway lines, telegraph poles, plantations, factories, and towns, peopled with Javanese clerks and policemen and Dutch inspectors on horseback. Yogyakarta, where Mas Rahmat claimed royal relatives, was home to a Dutch club, musical societies, and a garrison. Javanese workers were putting in longer hours than ever before, financing Dutch invasions of Aceh and Bali and the expansion of colonial government departments for education, agriculture, forestry, irrigation, and public health. None of this is noted in the diary. The colonial world had no existence in this text of Javanese composed in Arabic script.

Letters written by Adriana de Stuers–de Kock from 1836 to 1840 record another world within the colony. Her father had headed the Dutch contingents that fought against Diponegoro's armies, and her husband had escorted the defeated prince from Magelang to Batavia in 1830 as he began his journey into exile. Adriana left no personal record of the politics of Java. Women's lives, where they are recorded, depended on education. Adriana is known through letters she wrote from the Indies to her father following his return to Holland.

Adriana was born in Surabaya in 1809, grew up in Batavia, and married her father's adjutant in 1828. In 1837 her husband was appointed governor of Maluku, at a time when the Dutch were facing revolts. The ship carrying the new governor and his family, passengers, and crew of 140 was wrecked on a coral reef, where they were stranded for four weeks. Adriana, who was expecting her fifth child at the time, composed letters to her father in the formal French of the Dutch elite, describing the weeks of waiting to die as Indonesians and Dutch clung to the reefs. The shipwrecked were eventually rescued and brought to Ambon, where Adriana survived the births of more children and continued the correspondence with her father.

Adriana's letters show that Dutch women in the Indies saw themselves at the heart of a domestic circle with its endless concerns for the health of its members, the raising of children, love for relatives far and near. They also show how literacy oriented women to Europe. She has nothing to say to the retired military commander about colonial politics, race, or her husband's career in a tense period of Maluku history. Her world is as separated from the colonial as Mas Rahmat's. Pesantren education enabled Mas Rahmat's observations to be preserved in Javanese written in Arabic script and sealed him off from contact with the Dutch; European language schooling sealed Adriana off from the Indonesian world.

Some Indonesians, like Tuanku Imam Bonjol, were very conscious of the colonial world and stood in total opposition to it. Others were seduced by European culture. Their disposition and talents made them people of two worlds, accepted fully by neither. Such a person was the painter Raden Saleh, whose life spanned the nineteenth century. He was descended from Yogyakarta nobility and Arab immigrants; his uncles were princes and hajis. Some of his relatives were on the Dutch payroll as district government head and chief religious officer; others joined Diponegoro in his war against the Dutch and their Javanese friends. The war made colonial rulers want to attach important Javanese families to themselves. As a boy, Saleh was taken to Batavia as a candidate for the colonial civil service and given an education that included Dutch language, drawing, and draftsmanship. In 1829 he was given the job of accompanying a Dutch official to the Netherlands and, during the long sea voyage, of teaching him Javanese and Malay.

Raden Saleh's trip extended to twenty-three years in Europe. The Dutch government financed his studies in painting, and Saleh supplemented his income through commissions to paint portraits of the rich. He presented himself as an "eastern prince," dressed in a tightly fitting black jacket with elaborate brocade, a richly batiked sash, Javanese headdress, gold, and diamonds. He was guest of the royal houses of Europe. He painted large canvases of wild animals, horses, and nature in violence. His paintings were hung in public galleries and exhibitions across Europe. His connections to the official world made him the painter of former governors-general, including Johannes van den Bosch, creator of the cultivation system, and J. C. Baud, founder of Javanese studies in the Netherlands, whom Raden Saleh honored as his stepfather.

In 1853, Saleh returned to Java to take up residence in Batavia, where he attempted to introduce the latest in Western painting tastes and techniques to European and Javanese artists. He mixed in elite circles which, in the colonial capital, meant with Europeans and Eurasians. He secured his financial position by marrying a Eurasian woman who was heir to large property in the Cikini area of Batavia. It is not clear from colonial or Javanese records how this interracial union was viewed in Batavia and Yogyakarta, or whether the wedding ceremony was Muslim or Christian. On his property the new husband built a house of Gothic fantasy which can be seen in old photograph albums, and he copied the rulers of Java in maintaining on his grounds an animal collection, which later formed the core of the Jakarta Zoo.

When Raden Saleh returned to Java in 1853, the Indies government had just legislated the right of Indonesians to government schooling. Saleh, who had been named royal painter to William III in 1850, was appointed curator of the colonial government's art collection. One task was to restore the paintings of VOC-era governors-general. He continued to paint for royal patrons in Europe. In 1857 Raden Saleh completed for the king of Holland a painting symbolizing Java's subjugation: he painted the arrest of Prince Diponegoro. He also indulged in the scientific interests of the cultivated European in Java, collecting babads and fossils and becoming the first Indonesian to join the Batavian Academy of Arts and Sciences.

In 1866 Saleh divorced his Eurasian wife to marry a woman connected to Yogyakarta's royal house. He painted portraits of the Yogyakarta royal family and of his own near relatives. The men he painted were those whose incomes were derived from salaries or pensions paid by the Indies government and whose affinity for the colonial world inclined them to disregard the Islamic prohibition on representational art. They included Raden A. A. Koesoemoningrat, chief official of Cianjur; his grandfather, Kiai Bustam Kertodiningrat who was the chief official of Majalengka; and Sultan Hamengkubuwono VI. With his raden ayu, Saleh made a second, brief tour of Europe in 1878–79. He died and was buried in Bogor, site of the governor-general's hill palace, in 1880.

Nationalist history has few words for men such as Raden Saleh. He has no place in a past presented as continuous opposition between European and Indonesian. Where class is introduced into analysis, it is not difficult to perceive how men of different races and religions shared common intellectual interests and hobbies and felt a sense of distance from itinerant coolies and tenant farmers. Raden Saleh belonged to the elites that ruled Java. He lived in an era when only "fanatics" opposed the alliance of Dutch and Javanese aristocracy.

A generation later, the sons of privileged classes began to devise a different set of alliances to rule the state created by the Dutch. Some sought a revival of Javanese culture and ancient territorial reach; some thought of allying with the sons of datus and rajas and creating an Indonesian identity out of the many ethnic groups crowded into colonial space. Others considered using ulamas to deliver to their followers a vision of an independent state subordinated to the ruling classes of "tradition," with the new subordination made acceptable by being dressed in Islamic language and appeals to Muslim solidarity. In the last years of colonial rule they mixed the practices of modernity with the claims of class and birthright to rule. The many male voices raised to condemn colonialism, imperialism, and government by non-Muslims almost drowned out the few female voices that understood modernity to include women's rights to monogamy, health, and education. These new women shared with men of their class the view that Indonesia's common folk needed to be controlled and guided by ruling classes who combined inherited privilege and Western schooling.

10

BREAKING DEPENDENCE ON FOREIGN POWERS

During the first fifty years of the twentieth century, as Indonesia's ruling classes diversified in composition and outlook they experimented with new alliances. Sultans tried cautiously to relaunch themselves by patronizing the new cultural clubs and political organizations of young men freshly graduated from European and Middle Eastern schools. They lent their covert support to groups the Dutch perceived as "troublemakers," while feigning partnership with the Dutch. Young reformers found adat chiefs and sultans to be in their way; like Dutch men, the protected rulers monopolized top honors and positions in the colony. New graduates formed associations whose Dutch or Arabic names reflected their educational experiences. They tried alliances of men based on shared education, ethnicity or region of origin. They experimented in combining associations into federations, making political ideology or religious commitment the basis for union. These organizations challenged the alliance of Dutch colonials and Indonesian royals. Young women of the Indonesian elites formed associations based on their relationship to men as wives, daughters, and mothers. New groups and old minorities renegotiated alliances. Christian Ambonese demanded partnership with the Dutch because their soldiers had helped expand and enforce Dutch military power across the archipelago. Chinese Indonesians began rethinking their relation to their ancestral homeland and the land of their

Pakubuwono X in Batavia. This photograph tells three stories: the wealth and privilege of colonial-era kings; the incorporation into popular images of symbols of modernity; and the retention of royal prerogative. Photographic Archive, Royal Institute of Linguistics and Anthropology, Leiden, No. 13,368. Photo courtesy of the KITLV.

birth. The Dutch ruling class diversified too. Locally born Dutch men attempted to form partnerships with Javanese nobles, Eurasians, and Chinese to wrest power from Holland. Some Eurasians wanted to end their partnership with the Dutch and create their own state within the colony.

The Netherlands Indies still made money for Dutch companies. The colony's working poor were bound to Holland's new factory workers. Javanese, Minangkabau, Batak, and Toraja farmers grew coffee, tea, sugar, and tobacco that were hunger killers for Holland's workers. Chinese coolies and Indonesian smallholders produced rubber for the bicycle tires that took Dutch workers to jobs and shops. Dutch factory workers produced the cheap clothing, matches, kerosene lamps, and sewing needles that Indonesian plantation workers purchased with their wages. This was not an alliance that the working poor could break.

There was great competition and jockeying for power within the colonial state. Young graduates of Western schools who became acquainted with socialist concepts, denounced their elders as "feudal" and the Dutch as "imperialist." Some romanticized the "little people" and debated in clubs how to raise their living standards and cultural level. Men who had never known manual labor set up unions for working men (but not for working women). Identifying colonialism as the cause of low wages and unregulated work sites, they offered anticolonial struggle to workers, but not a sharing of privilege. New Muslim leaders attempted to break the hold of old-style kiais on their followers. They offered modern schools, health clinics, and study groups in place of cures, amulets, and night vigils at graves. The silent partners in these alliances, working men and women, were encouraged to hate foreign minorities, to condemn the "sinful capitalism" of European and Chinese bosses, and to accept the indigenous capitalism of Muslim landlords and factory owners. Ordinary men, tired of waiting for the promised land, sometimes sought immediate relief in arson, random murder, tax revolts, and mutinous gatherings.

The colonial government permitted public debate through municipal, regional, and national councils that it set up and monitored. The press was censored; political meetings and organizations required permits. The government sought to attach new groups to itself by offering jobs and influence to those who would cooperate. It promised change but controlled the scope of the discussion and the timetable for reform.

In 1942 the Japanese military took over. Indonesian ruling classes of all kinds quickly made accommodation with the new foreign ruler. They discovered that although Indonesian and Dutch soldiers could defeat Indonesian fighters and keep public order, they did not have numbers, supplies, or training to overcome Japanese soldiers. Holland was already a slave state in the German empire; the Netherlands Indies became a slave state in Japan's Asian empire. The Japanese wanted Indonesian resources of rice, rubber, tin, and oil and the unpaid labor of the Indonesian poor. They could not spare Japanese men to obtain what they needed, so, like the Dutch, they offered a partnership to Indonesia's ruling classes. Indonesian elites would deliver men, women, and products to the Japanese; the Japanese would eliminate the Dutch from Indonesia.

In the first half of the twentieth century increased Dutch emigration affected all archipelago societies and classes. The VOC had restricted immigration from Holland. Around 1870, changes in law, communications technology, and medicine combined to produce a sudden increase in the number and kinds of Dutch people in Indonesian societies. The Agrarian Law of

1870 opened the Indies to private entrepreneurs. Steamships traveling through the newly cut Suez Canal landed in Batavia within four weeks of leaving Holland. Underwater cable connected Java to Europe by 1871 and linked European headquarters to Indies businesses and families in Holland to relatives scattered across the archipelago. In 1854 the world's first cinchona plantation had been laid out in west Java, and by the 1870s quinine was being produced from cinchona bark, and daily doses were protecting immigrants from malaria. In the second half of the nineteenth century European suburbs in Indonesian cities got sewage services and clean water supplies. These improvements transformed the archipelago, in the minds of many Hollanders, from a place of fevers, wildness, and sudden death, fit only for bachelors, misfits, the destitute, or the foolhardy, to a landscape remade in the image of Holland. Indonesia became a place where Dutch men, women, and children could spend a short interlude and live Dutch lives. Between 1870 and 1880, 10,000 migrated from Holland. By then the number of people counted as European (a figure including Asian spouses) was approximately 43,000. By 1930, 225,000 people had European status; 60,000 of them were immigrants.

The bridging of distance revitalized a sense of Dutchness in immigrants long resident in the archipelago and created a knowledge of Dutchness among Eurasians. Newcomers took less interest in Indonesian cultures when they had books, music, and friends from home. Female migration meant that more households had a Dutch center. Colonial officials, who previously had wide discretion in policy and were influenced by Indonesian palace and merchant elites in VOC days, could not ignore telegraphed instructions from the minister of colonies. Books and magazines from the Indies informed a Dutch public of colonial affairs and prompted scrutiny by politicians and journalists.

After 1870 Dutch communities scattered across the archipelago had changed. Men employed by private companies or in business for themselves outnumbered government employees and soldiers; there were more women, and there were more households where the partners were married than before. More newcomers meant a greater diversity of opinion and manner of adjusting to Indonesian contexts. Migrants came from a Holland that was transforming itself into a semi-industrialized country, where rights of competing classes were being canvassed and where colonial affairs had become a matter of public debate and political campaigns. By the end of the nineteenth century the parties controlling the Dutch parliament had made moral responsibility the guiding principle for managing "our Indies."

DEBT OF HONOR AND THE ETHICAL POLICY

Batig slot and *batig saldo* are Dutch terms for a credit balance. In colonial history they refer to the profits generated from government plantations on Java and transferred to Holland's budget in the mid-nineteenth century. From the 1840s some Dutch men argued that profits generated by Javanese farmers should be spent on public works in Java rather than on roads and railways in Holland. The transfer from Java to Holland of profits made by the colonial government stopped in 1875. In 1899 a parliamentarian and owner of sugar plantations in Java, Conrad van Deventer (1857–1915), proposed that Dutch taxpayers assume a "debt of honor" and now reimburse Javanese laborers by sending 750,000 guilders annually to Java. Ethical policy was the term that characterized these new directions in colonial government. The term came from a pamphlet entitled "The Ethical Course in Colonial Policy" written by Pieter Brooshooft, a journalist in Java from 1877 to 1904.

Proponents of the ethical policy, called *ethici,* included writers, journalists, lawyers, and government officials in Java. They represented a new middle class of Dutch men who had connections of friendship and affection to the Indonesian world. J. W. Th. Cohen-Stuart, a journalist and lawyer, had a Javanese mother. The Islamic scholar, haji, and government adviser Snouck Hurgronje, was married to daughters of ulamas. The journalist C. E. van Kesteren had been a live-in tutor to the children of the Javanese head of Demak. J. H. Abendanon, a lawyer and government official, raised funds for Indonesian students in Dutch universities and established a foundation to finance schools for girls in Java. These men advocated the expansion of Western-type schooling for Indonesians in Dutch and regional languages. They campaigned to end the import of opium into Java, to abolish unpaid labor services, to develop local crafts and industry, and to expand public health services. On their return to the Netherlands they took up university appointments or entered politics and continued to promote their notion of colonial rule as having a special mission to "uplift" the Natives.

The ethical policy was declared the official agenda of government in 1901. A network of public services, initially on Java, created three-year primary schools in the vernaculars for farmers' and laborers' children, public irrigation works to bring more land under cultivation and increase yields, and rural banks and cooperatives to provide information and loans to small businessmen.

Reformers perceived Dutch leadership to be necessary for Indonesians to achieve the ultimate goal of ethical government, which was self-rule as a province of Great Netherlands. They called for archipelago peoples to be freed from exploitation by their hereditary rulers and from the "fanaticism" of their ulamas. The ethici enthusiastically backed military campaigns to extend Dutch power throughout the archipelago in order to end widow burning and headhunting. They failed to sympathize with Indonesians who wanted uplift, welfare, and self-rule through Indonesian leadership and Indonesian solutions.

Dutch women emigrated during the years when public rhetoric spoke of mission and civilizing duty. Single women who migrated to the Indies could sell their skills to Dutch and Indonesian elites. Teachers of piano and elocution, boutique owners, housekeepers, and seamstresses advertised their services in the colony's newspapers. Some women taught Indonesian and Chinese children in the Dutch-language schools that were multiplying in the early twentieth century. Other women found a place in Christian missions serving regions remote from the busy centers of Muslim populations. Most women accompanied husbands or came to join them.

Dutch wives took up residence in towns where individuals of many races and religions lived close together. To the newcomer, the Indies had an air of sexual licentiousness. Wealthy Indonesians were polygamous, poor Indonesians divorced and remarried, and Dutch men lived with Indonesian partners to whom they were not married and whom they frequently replaced. Dutch women noted with disapproval that mixed-race children born out of wedlock represented the largest group in the birth registers of Europeans and that children of all statuses were left to the care of servants. Wives of colonial reformers contributed their part to Holland's civilizing mission. They offered a vision of womanhood as public wife in a monogamous marriage. They celebrated motherhood as a full-time duty and vocation. They involved themselves in charities on behalf of the colony's Natives. Many had formal relationships with elite Indonesian women that in some cases developed into intimate friendships. Dutch women introduced into the colony's public discourse the rights of Native girls and women to schooling and medical care and they campaigned to end prostitution.

At the time women migrated to the colony, schooling for all social classes and for girls as well as boys was considered the duty of government in Holland, and the right of women to vote was being hotly debated. As soon as they had babies the new female immigrants demanded the Indies government open coeducational schools that taught in Dutch and offered subjects identical to schools in Holland. Histories of Western education in the Netherlands Indies usually explain the new colonial schools by reference to ethical policy ideals and the need for a cheap work force to staff government's multiplying departments. But European primary and secondary schools opened after Dutch women arrived in the colony. From the first, for reasons of economy, schools for Europeans admitted upper-class Indonesian children too. The legacy of Dutch female immigration for modern Indonesia is the formation of a secular and coeducational public school system.

DUTCH SCHOOLS AND COLONIAL RULE

Schools founded by the Dutch are discussed in two ways in the scholarly literature. First, Western schools are said to have produced a modern elite of teachers, doctors and veterinarians who then led the nationalist movement to end Dutch rule. Second, the numbers of schools are counted and the 1930 census used to show that only 6 percent of Indonesians (that is, 250,000 out of a population of around 48 million) were literate. Colonial rule is judged a disgrace for its failure to introduce universal, mandatory schooling, while at the same time it is argued that by spreading Western education, the colonial government buried itself.

This approach focuses on one kind of school. It recognizes as nationalist leaders only graduates of Western schools, and it is vague in its definition of literacy. The 1930 census takers were not instructed to count Indonesians who could read, but not write, Arabic or Malay or Dutch; nor did they count Indonesians who could write in Batak, Javanese, Chinese, or Arabic alphabets. The 1930 census recorded the numbers of Indonesians describing themselves as competent composers of an original letter or document in any language using the Roman alphabet.

Dutch schools occupied specially constructed buildings; pupils progressed through a standardized, graded curriculum; and they were taught by salaried teachers who had an academic diploma. The schools differed from Muslim schools where boys sat together on the floor in their teacher's home, reciting from memory or sharing one book. The Dutch introduced a new kind of school; they did not displace schools that already existed.

Dutch schools had a multiplying effect: their graduates opened private schools modeled on Dutch government schools, as did Christian missions, the Theosophical Society, and Indonesian cultural associations. New Islamic schools also followed the Western model and offered secular subjects as well as religion.

Schools were based on religion, class, or race. The most prestigious government schools were based on class: they admitted Dutch and upper class Indonesian children. The second tier of government schools was based on race. Separate schools for Indonesians, Arabs, and Chinese taught children in Dutch with a Dutch curriculum. Government schools for ordinary Indonesians taught in Malay in the Roman alphabet and "link" schools prepared bright students from the Malay-language stream for entrance to Dutch-language schools. The Taman Siswa schools, founded in 1922 by Ki Hajar Dewantoro, admitted only teachers and pupils defined as "indigenous." Christian and Muslim schools which offered an accredited curriculum also received funds from the colonial government for teachers' salaries and equipment. Christian schools admitted

Muslims and Animists as well as Christian children, but Christians rarely sought admission to the new-style Muslim schools.

Underlying discussion of colonial schools is the question: who should go to school? In Indonesian societies the ability to read and write had been restricted to a few mobile men. VOC schools had used Malay, written in the Roman alphabet, as the language of instruction and aimed at teaching Christian children the fundamentals of church belief and practice, as well as the basics for jobs in navy, army, and trades. Specialized schools for boys included Latin in an academic education, and there were schools for young ladies. From the early nineteenth century, the Indies government established vocational training programs. The colonial constitution of 1854 stated that colonial government had a duty to provide schools for (some) Natives.

Indonesia's constitution of 1945 affirms schooling as a right of all citizens. In 1984 primary school was declared mandatory for all boys and girls; in 1993 the requirement was extended through junior high school. Indonesian government schools have had a multiplying effect, as did colonial government schools. Today, alongside the government secular and religious streams of education, religious organizations and private entrepreneurs operate individual schools and school systems.

The Indies government set up schools and training programs as soon as it had specific needs for clerks, vaccinators, and foresters, but they were for Natives only. In the view of colonial officials, Chinese and Arabs should look to their homelands and governments to educate their children. Neither the vocational schools established during the nineteenth century nor the primary schools opened as part of the ethical program admitted groups the colonial government designated "Foreign Orientals." Government schools therefore perpetuated a sense of difference between people of indigenous and foreign ancestry.

Colonial officials who established schools were employees of an expanding state. They were beginning to conceptualize the Indies as Java plus Outer Islands, whereas formerly the Indies had meant Java alone to them. Now they had to think of the colony as a single work space through which Dutch and

Native would circulate in the course of government service. Prior to 1870, all government schools and training programs had included a course on Malay so that graduates could communicate with groups from other regions who came to Java. Now the directorate for native education had to introduce teacher training and textbooks into an archipelago state containing hundreds of language groups. Government officials settled on one language for one colony and determined what was "standard Malay." In 1908 the colonial government established a publishing firm, the Balai Pustaka, to print grammars, schoolbooks, and novels in this officially approved version of Malay.

Maps, atlases, and globes in the twentieth-century classroom presented students with the new Dutch view of the archipelago as a single state, stretching from Sabang, the northernmost island off Aceh, to Merauke, a town on the border separating West from East New Guinea. "From Sabang to Merauke" became one of Sukarno's slogans in his campaign for independence. Even before children entered colonial schools, they had already entered colonial space. Their parents allowed them to mix with people that religious leaders scorned as kafirs; they tolerated girls and boys together in the classroom; they accepted Dutch and Eurasian women as schoolteachers; and they permitted their boys training that could help them escape manual labor and launch into colonial careers. People who worked for the Dutch as village heads, plantation foremen, soldiers, and domestics were the first to enroll their children in government Malay schools. For them, colonial schools, rather than pesantrens, offered the promise of salaried employment for their children.

From the 1860s training for employment in the colony's civil service was organized into two branches. Senior positions required a five-year university degree and qualifying examination in Holland; lower positions could be filled by men with secondary schooling and examination in the Indies. In practice, the senior positions were held by Dutch immigrants, the lower ones by men born in the colony. Job requirements were standardized as district officials became salaried members of a ranked bureaucracy. Javanese men administering the colony for the Dutch had previously paid themselves by keeping a percentage of the taxes and monopoly crops they collected. They also drew on unpaid labor of people in their districts. After 1867, the colonial government attempted to suppress these "informal" means of raising income and to remake its Javanese employees into professionals whose careers and income were dependent on Batavia.

Many new government schools were opened in the far-off Ambon cluster of islands (Ambon, Haruku, Saparua, Nusa Tenggara). Together with the south and west coastal areas of Seram and Buru, they form the Ambonese cultural area. Ambon's population was roughly split between Muslims and Christians, who lived in separate villages under the control of hereditary rajas and their Christian or Muslim teachers. In 1863 the Dutch gave up their monopoly on the growing and sale of spices. For a few years Ambonese profited from free market sales, but when world prices sank they had no alternative cash crop to incorporate into their fishing and sago economy. At the same time, colonial government was expanding its departments, territories, and functions and accepting the need to recruit Indonesian staff. In Christian villages of Ambon, the colonial government introduced two streams of schools that would produce Malay- and Dutch-speaking graduates. The Malay schools provided former agricultural laborers with careers as soldiers, while the Dutch schools were to make sons of Christian rajas, teachers, and townspeople into civil servants.

Spice growing had kept Ambonese at home on tiny islands at the distant terminus of long trade routes. From the 1890s, colonial schooling drew Christian Ambonese out of Ambon; it made them partners of the Dutch in expanding and administering colonial space. Christian Ambonese who stayed behind and those who traveled into colonial space believed they had a special relationship with the Dutch monarchy. Colonial schooling did not make them into nationalists; rather, it sharpened their awareness of difference from Muslim Ambonese and gave them a sense of superiority over the archipelago's Muslim communities.

Ruling classes did not need colonial education to distance them from manual labor, but a Dutch-language education cemented their alliance with the colony's governors. Rajas and datus were aware that bright young men could rise through education, making a Dutch high school certificate necessary to preserve aristocratic privilege, for Dutch reformers and graduates of Dutch schools all too quickly labeled aristocrats feudal and outdated. Aristocrats sent their children by preference to schools for Europeans. Town dwellers who could afford it sent boys to the Dutch Native Schools. From 1914 there were also widespread demands for university-level education in the Indies. By 1940 colleges for law, medicine, engineering, and agriculture and teacher training institutes had opened. European and Native schools charged tuition, but advanced study in medicine and education was fully financed by the colonial government.

From the last decades of the nineteenth century, a few ruling families with close ties to the Dutch government elite sent their girls to European primary schools, but advanced schooling was closed to Indonesian female students. The medical colleges in Batavia and Surabaya would not accept female applicants, because graduates could be sent as staff doctors to army units in Aceh or

Lombok. Most Indonesian women were full or part-time farmers when the Agricultural Faculty was opened in Bogor in 1941, but no women students were accepted. Colonial officials judged that few rural communities would accept women as agricultural extension agents or supervisors of commercial fishing ponds. Girls wanting careers were directed to kindergarten teaching, midwifery, and public health jobs.

Dutch schooling was outside the daily experience of ordinary Indonesians, but, increasingly, colonial rule bound them into new public and private behaviors in dealing with illness. Ethical policy health programs aimed to reach the entire colonized population. Government health services had their origins in the first decades of the nineteenth century when medical staff were employees of the Military Medical Service. From around 1804, Batavians were vaccinated against smallpox. The Indies government introduced mass vaccination of children up to age five everywhere under its control. By 1870 smallpox ceased to be an important killer on Java, although it attacked communities elsewhere until the late 1920s when the entire archipelago had been brought into the colonial state.

Indonesians were trained as vaccinators. They had to be literate, for they were required to submit to their superiors lists of the names of those they vaccinated. Dutch records include the description "Muslim leaders" and women's names among those who responded to this new job opportunity. Between 1840 and 1900, 377 vaccinators and paramedics were trained in a Batavia hospital. Smallpox vaccination training became the core of a broader program in 1851 producing the "Java Doctor," a man trained in public health care. Java indicated the location of the school, not the ethnicity of the students. Students were Sumatrans and Ambonese as well Javanese. The school included Malay language in the curriculum, allowing its graduates to work anywhere in the archipelago. In the twentieth century paramedical training was upgraded to a full medical degree. Because the long medical education was paid for by the colonial government, a career in medicine attracted men wanting Western schooling. Many of Indonesia's first political leaders were graduates.

The Public Health Service was founded in 1925 to train community health workers, educate people in sanitation, hygiene, and first aid, and to coordinate combating outbreaks of cholera, influenza, and the plague. In 1936 the service employed 316 Indonesian physicians, 177 European doctors, 1,210 Indonesian nurses, and 150 European nurses. There were also 156 public health specialists (for instruction), 435 vaccinators, and 415 plague personnel. Alongside these staff were medical and paramedical workers employed by private institutions such as the Muhammadiyah, Christian missions, and plantation companies. In 1933 a two-year school for training hygiene specialists opened. Between 1935 and 1939, Indonesian inoculators vaccinated 2.9 million people and administered 6.5 million follow-up vaccinations in a population of around 50 million.

WESTERN MEDICINE: COLONIZING THE BODY?

Unlike American and Australian indigenous populations, Indonesians did not die from their exposure to Europeans in the sixteenth century. Indonesians, through their centuries of contact with India and China, had degrees of immunity to diseases of the Eurasian land mass. The impact of disease operated the other way: Europeans died from Indonesian fevers.

Epidemic diseases appear, from Dutch records, to be a phenomenon of the nineteenth and early twentieth centuries, when transport systems introduced new diseases such as cholera into the archipelago and accelerated the spread of known diseases such as smallpox. The influenza epidemic that broke out in Europe in 1918 reached the Indies that same year, and between one and two million people died.

The colonial government imposed drastic measures on areas of Java where plague was prevalent between 1910 and 1940. Infected people were isolated in camps, their houses burned, and autopsies performed where cause of death was not established. The Plague Service, created in 1915, enforced these measures and ran campaigns to boil drinking water and enforce sanitation laws. Despite a government program that rebuilt 2.5 million houses, antiplague measures roused popular hostility. Autopsies caused riots in communities that understood dissection as Christian defilement of Muslim bodies. Relatives sometimes buried bodies clandestinely to avoid autopsy.

The view of Western medicine as another arm of European empire overlooks certain realities in the colony. There were few Western hospitals, clinics, and trained staff; in 1930, for instance, there was only one Western-trained doctor for every 62,500 people in Java. Archipelago populations drew on all kinds of medicine—indigenous, Chinese, Western—and all groups visited holy places for cures of body and mind. Eurasian women wrote medical books on Javanese herbal remedies in Malay and Dutch. It was only after the revolution in medical science in Europe in the second half of the nineteenth century that European doctors grew disdainful of indigenous medical practitioners and left the study of indigenous medicine to anthropologists.

European medical advances assisted in the colonizing of the archipelago, but Indonesians did not turn away from Western medical treatments, such as vaccinations, that could save their children's lives. The doubling of the archipelago's population in the years of ethical policy health programs suggests receptiveness of Indonesians to Indonesian specialists in Western medicine.

Medical schools in independent Indonesia teach Western medicine and practice, including surgery. Community health programs aim at self-help and prevention. Under the Suharto government, as in colonial times, public medicine was under the command of an authoritarian government. Government-sponsored family planning agencies for the poor were particularly coercive.

Indonesians also experienced colonialism as the agent for the transfer of technical training. European economic activity in the Indonesian archipelago promoted crafts already practiced by local craftsmen and women by increasing demand for their services. Government primary and mission schools often taught pre-industrial crafts, too, and included instruction in crop rotation, animal husbandry, plowing, sewing, and first aid to the boys and few girls who attended. But the colonial government also established trade schools and apprenticeship programs for such modern middle-level jobs as surveying, draftsmanship, typesetting, telegraphy, and machine repair. Queen Wilhelmina High School opened in 1900 in Batavia to train machinists, engineers, and miners. Because instruction was in Dutch, the development of scientific and technical vocabularies in Malay was delayed, and many students came from well-to-do households. Technical education gave them a path for social advancement alongside the academic education in law and medicine preferred by those who inherited rank.

The Indies government opened teacher-training institutes in north Sumatra, Manado, and Ambon, but most higher-level schools were in Java. Men from territories incorporated into the Indies between 1860 and 1914 came to consider advanced schooling a purpose of rantau. While sons of farmers and traders embarked on commercial ventures for months of the year, sons of district chiefs and lineage heads spent years of study in Batavia, Bandung, or Surabaya. They boarded with relatives already in place through the rantau network or with Dutch and Eurasian families who took in lodgers. On Java they encountered the visible signs of a long colonial presence and power. They also experienced the force of Javanese numbers, Javanese culture, and Javanese ambitions.

Men from Sumatra and Sulawesi soon discovered that the Javanese were forming organizations, such as Budi Utomo, Muhammadiyah, Sarekat Islam, and Nahdatul Ulama which gave aspects of Javanese tradition modern form and modern insistence. Budi Utomo, which means Glorious Spirit or Endeavor, celebrated the philosophical heritage of Java's Hindu-Buddhist past. It was founded in 1908 by men with aristocratic titles and Dutch schooling who wanted to revive monarchy, remake Javanese culture for the twentieth century, and "raise up" ordinary Javanese. The Muhammadiyah began in the sultanate of Yogyakarta's old religious quarter with the patronage of Sultan Hamengkubuwono VII in 1912. It aimed to help men model themselves on Muhammad in their daily lives by training missionaries and sending them to local mosques. It set up schools, clinics, and charitable organizations parallel to colonial institutions so that Javanese could receive modern schooling, medical care, and assistance without having to submit to Christian staff. Muhammadiyah planted branches in the wider colonial state to give Javanese leadership to the reform of Sumatran and other Islams. By 1938 Muhammadiyah claimed 250,000 members across the archipelago, a network of mosques, schools, clinics, and libraries, and 7,630 missionaries.

Muhammadiyah schools were established as separate institutions with teachers hired and paid by the organization. Students followed a curriculum that gave priority to mathematics, geography, and science over religious subjects. By 1925 the organization was running fifty-five schools with four thousand pupils. Schools separated boys from girls and introduced Islamic clothing that enveloped the body and covered hair and neck for female students. Advanced Arabic classes prepared bright students for study in Egypt. Egyptian schools for girls were regarded by wealthy Muhammadiyah parents as safe places for study. They paralleled the colony's convent boarding schools that sheltered upper-class girls from public scrutiny as they continued their studies beyond primary level.

Budi Utomo and Muhammadiyah were male organizations. Muhammadiyah promoted the segregation of women from men in public life, yet it wanted to remake women Muslims, too. Its solution was to establish a separate organization for women, to found schools and study sessions for girls run by female teachers and preachers. The women's organization took the name Aisyah, after a favorite wife of Muhammad. She represented a model of Islamic behavior not found in Javanese Islam. By 1929 the Aisyah oganization had forty-seven branches and five thousand members, ran thirty-two schools for girls and employed seventy-five female teachers. Budi Utomo also solved the problem of female membership through a separate organization. In 1912 it helped found Puteri Mardika, which means Independent Young Ladies. Through this organization the Dutch-educated sisters of Budi Utomo men could pursue high-minded discussions of uplift for Native women. They were less concerned with Java's past than with its present, and felt a duty to wipe out the ignorance, dirt, disease, and superstition that gripped Java's masses. Neither Budi Utomo nor Puteri Mardika attempted to colonize the Indies' newly acquired territories. They were for upper-class Javanese, but they did join federations such as the Agreement of Indonesian People's Political Associations in 1927 and the Party of Great Indonesia in 1935 to press for more welfare for the masses and increased leadership roles for themselves.

Sarekat Islam, which means Islamic Union, was founded in 1912. It grew out of the Islamic Trading Association set up by Arab and Javanese traders in 1909 but declared in 1913 that only indigenous Muslims could join. Some scholars thus consider Sarekat Islam as more a nationalist than a religious organization, but this interpretation needs qualifying. The Arabs of the Islamic Trading Association had been born in Java; they had Javanese mothers. Sarekat Islam's decision shows that, in the view of political leaders (and scholars of Indonesia), identity and belonging derive from fathers only; wife and mother transmit no nationality. Sarekat Islam was for men.

The Islamic Union tried to raise living standards for its members, who were foremen in factories and plantations, landowning farmers, bank tellers, clerks, Muslim soldiers in the colonial army, food sellers, traders, and manufacturers. Leaders worked for economic goals that were within the reach of their followers: they promised cement houses, opposed taxes levied by a Christian government, and advocated breaking Chinese control of textile and cigarette manufacturing. They urged Muslims to buy only from fellow Muslims and organized boycotts of Chinese businesses. The association helped poor members pay for Muslim funerals; it organized mosque gatherings; its youth wing took on members of Chinese gangs and imposed "street justice," rather than solve community disputes through colonial courts, police, or charities. It spread rumors that it would drive all foreigners out of Java and elevate Pakubuwono X of Surakarta as emperor of Java and caliph. Sarekat Islam was essentially an organization of Javanese, but it wanted to end Christian government throughout the archipelago. The organization signaled its wider views by changing its name to Party of the Islamic Union of Indonesia in 1929 and it briefly joined the Agreement of Indonesian People's Political Associations to hasten the collapse of the Netherlands Indies.

Nahdatul Ulama (alternative spelling: Nahdlatul Ulama), meaning Rise of the Scholars (of Islam), formed in the pesantren of Kiai Haji Hasyim Asy'ari (1871–1947) in east Java in 1926. Its members were landowning farmers, urban-based traders, paralegal workers, pilgrimage organizers, and labor brokers who shared common origins in east Java. Their Islam was rooted in the consensus of east Java's Muslim communities, guided by their kiais, rather than in the reinvented seventh-century Islam imagined by Muhammadiyah missionaries. Nahdatul Ulama members rode Dutch trains and boarded Dutch steamships to Mecca; they copied Christian models of public existence with their own pesantrens, hospitals, and politicking within colonial assemblies, but for them the colonial state was irrelevant. East Java was the limit of their world and organizing; they sent no kiais to Gorontalo or Ternate. Members lived in east Java and in migrant communities of east Javanese in south Kalimantan. Nahdatul Ulama leaders ensured space for their operations by reaching a political accommodation with the Dutch, the Japanese, and later with the leaders of the Republic.

Sumatrans and others who came to Java's principal cities to study were confronted by royal Java, modernizing Islam, pesantren-focused Islam, and old-style hatred of non-Muslims. At the same time, those they left behind were confronted by Javanese moving into their homelands as migrant farmers, soldiers of the colonial army, government staff, leaders of reform movements, and adventurers. Students influenced by Islamic reform movements at home in

Aceh or Makasar encountered in Java reformers who wanted unveiled women in public life and the professions and politicians seeking revivals of Javanese culture that either actively opposed Islam or ignored it. The feminist Raden Ajeng Kartini, the European theosophist Dirk van Hinloopen Labberton, and the educator Ki Hajar Dewantoro typified for them the "modern" attitude that Islam was irrelevant.

Raden Ajeng Kartini (1879–1904) was a member of the Condronegoro family that monopolized jobs in the colonial civil service in north-central Java. They hired Dutch men and women as live-in servants to tutor their children, enrolled daughters and sons in European primary schools, and sent the boys to Dutch high school and one to university in Holland. They were subscribers and contributors to Dutch-language magazines and corresponded with ethici. Kartini and her sisters, Rukmini and Kardinah, drew from their experience of European primary school and intimate friendships with Dutch women a model of personal freedom, convictions that women should have the right to schooling, careers, and monogamous marriage, and a sense of their duty to "uplift" Native women. They wrote under the pen name "Cloverleaf," but they were easily identified and accused of abandoning Islam and Javanese culture. Family opposition prevented Kartini from accepting the Dutch government scholarships offered her for study in Holland or Batavia, but the friendships the sisters cultivated with wives of important Dutch men in the colony made ambitious Javanese officials want to marry them, despite their notoriety. Male and female members of the Javanese elite shared a vision of the Indies ruled by an alliance of Dutch and Javanese working together to raise Javanese standards of civilization and engender respect for Javanese among Dutch people in the colony and Holland.

Dirk van Hinloopen Labberton was a Dutchman who arrived in Java early in the twentieth century to work at a sugar factory at Probolinggo, but he soon moved into government service. In Holland he had joined the Theosophical Society, and in Java he joined the Bogor and Batavia branches and became the leading member of a group of Dutch men and women who were Buddhist, vegetarian, fascinated by mysticism, and in love with an imaginary past of Eastern wisdom and ancient nobility. The Theosophical Society, which worked for universal brotherhood and an end of discrimination, opened membership to Javanese, Chinese, Eurasians, and Dutch, to men and to women, and its lodges provided one of the few places where Javanese and European met socially as equals.

Van Hinloopen circulated his views through many channels. He was a member of a government committee to promote popular literature, a high school teacher, magazine editor, author of a manual on Sanskrit, and, in 1922, founder of the Movement to Combat Illiteracy. He helped start the Batavia branch of Budi Utomo and expanded the activities of the Java Institute for the study of Javanese language and culture.

Although van Hinloopen's principal interest lay in his imagined Hindu Java, he took up causes that advanced the movement for a self-governing Indies. He nurtured among Javanese men who were interested in the roots of their culture his view that Islam was a foreign imposition, and that Javanese had to revive knowledge of their ancient culture as the basis for regaining self-rule. He promoted Malay language for scholarly discourse, public debate and

KARTINI: NATIONAL HEROINE OR CREATURE OF THE DUTCH?

Kartini's Dutch friends ensured her survival in Indonesian histories because they preserved her letters and published them, and raised money to open schools for girls in Java. President Sukarno elevated her to the status of National Heroine as Ibu (mother) Kartini in 1964. Dutch admiration and Kartini's Java-centrism ensured that she would be a controversial choice for heroine of independent Indonesia. Detractors argued she was an apologist for colonialism, and that her revolt against Javanese feudalism was meaningless elsewhere in the archipelago. They proposed as more appropriate models for female behavior veiled women such as the Minangkabau Rahma El-Yunusiah, who taught Arabic and Koran to white-clad women, founded the Indonesian Association of Female Teachers of Islam in 1933, spurned colonial rule, and considered contact with Dutch people a personal insult. Rahma El-Yunusiah's vision was not preserved, so it is Java's Kartini who writes women into Indonesian histories as individuals yearning for personal freedom and a Western-style education with the opening lines of a letter to a Dutch woman pen friend in 1899: "I have so longed to make the acquaintance of a 'modern girl,' the proud independent girl whom I so admire."

common language for the entire colony. The Indies government, judging van Hinloopen a public danger, closed down his literacy program and brought his Indies career to an end in 1923. Although he espoused a multiracial society that Indonesians were to reject, van Hinloopen and his fellow Theosophists, Javanese and Dutch, made a lasting impact on Indonesia's modern history through the multiplying effects of their educational efforts. Graduates of Theosophical Society schools became teachers in new schools set up to promote national identity. The funds Javanese Theosophists raised for scholarships, schools, books, and study clubs equipped a generation of leaders who acted without Dutch support and led the country against continuing Dutch rule and association. Men such as Muhammad Hatta (1902–1980), Indonesia's first vice president, studied and politicked in Holland, supported by a Theosophical scholarship.

Ki Hajar Dewantoro (1889–1959) was another prominent member of colonial society who put Java above Islam. He belonged to the Pakualaman court within the sultanate of Yogyakarta. Pakualaman princes were known for their interest in European culture, cultivation of Dutch acquaintances, and pursuit of Dutch education. Dewantoro's first political vision took form in the Indies Party, when he was still known by the name Suwardi Suryaningrat. The Indies Party, founded around the same time as Budi Utomo, Muhammadiyah, and Sarekat Islam, took the colonial state, rather than Java, as its frame of reference, campaigned for independence from Holland, and proposed as leaders men born in the colony who had a Dutch-language education. Eurasian and Javanese men were drawn to the Indies Party, the first to propose a secular nation-state and the first to be dissolved by the colonial government. Its leaders were temporarily removed from the colony to Holland.

Suwardi spent the years 1913 to 1919 in Holland. When he returned to Java he had a new name, Ki Hajar Dewantoro, and a new vision. As qualification to rule, he substituted Javanese ancestry and culture for birth in the Indies. A Java-based nationalism would form the foundation of a state that he saw as Java plus Outer Islands. He rejected Islam as a basis for national unity in favor of an indigenous culture that had absorbed Islam into itself. In 1922 Dewantoro established the first of the Taman Siswa schools, which were immediately popular with parents who feared years in a Dutch classroom would produce pseudo-Europeans and who avoided Islamic schools as centers of fanatical hostility to Javanese culture. By 1932 Taman Siswa had 166 schools and eleven thousand pupils. It established secondary-level schools and a teacher-training institute. Taman Siswa became the model for schools in other regions of the archipelago where local history, language, and arts were substituted for those of Java.

There was no equivalent of the Java-centric reformers among the Indies' other ethnic groups. None, for instance, proposed an archipelago state governed from Palembang, based on the Buddhist heritage of Srivijaya. The members of the Sumatran Union, formed in Batavia in 1918, of the Timorese Alliance, founded in Batavia in 1921, and of the Sunda group Pasundan, founded in 1914, saw their futures in an archipelago-wide union that no one ethnic group dominated. They campaigned for a federation of states based on the ethnic cores, with a weak central government to represent Indonesians to the world and leave each region to preserve its own identity and develop its economy for the benefit of its own population. Even the colony's Christian groups, who felt a close kindred with the Dutch, had leaders who saw their future inside a federal Indonesia, rather than in the kingdom of the Netherlands. From 1920, groups such as the Union of Ambonese (whose principal branches were in Batavia and Surabaya) promoted unity among Muslim and Christian Ambonese and a hitching of Ambon's fortunes to an Indonesian federation of Malay speakers that would jointly inherit the colonial state. Java's reformers and politicians could think of Java alone. All others had to figure Java into their calculations about the future.

TWO SUMATRAN PROPOSITIONS FOR AN INDONESIAN FUTURE: MUHAMMAD YAMIN AND HAMKA

Two west Sumatran intellectuals argued alternative paths to the future. Muhammad Yamin (1903–1964) was born into the class that emerged from Minangkabau's Padri wars to become administrators of the colonial state, guaranteed jobs, status, income and Western schooling in return for their alliance with the Dutch. Yamin's rantau took him from Sumatra to Batavia's new law school on a scholarship from the Theosophical Society. In the colony's capital, Yamin began to define his homeland as Sumatra, rather than his native Minangkabau corner of that island. By 1928 he was calling his homeland the colonial state itself, recast as Indonesia. He was one of the drafters of the Youth Oath of 1928 that called for one state (Indonesia), one people, and one language (Malay, to be called Indonesian). He represented Minangkabau in the colony's People's Council in 1938 and was a principal author of the independence constitution of 1945.

Yamin was receptive to prevailing Dutch and Javanese conceptions of archipelago history that cast Java as the site of a splendid reworking of Indian civilization. The great cultural treasures were those inspired by Hindu epics, and the preeminent empire was Majapahit. Yamin saw the rest of the archipelago as outer islands to the Java center. He argued that Java shared with the outer islands six thousand years of culture, custom, and spirit, and that this unity had been undermined by the Dutch strategy of recognizing the archipelago's many kings and by revival of interest in regional languages. The work of modern politics was to recover this imagined past. Yamin did not wish to restore monarchies. He wanted one single state created out of all the lands he believed had once been subject to Majapahit. Yamin's Indonesia included East Timor, all of present-day Malaysia, and southern Thailand. Shared culture, a common history of Javanese conquest, and the Malay language would be its pillars.

Hamka (1908–1989) was also a Minangkabau, but he belonged to the class that opposed the Dutch and their Minangkabau allies. His male line for five generations back had sought distinction through Islam. Whereas Yamin's formal schooling was lengthy and took place in Sumatra and Java in the Dutch language, Hamka's formal schooling was short, local, and in Malay and Arabic. Travel took him to Mecca, not Batavia. Hamka joined the Muhammadiyah, and by 1930 called himself a nationalist. Pilgrimage and politics made him see a unity in the archipelago state the Dutch ruled, but the basis of unity was Islam, not a Javanese Hindu past. In Hamka's view, his contemporaries were the product of a history of conversion to Islam, life experience as Muslims, and connection to Islam's core. Pre-Islamic pasts had no contribution to make to a new nation. His heroes were not Javanese Hindu conquerors, such as Gajah Mada, but men such as Banten's Sultan Hasanuddin who had conquered Hindu lands for Islam.

At first, Yamin's vision prevailed. He lived to see Indonesia become an independent republic, dominated by Javanese and Java, although not filling all of Majapahit's supposed space. Hamka's argument, that Islam, not Java, is the basis for Indonesian unity, is vigorously shaking the Indonesian state at the beginning of the twenty-first century.

Across the archipelago were Muslim leaders who judged the concepts of nation or homeland un-Islamic. For them identity was grounded in religion alone, and political allegiance was owed only to the man who ruled in the name of Islam. Some pursued the logic of their beliefs by withdrawing from the colonial space of the Dutch and from nationalist politics to found *Darul Islam,* the House of Islam. It was not enough for them that political parties such as the Nationalist Party of Indonesia (founded in 1927), or the Indonesia Party (founded in 1930), or the Socialist Party of Indonesia (founded in 1948) would replace Dutch Christians with Indonesian Muslims and substitute the Republic of Indonesia for the Netherlands East Indies. Republic and rule by Indonesian politicians were irrelevant to the goal of founding a society ruled by Islamic law and guided by experts in Islamic religion. Adherents of Darul Islam turned their backs on nationalist politicians and colonial officials alike. During the war for independence, Islamic Armies of God fought against soldiers of the People's Army of Indonesia as well as against soldiers of the Dutch colonial army in west Java. After Indonesia was internationally recognized as an independent, secular republic, governed by politicians from the nationalist parties, Islamic Armies of God fought against the (renamed) National Army of Indonesia in west Java, Aceh, and south Sulawesi.

Dutch people in the Indies organized too. The Fatherlands Club was founded in 1928 to represent the 60,000 Dutch immigrants within the larger European community composed of Eurasians, Indonesian and Chinese spouses of Dutch men, and Asians who had been declared Europeans in legal status by courts of law. Members perceived their interests to be threatened by communists, nationalists, and ordinary Indonesians living off government welfare. At its peak in 1930, the Fatherlands Club claimed 30 percent of all adult Dutch male immigrants as members.

In the mid-1930s the Fatherlands Club emphasized maintenance of Dutch character and traditions more than race. It supported an Indies univer-

KARTOSUWIRYO AND DARUL ISLAM: THE DREAM OF WITHDRAWAL

Kartosuwiryo was born in 1905 into a family that could afford him a Dutch-language schooling. As a young man he joined the Party of the Islamic Union of Indonesia but was forced out in 1939 on account of his condemnation of cooperation with colonial institutions. Kartosuwiryo settled in his wife's village in the Sunda territory of Garut where he began to teach withdrawal of Muslims from contact with the colonial state.

In 1940 Kartosuwiryo founded the Suffah Institute as an agricultural commune. Kartosuwiryo ran his Islamic community through deputies and screened himself from followers, so that rumors began to circulate. People said that Kartosuwiryo had acquired unusual powers through meditation and ascetic denial. He could render himself invisible; amulets that he fashioned made their bearers invulnerable to bullets. Young men hailed him as warrior of Islam. They launched raids for the extension of the House of Islam against all who stood in their way: ulamas and villagers who did not acknowledge Kartosuwiryo's leadership, Dutch troops, and representatives of Sukarno's government. In 1948 he took the title imam and proclaimed the Islamic State of Indonesia. After the Dutch left, Kartosuwiryo continued the fight against Indonesia. He designated Sukarno as the enemy because he appointed non-Muslims to positions of authority over Muslims. Kartosuwiryo's armed bands welcomed men dismissed from the national army and members of marauding militias that were the legacy of the revolution. They burned down mosques and houses of local opponents and terrorized west Java with random murders and display of heads.

With Kartosuwiryo, the divorce between leadership and government was complete. His learning and holiness had a local renown only. Sharia-trained officials denounced Kartosuwiryo's brand of Islam that stressed magical qualities of the leader; they pointed to his slight formal Islamic education and decried his rejection of wealth and connection to urban cosmopolitans.

For many Indonesians, attacks on fellow Muslims and on a government of Indonesians could not be justified. Darul Islam separatist movements asserted themselves again in the 1950s when regional aspirations clashed with the Javanese power holders of Jakarta. Because they were local, Darul Islam soldiers were no match for a military machine that carried the nation's goodwill as the destroyer of Dutch rule. West Java's Darul Islam movement collapsed in 1962 when Kartosuwiryo was captured by the Indonesian army and shot.

sity and promotion of qualified Indonesians to higher positions. It left exclusion of Indonesians to the National Socialist League, which was the Indies branch of Holland's Nazi Party. The Fatherlands Club campaigned for a self-ruling Indies within the kingdom of the Netherlands. It attracted Eurasian men to its membership when it proposed West New Guinea as a separate homeland for Eurasians. It campaigned for the build-up of defenses against Japan in the People's Council, where it voiced similar demands to Indonesian nationalists. Ultimately, the Fatherlands Club, which began its political life in opposition to the ethical policy, ended up espousing many of the ethical policy's ideals, including ultimate power-sharing with Indonesians.

All kinds of groups organized in the 1920s and 1930s. The Communist Party of Indonesia established itself in 1920. By late 1926 branches in Batavia, Banten, and Priangen thought the time ripe to pull down the colonial state. Communists in West Sumatra rebelled in January 1927, and 13,000 communists were arrested. The Dutch jailed 4,500 and sent 1,308 into prison camp in West New Guinea. Alert Wives, founded in Bandung in 1930, demanded equal rights for women. By 1938 the Indonesian Women's Congress had been pushed by Alert Wives to demand the right for women to vote and to run for public office. The Association of the Subjects of Yogyakarta, founded by Prince Suryodiningrat in 1930, fueled old yearnings of central Java farmers for a just king who would inaugurate a golden age. It had no Indonesia focus, no program of reform, and nothing to say to Sumatrans, but its membership of 260,000 in 1939 made it the largest political group in the colonial state.

Sukarno (1901–1970) found the right mix for the time. He campaigned for a state that would extend to the colony's borders and that would be the possession of the little person. The past he imagined was not Hindu or Islamic monarchies, but village republics, where everyone was more or less equal. He argued that for 350 years the Dutch had taken over Indonesian history, and Indonesians everywhere had lost the power to rule themselves and the ability to see their common culture. Sukarno called himself a poor man of the people, but his father was a government school teacher, able to raise his son in a large house in Blitar and pay for an expensive Dutch-language education through engineering college. Sukarno regarded Islamic pieties as old-fashioned, boasted that he trampled on the Islamic etiquette of segregating the sexes in public, and announced that the modern face of Indonesia was the man in the Western suit and shoes. Self-rule would automatically resolve all social and economic problems. He rejected as "housewife issues" the civil rights stream within the nationalist movement that the women's parties represented. He rejected demands from ulamas for a sharia-based state.

Sukarno surrounded himself with young men who wore Western dress, were graduates of Dutch schools, and wanted a secular republic with elected parliaments. He began his political life in the second decade of the twentieth century when regional, ethnic, and religious models of government were competing. Sukarno rejected them all. His goal was an Indonesia of believers, not of belief. He understood Indonesia to mean a state naturally organized from Java, oriented to Java, a state based on the reach of Dutch armies and navies. He wrapped his message in impassioned speeches, overawed his rivals, cowed many others by the force of his personality, and convinced fellow politicians that he was the spokesman of the masses. He dropped into Indonesian discourse the word *merdeka* (independence) as slogan, greeting, rallying cry, and aspiration.

MERDEKA: A WORD FOR SUKARNO

Merdeka, a powerfully emotive word in modern Indonesian, means free, independent. Sukarno used it in the 1920s as a call to action to create the nation; his daughter, Megawati Sukarnoputri, used it in her 1999 presidential campaign to preserve the nation occupying the space of the old colonial state. In the early months of Indonesia's war for national independence, "merdeka" became a common greeting.

Although *merdeka* in its modern form entered the nationalist discourse in the 1920s, it has a long history in Indonesian languages. The Sanskrit word *maharddika,* meaning a man who is eminent, wise, rich, and illustrious, entered Javanese texts in the tenth century. The oldest writing preserved in Malay, the seventh-century stone inscription of Srivijaya, contains the derivative *murdhaka,* meaning leader of a group of subjects or bondspeople. The word indicates a social class intermediate between slaves and rulers in some languages of Kalimantan and Sulawesi. Frederik de Houtman included the word *mardeka* in his 1603 Malay-Dutch word list, translating it as "free man." The Dutch derivative, *mardijker,* designated freed slaves and was used for men of Indian and Portuguese parentage in VOC towns. Eighteenth-century Javanese texts used other derivatives from the Sanskrit word to mean old, wise person.

The Sanskrit word *maharddika* is also the origin of the Javanese word *pradikan,* meaning a tax-exempt village. The *wong mardika* was a person exempt from paying taxes to the king. The free person was a rich male, one commanding the labor of others, acknowledging no superior. He was not a democrat. In 1914 the Samin movement in north-central Java, which opposed entering any relation with the colonial government, including paying taxes, defined its stance as merdeka.

Merdeka expanded its meaning in the writings of poets and politicians to include personal as well as political freedom. Male poets used it to mean release from responsibility to society. The first modern association of women took the word in its name Puteri Mardika. Members understood it to mean freedom for personal development realized through duty to society.

Sukarno voiced a kind of nationalism in the 1920s and 1930s that was different from his local competitors and from the nationalisms of neighboring colonies. In Vietnam, Burma, and Malaya the majority ethnic group claimed inheritance of the colonial state and demanded that Cham, Khmer, Yeo, Karen, Kachin, and Temiar minorities assimilate to the dominant Vietnamese, Burmese, and Malay. Sukarno did not proclaim a Javanese takeover of the Indies in 1945, he did not order Sumbawans, Manadonese, and Savu peoples to become Javanese. The ethnic base he set for Indonesia's nationalism was the indigene, which he defined as all peoples whose (paternal) ancestors had been born in the archipelago. His definition of Indonesian included Hindu Balinese, Christian Batak, Muslim Sasak, and Animist Dayak. Sukarno drew the divide between Indonesian and Dutch. In the 1950s he was enamored with modernity, intoxicated with his nationalist rhetoric, flirted with communist visions for Indonesia, embarrassed by kiais, suspicious of Muslim reformers, and angered by regional leaders unwilling to subordinate themselves to the capital in Java. Sukarno's romanticized notions and conviction in his own leadership led him to believe he could reconcile left and right, secularist and Muslim, and achieve a permanent union of Indonesian differences through a nationalism focused on love of Indonesia.

Elite Batavia-based politicians were sure that they represented the little man, the pious Muslim, the clerk, the overburdened mother, the factory worker, and the Torajan. Dutch ethici thought they knew what most troubled ordinary people. Official investigations showed that poverty was increasing along with population. The colonial government feared there would soon be no space left in Java or Bali, and began establishing colonies of farmers in Sumatra, Sulawesi, Kalimantan, and West New Guinea. The Dutch press reported the hostility of ordinary folk toward colonial rule, expressed across the archipelago through arson, tax protests, the sudden massing of armed men, and murders of isolated Europeans.

It is doubtful that ordinary Indonesians believed privileged Batavia politicians or Dutch do-gooders represented them or could solve their problems. What is clear is that, in small groups, rallying behind local heroes, Indonesian men and a few women vigorously protested immediate concerns. Anger exploded in a show of knives and sharpened bamboo. In many Indonesian communities it was established practice for aggrieved commoners to go as a group to their sultan or district chief, sit on the ground outside the boss's residence, and wait to submit their complaint and be spoken to. Often a single Dutch officer and two or three Indonesian assistants were confronted by fifty to one hundred men armed with machetes and amulets, who failed to disperse after authority had made its public appearance. Pistol and musket shots scattered such groups. Protest collapsed when leaders were arrested and jailed or exiled. Batavia-based politicians did not coordinate haphazard, local protests into one sustained island or archipelago-wide rebellion. They perceived the Dutch grip on power as unshakable, and they feared armed, angry commoners who followed leaders of their own choosing.

KIAI KASAN MUKMIN, A.K.A. IMAM MAHDI

In 1903 his disciples proclaimed Kiai Kasan Mukmin an incarnation of the tenth-century Imam Mahdi. Mukmin called on his followers to kill all Europeans living in his home base in east Java, which would then become a Muslim land where only taxes sanctioned by the Koran would be levied on believers, and where the observance of sharia would automatically bring peace and prosperity. Kiai Mukmin was not a mosque official who drew his salary from the colonial government, nor was he a learned man by Islamic standards, for his knowledge of Islam had been gained through contacts with hajis and pesantrens in the course of trading. He settled in Krian district, married a local woman, and, around forty (the age when Muhammad received the first of the revelations), began teaching and healing.

The districts in which Mukmin traveled were the center of the colonial sugar industry. Plantation companies were seeking more land and hiring laborers at wages higher than Javanese farmers and entrepreneurs were willing to pay. The 124 men who followed Mukmin into battle were landholders, fishpond owners, manufacturers, and traders. Many were hajis. Mukmin's first move was to send a letter to Javanese officials in the area proclaiming a holy war against Europeans and announcing the reign of the Mahdi that jihad would install. Then Mukmin and his followers marched against a sugar mill where a European manager headed a staff of Eurasians and Javanese. Colonial troops had little difficulty putting down the rebellion, for the plantation's wage laborers and small farmers in the neighborhood did not join in. The kiai was killed in battle, and a few men were imprisoned. The revolt was over.

Some aristocrats, urban technicians, and rural prophets experienced colonial rule as exile. Exile was the colonial government's preferred method of distancing a leader from his followers, for it silenced the man who had lived by public speaking, rallies, or the more intense persuasion of study circles. Men exiled to Bangka or to Banda Neira had personal freedom of movement; they received a monthly pension from the colonial government, could send for wife and children, could take a job, join a local church or mosque, and attend public meetings, but the weight of official disapproval often deterred local people from much contact with them. Political exiles were often distrusted; they felt ill at ease among ethnic groups that were strange to them. The Ambonese Christian nationalist A. J. Patty, for instance, was exiled to the Muslim community of Palembang in 1926. There he took a government job and joined the local branch of Sukarno's Indonesian Nationalist Party, but he was regarded with suspicion by Dutch officials and colonized community alike. Men who chose to spend their term of exile in Holland involved themselves in Dutch social causes that estranged them from fellow Indonesians. Tan Malaka, for instance, joined the Dutch communist party and ran for election to the Netherlands parliament, whereas in the colony most ulamas taught their congregations that communism was the enemy of Islam and urged Muslims not to participate in European institutions. Exiles were not always shunned by their host communities. The socialist-leaning Syahrir adopted two children during his period of exile in Banda Neira (1936–1942) and took them back to Java with him on his release. Sukarno developed his career of serial marriages in his Bangka exile.

Two camps on the Boven Digul River in the thickly forested interior of West New Guinea occupy a special place in Indonesian histories of colonial rule. They were opened in 1927 as holding sites for the landowning farmers, Islamic religious leaders, and communist party officials who had thought the time was ripe in 1925 to overthrow Dutch rule. By mid-1935 death from jungle diseases or release had reduced the number of political prisoners to 442. Prisoners then included officers of nationalist, socialist, and Islamic parties. The government described this jungle exile as a reeducation site, a place where agricultural labor could reorient the energies and ambitions of inmates. Schools, a hospital, a movie theater, and sports re-created the colonial town, as did the multiethnic inhabitants and the stratifications of colonial society. The Dutch-educated, Dutch-speaking intellectuals received subsidies from the government; they were installed in better class housing with their libraries; they wrote for Indonesian and Dutch magazines. The underclass of small business people, hajis, and kiais who did not know Dutch received government pensions for a short time only. They had to support their exile by turning jungle into cultivated fields, raising their own food crops, and building their own houses.

By 1940, politically active urban Indonesians were divided into two camps, those who worked through colonial institutions to achieve self-rule and those who refused to cooperate with the Indies government. There was still no directly elected parliament, only a council for grandstanding; there was no army trained for national defense, only an army geared to keeping civilians in order. The Indies government pursued its own path. In 1935, for instance, it had appointed the first woman to the People's Council, even though men of all ethnic groups had voted in the Council to deny women the right to vote and to run for public office and the majority of Indonesian political parties refused to admit women to their public congresses. Only a handful of the smallest parties wanted a secular republic with an elected parliament and guarantees of equality for all citizens. The largest parties, the Muhammadiyah and the ethnically based parties, stood for quite different directions in national life. Most Indonesians had no political affiliation. The old ruling classes of sultans and rajas were still allied with the Dutch, pushing to retrieve some of their lost authority, but holding up their end of the Dutch blueprint for rule.

In January 1942 Japanese troops landed in Ambon. Colonial and Allied troops fought to defeat in Timor, Ambon, and Borneo and on the Java Sea. In March the Japanese 25th Army invaded Sumatra, the 16th Army fought its way into Java. The colonial state ceased to exist. Its government went into exile in Australia, its army of 65,000 were prisoners of war. From May 1942 the Japanese removed Europeans from Indonesian life. Dutch civilians were forced into camps in all the major cities. Indonesian soldiers were detached from the colonial army and sent home. Dutch soldiers and male civilians were transferred to slave labor camps in Indonesia, mainland Southeast Asia, and Japan. When Allied troops defeated the Japanese in 1945, only 40 percent of the men were still alive. For three and a half years the colonial state was split into three separate regions under Japanese army and navy rule. All the political parties permitted by the Dutch were banned by the Japanese. Political organizing to achieve an Islamic or a democratic state, or the right of women to vote was now a prohibited activity. The old colonial pyramid of a tiny Dutch ruling class, a layer of Indonesian elites, a layer of Eurasians and Christian Indonesians, a layer of Chinese and Arabs, and a base of Indonesian business and working classes was rearranged. Now Japanese were at the pinnacle, then Indonesian elites, then the base of Indonesians. Dutch and Eurasians were eliminated from view; Christian Indonesians were harassed as spies; Chinese were persecuted. Race, religion, and class continued to determine government policies under the Japanese. Indonesian politicians who welcomed Japanese military rule counted on the Asia war to smash alliances with the Dutch forever and looked to Japan to give them control of archipelago communities and their resources.

11

REARRANGING MAP AND MIND
Japan and the Republic in Indonesian Histories

Indonesian politicians viewed the sweep of Japanese armies across mainland Asia in the 1920s and 1930s with mixed feelings. They admired Japan's independence, modernization, and military prowess and wondered if Japan could hasten the overthrow of Western colonialism in Asia. The Dutch and Chinese living in Indonesia viewed Japanese expansion with alarm. Invasion, when it came, was sudden and complete. By March 1942 the colonial state had vanished. In places such as Bali, where no Dutch soldiers were stationed in 1942, there was no fighting. The fiercest fighting for the defense of the colony took place at invasion points in the Christian fringe of Ambon and Timor, in Kalimantan, and on the Java Sea. In the weeks between the collapse of the colonial state and the arrival of Japanese troops, local conflicts erupted. Chinese- and Dutch-owned properties were looted and burned. There were killings among Indonesian rival groups; people went into hiding or vanished.

Japanese shopkeepers, gardeners, and pearl-fishers in the Indies emerged in military uniform. Japanese troops swiftly took control of government buildings, radio stations, railway terminuses, the postal and telegraph system, ports, and interisland shipping. Occupying forces permitted the display of national symbols that the Dutch had forbidden, and Japanese troops paraded through streets lined with cheering crowds whom they provided with red and white flags. Senior Dutch officials of the colonial government went into exile ahead of the invasion of Java, taking political prisoners, family, and personal attendants to Australia. The colonial government had given prominent prisoners the choice of release into a country awaiting conquest or relocation of their place of exile. Sukarno, Hatta, and Syahrir chose to remain and made their way to Java, where they calculated how Japanese rule could fit into their plans for an independent Indonesia.

For Japanese officers who led the conquest of the Indies and for Japanese planners in the war ministry in Tokyo, Indonesia's islands were part of a larger plan for Asia. They welcomed the offers of cooperation made by Indonesian ruling classes and politicians. They kept local elites in place and through them supplied Japanese industries and armed forces. Indonesian cooperation meant that the Japanese could focus on patrolling the archipelago's waterways and skies and building Indonesia's islands into forward posts protecting Japan from Allied attack and invasion. Throughout their occupation, the Japanese controlled information and all news sources. Japanese news services pumped a rhetoric of Japanese victories, Asian identity, Asian command of Asian destinies, and a denigration of Westerners and Western culture. The demands for sacrifice, displays of loyalty to Japan's emperor, emphasis on military culture, and scorn for civilian government, combined with terror directed against segments of the population, generated a climate of fear, but also excitement and possibility, especially for young Indonesian men.

Under the Japanese, the colonial state shrank to Java, the only island that the Japanese considered qualified for a degree of independence. Sumatra, Kalimantan, and east Indonesia counted only for their agricultural and mineral potential. It was on Java that archipelago politicians were channeled into Japanese organizations and permitted to address rallies. Java-based politicians were taken into Japanese imperial space and sent to Japan, Singapore, and Saigon. It was on Java that they were assembled by Japanese command, in June 1945, to discuss a common future for the whole of the Indies.

Indonesian experience of Japanese rule varied by region, ethnicity, class, and gender, but all inhabitants of the archipelago shared one common experience, the elimination of Europeans from Indonesian landscapes. Few archipelago residents regretted their disappearance as they coped with the new ruling class. When Japan's defeat came, as sudden as their earlier defeat of the Dutch, few hoped that the Dutch would return. The fighting again took place in the fringe territories of Kalimantan, Morotai, Ambon, Timor, and West New Guinea. Japanese defeat was invisible to Java. Japanese soldiers remained, fully armed, there and on Sumatra. They stood aside as Chinese shops burned, as neighboring villages turned on each other, as militias scrambled for weapons and territory, and mobs imposed "revolutionary justice." Sukarno and militias associated with him quickly secured control of the airwaves in Java, and it was there that Indonesia was proclaimed before most archipelago inhabitants even knew the war was over. The new state was presented as Java-Sumatra, with Sumatra standing for the Outer Islands, and the Sumatran Hatta deputy to Java's Sukarno.

When the Dutch tried to reclaim "their Indies," the major battles of the struggle for independence were fought in Java, where the republic's capital was and negotiations to preserve the republic conducted. Elsewhere, the old alliance of ruling classes and the Dutch partially revived in the form of Dutch-sponsored states established to entrench ethnic interests and promote alternatives to a single, Java-dominated state. Circling the Java heartland were states in Sunda, Sumatra, Kalimantan, and eastern Indonesia that had assemblies, cabinets, and government departments in which Indonesians pursued regional ambitions with Dutch military and civilian advisers. The republic, which had no Dutch officials, contracted into central Java. Republican politicians set up parties, committees, assemblies, held congresses, and competed with military men for control of the armed bands operating from mountain hideouts. Sukarno focused on being what he later called himself, Mouthpiece of the Revolution, symbol of one nation.

Indonesia's riches of oil, tin, rubber, rice, and people were important to Japan as it recast its place in the world in the twentieth century. In the last years of the nineteenth century, Japan had seen itself as naturally one with Western countries because of its modern army and navy, modern education system, and new industries. Japan viewed other Asian countries as inferior in culture and development. Imperial expansion brought Japan into conflict with Western colonial powers. Japan now began to see itself as the natural leader of Asia, destined to expel Western countries and to create in former Western colonial space a Japanese-dominated political and economic zone that could compete with Europe and the United States. Asia's resources would be channeled to Japanese industries and Asian countries would purchase Japanese manufactured goods and import Japanese culture and Japanese forms of modernity.

The boundaries of Japan expanded into Asia. Taiwan became a colony in 1895, Korea in 1910, and Manchuria in 1931. Japan's advance into China began in 1937. The advance into Southeast Asia followed: Indochina in 1940, Malaya and Singapore in 1941, and the Philippines, Indonesia, and Burma

(Myanmar) in 1942. Western expansion and conquest that occurred piecemeal over three hundred and fifty years took fifty years in Japan's case. The speed of this imperial expansion was a direct consequence of Japan's inheriting Western science and technology and adapting its management and organization methods.

Japan's campaign for leadership of China and China-influenced Asia (Korea, Taiwan, and Vietnam) was the product of centuries. Japanese armies conquered the "outer barbarians," Japan's term for the countries of Southeast Asia, in preparation for war with the United States. Until 1940 America had supplied Japan with 60 percent of its oil. Conquest of Southeast Asia brought Japan new sources for fuel and food. Early in 1942 Japanese troops seized Sumatra's oil fields. As the region's new imperial power, Japan redrew the borders of Thailand, Cambodia, Malaya, and the Netherlands Indies.

The new Asia was devised while Japan was carrying war overseas; it was implemented as Japanese forces suffered major defeats from the middle of 1942 and as Japan itself became a target in the war. In November 1943 representatives from China, Manchukuo (Japanese-conquered Manchuria), Thailand, the Philippines, Burma, and India attended a conference on the Greater East Asia Co-Prosperity Sphere in Tokyo. The final communique promised that the sphere would achieve independence from Western control, the abolition of racial discrimination (understood to mean European race policies directed against Asians), and a prosperous coexistence. Not invited were representatives from Indonesia, Malaya, Vietnam, Korea, or Taiwan. They were to have no part in determining Asia policy.

The Japanese had not initially intended to displace the Dutch. They offered the colonial government a new alliance: provision Japan's war industries and forces and, in return, remain in control of Indonesian lands and peoples. The Dutch refused this deal. The cabinet went into exile, and the governor-general remained to be arrested and imprisoned. Instead of receiving a steady transfer of Indonesian goods and laborers from an Indies puppet government, Japan's war planners had to devise their own means of administering the archipelago. Until May 1940, the Dutch colony had been administered as a single state under civilian rule, with a small army and police force, an emphasis on "order and stability," a tightly supervised public life, a gradual introduction of indirectly elected councils, a slow decentralization of powers, moving toward semi-autonomous status within a Netherlands union at an unspecified date in a far-off future. The colony would be "developed" when its political life was channeled through Western-style parties, when religion was separated from politics, and when people were Western in outlook and habits. Colonial policy was determined in Holland and was the product of generations of "Indies hands" who saw themselves as ruling for Indonesians' own good, enduring the rebuffs of ungrateful Indonesian graduates of Dutch and Indies colleges, ever vigilant against the plots of fanatics.

In place of the leisurely formulation of policy through the Dutch parliament, which answered to elected taxpayers in Holland, Japan's war ministry, responsible only to the emperor of Japan, had to decide quickly how to run the colony, fill quotas for oil and rubber, and resolve tensions between the rhetoric of liberation and the reality of military exploitation. Within weeks, the symbols of Indonesian national unity, such as flag and anthem, were banned by the new rulers. The colony's political parties, suspended by the Dutch at the beginning of the war, were dissolved by the Japanese. Japanese war administrators divided the colonial state into three parts under three distinct administrations and three capitals. Sumatra was placed under the Twenty-fifth Army and joined with Malaya and Singapore into a single administrative unit, with its capital in Singapore. Java was administered by the Sixteenth Army. Batavia, renamed Jakarta, shrank in importance and function to Java's capital. The Second Southern Squadron of the Japanese navy took over administration of Kalimantan and east Indonesia and located its headquarters at Makasar. The grids of post, telegraph, and shipping service that had linked the archipelago and led to Batavia were broken up. In place of one cross-archipelago state, linked to Holland, regions were sealed off from each other and linked individually to Japan. Food, goods, and services were to circulate only within each region and to leave the region for Japan; all interisland trade was officially terminated.

In 1943, the Twenty-fifth Army command abandoned the idea of a new state in the western archipelago and separated Sumatra from Malaya. It saw Sumatra as a rich supplier of resources and tolerated very limited advice-giving from Sumatran ulamas, datus, and sultans. The navy opposed any form of self-government for east Indonesia. It viewed Christian communities there as supporters of the Dutch and potential spies, and replaced Christian administrators with Muslim Indonesians. In 1943, West New Guinea was detached from the navy's Indonesian administration and placed under the Fourth Southern Squadron. There was little Indonesian participation in government anywhere in the navy's jurisdiction.

The Sixteenth Army viewed Java as a source of rice and labor and as the home of a dangerously unruly population. It first tried to harness Java's people resources into Japanese mass organizations and to control them through intensive instruction in Japanese war doctrines. By late 1944, when defeat was anticipated, Japanese officers decided on a three-pronged policy for Java. They would create militias to take the first waves of Allied attacks and shield Japanese forces; they would create an Indonesian state on Java that would leave no room for the Allies to set up their own administration; and they would stir up an already volatile population to such frenzy against Westerners that would prevent the Dutch from ever resuming past privileges and powers.

The ruling Japanese were divided between army and naval commands, between Tokyo and field, between senior and junior officers, and by degrees of sympathy with Indonesian aspirations. But time, language, and information were uniformly controlled for all archipelago inhabitants. The Japanese calendar, which numbered years according to the reigns of Japan's emperors, was made the official dating system in place of Christian, Muslim, and Hindu calendars. From Aceh to Timor, Indonesia was made a single time zone (on Toyko time), and Japanese time, rather than Muslim time or Dutch divisions of night and day, ruled workers' lives. The official language was Japanese. The speaking and teaching of Dutch were prohibited. Japanese was the language of the rulers, and Malay-Indonesian the language of public rallies, propaganda pamphlets, newspapers, films, and public announcements. Japanese ships sealed the archipelago off from its neighbors. Suppression of all independent sources of news wrapped archipelago inhabitants in a world the Japanese wished them to know. Military police pursued people who could challenge the Japanese version of reality. They took over radio repair shops and required owners of radios to submit them for alteration so they could be tuned to Japanese stations only. Possession of a short-wave radio was punishable by execution. Military police raided houses for spies and staged trials and executions of traitors they found among Indonesian communists, socialists, Christians, and Chinese.

Most texts on the Japanese occupation focus on the long-term consequences of Japanese rule rather than on how the Japanese governed and how ordinary Indonesians experienced the Pacific War. In these texts, Japan's role is to end Dutch rule, to foster military values, and to pave the way for independence by forming militias and filling them with notions of glory, sacrifice, no compromise, and no submission to civilian command. Memoirs of Japanese rule by Indonesia's first generation of leaders tell of school, jobs, politicking within Japanese-approved organizations, scholarships to Japan, optimistic prophecies that Japanese rule would be short and altruistic. Their wartime problems were how to contrive proper celebration of weddings when ceremonial foods and textiles were in short supply. Recent studies of Japanese rule by Japanese and Western scholars have focused on the organization of economies within the sealed-off regions, the requisitioning of labor and rice, the regional famines, the uprisings by scattered groups of farmers, the export of between two hundred thousand and five hundred thousand Javanese to Japanese labor camps in mainland Asia and Japan, the drafting of girls into brothels, and the terrible shortages of food and basic clothing. Politicians who were sent on speaking tours by the Japanese to urge Indonesians to greater effort to supply Japan's army had no personal connection to the war miseries of the majority. Young men getting their first jobs and scholarships found wartime exciting. They enjoyed the staged rallies denouncing the West, the glamour of military uniforms, the imperial songs. They were glad the Japanese put village girls into brothels, so that girls of their own class were safe.

Indonesian members of nationalist parties the Japanese banned struggled to keep alive the dream of an independent nation occupying the same territory as the former Dutch colony. Java organizations that had planted branches in Dutch colonial space became separated from them and had no knowledge of local conditions, local developments or local sentiments. Leaders of regional groups caught in Java by the war were drafted into Japanese mass organizations for support of Japanese goals, while followers in their home regions were left without direction and encouragement and began to see Indonesian futures in terms of separate regions rather than in a Java-led state.

Prewar, preparatory studies taught Japanese war planners lessons that Indonesian urban elites had already learned: the route to ordinary Indonesians was through their labor bosses, village headmen, and ulamas. Labor bosses who controlled working-class sections of Indonesian cities recruited workers for a fee, charged workers for employment and lodging, and kept order on the work site or caused trouble, depending on the inducement. If labor bosses joined a political party or union, the workers in their detail joined also. Rural people lived in communities where the leading families who controlled village government and land were mosque leaders and teachers. If these village gatekeepers joined a branch of a national organization, they brought along their tenants, dependents, assistants, students, or congregation as members.

The task for politicians aspiring to mass support was to win over targeted members of urban and rural communities by framing their message to match local knowledge, interests, and concerns. The central leadership of the Indonesian Communist Party, for instance, had campaigned against taxes imposed by a Christian government to appeal to rural religious leaders. It had not preached Marxist dialectics, opposed private ownership, or mocked God. For a brief period in the second decade of the twentieth century, Sarekat Islam branches in west Java had admitted members of the communist party, and "Islamic communism" had been taught by kiais. In 1927 the Dutch had exiled hajis and ulamas to Boven Digul for leading communist rebellions. Sukarno's Nationalist Party of Indonesia had substituted promises of brick houses, rice fields, and buffalo for its analysis of imperialism in reaching out to the Java countryside.

Japanese officers charged with internal security kept urban elites busy and dealt directly with labor bosses and community leaders. They herded men with national reputations into Japanese-sponsored organizations to control and contain them. Sukarno was allowed to make speeches in Java promoting an Indonesian state within the Japanese empire. The Japanese authorities courted Muslim leaders with a Java-wide reputation and opened an Office of (Islamic) Religious Affairs in 1942. Muslim leaders were organized in October 1943 into the Masyumi (a contraction for Consultative Council of Indonesian Muslims), with the founder of the Nahdatul Ulama as its head. From 1944 his son headed the Religious Affairs Office. Japanese security (unsuccessfully) pressured these Muslim leaders to declare Japan's war a jihad. Promoting an Indonesian Islam sufficient in itself, they advocated a ban on Arabic in Islamic schools and published an Indonesian translation of the Koran in June 1945. In July 1945 they founded the first Islamic university in Jakarta.

Internal security officers replicated at the local level methods of population control, monitoring, and indoctrination already in force in Japan. Headmen of urban neighborhoods and villages had to register residents, record visitors, update lists regularly for Japanese inspectors, and set up and supervise neighborhood associations covering every three streets. Headmen were responsible for filling quotas of workers and goods and for displaying Japanese posters, banners, and flags in their areas. They had to install radios in public places so that Japanese versions of news and exhortations filled public space. Security officers also targeted rural religious leaders who had substantial followings. One thousand ulamas on Java were sent to Jakarta for month-long training sessions where Japan's war was presented within an Islamic framework. Their pesantrens were inspected, and ulamas were ordered to introduce Japanese language and approved subjects into their curriculum. Detailed study of ordinary people, plus a network of informers and military police, enabled the Japanese to monitor town and countryside.

TOOLS OF MILITARY OCCUPATION: ACADEMICS AND THE MILITARY POLICE

Japanese academics who accompanied the Sixteenth Army to Java made close studies of four villages. The study of Cimahi village in west Java conveys the degree of impact of " three hundred and fifty years" of Dutch rule as much as the extent and nature of Japanese inquiries. Members of 574 households (out of 938 total) in seven of the twelve hamlets comprising the village were interviewed. Indonesian local government staff attended preparatory meetings conducted by Japanese military and the investigating team to encourage cooperation. Payment was in difficult-to-obtain textiles.

The investigators reported that most villagers were unable to write (defined as signing one's name) in either the Roman or Arabic alphabets. Only officials of local government knew Indonesian, and there was no village resident with a knowledge of Dutch. Primary schools established by the Dutch had taught children in the Sundanese language and writing system. Many adults, male and female, had made the pilgrimage to Mecca. Cimahi supported its own mosque and graveyard. The Japanese researchers concluded that the several pesantrens in the area had little influence on Cimahi life. None of their students came from the village itself, and the self-sufficient pesantrens had little contact with the village.

The Japanese record depicts a village operating in a Sundanese world. Villagers could move into colonial space if they had funds and ambition for study in high school or sought work outside. Those who stayed put were walled off from contact by economic self-sufficiency and by a language and schooling system that perpetuated a regional identity while closing the window to the worlds of Indonesia and Europe. The Japanese academics concluded that agricultural production could be increased and village farmers kept docile if responsibility for filling Japanese quotas was assigned to the village leadership and Japanese authority was kept invisible.

Kenpeitai (alternative spelling: *kempeitei*), meaning military police, was established in Japan in 1881 to keep order within the armed forces. Military police traveled with the armed forces as they pushed the boundaries of Japan into China and Southeast Asia. Military police monitored Japanese as well as Indonesians in occupied territories for signs of subversion.

The military police classified the population of conquered Java into Dutch, Eurasians, "Overseas Chinese," Indonesians, Ambonese, and Manadonese. Eurasians and Ambonese were considered virulently anti-Japanese as a result of Dutch indoctrination, while the other enemy identified, the Overseas Chinese, were classified as hostile because of their attachment to China. The kenpeitai recruited Indonesian informers to reveal identities of enemies by provoking demonstrations or incautious remarks. They used the suggestion of menace, as well as swift, public punishment of opponents, to keep Indonesian populations under control.

The Japanese military set up organizations such as the Triple A Movement, the Center of People's Power, and the Java Service Association and appointed politicians such as Sukarno to head them in order to know what Indonesians were saying and to control and contain their messages. The Japanese also sponsored organizations for wives of the well-placed. Before the war, federations of women's organizations such as the Indonesian Women's Congress had debated the role of women in an independent Indonesia and had championed women's rights to public office, education, careers, monogamy, protection against arbitrary divorce, and minimum age for first marriage. The Japanese organization for women, Fujinkai, set as female goals service to husband, devotion to emperor (of Japan), sacrifice for the war against the West, and teaching lower-class women how to work harder and raise more food crops. Magazines and films promoted Japanese styles of costume and femininity.

Young males, who were not attracted to organizations led by middle-aged professional politicians, were regarded by the Japanese as potentially dangerous, a floating group in society, detached from family responsibilities and often unemployed. Some came from the criminal underworld where they controlled laborers, opium, gambling, and prostitutes. They were eager to emulate young Japanese men in uniform. As Japanese security saw it, Indonesian youths had no fixed views and could spontaneously form a group for any number of causes, to rob, to set up an Islamic state, or to attack the Japanese. Such young men were drafted as auxiliary forces into the Japanese armies in Java and Sumatra. They received the same physical training and indoctrination as Japanese soldiers but were not given rifles. Draftees were assigned to guard prison camps, to monitor Indonesian communities as police, and to provide fire and air-raid defense services. In October 1943 the Japanese created Protectors of the Fatherland, a volunteer force outside the Japanese armies known by its acronym Peta. Recruits received instruction from Japanese officers in guerrilla warfare techniques and were trained to see themselves as helping the Japanese bring independence to Indonesia.

In 1944 youth militias were attached to organizations designed to control civilians. The Vanguard Column was intended to make all Javanese men over the age of fourteen promoters for the Java Service Association. Java's military governor was its head; Sukarno and Nahdatul Ulama's Hasyim Asy'ari were its advisers; Hatta and Kiai Haji Mas Mansur of Muhammadiyah were its managers. In May 1945, as Allied invasion seemed imminent, the eighty thousand members of the Vanguard Column received guerrilla training. Youths committed to Islamic causes were channeled into the Army of God Column. This Barisan Hizbullah was set up as the military wing of Masyumi. Overall, fifty thousand young men were trained and armed in 1945.

The Japanese military attempted to shape all these armed groups into the first line of defense against the invading Allies. They contained unruly youth by imposing military discipline on them, subordinating them to Japanese officers, and giving them duties that could be monitored. Japanese officers glorified war and violence as solutions to social problems, setting a pattern for public life in the Indonesian republic: political parties entered independence with military wings; the nation's armed forces consisted of a professional army and an array of associated militias, armed and trained by the standing army to be unleashed on specific targets.

Japan offered a political model of sacred emperor at the pinnacle of government, military executors, and a network of patriotic associations that caught up all social classes. In occupied lands, such as Manchuria and Vietnam, the Japanese reinstalled emperors as subleaders to their own imperial ruler. They expected to find Javanese calling for the elevation of Surakarta's Pakubuwono XI (r. 1939–1945) as emperor of all Java. But politicians who cooperated with the Japanese did not want to subordinate themselves to princes. Neither Sukarno nor the kiais heading Muhammadiyah and Nahdatul Ulama wanted to bow before a Javanese emperor. Nor did Ambonese, Batak, or Minangkabau politicians in Java. Even Javanese supporters of monarchy were divided in allegiance between the kings of Surakarta and Yogyakarta. Sukarno said the soul of the nation was the *rakyat Indonesia,* the Indonesian (common) people; Muslim leaders said it was the *ummat Islam,* the Muslim community. Most politicians opposed "feudalism" as well as colonialism, so that the Japanese could not find attractive candidates to promote an imperial system for a Javanese substate within the Japanese empire. Two Javanese, Sukarno and Ki Bagus Hadikusumo, chairman of Muhammadiyah, and the Sumatran Hatta seemed to Japanese officers the most able and popular of the political leaders on Java. They, not monarchists, were chosen to go to Japan in November 1943 to pay homage to Emperor Hirohito. It was Sukarno's first journey overseas. He did not return a monarchist.

Indonesian leaders who cooperated with the Japanese expected to win political concessions in return for deliveries of goods, laborers, and girls. They calculated that there would be a faster transfer of power in wartime under Japanese occupation than in peacetime under the Dutch. Sukarno and fellow nationalists pushed for permission to display Indonesian symbols and to nourish ambitions for independence for Indonesia, rather than for Java alone. Islamic leaders such as Mansur and Hadikusumo and the Sumatran Haji Agus Salim pushed until the Japanese withdrew the requirement that congregations bow in the direction of Tokyo during Friday prayers.

Political concessions, when they came, were not the result of Indonesian eloquence, nor of goods and laborers drafted for Japan's industries. American defeats inflicted on Japanese naval bases in 1944 altered Japan's Indonesia policies. In September 1944, as American troops made their first landing in the archipelago, on Morotai off Halmahera, Japan's Prime Minister Koiso promised independence for the Indies "in the future" and authorized the immediate flying of the Indonesian flag alongside the Japanese imperial flag on offices of the Service Association in Java. In March 1945, American forces won their first victories over Japanese troops on Japanese soil at Iwojima. In that same month the Japanese military administration on Java announced it would form a Committee for Investigating Independence for Indonesia to recommend models for an independent state to the local Japanese authorities who would forward them to Tokyo for review. After the emperor selected a model, a committee to prepare for the transfer of independence would be established in Jakarta.

The military command named the investigative committee's Indonesian and Japanese members on April 29. The sixty-four Indonesian members were selected from politicians in Java and prominent members of Javanese society. Because the colonial state had incorporated so many ethnic groups with varied cultures and orientations, Sukarno and Muhammad Yamin recommended the most inclusive definitions and the vaguest guidelines. Sukarno delivered their joint proposals in his Panca Sila (Five Pillars) speech to the committee when it met in June 1945. He proposed that the founding principles of an Indonesian state should be (in this order) nationalism, internationalism, government by consent, social justice, and belief in one God. He argued that these five pillars constituted *gotong royong*, which he defined as the Indonesian principle of co-operation unifying rich and poor, Muslim and Christian. Sukarno made no specific statement about the rights of women, children, workers, or any other category. He called for a society in which sovereignty resided in "the people" undifferentiated by class, age, wealth, religion, or gender. He specifically rejected a bill of rights, arguing against fellow committee member Maria Ulfah Santoso that such guarantees were unnecessary since the state would embody the people.

The committee debated three issues fundamental to the new state: the space it should occupy, who would belong as a citizen, and the role of government in enforcing Islamic law. Thirty-nine members voted for an Indonesia consisting of the Netherlands Indies, British Malaya, Singapore, British Borneo, Portuguese Timor, and West New Guinea. Nineteen wanted the territory of the Netherlands Indies. Six wanted Malaya and the Netherlands Indies minus West New Guinea. The majority recommended granting automatic citizenship to "native Indonesians," whom they defined as people born in the archipelago to native fathers. People born in the archipelago to Indonesian mothers, but whose fathers had foreign ancestry, could apply for naturalization. Fifty-five voted for a republican form of government and six for revival of monarchy. The model of an Islamic state guided by imams was not put to the vote. Instead, the committee attached to the draft constitution a document which has become known as the Jakarta Charter. It guaranteed that only Muslims would be eligible to be head of state and required the government of Indonesia to monitor and enforce observance of Islamic law by Muslim citizens.

On August 7, 1945, one day after the United States dropped the first atomic bomb on Hiroshima, the head of Japan's Southern Territories Command proclaimed imperial permission for the formation of a Committee to Prepare for Independence and promised Indonesia would be born in September. He announced that the new state would immediately declare war on the

Allies and fight under Japanese command. Japanese military officials would continue to guide and supervise the new country, and control its foreign relations. The new state would occupy the same territory as the Dutch East Indies but initially would govern only Java. General Yamamoto, head of the military administration on Java, disbanded the investigative committee and appointed twenty-one men to represent the Japanese zones of Java, Sumatra, and East Indonesia, and the Chinese community in the new Preparatory Committee. Their first meeting was set for August 18.

On August 9, the day the second bomb was dropped on Nagasaki, Sukarno, Hatta, and Dr. Rajiman Wedioningrat (a leader of the prewar Budi Utomo) flew to Japanese military headquarters in Saigon to receive further instructions. They carried back to Jakarta such a conviction of Japanese might that they refused to believe Indonesian clandestine radio operators who by August 12 had picked up Allied broadcasts that Japan would officially stop fighting and surrender on August 15. (The Japanese did not announce their surrender until August 21 in Java and until September in Sumatra.) Japanese monopoly of information had kept politicians in Java unaware that Allied bombing of Japanese airfields had begun in Ambon in 1943, and that Japanese troops had lost control of territories in Kalimantan, east Indonesia, and New Guinea to Allied forces in 1944. Java politicians did not know that Dutch and British commandos had been operating in north Sumatra since June 1945.

Youths in Java who tracked the skies and could identify Allied from Japanese aircraft knew what Java's politicians and ulamas, in their Japanese cocoon, could not know, guess, or believe. On August 16, Jakarta youth groups kidnapped Sukarno and his immediate circle forced them to declare Indonesia's independence unilaterally, rather than accept independence as the gift of an already defeated Japanese emperor. On August 17, 1945, standing in front of his house before a small group of political allies, and under watch of Indonesian militias, Sukarno proclaimed Indonesia's independence in the name of the Indonesian people. He and Hatta signed the declaration. Indonesian staff briefly seized control of Jakarta radio from their Japanese supervisors and launched the news into Java's airwaves.

The Japanese empire was seen to be defeated in fierce fighting in 1944 and 1945 in the Philippines, New Guinea, Ambon, Timor, and Kalimantan. Elsewhere, Japanese defeat by the Allies was not apparent to ordinary Indonesians or to Indonesians who staffed government agencies and headed wartime organizations for the Japanese. People received the news from fully armed Japanese soldiers who guarded ammunition supplies, tanks, and trucks. Japanese soldiers retained control of cities, transport, and communications systems, flew the Japanese flag, and continued to issue orders to politicians and the populace at large. On Allied instructions they had to maintain public order until Allied troops could arrive to disarm them, select individual officers for war crimes trials, and arrange for the rest to be returned to Japan.

In August 1945 there were seventy thousand Japanese troops in Java. Sukarno feared that mass rallies celebrating war's end and independence could result in Japanese guns being turned on unarmed Indonesian crowds and that independence leaders would suffer immediate retribution. Indonesian political leaders could not stop youth gangs from attacking small guardhouses in a grab for weapons; they could not prevent mob actions against village heads who had pressed farmers for rice to fill Japanese quotas while their families went hungry; they could not halt the lynchings of friends of the Japanese or the public humiliation of brothel girls. They could only sit indoors and build a government on paper, while outside youths ran through the streets shouting "Merdeka!" (Freedom!) and "*Bersiap!*" (Watch out! Be alert!), painted slogans on walls, attacked alleged traitors, and battled for turf and weapons.

The sixty-four Indonesian members of the investigative committee had debated in the name of all Indonesians, but they did not represent the archipelago's sixty million in age, class, education, religious conviction, region, or gender. In a young population that grew by twelve million births between 1930 and 1945, committee members were old, their average age forty-eight. All were graduates of secondary schools and universities at a time when most Indonesians could not read or write. Fifty-seven of the sixty-four were graduates of Dutch-language schools. Eighty-seven percent of the population was Muslim, but only seven of the committee had been educated at Islamic colleges in Java, Egypt, or Mecca. The largest prewar organization had been the Association of the Subjects of Yogyakarta, promoting Javanese ethnicity and submission to royalty, yet monarchists were represented by a single delegate, and there were no representatives of groups that wanted independent Indonesia to be a federation organized around ethnic cores. Fifty percent of the population was female, but only two committee members were women, and they represented the three thousand Indonesian women who had a Dutch education. They were Maria Ulfah Santoso, who was the first Indonesian woman to graduate from law school in Holland, and Soenaryo Mangunpuspito, who had been appointed by the colonial government to the Semarang municipal council. Both women were Javanese Dutch-speakers. They had a record in public life and careers devoted to securing rights for women in schooling, marriage, and work through colonial legislation. There were no representatives of

Aisyah, the largest prewar women's organization, or of any other women's groups that had wanted reforms to be compatible with Islamic prescriptions and initiated through Islamic courts. Although the Japanese had allocated them two delegates, youth organizations rejected membership because seven Japanese were also on the committee. Left-wing leaders were also not represented, because, like Syahrir, they refused to participate in Japanese-created associations, or because, like Amir Syarifuddin, they were in Japanese jails. Committee members represented no one in Brunei, Thailand, Malaya or Portuguese Timor, although they claimed these territories for Indonesia.

Despite their differences from the population at large, committee members believed themselves to represent the aspirations of every inhabitant of the archipelago in designing a future where Indonesians would govern themselves. On August 18 they transformed themselves into the National Committee of Indonesia, adopted the constitution drafted by the investigative committee, and named Sukarno president and Hatta vice president. Sukarno added more delegates to the National Committee to broaden representation until the number reached 135. In December 1946 it was expanded to 514. The committee regarded itself as a quasi-parliament and promised to hold elections as soon as conditions permitted. Politicians did not check if they indeed represented Indonesians until 1955, when every male and female citizen aged eighteen or already an adult through parenthood was eligible to vote without qualifications of literacy, property ownership, or religion. The politicians legislated election rights that most prewar parties had not demanded but to which ordinary Indonesian men and women responded. Thirty-nine million registered to vote, and 91.5 percent of them turned up to cast their votes by secret ballot.

While middle-aged, affluent politicians passed orderly and high-minded resolutions in August and September 1945, the situation in streets, towns, and villages was violent and unpredictable. Dutch people who had survived disease, labor, and starvation staggered out of Japanese prison camps into newly proclaimed republican space. Some tried to reclaim houses and property taken from them in 1942; some avenged deaths of relatives on enthusiasts for revolution. Most women and children drew back into the camps for safety. Many Indonesians were angry at the appearance of Dutch people, who were attacked, and there were witch-hunts for Indonesian traitors among Christian minorities. Many Indonesians have preserved a record of the tense "Bersiap" period in Java in memoirs, short stories, and poems. There is less information on this period from communities in other islands, but a Japanese officer with the Twenty-fifth Army has left a memoir, valuable because it shifts attention from Java to Sumatra.

TAKAO FUSAYAMA: AFTER THE FALL

Takao Fusayama was conscripted into the Japanese army, trained in wireless communications, and sent to China in 1940. He accompanied Japanese units invading Vietnam, Cambodia, Thailand, Malaya, and Singapore. By early 1942 Fusayama was in Sumatra, posted to Medan and Aceh. In July 1946 the Allies repatriated Fusayama to Japan, where he resumed his civilian career.

Fusayama begins his memoir late in August 1945, after Japan's surrender. (His recollections of war service in Sumatra from January 1942 until August 1945 relate only to learning Indonesian and collecting folklore.) He portrays the Bersiap months from the perspective of Japanese trapped in Sumatra by the end of war, menaced by Indonesian revenge seekers, obliged to coerce farmers and market sellers into continuing to supply them with food. He describes Japanese officers attempting to ensure Indonesia's independence by maintaining public order and keeping warring factions apart. He describes the Allied victory as bringing a tragic interruption to the Japanese program of liberating their "little brown brothers" from foreign rule.

Indonesian histories record a nation galvanized into unity to defend its independence. Fusayama's account shows republican leaders in far-off Yogyakarta struggling to control day-to-day events in Sumatra. Sukarno's representatives had to contend with local gangs, youth militias, and ulamas in the contest for power. Angry mobs attacked their sultans, Europeans, and isolated Japanese. Armed men denounced, robbed, and attacked in the name of revolution. Upper-class women who had attended Dutch schools and wore Western costume were murdered; ordinary women who had worked in Japanese brothels were stripped naked and paraded through the streets. Indonesian men who were graduates of Dutch schools vanished after being accused of spying. Chinese and Indian shopkeepers were robbed of their stores in the name of revolutionary action. Fusuyama records that wealthy men sent their adult children to

Holland, that locals attacked migrant workers on plantations, and that squatters moved on to private lands. Entrepreneurs smuggled republican government assets to Singapore for their own profit. Youth groups fought among themselves for control of towns. Rice fields were left uncultivated as the countryside became unsafe, and internal trade was killed off by armed men who set up road blocks and imposed levies. The revolution proceeded by terror.

In the last weeks of war the Japanese promoted Indonesians within the bureaucracy to senior positions such as province head. The new republican government confirmed these appointments, giving officials the dual status of Japanese and republican staffers. The republican government also adopted the Japanese model of a single mass organization to channel emotions into service to the new state. It gave the president emergency powers and made all officials personally responsible to him. Soon the need to present an acceptable face to the West superseded the need to be acceptable to the Japanese. A British force was due in Java in September, and war trials of Indonesian collaborators were anticipated. Some politicians urged that Sukarno and Hatta withdraw from public view and that fascist features of the new republic, such as the single party, be dismantled. In October 1945 Sukarno turned over to Syahrir the task of creating an acceptable Indonesia—acceptable that is, not to the new republic's citizens but to another set of foreign outsiders. Syahrir, as Indonesia's first prime minister, created forms of government that were recognizable to Allied military commanders and civilian policymakers. He reduced the emergency powers of the president and selected a cabinet from the National Committee that was responsible to the committee as a temporary parliament. He encouraged the formation of political parties and workers' unions, attempted to cultivate the principle of civilian control of the armed forces, and tried to establish open procedures and forms in the conduct of political life.

Indonesians with guns had little sympathy with the National Committee's policies. They did not care what Westerners thought of Indonesian public life. They wanted to get weapons, prevent the re-imposition of Dutch rule, and establish their group's prerogatives in an independent Indonesia. Many Muslims in parties and militias also opposed creating an Indonesia that replicated either Japanese fascism or Western democracy. They wanted Indonesia to be the

SYAHRIR: WESTERN EDUCATION VERSUS EASTERN SUPERSTITION

Sutan Syahrir (1909–1966) was born into a Minangkabau titled family. His father was adviser to the sultan of Deli and chief public prosecutor in Medan, serving the twin bases of the colonial state, Indonesian monarchy and colonial bureaucracy. Syahrir attended the primary school for Europeans in Medan, secondary school in Bandung (west Java), and law school in the Netherlands. Syahrir was committed from the beginning to a republic replacing the colonial state. In 1926 he founded Young Indonesia, and he was a member of the youth congress that produced the commitment to one nation in 1928. While a university student, Syahrir was a member of Holland's Social Democratic Party and the Indonesian Association that had grown out of Abendanon's Indies Association. He had a brief marriage to a Dutch woman.

In 1931 Syahrir returned to the colony to take up political life. His approach was to form study circles to mold Dutch-speaking young men into intellectuals and leaders. He wanted a strong Sumatran contribution into the new Indonesia to counter the flamboyant emotionalism of Sukarno. For Syahrir, "Javanese" was synonymous with "backward." He had little sympathy for feudalism and superstition, or for the crowd in political decision-making. Indonesians, he thought, needed guidance and firm leadership, but not from the Japanese. An opponent of emperor worship, glorification of warrior virtues, and rule by the military, Syahrir did not seek or accept leadership positions in Japanese-sponsored mass organizations. His prewar political action and six years' exile qualified him for the privileges and prominence enjoyed during Japanese rule by Sukarno, Hatta, Rajiman, and Asy'ari, but the Japanese interned him as an enemy before placing him under house arrest in Cipanas. There Syahrir attempted to be invisible to the Japanese and concentrated on forming Sumatran students, caught in Java by the occupation, into cadres for his political future.

As prime minister during the first years of Indonesia's independence struggle, Syahrir chose negotiation over military struggle. He signed the first of a series of agreements with the Dutch that shrank republican territory to Java and Sumatra. He experienced the revolution as terror. A militia operating for Tan Malaka kidnapped him in 1946, and Dutch troops arrested him in December 1948 and imprisoned him with the civilian leadership of the republic. Syahrir did not welcome the Indonesia that was eventually won in 1949. His Socialist Party of Indonesia proved to be the party of only two percent of the electorate in 1955. He aligned himself with Sumatran reformers in Masyumi and Sumatran army leaders in opposition to Javanese politicians and Javanese ambitions. In 1962 Sukarno placed him under house arrest. Syahrir was allowed medical treatment early in 1965 in Europe, where he died in April 1966 as Indonesia was convulsed by youth squads and militias eradicating Sukarno's legacy through systematic intimidation and killing.

House of Islam. Tenant farmers wielding machetes and bamboo stakes turned against landlords and the Chinese shopkeeper-banker. Town youths set on officials who had served Dutch and Japanese administrations and were now calling themselves servants of the republic. All these groups used revolutionary times to stake out their space and impose their solutions. Central leadership had pride that the people whom the Dutch had derided as "the weakest folk on earth" were capable of fighting but also fear of the popular anger so readily turned against all authority.

In some parts of Indonesia there was no fighting against the Dutch. Early Allied possession of Ambon and return of Dutch troops there, for instance, meant the absence of fighting through the years 1945 to 1949. But in periods of transition hostility between Muslim and Christian villages took violent form. Between the collapse of Dutch authority and imposition of Japanese in 1942, Muslims looted and burned houses and businesses of Dutch residents and their closest Christian Ambonese supporters. In 1945, as the Dutch returned, Christian Ambonese took revenge on Muslim Ambonese. To the rajas and Christian communities the republic meant domination by Javanese and Muslims. They heard with alarm the People's Army of Indonesia declare guerrilla and economic warfare against Dutch, Eurasians, and Ambonese in October 1945 and were fearful when the Nahdatul Ulama and Masyumi parties declared the war against the Dutch a war to establish Islamic life and government throughout Indonesia. Christian Ambonese soldiers reenlisted and new recruits signed up to fight for the Dutch cause throughout the archipelago. Christian Ambonese saw more secure futures in a colonial state than in a Muslim Indonesia. Muslim Ambonese, who had never had equal access to school and jobs under the Dutch, supported the republic.

There was no struggle against the Dutch in Aceh, for Dutch troops did not reenter the province. Instead, Aceh exported men and funds into contested territories. Within Aceh, fighting was between Acehnese. In 1942 the All-Aceh Union of Ulamas had welcomed the Japanese, but the Japanese had kept the uleebalang administrators of the Dutch system in place and the republican government in Jakarta confirmed them as its regional representatives in 1945. As Aceh's ulamas saw it, in every territory the Dutch reoccupied, the old elites left republican service to work for the Dutch. So, in Aceh, in March 1946, the killing began. Ulamas led armed bands against landowners and officeholders and their families. Tenants seized their rice lands. By the end of 1946, the uleebalang class was eliminated from Acehnese society. Ulamas controlled military power and civilians, the region was autonomous throughout the revolution, and Aceh resumed its old trading relations with the Malay Peninsula and Singapore that the Dutch colonial state had broken off.

In reoccupied areas the Dutch immediately reestablished contacts with local elites, offering an alternative to the single state offered by the republican leadership on Java. The State of East Indonesia, consisting of Sulawesi, Maluku, and Bali, was formed under President (and Prince) Anak Agung Gde Agung in December 1946, with its capital in Makasar. In May 1947 Sultan Abdul Hamid II of Pontianak became head of the State of West Kalimantan. In December 1947 the State of East Sumatra was formed, followed by the States of Madura and of West Java in February 1948, and the State of East Java in November. All were headed by Indonesian nobles whose administrations rested on the Royal Netherlands Indies Army. In July 1948 the Dutch drew the Indonesian heads of states into an Assembly for Federal Consultation. The assembly was, under Dutch leadership, to design a federation that would be admitted to a Netherlands Union consisting of the Netherlands and its former West Indies colonies of Surinam and Curaçao.

Pro-republican youth groups and militias disbanded or were killed by soldiers of the colonial army in reoccupied territories. Three thousand died in south Sulawesi between November 1946 and February 1947. The Indonesian nationalist cause was kept alive in the web of organizations the Dutch created. Pro-Republican Ambonese, for instance, took part in Dutch-sponsored councils in East Indonesia during the revolution years, and they won the majority of seats in the Council of the South Moluccas when Muslim and Christian Ambonese voted in 1947 and 1948. Most Indonesians ended up spending the revolution under Dutch rule.

In Java, Allied forces landed in the major north coast cities in September and October 1945. They initially recognized the republic, but soon concluded that its appointees were unable to keep order and began turning over government buildings and army bases to the Netherlands Indies Civil Administration and Army. Although republican support had been highly visible and vocal in Jakarta, in Surabaya the depth of commitment to an Indonesia free of foreign rule was most dramatically demonstrated. Surabaya was Java's second largest city, the site of dockyards, factories, schools, and army bases. Workers, students, laborers from surrounding plantations and mills, men attached to the many pesantrens in northeast Java, and the unemployed all converged in Surabaya as 6,000 British Indian troops entered the city on October 25 to evacuate Dutch survivors of prison camps and disarm the Japanese. They were quickly confronted by 20,000 Indonesian soldiers of the republic's army and about 120,000 other men grouped in bands and militias who responded only to the orders of their own heroes and to the appeals of Sutomo (Bung Tomo), whose militia controlled Surabaya's airwaves. The British flew in republican leaders they hoped could prevent fighting: Sukarno, Hatta, and Amir Syarifuddin (whom the British had just freed from a kenpeitai gaol and who was now Sukarno's minister of information and vice president of the caucus of the National Committee). Their influence brought about a ceasefire, but could not keep the ceasefire in force after a British plane bore them back to Jakarta.

British air and naval bombardment of Surabaya began on November 10, 1945. Barely armed men responded to Bung Tomo's appeals in the name of Islam as well as of the republic. It took the British three weeks to end the fighting, by which time thousands of Indonesian men were dead, much of the population had fled, and Surabaya was badly damaged.

November 10, which has become enshrined in Indonesia as Heroes' Day, was one of the two large-scale battles of the war for independence in Java. Afterward, army and militias withdrew into the hills. From hidden bases they harried Dutch troops with ambushes, sniping, bridge explosions, and damaged roads. Civilian authority over army and militias ended, and the war was fought by guerrilla bands operating in their own territories. Dutch-trained Indonesian army officers, who thought in terms of battalions and coordinated strategy, lost out to men who had learned their army skills from Japanese instructors and to men who emulated warrior traditions of Trunajaya and Surapati and surrounded themselves with followers who spread rumors of their leader's holiness and special powers.

SUDIRMAN: PESANTREN IN ARMS

Sudirman (c. 1915–1950), an Islamic schoolteacher, was hostile to the rule of Dutch Christians and to Surakarta's royals and all Javanese who worked with the Dutch. In 1943 the Japanese recruited Sudirman to train as an officer in Peta. There he furthered his skill in martial arts and was attracted by the union of warrior and spiritual belief in the Japanese military code. Sudirman's followers saw in his ascetic conduct, meditation, and personal discipline the signs of holiness. Militia men elected him supreme commander of the army in November 1945. They shared his contempt for civilian government and refused to recognize the army leaders appointed by the republic's prime minister and cabinet.

Sudirman worked through militias. He unleashed them against Pakubuwono XII and republican politicians. Forces loyal to him seized control of Surakarta. Sudirman pressured the republican government to strip Surakarta's royals of rights beyond their palace walls. He opposed negotiating independence and sent a militia to kidnap Prime Minister Syahrir. He established the Indonesian army's tradition of opposing representative government.

In 1949, the Dutch captured the entire republican government and swallowed its remaining territory. Sudirman directed the uprising of militia squads that contested the Dutch. He was by then dying of tuberculosis, and followers carried him on a litter to rally his militias. Thus his legend was born. The foe of civilian politicians now lends his mythic holiness to Sukarno. In the Blitar museum, portraits of Java's walis, Diponegoro, and Sudirman occupy commanding positions around Indonesia's first president. Photographs of world leaders meeting with Sukarno are shunted into a corner.

The republic's leaders saw in the charisma of Bung Tomo and wild fervor of the Surabaya fighters fearful evidence of what ordinary Indonesians really felt. They recognized the power of appeals phrased in Islamic language and the new importance of radio in the war for popular allegiance. After Surabaya, republican civilian elites on Java turned to negotiation with the Dutch to achieve independence. Even as they participated in long diplomatic sessions, they sensed the enormity of popular passion in town and countryside. They heard daily of kidnappings and murder and feared physical threat to themselves.

Revolutions, like colonies, attract all kinds of misfits, adventurers, people detached from family, and individuals on the fringes of the law. Such types often brought a passionate commitment to the republican cause, but they were too full of themselves to subordinate personal gratification to the central civilian leadership and too busy finding personal meaning in drama to be good citizens.

SOLO REVOLUTIONARIES OF THE FRINGE: THE CASE OF K'TUT TANTRI

Revolution offered a few women the chance to live free of home, husband, and family. K'tut Tantri is the Balinese name taken by a British woman who found in Indonesia a territory for self-dramatization. She established herself in Bali in the 1930s where, as a hotelkeeper, she helped invent and sell exotic Bali to wealthy tourists. Under Japanese military rule in 1942, she made English-language radio broadcasts that were vehemently anti-Dutch for Japan's Java war propaganda bureau. In 1945 she began broadcasting appeals to the English-speaking world to support the republic and traveled with Bung Tomo's set. In 1947 she ventured into arms dealing on behalf of the nationalist cause. The republican leadership eased her out of Indonesia.

K'tut Tantri continued as traveling spokeswoman for a free Indonesia. In 1960 her book *Revolt in Paradise* found a ready audience. It was reprinted and translated into a dozen languages, including Indonesian. Following independence, the government brought K'tut Tantri to Indonesia for a sentimental tour and meetings with former militia leaders and President Sukarno. It paid her a pension until her death in Australia in 1999. K'tut Tantri's role in Indonesia's revolution survives only in her own memoir and imagining. No history issued by Indonesia's ministry of education includes her name.

Dutch civilian and military officials who entered Java alongside British forces in 1945 quickly set up an administration in Jakarta. They renamed it Batavia and began scouring the city for republican supporters, especially young men, and jailing them. Former employees received offers of jobs and resumption of pensions. Dutch troops set up barriers on roads leading into the city to prevent infiltration of guerrilla fighters and patrolled streets, markets, and railway stations. The battle for Surabaya and the killings in Sumatra pressured the Dutch to reach an accommodation with the republicans before the withdrawal of British forces in December 1946. In November that year they signed a cease-fire with representatives of the republic. The Dutch recognized the Republic of Indonesia as occupying Sumatra, Java (except Batavia and environs), and Madura. Republicans conceded the Dutch occupation of east Indonesia and agreed to work with the Dutch to form a Republic of the United States of Indonesia within a Dutch-Indonesian Union by 1949. It was called the Linggajati Agreement and signed, on behalf of the republic, by Prime Minister Syahrir. His personal dissatisfaction at events and awareness of popular anger at concessions ended his role in republican politics.

The Dutch formed their first federal state one month after Linggajati and the second in July 1947. By then the Indies army had been rebuilt to one hundred thousand men. It seized Java's north coast ports and Madura, west Java with its tea and coffee plantations, and east Java with its sugar plantations. The Indies army also captured Medan, Palembang, and Padang. Once in control of

Sumatra's oil fields, its rubber and tobacco plantations, and its tin deposits, the Indies army took over the entire island with the exception of Aceh. The republic's civilian leaders again signed their acceptance of shrinking space in the Renville Agreement of January 1948. Once more, signing led to the loss of the prime minister, this time Amir Syarifuddin. The republic was now confined to central Java, cut off from contacts with its constituents across Indonesia, access to oil, rubber, and rice, along with export and import revenues. The population under Dutch command swelled as refugees fled guerrilla fighters in the countryside or sought food, medicine, schooling, and jobs in Dutch-controlled cities. Soldiers of the republic's Siliwangi division in west Java withdrew to central Java. In official Indonesian histories this abandoning of the Sundanese population is dignified by the Arabic word *hijrah.*

HIJRAH: THE MAKING OF A NATIONAL MYTH

Hijrah signifies the withdrawal of Muhammad and his followers from Mecca in the year 622 C.E. They fled hostile Arab tribes for the city of Medina, where Muhammad was able to build up a society governed by Islamic law and plan the reconquest of Mecca. Muslim time signals the significance of this withdrawal by naming it Year 1. In the Indonesian context, hijrah signified that Siliwangi troops would in time return to throw out the Dutch after a strong republic had been established in its core area of central Java.

In west Java, Muslim militias did not wait for the return of Siliwangi troops. In 1948 they led attacks on the Dutch. The republic's shrunken territory now held over one million armed men, competing army staff commands, and militia leaders who recognized no superior authority. East Java launched its own war for a communist state centered at Madiun. Militias, regular troops, and civilians fought, killed their prisoners, murdered opponents and fellow villagers. Communist, Masyumi, and Nahdatul Ulama supporters hunted each other down. Amir Syarifuddin, who had joined the communists, was captured and executed by Siliwangi men.

In December 1948 Dutch troops invaded the republic's remaining territories, captured its civilian leaders, took them deep into Dutch space in Bangka, and raised the Dutch flag in the republic's heartland. Sukarno's tactic of focusing international attention on a captured leadership worked. The United States pressured the Dutch to include Sukarno's republic in the Republic of the United States of Indonesia and to transfer sovereignty in December 1949. But Indonesians with guns were not convinced that civilians were to be respected or trusted. Sudirman proclaimed a military government as soon as Sukarno and his cabinet allowed themselves to be arrested. Guerrillas assaulted Dutch positions from their mountain hideouts; the Siliwangi fought its way back into west Java to confront the Dutch and Darul Islam forces. Men who fought the last battles of the independence war saw themselves as saviors of Indonesia and its rightful leaders.

There is no single moment when Indonesia's struggle for independence ended. To the world, the struggle was over when the Republic of the United States of Indonesia accepted transfer of sovereignty from the Netherlands on December 27, 1949. To many Indonesians the struggle was not over until August 17, 1950, when, after steady pressure from Jakarta, the states that the Dutch had created dissolved themselves into a unitary Republic of Indonesia. From another perspective, the struggle continued as battalions of the National Army of Indonesia fought in Ambon in 1950 to suppress a movement for independence from Indonesia. They fought again through the 1950s in Aceh, Sulawesi, and west Java to suppress Darul Islam rebellions and revolts against Java's dominance of regional economies. For some, the struggle for independence ended only in 1969 when West New Guinea was incorporated into Indonesia (or reunited with Indonesia) as its twenty-sixth province.

Alternatively, the struggle for independence could be said to have ended in 1957 when President Sukarno expelled the forty-six thousand Dutch citizens still living in Indonesia, nationalized Dutch-owned businesses, and turned them over to Indonesia's army to manage. In another sense the struggle for independence continued as Sukarno and sections of the army attacked the republic's parliament as a Western device alien to Indonesian national identity, a leftover from the Dutch that was derailing national life. From this perspective, the struggle ended when Sukarno decreed martial law in 1957, suspended the elected parliament, and began implementing Guided Democracy. In 1959 Sukarno and the central army leadership defeated fresh independence movements in Sumatra and Sulawesi. After that none could challenge the dominance of Java and Javanese in Indonesia's political, economic, and cultural life.

With the Dutch eliminated and the Outer Islands merged with Java, Sukarno began creating new forms of government that he thought would fit with Indonesian history and Indonesian personality as he understood them. He rejected the conception of society being composed of individuals or social classes in favor of an "Indonesian" sense of society composed of "togetherness" groups. He did not see public life as a competition between opposing class interests. He discovered the "Indonesian" way as incorporating opposites within a single government, reconciling opposing goals by consensus, not by voting, and leaving no group outside. In 1960 he called such an alliance of forces Nasakom government, meaning a fusion of nationalists, religious people, and communists. He expanded this concept later to "four-footed government," drawing in the armed forces. He revived the Japanese-era constitution that gave the president extensive powers and made the cabinet responsible to him rather than to elected representatives of voters. His inclusive cabinet grew to more than three hundred members by 1965. He replaced the elected parliament with a council replicating the Dutch People's Council, because it included members elected from government-approved slates of candidates and members appointed by government to represent "functional groups": women, peasants, youth, the military, lumped together across class, generation, region, ethnicity, and religion. Opponents who refused to join were jailed without trial and their parties banned.

All this proved acceptable to many in the Javanese communities stretched across the archipelago and to Beijing. Sukarno's Guided Democracy was not welcomed by the West, by many Indonesian ethnic communities, by important segments of the armed forces, or by Indonesians who had fought for independence in order to replace colonial rule with Islamic government. In the early 1960s their voices could not be heard as more unfinished business of the Indonesian struggle against colonialism was found in British sponsorship of the formation of Malaysia in the western end of the archipelago.

WHAT'S IN A NAME? DECLINE VERSUS ABERRATION

When the National Army of Indonesia took control by presidential decree in 1957, political parties, campaigning, elections, and elected assemblies were banned and the civil courts of justice were suspended. Looking back at the vigorous political life of the Dutch-era parties, of the revolution, and of the multiparty governments of the first seven years of independence, the political scientist Herbert Feith discerned a decline in constitutional democracy in Indonesia. He attributed this decline to fragile commitment to democratic procedure, the use of government to advance party and partisan causes, and the willingness of political parties to call on their militia affiliates to intimidate opponents and bring bully law to the streets.

While politicians plotted in Jakarta, ordinary people faced the problems caused by rapid population growth and economic crisis. Feith established the context. Between the fall of the Dutch in 1942 and the birth of the Republic of Indonesia in 1950, the number of Indonesians rose by 17 million. By the time Sukarno introduced Guided Democracy in 1960 Indonesia's population had grown to 97 million. Indonesia's politicians, engaged in the politics of grabbing resources, did not devise ways to feed, clothe, house, and educate Indonesia's millions. Constitutional democracy declined until it was cancelled by authoritarian government. In Feith's analysis, pragmatic politicians who tried to implement reforms were swept aside by the "solidarity-makers," who promoted national spirit, ongoing revolution, and continuous struggle as answers to unemployment, low literacy rates, and high inflation.

The historian Harry Benda challenged this conclusion of decline and failure, arguing that the 1950s were not years of decline of democracy, but of aberration. From Benda's perspective, the years of constitutional democracy were a radical departure in Indonesian public life. There had never been democratic institutions in Hindu or Islamic monarchies. Nor had colonial government been accountable to its subjects. The Dutch had not guarded individual rights or instituted democratic procedures. According to Benda, when Sukarno and the army dismantled democratic rights, Indonesian public life flowed back into its inheritance of authoritarian rule, monopoly of power, exclusion of the many from the privileges of the few, reliance on bullies (hired thugs, militias), and rule by terror.

Since the overthrow of President Suharto, this bleak assessment of the 1950s has been replaced in some Indonesian quarters by nostalgia. In this twenty-first-century imagining, political life in the 1950s was free, vibrant, untrammeled by heavy government, censorship, and the application of terror through the "mysterious killings," disappearances and mass murder of the Suharto years.

12

MAJAPAHIT VISIONS
Sukarno and Suharto in Indonesian Histories

From January 1950 the Republic of Indonesia occupied the space of the Dutch colonial state, excepting its West New Guinea territory. From Jakarta President Sukarno surveyed the archipelago state. The solid core of Java contained half of the new nation's population, most of the nation's men with modern educations, and the highest concentration of politicians committed to a unitary state. Java was also the region most damaged by guerrilla warfare and most divided within itself. Two civil wars had been fought there, pitting republican troops against Muslim soldiers and communist partisans. Java's inhabitants had been most galvanized by the years of Japanese mass mobilization. Java was also where the contest between civilians and military for control of government had been most dramatic.

Looking out from Jakarta, Sumatra had natural resources, militias that had operated independently of any coordinating authority, recognizing no superior power, and the history of killing as the means to eliminate designated classes. Aceh showed no signs of wanting to accept equal status with other regions under Jakarta's rule. Eastern Indonesia, the oldest and best functioning of the Dutch-sponsored states, had its many princes and its ambivalence toward the Javanese. The Christian fringe included men with secondary schooling, modern skills, and experience in administering an archipelago state. This region's soldiers, the most experienced in policing an archipelago state and

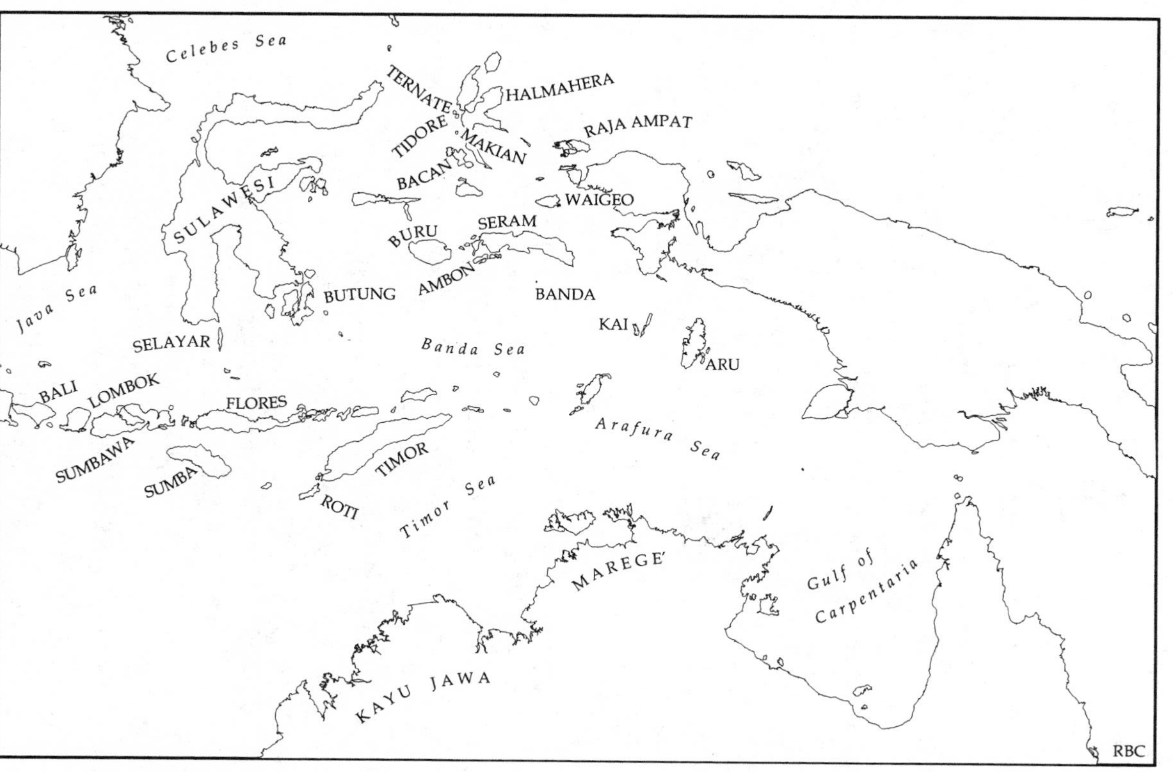

The Eastern Archipelago

putting down trouble for its ruling elite, were demobilized now and discredited owing to their partnership with the Dutch. Semi-nomadic peoples remained outside the organized religions of Islam and Christianity for the most part or followed forms deemed highly suspect by Jakarta authorities.

Encircling this fringe were other countries: Malaya, still a colony in 1950, the new countries of Burma and the Philippines, and Vietnam convulsed by fighting for independence. From Jakarta it seemed as if Indonesia was in charge of its own destiny. Historians were called on to recast past time into the service of the new state. The struggle for independence, that had taken place largely on Java, became the new history's center. Indonesian regional histories yielded center stage to the Dutch, and Indonesian roles in this drama were confined to resistance, courageous failure, and misery. National heroes were Muslim men who led armed bands against Dutch troops. There was no place in national history for parallel histories of Indonesian societies, no perspective that showed the Dutch occupying a tiny space while Indonesian actors assumed the larger roles. In this new history, loyalty to Islam and hatred of European domination had motivated Indonesians in all times and places.

This national history contrasted dramatically with the history Dutch-educated politicians had learned in school. Colonial history began in the Netherlands, located authentic Indonesian pasts in the pre-Islamic period, and recorded Dutch military victories and innovations in technology and welfare. Archipelago oral and manuscript traditions located ancestors in sky or on mountaintops and explained why kings should rule and everyone else obey. The history constructed in pesantrens began with Adam and Eve, named Indonesian ancestors who pointed the way to Islam, and identified society's true leaders as descendants of Muhammad or of renowned theologians.

Outside Java armed groups menaced regions preferring federation to a unitary state. Java-based elites seemed insensitive to local conditions. The Dutch still managed plantations, ran oil drills, operated banks, and taught college. Ordinary people had acquired, through independence, the obligation to repay the Netherlands' treasury for the cost of delaying independence through their taxes. They still could not gather housing materials and firewood from state forests or cut down trees to plant food crops. Plantations remained the private property of foreign companies, their cultivated, fertile soils off-bounds to landless Indonesian farmers. There were not enough jobs off the farm and not enough places in school. Everywhere there were men who had been shed by the national army, without jobs, recognition, or futures. The grand houses of the Dutch and their showy symbols of status, such as cars, now belonged to Jakarta politicians. Prosperity was not trickling down to ordinary Indonesians.

Government revenues found their way into the pockets of the new rulers or were spent on "prestige projects" in Jakarta. Christians still ran government ministries and army commands, although they were now Indonesian Christians. An Indonesian government suppressed regional languages and identities by doing away with textbooks and language instruction in native tongues.

Protest was difficult. Colonial-era laws restricting rights to assembly and expression remained in effect. Criticism and dissent were deemed treason, opposing the tide of nationalism and world history. No culture of loyal opposition existed. While schoolbooks and the government-controlled news industry presented the revolution as a shining, selfless moment, to ordinary people it seemed a power grab. From the beginning, the national army leadership opposed the free participation of ordinary Indonesians in public life. In 1952 the army, under Colonel Nasution, pressured Sukarno to dismantle the transitional parliament. In 1957 the army expanded into managing the economy and policing the state. It closed down political parties, found enemies within, and set up a military administration by placing officers at the head of every unit of local government.

Sukarno dominated the republic's first twenty-one years, Suharto its next thirty-two. Both men were committed to a Java-dominated state and expected regional politicians to pay homage in their capital. They broadcast the glories of the state to the furthest corners of the archipelago. They sent the armed forces into rebellious regions in the 1950s, and to extend Jakarta's rule into West New Guinea in 1963 and into East Timor in 1975. They paid television directors and museum curators (modern-day palace poets) to expound and commemorate their version of the state. Ordinary citizens, whose ancestors had "read" carved panels on temples, now "read" the state's progress through its public buildings, stadiums, statues, arches, war memorials, and billboard art. The governments of Sukarno and Suharto made promotion dependent on patronage from Jakarta and transplanted communities of Javanese into "empty spaces," throughout the archipelago, ensuring Java loyalties within the regions.

Sukarno and Suharto dominate the second half of Indonesia's twentieth century, but they were not alone. Java crowds loved Sukarno. They admired his lengthy speeches about struggle and revolution, believed he would deliver food, school, and jobs when politicians and army men could not. They overlooked his enjoyment of luxuries to claim him as one of the "little people." Middle classes tolerated or loved Suharto. They wanted him to protect their lives, ensure comfortable futures and foreign degrees, keep Indonesia's huge population under tight control, and eliminate troublemakers who wanted to launch jihad or seize landed estates.

The governments headed by Sukarno and Suharto are often characterized as monolithic regimes, but both administrations were composed of many groups, each working for its own vision of Indonesia. Within the model Majapahit, there had been disaffected vassals, resentful taxpayers, and a Muslim minority within the Hindu palace elite. In the Indonesia of Sukarno and Suharto, opposing forces also battled beneath the surface of homage and apparent acquiescence.

One institution imprinting its vision for Indonesia on the citizenry was the ministry of religion, the first ministry to be established by the republic. Dutch and Japanese governments had run offices of religious affairs in order to contain the diverse strains of Indonesian Islam. The ministry of religion saw itself as the arm of a Muslim state, whose job it was to right past injustices, expand Islam, and contain the state's non-Muslim minorities. While Sukarno advocated an "Indonesian identity" in the 1950s and Suharto promoted economic development in the 1970s and 1980s, the ministry of religion laid the foundations for an Islamic state.

The ministry introduced Islamic education into the public school system, established Islamic universities and institutes, and brought supervision of marriage law and the organization of religious courts into government. It appointed Muslims to inspect Islamic schools, oversee religious foundations, and handle pilgrims. The ministry encouraged greater Islamic religious observance at home and stronger links with world Islam. It financed pilgrimages and religious studies overseas, imported missionaries from Egypt, and ran programs to promote Arab culture in mosque design, domestic architecture, and personal dress. It promoted Arab political causes through pamphlets, Friday sermons, and pressure on government foreign policy.

In the tradition of Islam, the ministry defined what place non-Muslims should have in the state, setting up sections within the ministry for tolerated religions (Christianity, Buddhism). Its early definition of "paganism" meant that Bali's Hindus, Nias islanders, Tengger, Dayak, and Irianese peoples had no place in a state based on belief in one God. In 1962 the ministry recognized Bali Hinduism as a tolerated religion, but it continued to view worshippers of local spirits as "potential Muslims" and sponsored conversion programs among them. In Kalimantan, Minahasa, Ambon, Irian and, until 1999, in East Timor, the ministry supported transplanting Muslims into non-Muslim communities and appointment of Muslims to positions of authority.

For many, Indonesia seemed to be on the right course. The Jakarta Charter had been dropped from the constitution, but belief in one God had been made the first (rather than the fifth) pillar of the nation's ideology. There was the seduction of the new state, and spoils to seek. Under Sukarno, Nahdatul Ulama politicians got their hands on the resources of the state in coalition cabinets with members of Nationalist and Christian parties. Under Suharto, orthodox Muslims were appointed to government jobs and advisory councils; prefabricated mosque packages were distributed, and loudspeakers were installed so that all would hear the Muslim marking of time.

Other Muslims were disappointed by the new republic. Christians were still in government and army commands. Islamic political life was hobbled. In 1960, Sukarno banned Masyumi, Indonesia's largest Muslim party. In 1973, Suharto required all legal parties with Islamic agendas to coalesce in the Unity and Development Party. The new coalition was not permitted to attach Islam to its name or to display Islamic symbols. Western scholars elaborated on the difference between santri and *abangan* Islam—orthodoxy versus accommodation with Indonesian customs—and focused on Islam in Java. Inside independent Indonesia, in all regions, the debate was often framed in other terms. The proponents of Darul Islam were not satisfied with a greater share of public money for Islamic causes as the gift of a secular state and wanted to substitute sharia for Dutch law. Muslims outside the circles of patronage and Muslims offended by Christians in government felt as if Islam still had a minority status in Indonesia.

In the early years many people took pride in being Indonesian, and part of a global trend in defeating Western imperialism. The media presented Sukarno as a world leader. People who had lived under the colonial term "Native" now had a territory and a status of their own. In 1955 heads of state and foreign ministers from India, Africa, and China journeyed to Bandung in west Java for the first Conference of Non-Aligned Nations to acknowledge the vision of Indonesia's new leaders and endorse the message that two-thirds of the world's population rejected the leadership of the United States and the Soviet Union.

In the past, Indonesia and Indonesians had been presented in Dutch terms in exhibitions in Europe's capitals. In Paris and Amsterdam, in "Indonesian-style" buildings, designed by Dutch architects, live Indonesians were posed among stationary exhibits of the colony's commercial enterprises. The live exhibits demonstrated "traditional" handicrafts for spectators accustomed to the modern world of mass manufacturing. They were presented as subjects of Dutch military might and modern management. Now Java was the site for exhibition of Indonesians. Instead of native crafts, there was a national army with modern weapons, the mastery of press and information, the management of great numbers of leaders, aides, and security staff. The setting was authentic, not a Dutch version. The colonized challenged the former colonizers, denouncing Western influence on youth cultures and attempts to continue controlling Asian and African economies.

To Indonesians enthralled by a revival of Majapahit "glory," rancor and rebellions were the product of external forces. Regional groups challenging Java's domination of local politics and resources were derided in the controlled press as pawns of the West, which begrudged Indonesia control of international water highways. According to readily accepted conspiracy theories, the West was working for the breakup of Indonesia, or wanted to dismember the world's largest Muslim country. External enemies explained breakaway movements in Sumatra, Sulawesi, and Ambon in the 1950s.

ANOTHER PATH TO PARADISE: THE REPUBLIC OF THE SOUTH MOLUCCAS

For Christian Ambonese the republic meant domination by Java and Muslims and loss of status. Some saw a solution in a "Christian Indonesia" to be composed of Ambon, Manado, and Timor, whereas others wanted to become part of the Netherlands; most pinned their hopes on regional autonomy within a federal republic.

For Muslim Ambonese, independent Indonesia offered an authenticity of belonging, and the chance to seize power in Ambon. The nationalist movement of the 1920s and 1930s had enabled them to break away from their rajas and brought them greater contact with other Muslim communities in the archipelago. Ambonese Islam had been isolated in its own beliefs and practices. Local tradition said Muhammad had journeyed there and was buried in Ambon's hills. Dutch government schools were built in Christian neighborhoods and shunned by Muslims, so that the wider colonial world remained unknown to them. In 1924 the first madrasah opened in Ambon. Muhammadiyah established a branch there in 1933, and an array of political parties began challenging the comfortable alliance of Dutch, rajas, and Christian religion teachers. During the struggle for independence, prorepublican Muslim Ambonese looked to a Republic of the United States of Indonesia to guarantee a place for them within the nation and superiority at home in Ambon.

In the last months of 1949 units of Christian Ambonese that had fought against independence guerrillas across the archipelago pulled back to Ambon to await the independence agreement being negotiated between Sukarno's government and the Dutch. They were fully armed and apprehensive about their pay, pensions, and integration into the new nation's army. Individual soldiers attacked prorepublican Muslim youth who were parading with Indonesian flags and training with sharpened bamboo stakes in Ambon's capital. In 1950 there was enormous pressure to replace regional autonomy with rule by Jakarta as the Indonesian solution for independence. In March large demonstrations in Makasar supported the dissolution of federalism. In early April, Ambonese of the former colonial army seized Makasar to prevent the arrival of troops from Java. By April 19 their profederalist revolt was put down and their leader arrested, prompting a set of Christians to declare the birth of the Republic of the South Moluccas in Ambon on April 25.

The movement claimed the Ambon islands, Seram, Buru, the Aru and Kei islands, and points on the West New Guinea coast. It did not seek provincial status within the Netherlands, but it appealed to the Dutch for help. The breakaway republic also tried to get Western support against Sukarno, who in 1950 was jailing opponents without trial.

The Jakarta government and military circles had little sympathy for Christian Ambonese. When negotiations failed the navy imposed a blockade to strangle the republic's economy. Battalions of the national army, with air support, were sent in. As Ambonese waited for the invasion, rumors spread that the army would force Christians to convert at gun point, burn down Christian property, and replace Ambonese officials with Javanese. Soldiers sent killing squads into Muslim villages. Between 1,500 and 2,000 soldiers for an independent South Moluccas kept ten national army battalions fighting for four months before being forced to flee into the Seram hills and West New Guinea or to Holland. Trials of twelve separatist leaders began in Jakarta in 1955. President Soumokil of the Republic of the South Moluccas was captured in 1962. Suharto's government concluded this Indonesian history by executing him in 1966.

Within Indonesia, Ambonese became synonymous with soldier and servant of the Dutch. History books recorded that Ambonese fought for the Dutch, but omitted mention of units of Buginese and Javanese in the colonial army. In Ambon itself the new nation gave Muslims the opportunity to gain modern educations and compete with Christians for jobs in the bureaucracy. The Suharto government invented the history of Ambon as a place of harmony, where Muslims helped Christian neighbors to build churches and Christians assisted in the construction of new mosques. But, from 1968, the government also pursued the policy of placing Javanese Muslims at the head of government and army commands in Ambon. The Suharto era of development promoted the circulation of Indonesians through the archipelago and planting of Muslims in Christian territories. In 1930 65 percent of ethnic Ambonese were Christian, 32 percent were Muslim. Already it was a territory for immigration of Muslims from Butung, so that Christians were barely in the majority at 56 percent of the total population. By the 1980s Christians were the minority in Ambon. They had lost their monopoly of government jobs and patronage. Ambon had become a space for Muslims.

With the overthrow of President Suharto in May 1998 violence exploded in many places across the archipelago, destroying the state's rhetoric of a harmonious, classless society. Burning and killing began in Ambon in December. Java became the recruiting ground for jihad against Ambon's Christian communities. Armed gangs of Christian and Muslim youth carried the fight for turf and spoils into churches, mosques, and homes. The paradise jihad soldiers fight for at the opening of the twenty-first century is a Muslim Ambon that will obliterate the Christian haven colonial soldiers fought to establish in 1950.

Other enemies were found. Chinese filled this role as a foreign minority that had been in partnership with the Dutch. In many ways Chinese communities mirrored the larger Indonesian society. Like Indonesians, Chinese were very diverse. Their forebears came from several regions and lineages of southern China. Although some still spoke a Chinese dialect, many spoke Indonesian languages. Some had converted to Islam, others to Christianity. In the early twentieth century some consciously identified themselves as Indonesian Chinese. In 1927 they showed their identification with the nationalist movement by substituting Indonesia for Netherlands Indies in the name of their federation, the Union of Associations of Young Chinese in Indonesia. Others supported causes in China. Most tried to avoid commitment to any political cause. "Chinese," like "Indonesian," was a single label covering a great variety in origins, classes, religions, occupations, and political sentiments.

Indonesia's founding constitution identified all people of Chinese ancestry as foreigners until they applied for naturalization. In 1955, in an agreement signed between the People's Republic of China and Indonesia, China agreed to relinquish jurisdiction over all who opted for Indonesian citizenship and to offer consular services only to those claiming Chinese citizenship. The first of several large groups to repatriate to China numbered 119,000. They saw no future for Chinese in a Muslim Indonesia. Those who stayed could not free themselves from the perceived taint of Dutch privilege. Young men wishing for military careers found the armed services closed to them, except for the medical corps. There were quotas in universities and pressure to change names to Indonesian forms. In 1960 the army ordered foreign Chinese out of rural towns across Java and herded them into clusters in cities.

People of Chinese origin also were targets for killings and arson whenever government authority weakened and local heroes marshaled armed supporters. Like Madurese in Kalimantan or Ambonese in Java, they were readily identifiable. Even those who had shed Chinese costume, name, and diet did not escape mob attack. Chinese shops, houses, churches, and cars were set on fire in Tanggerang in 1946, Sukabumi in 1960 and 1963, Bandung in 1965–1967 and 1973, West Kalimantan in 1967, Ujung Pandang in 1980, Surakarta in 1982, Medan in 1994 and 1998, and Situbondo and Tasikmalaya in 1996. In May 1998 Jakarta's Chinese were victims of organized mobs who looted and burned businesses, raped women, and killed for the military and political groups pushing for President Suharto's downfall.

Indonesian Chinese appear in scholarly and popular literature as a "problem," obstructing Indonesian entrepreneurs from expanding their businesses.

The Indonesian nationalist elite in the 1950s, with no specific economic program of its own for the new country, inherited sentiments opposing "foreign capitalism" and favoring "socialism." The republic's Labor Ministry, created in 1946, drew up legislation to protect workers' health and safety, set living wages, and provide for meals, bus fare, and holiday and festival leave. Prewar labor unions had taken up workers' issues, but their agendas had been diverted to opposing colonialism. In the new Republic of Indonesia, rallies, strikes, and education programs filled work sites and streets in the early 1950s. Every major political party had a labor branch.

Labor groups' vision of a workers' Indonesia differed from Sukarno's vision. All around him his dream of a united Indonesia was shattered. Indonesians had replaced the Dutch as enemy in Ambon, Aceh, west Java, and Sulawesi. Cabinets in Jakarta lasted only a few months. Army officers seemed poised to take over, and the relative prosperity of what some people were calling "normal times" (*zaman normal,* meaning the Dutch period) had failed to take root in a free Indonesia. Sukarno's solution was to harness popular anger for causes far distant from the immediate problems of earning a living. Javanese had become used to mass mobilization. In the late 1950s Sukarno revived this model of state control, drawing on unionized labor, the Communist Party, and the unemployed. In 1960 he created the Front for the Liberation of West Irian, which he presented as the unfinished business of the Indonesian revolution. He blamed continuing Dutch rule of West New Guinea for Indonesia's problems and used the microphone to whip crowds into a frenzy.

West New Guinea raised the question: what was Indonesia? For nationalists, Indonesia was everything touched by the Dutch. Common experience of colonialism had forged a single identity from Sabang to Merauke. Not everyone, however, accepted that Dutch treaties and conquests were a sufficient basis for a nation, arguing that Indonesia had to rest on a prior history of unity. Some looked to Prapanca's record of Majapahit conquests to establish their Indonesia; Yamin wrote that Indonesians had shared cultural symbols for six thousand years. Others contended that the experience of Islam was what held Indonesia together. To some Indonesians, West New Guinea was wild territory inhabited by tribes of seminomadic foresters who had not followed Indonesian histories of city- and state-building and had not begun the intellectual journey of borrowing a writing system and adopting a monotheistic religion. West New Guinea had no Majapahit connections, no folk memories of links to Java. Seen from Sumatra, there was nothing to tie New Guineans into Indonesian histories of Islam and Malay culture.

West New Guinea coastal peoples did live inside Indonesian histories. The archipelago's trading networks ended on New Guinea's northwest coasts. Through traders from the Seram, Aru, and Kai islands, villagers had acquired foods native to the Americas. Imported metal tools and textiles replaced stone tools and bark clothing. From the sixteenth century sultans of Tidore and Bacan had stationed agents in New Guinea villages, designated village headmen their vassals, and given them titles, flags, guns, tobacco, and rice. Their agents married local women. Within coastal villages there developed communities of Muslims who lived in Malay-style houses on stilts, wore Malay clothes, and looked to Maluku sultanates as the cultural, political, and economic center of their world. In the late nineteenth century Maluku sultans signed contracts transferring to the Netherlands Indies suzerainty over all their territories, so that the Dutch inherited east Indonesian claims to West New Guinea's coasts. From 1907 military patrols expanded Dutch political authority into the mountainous interior. In the 1920s the colonial government carved out of West New Guinea jungle exile sites and sent there political and religious campaigners for an independent Indonesia.

Peoples of West New Guinea had entered Indonesian histories as slaves, as suppliers of trade goods, as purchasers of Indonesian manufactured goods, and as taxpayers to east Indonesian sultans. Their territory had served as prison for leaders with Indonesia visions. West New Guinea had also shared the colonial experience in providing a field of activity for Dutch civil servants, businessmen, and Christian missionaries. Its long coastline was home to communities of archipelago Muslims, Christian Ambonese, and Chinese. West New Guinea shared an archipelago-wide pattern in the relationship of coastal and mountain peoples. Its multiethnic coastal population belonged to mobile sea worlds; they acted as gatekeepers and suppliers for land-bound peoples who harvested forest interiors.

From the point of view of Jakarta's elites, West New Guinea had much in common with Sulawesi and Kalimantan. In southern Sulawesi, coastal communities had for centuries been mobile, literate, Muslim, while behind them, in the mountains, were Torajans (meaning "people of the hills"), who were tribal headhunters, animists, and harvesters of the forest. Similarly, Kalimantan had a Muslim coastal fringe linked to archipelago histories and a forested interior of Dayak tribes. For Jakarta West New Guinea unquestionably belonged to Indonesia. Jakarta politicians who had discussed Brunei, Malaya, and southern Thailand as potential Indonesian territories in 1945 without consulting their inhabitants were in power in Jakarta in 1960. They did not consider it necessary to ask West New Guineans whether they wished to become part of Indonesia. Sukarno had abolished voting as un-Indonesian.

Jakarta politicians also knew, by 1960, how to use the nation's army against citizens who revolted or disagreed. Ambon had been brought into the republic by force; Sumatra had been bombed; it was time to bring in West New Guinea.

Inside West New Guinea, small groups wanted union with Indonesia to get jobs and careers that were monopolized by Dutch, Eurasians, and Christian Ambonese. Indonesian militias were launched into West New Guinea space. Sukarno turned up the frenzy of demonstrations in Java. In 1963 he appointed then Lieutenant-General Suharto to head units of the national army and incorporate West New Guinea into Indonesia by conquest. In 1969, for the benefit of the West and the United Nations, 1,022 selected tribal chiefs made an "act of free choice" for integration into Indonesia or for autonomy.

The incorporation of West New Guinea, renamed Irian Jaya (Glorious Irian), as Indonesia's twenty-sixth province was begun by Sukarno to finish Indonesia's revolution. Incorporation was completed by Suharto, who sent Javanese to settle the "empty spaces" of Irian. Immigrant rice farmers cut down New Guineans' forest habitats. Java supplied the civil servants and army commanders to govern Irian space, and Java-based entrepreneurs with their foreign investors mined Irian's copper. Indonesian symbols, architecture, and festivals marked towns; government schools and colleges instructed students in Indonesian history, manners, and speech. Irian became Indonesian space for Muslim peoples to pass through. Irianese appeared on Jakarta stages showing specimens of their "primitive" arts to Indonesian audiences. Just as the Dutch had determined what were "true" Balinese and Javanese styles, Jakarta standard-enforcers clothed naked Irian bodies in batik for command performances of "traditional" dances.

The passions roused in the Irian campaign were channeled into the Crush Malaysia Campaign. At the western end of the archipelago Sukarno found threats to Indonesia's existence in the formation of Malaysia in 1963. The gluing of Britain's Borneo colonies onto Malaya seemed a British ploy to dominate the region. The formation of Malaysia also meant that Indonesia would share a land border with an Asian neighbor that had the appearance of an Islamic state with its council of sultans and its constitution guaranteeing Muslims control of government and the prerogative to restrict non-Muslim space and rights. Many groups desired this model of government in Indonesia. And Malaysia was a federation, a form of government for which many Indonesians had been willing to rebel against Jakarta. In 1964 militias were sent into the Borneo territories and the Malay Peninsula. In calling on Indonesians to follow him and (hoping they would) forget about inflation, corruption, and arbitrariness in government, Sukarno found his constituency in the Communist Party of Indonesia.

The origins of Indonesian communism lie with Dutch socialists in the Indies who set up labor unions, study clubs, and political parties. Indonesian political exiles in Holland joined the Dutch communist party and ran for elected office. The Communist Party of the Indies was born in May 1920 out of the Indies Social Democratic Union, founded in 1914. Very early on the colonial government took steps to root out communism by close surveillance and exiling the party's leaders. In 1922 Tan Malaka was sent to Holland; his colleague Semaun was exiled the following year. In 1927, just ten years after the triumph of communists in Russia, the Indies government was building a prison camp deep in West New Guinea to isolate Indonesian communists.

From the first, Indonesian communism tangled with organized Islam. In the second decade of the twentieth century, party leaders pursued a strategy of "Red Islam." Members joined branches of Sarekat Islam. When they lost the contest for control of Sarekat Islam's central leadership, they formed Sarekat Rakyat (People's Unions) and pitched their appeal to farmers. In 1924, following orders from the Comintern to break off relations with bourgeoisie and peasantry, Indonesia's communists organized wage workers to strike in preparation for a colony-wide uprising that would begin in east Java. Colonial security agents put an end to the plans, but party branches in the northern Banten districts of west Java launched an uprising late in 1926. Branches in west Sumatra followed in January 1927.

Central leaders of the Communist Party were men of privileged backgrounds who made trips to Russia, but local leaders had firsthand experience of rural and urban life. They knew that ordinary people were bound by custom, debt, and inherited obligation to village landlords and labor recruiters, burdened with care of siblings, family, and dependents, and consumed with hatred for Christian rulers. Villagers and slum dwellers knew that they were casually dismissed as lazy and unreliable by European managers and as stupid and impious by Javanese entrepreneurs and landowners who advertised their worldly success by becoming hajis. The ordinary dispossessed struggled to earn a living at the bottom of society, but they also knew they were feared when they reached for machetes, bamboo stakes, and fire to right immediate wrongs.

During the war for independence many of central and east Java's poor followed the call of communist leaders. Not all of them understood the intricacies of republican politics in pursuing independence, but they were hostile to Muslims wishing to impose their version of Islam, as much as they envied Muslim landlords their wealth in farm property. The communist uprising of

Madiun in 1948 pitted militias supporting the Communist Party against the republic's army. It was also a fight in villages. Killing squads of young men cut down landowners and looted their possessions; revenge squads of landowners killed men identified as communist and burned down their huts. Both sides mutilated the bodies of their enemies, flung them into rivers, and displayed heads in public places so they could be recognized. Around eight thousand died. Communism evolved, in Indonesian settings, from the detached debates of the well-born to frenzied attacks to protect space and repel neighbors who were slightly better off.

Communism in independent Indonesia attracted most of its followers among the Javanese. In the elections of 1955, 85 percent of the Communist Party's vote came from Java. The party won 16.4 percent of the national vote, making it one of the "big four" along with the Nationalist Party, the Nahdatul Ulama, and Masyumi. In elections conducted in Java in 1957 for district and municipal boards, communists won 35 percent of all votes cast. The Communist Party began its career in independent Indonesia reviled by army leaders for having launched civil war during the larger war against the Dutch. It was perceived as the enemy by those wanting a state ruled by sharia. In 1950 communists were still being rounded up and jailed without trial by the new republican government.

Jakarta's elites were astonished by Java's voters in 1955. The party they thought so thoroughly discredited was the first choice of half the voting population of east and central Java. By contrast, the party that had pushed Indonesia to independence through negotiation, the Socialist Party, almost disappeared. It appeared that Sukarno's *Marhaens* (the ordinary people) thought the communists most likely to care about their concerns.

Many have tried to explain why communism had little appeal to the non-Javanese, often drawing on Outer Islands-Java divisions. Outer Islanders were said to be more Muslim, more pious, less likely to be deceived by communists, or lulled into believing they would respect religion. For Indonesia the crucial point was that communist voters were numerous in Muslim Javanese neighborhoods. In east Java, voters split almost evenly between the Nahdatul Ulama and the Communist Party. This fact meant that within the one village, landowners, entrepreneurs, traders, and religious leaders were likely to be Nahdatul Ulama supporters, while their tenants, renters, purchasers, and potential congregants were likely to back the Communist Party. Political difference was personal; it affected villagers' very existence.

As the Communist Party gathered confidence by aligning itself with Sukarno in the late 1950s, cadres began supporting demands for land reform.

In villages of east Java, land reform meant the classification of neighbors into rich and poor peasant categories and the forcible seizing of one man's few hectares for distribution among his tenants. From Madiun came memories, not just of national betrayal, but of land grabs and killings by people who had previously assumed the guise of deferential client. The Madiun case also showed that people who owned a little would kill neighbors to defend their property.

The long-term consequences of turning politics personal in the village were not apparent when the new communist bosses of the 1950s began courting Sukarno and providing him with a constituency. Under government by parties and cabinets (1950–1957), coalitions of nationalist, Muslim, and Christian parties controlled power and communists were excluded from office. Even after the 1955 elections Jakarta's politicians excluded elected representatives from the Communist Party from cabinet ministries. In response the party, under Chairman Aidit (1923–1965), formed mass organizations that dwarfed membership of all the other parties and dominated public life with banners, marches, and demands. In 1960 the party had two million members. By 1965 it claimed to have thirty thousand trained cadres, a general membership of almost three million, and a further fifteen to twenty million supporters in organizations associated with it. It positioned itself as the party behind Sukarno, supporting all his policies.

The Communist Party rose in numbers and dominated public forums during a period of sharpened hostility between parties and during the push, on all sides, away from government by elected representatives to government that shut out individual voices and favored consultation over voting. In March 1956, President Sukarno began his campaign for Guided Democracy. In October he made his "Bury the Parties" speech. In March 1957 he suspended civil law and instituted rule by the armed forces. That same year Indonesia's armed forces were turned against protesters and rebels in Sumatra and Sulawesi. In September the All Indonesia Congress of Islamic Scholars declared it a sin for Muslims to be communist and demanded that the Communist Party be banned. In January 1960 parliament was dissolved, and in August the president outlawed the Masyumi and Socialist parties. In March 1962 Sukarno brought the Communist Party to the fringes of executive power by admitting Chairman Aidit and Politburo member Nyoto (1925–1965) to the outer cabinet as ministers without portfolio.

The demands for ongoing struggle, seizing land, liberating Irian, and crushing Malaysia silenced other voices in the early 1960s. Sukarno cut Indonesians off from Western contacts. In 1960 he broke diplomatic relations with Holland; in January 1965 he pulled Indonesia out of the United Nations, and in August he withdrew Indonesia from the World Bank and the International Monetary Fund. Academics went on study tours to Soviet countries and to Mao's China. At home, intellectual life was stifled as the Institute for People's Culture staked out the only acceptable forms of artistic and personal expression and harassed university teachers, writers, and journalists. Censorship blocked out Western news commentary, permitting only left-slanted news and analysis. Sukarno proclaimed the Jakarta-Beijing Axis on August 17, 1965, while his generals purchased Russian weapons, and loans from the communist world financed imports of rice and medicines.

In May 1963 President Sukarno lifted martial law. Toward the end of that year communist cadres in east Java launched "unilateral actions" for land reform: they redistributed land by seizure, brawls, arson, kidnappings, and killings. The intensity of conflict over land can be explained by population growth. There was simply not enough land for Java's population, which grew by seventy million in the twentieth century. The rapid growth following independence reflected the colonial mass vaccinations of the 1920s and 1930s that had brought an end to epidemics of cholera and smallpox. Penicillin and antibiotics, developed in Western laboratories in the 1940s and 1950s, treated pneumonia, dysentery, malaria, yaws, hookworm, and venereal diseases in the 1960s, while chemical sprays, such as DDT, reduced insect breeding grounds. By the 1960s infant mortality had dropped, and population densities in Java had reached five hundred people per square kilometer. The comparative prosperity of village elites exacerbated tensions. The government's land reform program could never have provided enough for Java's rural population, but the landless believed communist arguments that seizing property from village headmen and hajis would provide a permanent solution to their landlessness and hunger.

In 1965 the Communist Party demanded the creation of a "fifth force" to be formed from mass organizations of Sukarno's supporters. Communist leaders demanded expansion of the weapon supply and accumulation of weapons by civilian militias at a time when the chief Muslim party, its youth wings, and its militia remained outlawed, and the last Darul Islam movement had been defeated. In July 1965 the air force began training two thousand members of communist mass organizations in Jakarta, while Sukarno and his supporters continued to fuel anger in the population.

On September 30, 1965, Sukarno's presidential guard made a grab for power. They seized control of the national radio, rounded up generals commanding the army, and announced a program to save the nation from corruption and to preserve Sukarno's leadership. The generals arrested were murdered, their bodies concealed at Halim air force base, where the "fifth force" trained. Sukarno visited Halim before removing himself from Jakarta in an attempt to ride out events and remain in charge.

The revolt was put down by General Suharto, who quickly brought Jakarta regiments under his authority and identified the coup as the work of the Communist Party. News sources under his command accused communist men's and women's militias of mutilating the bodies of the nation's top army commanders. Suharto forced from Sukarno emergency powers to run government. He brought an end to the small-scale war against Malaysia and in 1966 rejoined the United Nations. By 1967 he was pursuing Western banks and investment companies for funds to import food supplies, rebuild the nation's infrastructure, and expand public education and the health system. In 1967 Suharto extracted resignation from Sukarno, made him an object of public disgrace, and held him under house arrest until his death in 1970. In the 1970s and 1980s Suharto made economic development the nation's goal and refined those institutions created by Sukarno for the suppression of political opposition.

In the interim period, as one government shook loose and before the other had full control, killing squads mobilized in Java and in Bali in the belief that a communist coup was under way and that communists would kill them if they did not strike first. When it became clear that the army had seized government, squads continued to kill, now to exterminate forever the perceived threat to their lives and property. In some areas, outsiders entered villages, their faces concealed, and made for houses of known communists and sympathizers. In other areas army units demanded lists of communists from village heads; they rounded up men, forced them to dig their graves, and shot them. Elsewhere, militias of Muslim and Roman Catholic youth groups were provided with army trucks and performed the executions with knives. Rivers, the sea, and roadsides became the dumping ground for bodies and the terrible public classroom for the evils of communism.

The nation's army supplied many of the executioners, but not all. Indonesia's armed forces included devoted supporters of Sukarno, officers appalled by the corrupt wealth of their superiors, and others who thought the armed forces should be trained for defense against external attack rather than assault on Indonesian citizens. The armed forces, as a representative institution that offered upward social mobility, also included men who wanted a government committed to Islam and willing to protect private property, as well as men whose families needed land, income, and a future. There is no single explanation why most of the victims were in Java and Bali. Local conditions produced victims and their executioners. Central army leadership, a relentless rhetoric demonizing communists, and local experience turned ordinary Indonesians into killers.

KILLING SQUADS IN BALI

Five percent, or eighty thousand, of Bali's population died in the killing that followed the Jakarta coup of 1965. In popular memory Bali's communists, sensing their time had come, dressed themselves in white and went out to face their attackers, or to die by their own kris. But mass suicide is a local fiction that shifts focus from attacker to victim and lifts Bali out of Indonesian histories as unique, exotic, and mysterious. Bali was different. It had no substantial community championing an Islamic state. In Bali opposition to communal Hindu celebrations came from Hindus who resented the exactions of time and expenditure, and the prerogatives of the "twice-born" caste of rajas, aristocracy, and ritual celebrants.

During Indonesia's first years of independence, Bali was a site of killings. Animosities inherited from the war for independence existed between those who had supported the Dutch and those committed to Sukarno's Indonesia, among militias controlled by rajas, militias controlled by political parties, and militias answerable to no one. There were also contests for jobs between those qualified by caste and those qualified by modern education. Nationalist, Socialist, and Communist parties battled in the political arena. The spoils of office—funds, patronage, right to grant business licenses—had fallen to communists in the last years of Sukarno government. Conflicts over land and tenants' rights changed to land seizures and killings when Aidit's Communist Party sponsored "unilateral actions."

As Suharto gained control in Java, Sukarno's governor was pushed from office in Bali. Military-controlled radio and press exacerbated tensions in a society already home to armed vigilantes by proclaiming Bali's communists to be traitors and atheists. Communists were specifically accused of aiming to destroy Bali's religion, culture, and character, and Balinese were urged to follow the example of Java in eliminating the enemy within. The arrival in December 1965 of the Army Paracommando Regiment and Brawijaya units, which had conducted killings in Java, altered the balance of power. Sanctioned by Javanese military commanders, Balinese squads killed until ordered to end the slaughter. Proportionately, more people died in Bali than anywhere else in the republic during the killings of 1965–1966.

Official history, composed by Suharto's New Order government, obliterated official memory of the killing of around 800,000 men and women. It emphasized the murder of the six generals by palace guard and communists. Commemorative statues, annual ceremonies, and the naming of streets for the generals created public memory. The government imposed silence about the mass killings on journalists, writers, and academics. The months of killings and the army sweeps for communists and their sympathizers cowed mourners. Around 250,000 people were removed from society to detention sites, where they remained without trial until 1979. Following release into their home communities, ex-prisoners remained under heavy supervision and disapproval. Silence continued inside Indonesia.

More than thirty-five years have passed since the killings. Most Indonesians of the twenty-first century were born after 1966, but fear of communism has outlived Suharto's reign and ideology. In March 2001, members of the Institute to Investigate the 1965–66 Massacres planned reburial, with religious rites, of the remains of twenty-six people killed in the Kaloran hamlet of Temanggung (central Java) in 1965. Death threats and mob action organized by Kaloran's Islamic Solidarity Forum prevented the reburial. In a world where most communist governments have collapsed, "communist" remains in Indonesia a deadly accusation to hurl against opponents.

Killing and the rounding up of communist sympathizers removed citizens with secular solutions to problems of hunger, unemployment, and religious conflict. The state eradicated all reminders of the time when communists seemed about to take over government. A tolerated mob burned down the embassy of the People's Republic of China. The state broke off relations with China in October 1967, banned the teaching of Marx, Weber, and Chinese language in universities, and removed socialist art from public places. At the same time the government turned West New Guinea and Buru Island into detention centers.

BURU EXILE: DEVELOPMENT THROUGH FORCED LABOR

Buru, which lies northeast of Java in the Banda Sea, became part of the empire of the sultanate of Ternate in the 16th century. Its coastal lowland population converted to Islam and its ports became home to Javanese, Buginese, Butung and Maluku islanders, and Arabs. Inland peoples were semi-nomadic forest harvesters. In 1949 Buru was incorporated into the Indonesian state. It was the site of the first major battle to defeat the Republic of the South Moluccas in 1950.

In 1967 the New Order government selected southeastern Buru as a prison camp for its outcasts. Buru now experienced a familiar pattern in Indonesian histories: the displacement of semi-nomadic farmers by sedentary food producers. Indonesia's political prisoners were the agents of displacement. Under brutal conditions they cleared Buru hunting grounds and forest farming plots of tree cover and laid out irrigated rice fields. In Buru, deprived of protection of law and the care of society, Java's rejects became targets for attacks by Buru islanders as well as by their army guards.

Prisoners were given the option, later in their detention, of sending for their wives and children from Java and becoming permanent residents of Buru. In 1987 out of 102,000 inhabitants of Buru, 23,000 were Javanese political prisoners and their families, now labeled "transmigrants."

With communism and communists extirpated, Suharto declared a total break with the past. The Old Order of Sukarno was noise, public tumult, high inflation, hunger, and insufficient skills for Indonesia to compete in the modern world. The New Order of Suharto should be quiet, conforming, its population mobilized for economic development and secured from communist envies by expanded education, higher living standards, and attachment to material things. To achieve a calm and prosperous Indonesia, Suharto took up Sukarno's tools of martial law, representation by functional group, tight controls on political assembly, organization, and publication, and Panca Sila ideology.

Sukarno and Indonesia's senior army leaders, such as General Nasution, had opposed government by a parliament of elected party members representing competing ideologies. Sukarno installed assemblies whose members were appointed by the president to represent people in clusters according to their officially designated (single) function in society: the armed forces, national entrepreneurs, workers, farmers, women, youth, religious scholars, intellectuals, the "1945 generation," and the regions. Functional groups compartmentalized society. Women, for instance, were isolated by gender from workers and intellectuals; farmers were separated from representatives of regions. Such groups were consulted by the president; they did not establish majority and minority views by voting on policy.

Suharto developed Sukarno's system of functional groups. In 1971, with Indonesia's leftists dead or imprisoned, Western loans financing food imports, and the armed forces firmly in control, he instituted a system of voting that would publicly affirm his leadership every five years. Suharto chose Golkar (an acronym for Functional Groups) as the vehicle. Founded as a federation of anti-communist associations by the army's senior leadership in October 1964, Golkar was shaped into the party of government and presented as the living capsule of Indonesian society. All employees of government were required to join. Quotas for Golkar representatives were set in councils at all levels of government. People who insisted on remaining outside this mini-Indonesia were herded into two other streams. Parties with Islamic agendas were required to amalgamate in the Unity and Development Party, while parties identified as nationalist or Christian, had to amalgamate into the Indonesian Democratic Party. The party of Indonesia and the two outsider parties contested elections every five years. The head offices of the Development and Democracy Parties had to submit candidate nominees for government approval. Only during election seasons could political parties campaign in villages. For the cycles between elections, only Golkar, the "natural" party of government, was allowed.

Golkar was often dismissed by foreign critics as the pliant agent of repressive government, and the crucial center of "connections" that led to corrupt practices in the awarding of government contracts. Starting in 1983 Golkar was opened to individual membership, and by the end of the decade more than ten million Indonesians had joined. From 1993 the organization replaced its leadership of senior military men with civilians and presented itself as a party with a mandate to protect the lives, property, and expectations of members. It has outlived Suharto and his generals, and continues to fight for its share of the spoils in Indonesia's politics of menace and mass rally.

Sukarno's Panca Sila was an emotive statement of what bound Indonesians together. Under Suharto it became a cudgel for control and conformity. Press and television operated within guidelines laid down by the state, so that a uniform message reached citizens of Indonesia of all ages, social classes, and regions. In 1975 political parties were required to incorporate the 1945 constitution and Panca Sila into their charters. In 1985 the government stipulated that Panca Sila was to be the sole founding set of principles of every organization in the nation. Month-long training courses in Panca Sila were instituted for all employees of government. National ideology and national history were introduced into the school system at every level from kindergarten through university. As a result, the present generation of Indonesians of all social and economic classes has had more formal instruction in history than any preceding generation.

A SINGLE HISTORY

During President Suharto's three decades in office there was an enormous expansion of public schooling at primary and secondary levels, alongside a great growth in private schools. The New Order government required public and private schools to teach the same nationally mandated syllabus to all schoolchildren. National history along with the Morals of Panca Sila were compulsory subjects, requiring four to six hours of study per week.

The message of official history was the essential unity of indigenous Indonesians. The ministry of education packaging obliterated any contests between classes or ethnic groups; social and religious conflict was with the Dutch alone. The classroom environment discouraged critical discussion of issues and alternative interpretations. Computerized tests reduced history to multiple-choice questions and true-false pairings. The history classroom functioned to suppress knowledge of difference.

Outside the classroom, citizens were drafted into mass organizations dedicated to furthering the goals of the state. The wives of civil servants and female government employees, for instance, had to join Dharma Wanita (Women's

Duty). This organization paralleled government bureaucracy, so that the wife of the department head was president of the branch. Members were kept busy by frequent meetings and by "good deeds" projects through which they explained government goals and taught home-based skills to lower-class women. The Women's Code, formulated by government, paralleled the five pillars of Panca Sila. Women, as auxiliary members of the state, were defined as supporters of the husband, managers of the household, bearers of the future generation, educators of children, and citizens of Indonesia. Poor women experienced the uniformity of development through the government's two-child policy, fostered by public posters, classroom instruction, health clinics, and government surveillance.

The New Order was based on the threat that the other side of development was the nightmare of communism and disorder. New Order government created a comfortable middle class and brought vast wealth to some. The culture of conformity and imposition of accepted opinion was also the culture of patronage. Licenses for imports, home manufactures, and construction were a function of government connection. The rights to do business were allocated as monopolies to family members of the president and favorites, or sold, as in earlier Indonesian societies, to Chinese.

TOLLGATES, PETROL STATIONS, AND FIRST FAMILIES

Toll barriers, which raise revenue and check the movement of individuals, have been a tool of government in Java for centuries. Under the government of President Suharto, a modern system of toll roads taxed travelers between west Java cities and the nation's capital. Again control of the toll booths was in the hands of modern royalty, the eldest daughter of President Suharto. Modern tollgates attract amenities in the network of gas stations along toll roads. They sell automobile supplies, bottled water, snacks, and souvenirs, and provide rest areas and prayer rooms for Muslims. The monopoly for gas stations was held in 2001 by the husband of President Megawati Sukarnoputri.

The public face of regulation in Suharto's Indonesia was symbolized in large theme parks, such as Jakarta's Taman Mini, where Indonesia's many peoples and cultures are represented through orderly examples of architectural and artistic diversity, and by small villages, officially maintained in a time warp, such as Kampung Naga in west Java. Steep stone steps, a gift from the government in 1980, connect villagers with the outside world of electricity, running water, mechanized transport, manufacturing, and supervision. Battery-powered radios, also a gift of government, bring in the noise of the outside, and buses stop daily at the village entrance to take children to primary school. The government-trained tourist guide explains that Naga people want self-sufficiency, the opportunity to continue their own Muslim adat, and to be model citizens. Villagers gratefully leave big questions to government. Their spokesman presents them to visitors as neat and conforming, almost a parody of the orderliness desired by the New Order.

Colonial administrations and the New Order shared a facade of calm, underneath which many groups jostled for space, competed for local allegiances, and resented the domination of Batavia-Jakarta. Suharto's government, like Sukarno's, brought as many opponents as it could into mass organizations. It entangled children of potential dissenters in the state's bounty of foreign scholarships and prestigious jobs. Through control of press, radio, television, and publications the government attempted to inculcate uniformity of opinion. New Order meant staged dramas of public life, such as commemorations of August 17, uniforms for civil servants, matching blazers for university staff, model villages, televised visits by the president and his suite to Jakarta's Istiqlal mosque on festivals, and "charitable foundations" that pressed donations from foreign businessmen and dependent Chinese. For groups that would not submit there was the armed power of persuasion. Government directed army units to shoot protesters at the Tanjung Priok dockyards in 1974, banned political organizing on university campuses in 1978, and intimidated labor organizers and activists in nongovernmental organizations with arrest and beatings. In the 1980s Suharto's government issued warnings to criminal and obedient alike with mysterious killings and the display of bodies in public. Few forums inside Indonesia allowed public discussion of difference or cultivated the habit of accepting difference. Instead, problems arising from the many opposing streams in Indonesian society were handled with violence.

From Jakarta, Aceh was seen as a wild area requiring full induction into the New Order state. Sukarno had designated Aceh a special region in 1959 after the armed forces had defeated a rebellion to form a federal Islamic State of

Indonesia. Acehnese could substitute their own laws on religion, custom, and education for rulings from Jakarta's ministries. In 1965 Aceh had appeared to march in tune with the Suharto faction in Jakarta when a congress of Aceh's leading ulamas issued a fatwah that allowed the killing of communists. Islamic youth groups joined units of the national army in killing thousands of Communist Party sympathizers, especially in Javanese transmigrant farming settlements. Once firmly in power, Suharto's government sought uniformity in administration, as well as outlook, and had little tolerance for a border territory pursuing its own course.

In Aceh the New Order applied its special combination of incorporation and violence. All parties with "Aceh first" platforms were banned. Acehnese were required to participate in elections, from 1971, through national parties whose headquarters were in Jakarta. From 1974 nominees for governor and officials down to district level had to be approved by Jakarta's minister for internal affairs, and they were accountable to the Jakarta ministry, not to Aceh's consultative assembly. From 1975 all government officials in Aceh were required to join Golkar. Jakarta supplied and controlled funds for building roads, bridges, and schools. Technical experts in regional economic development were employees of the central government, committed to building up Aceh for the benefit of Jakarta. The military and the ministry of the interior controlled industrial zones as a matter of national development and security. Ulamas were marshaled into the Aceh branch of the New Order's Council of Indonesian Ulamas and assigned the job of explaining and supporting Jakarta's development policies to their village followers through fatwahs.

Added to the old grievance of not being autonomous and Islamic enough were new objections against the relationship with Jakarta. Aceh's wealth in oil and natural gas turned Indonesia's economy around in the 1970s, but the profits flowed to Jakarta to support Java's development or Jakarta-based politicians and military men. Aceh's oil wealth could have made the province into Brunei, one of the world's richest states. Instead, it created more jobs for Javanese immigrants than for Acehnese. New Order technocrats regarded the industrial zones as agents for national development that happened to be located in Aceh, rather than as means to eliminate poverty in Aceh's north and east. Industrial zones in Aceh were enclaves of foreign and Indonesian entrpreneurs, sites of foreign manners and values, and islands of wealth surrounded by a disapproving fringe of Aceh tenant farmers, small contractors, and ulamas. Jakarta overlooked Aceh's special Islamic cast, and promises of autonomy over religious life stopped at the industrial zones. Aceh's ulamas could issue fatwahs binding only on Acehnese Muslims living outside the enclaves.

In such conditions some welcomed a Free Aceh Movement when it was proclaimed by Teungku Hasan Muhammad di Tiro in October 1976. He presented himself as descendant of the ulama and official national hero Teungku Haji Cik di Tiro of Pidie, who led militias against the Dutch from 1881 until his death (from poison) in 1891. In 1976, Hasan di Tiro argued, the struggle had to be renewed, because Aceh was still a colonial state. Javanese had replaced the Dutch as colonial rulers. His reading of history cast Aceh's sultans as kings of all Sumatra before 1873. This view underlay di Tiro's claim that in 1949 the Dutch should have transferred sovereignty over Sumatra to Aceh, not to Java. He repudiated Majapahit and Dutch constructions of the archipelago, denied the existence of historical links between the Outer Islands and Java, and called Indonesian nationalism a Western tool to contain Islam. In December 1976 his Free Aceh Movement declared the independence of Aceh-Sumatra, called for expulsion of Javanese-Indonesian "invaders," and promised that the new state would have the Koran as its constitution.

The Suharto government army soon stripped the movement's pamphlets, flags, and soldiers from public space, chased its remaining fighters into the forests, and coopted Aceh's elites. The movement reemerged again in 1989 with military commands in all four regions of Aceh, a government-in-exile in Sweden, an operational command in Malaysia, a public relations office in Singapore, and a core of 250 graduates of military and ideological training in Libya. In the Aceh rebellion of 1989–1992 and the struggle that started again in the late 1990s, militias and political movements had varied goals, from autonomy to complete independence from Indonesia to an Islamic Indonesia composed of states with strong rights. All groups saw the Armed Forces of Indonesia as the enemy of Aceh. Militias targeted police, soldiers, government officials, informers, and Javanese migrants. To subdue Aceh's disparate groups, the armed forces applied a uniform strategy of arrests, imprisonment, killings, dumping bodies in public places, burning houses, and rape. Villages were relocated. Men were made to accompany army sweeps of "enemy territory." Acehnese killed each other under the military's direction.

In the 1980s Aceh's ulamas toured with units of the national army, forbidding villagers to join independence movements and advising that it was permitted to kill supporters of the Free Aceh Movement (called Movement of Disturbers of the Peace by government spokesmen). But by the late 1990s many religious leaders backed independence in the light of changing circumstances. Ulamas could not overlook a national army run wild in Aceh, leaving mass graves, refugees, and orphans in its wake. They had to open up mosques to shelter Acehnese made homeless by the fighting and to educate children whose schools had been torched as part of the campaign to quell rebellions. Nationally, movements in Irian Jaya and East Timor sought to break away from the republic. Aceh's religious leaders also found a growing community of Muslims committed to an Islamic Indonesia, beneficiaries of Suharto's program to create "Panca Sila Muslims." There was also, in the months leading up to Suharto's overthrow and the chaotic succession of presidents, a multiplication of Islamic fronts, defense groups, militias, and prayer associations formed to defend particular interests and national causes. In this context, Aceh opposition groups maintained their rage against Jakarta's government and its armed representatives. Acceptance of autonomy and institution of Islamic law with its religious police now set Aceh on a distinct pathway within the Republic of Indonesia.

The Masyumi Party, created by the Japanese in 1943 as a mass organization for Islamic associations, claimed in the early years of independence to be the only party for Muslims in Indonesia. It proved to be Indonesia's second largest party in the 1955 elections, when it won 21 percent of the vote. It was also the only party winning votes almost equally across archipelago electorates. Although the Nationalist, Communist, and Nahdatul Ulama parties had won over 85 percent of their votes from people in Java and attracted less than 15 percent of voters in other parts of Indonesia, the Masyumi had won 51 percent of its votes in Java and 49 percent in Sumatra, Kalimantan, Sulawesi, and eastern Indonesia. Masyumi appeared to be the only truly national party. Masyumi members reflected a whole range of Muslim agendas from functioning in a secular state to sharia-based rule, but all opposed communism and supported regional rights against Jakarta. Such stands brought the national party of Muslims into direct conflict with the nation's president. In 1960 Sukarno ordered the dissolution of Masyumi. Suharto did not lift the ban.

As a result, constituent organizations of the Masyumi federation, such as the Muhammadiyah, accelerated social and educational programs that would create a more Islamic-acting population. They replaced short-term political competition with a long-term strategy for achieving Islamic goals. The strategy became known as *dakwah,* an Arabic word meaning efforts to improve thought and behavior so that they conform with Islamic ideals. Mohammad Natsir, a former leader of Masyumi, established the Indonesian Islamic Dakwah Council in 1967. In order to counteract forms of Indonesian Islam that emphasized mysticism and submission to a spiritual leader, the Dakwah Council supplied books to religious schools, trained missionaries for work among Muslims in Indonesia, provided scholarships for study abroad, and ran advanced courses for teachers of religion. The council tried to prevent proselytizing by Christian missionaries, which it saw as an intrusion of Christianity into Islamic space, a distraction or temptation to Muslims.

The Dakwah Council established close links with Muslim organizations worldwide. It sought to reform local Islams by being up-to-date with trends in world Islam. The Dakwah Council pressed Indonesia's foreign policy makers to join the "Islamic side" in international politics, and it took on issues confronting many Islamic societies, rather than dwell on specifically Indonesian issues of adat and local saints. Dakwah broadened Indonesian debate to include the place of women in the life of the nation and their right to hold jobs, run for public office, and participate in sports. It promoted Islamic dress codes for females.

In the 1980s, President Suharto began applying the resources of the state to supporting specific items on the dakwah agenda. He brought television cameras to film the first family in public prayer and alms-giving; he encouraged the increase in "Muslim" content on the state-owned radio and television networks and on the private networks owned within his family. He banned public lotteries, supported an Islamic bank, provided funds for more Muslim schools, promoted the adoption of an Indonesian Islamic dress code for women (personally represented by his eldest daughter), and allowed the publication of an Islamic newspaper. He also appointed men with reputations for Islamic piety and Islamic agendas to senior positions in the military. In 1990 Suharto sponsored the formation of the All Indonesia Association of Muslim Intellectuals. Under his chief aide for technological development and later vice president, Habibie, this association drew in civil servants, activists, and intellectuals to push for a more Islamic face to Indonesia through fewer Christians in prominent positions and fewer government contracts for Chinese. Suharto's greatest contribution to dakwah was in funds for mosques and prayer houses. As a result, urban and rural Indonesia became visually a more Islamic landscape, with Islamic architecture, places of congregation, prayer groups, boards with Arabic writing, and the public marking of Islamic time. Indonesia's streets became filled with men, women, and children in religious costume, and fund raisers working passing traffic for donations to support more mosque building and restoration. It was in such a landscape of confident and self-assertive Islam that other Indonesians sensed their own space contract, their visible difference become less comfortable.

In earlier times, mosques served as hotels. In addition to places for public prayer, they offered meeting space and sleeping accommodation. Mosques possessed the landscape as Muslim territory, enabled passage of people,

A MOSQUE FOR A PANCA SILA INDONESIA

Indonesia's contribution to Islamic architecture can be seen in the design of the roof of old mosques. In place of the Arabic dome, builders constructed the roof as a series of tiers, which is characteristic of pre-Islamic architecture and remains a feature of temple design in Bali. The three-, five-, and seven-tiered roofs of Indonesia's mosques also reflect a heritage of Chinese builders and Chinese Muslims. Many of Java's old mosques had wooden screens, pulpits and chairs for the local aristocrat carved with animal and floral motifs, kala heads, and lotus flowers. Some decorative elements such as tortoises also had a pre-Islamic significance as symbol of immortality. Other local design elements were the split gate without archway and the open-sided, pillared hall. The tower for calling men to public prayer was often attached, chimney style, to the mosque roof rather than built as a separate structure.

In the 1980s the New Order government introduced a uniform "Indonesian-style" mosque to Indonesian landscapes. It channeled funds to an agency that built prefabricated mosques in three sizes from timber, steel, reinforced concrete, and cement. These mosques incorporated pan-Islamic features such as pointed arches on windows, but in place of the dome was the Indonesian tiered roof. It was topped by a spire bearing the Arabic letters for the name of God bound into a pentagon representing the five pillars of Indonesia's official ideology, Panca Sila. Since the fall of President Suharto, the pentagon has gone, the Arab dome has become a dominant feature of new and renovated mosques, and domes are prominently displayed in stalls lining the main roads.

goods, and ideas, parallel to and entirely distinct from the institutions of the colonial state. In the same way, the multiplication of mosques created by Suharto's funds in the 1980s and 1990s fostered a distinct universe in New Order Indonesia. Mosques became centers promoting greater devotionalism and more self-consciously Islamic identification. Young women adopted religious clothing to set an example of Islamic behavior and difference. Mosques

Mosque with three-tiered roof, Indrapuri, c. 1875. Photographic Archive, Royal Institute of Linguistics and Anthropology, Leiden, No. 3780. Photo courtesy of the KITLV.

became fixed points of contrast to Suharto and all the New Order represented in Westernization, huge fortunes, and materialism. In neighborhoods where self-conscious Muslims gained a majority, they banned practices they considered un-Islamic, such as tending shrines for village spirits, wearing batik, and showing reverence for heirloom krises. Mosques also served as centers of opposition: Friday sermons examined the Iranian revolution and its relevance for Indonesia; the buildings housed refugees from New Order sweeps.

Dakwah was the product of Muslims excluded from government. The movement created the conditions for Islam's reach for power. In the 1990s dakwah won concessions from Suharto, who wished to build Muslim support as a defense against his armed forces, which included men with Islamic outlook and commitments.

As his armed forces appeared less manageable and less united in purpose than early in the New Order, Suharto made concessions to another group in Indonesia that felt excluded, the admirers of former President Sukarno.

Offering at Panataran Temple, East Java, June 2000. This offering, left by an unknown visitor, is marked by a three-tiered parasol. Photo courtesy of Iskandar P. Nugraha.

Sukarno's photograph was no longer displayed and his writings vanished from bookstores in the early years of the New Order. Beginning in the 1980s, Suharto moved to rehabilitate the man many Indonesians still revered as the creator of their independence. He named the new international airport Sukarno-Hatta, and he allowed the transformation of Sukarno's modest burial site in Blitar into a grand mausoleum of glass and marble.

Indonesia's first president now lies between his parents. (In keeping with burial patterns at Java's holy sites, and reflecting the dilemmas of polygamy, no wife's grave is sited near the great man.) In prominent place is a Balinese-style offering of fruits; an open Koran lies on a small stand in a corner. People who come to pay their respects are marshaled to purchase red and white flowers, scatter them at the designated spot, meditate, and then move on. The walled compound is approached through massive split gates. Concessions to Sukarno supporters encouraged boldness. The plaque advising visitors that Suharto created Sukarno's national monument was soon defaced.

For working-class Indonesians, the New Order brought a huge expansion of low-paid jobs in manufacturing that catered to a large home and export market. In 1990, for the first time in the archipelago's long history of exporting Indonesian products, manufactured goods exceeded agricultural exports

This portrait of President Sukarno hangs in his childhood home, now the Blitar Sukarno Museum. The president is flanked by photographs of his parents. Ceremonial gold and white parasols and a lance suggest his elevated status. Photo courtesy of Iskandar P. Nugraha.

in value. Factory workers entered a New Order workplace that isolated them from union organizers, kept them vulnerable to world prices and bosses, detached them from family and village work units, and made them consumers of global pop culture, instant foods, and modern appliances. Factories pushed along the transformation of cultures and manners by hiring unmarried girls and giving them an ambiguous status within their families as sources of cash and independent values. Farmers entered the world of chemical pesticides, genetically altered rice strains, state loans, and directives from agricultural research units, international banking, and investment agencies. By the 1980s Indonesia grew sufficient rice to feed its people. Income generated by Indonesia's oil and gas fields, industralization, the "green revolution" in agriculture, and perhaps also the state's birth control programs seemed, in the 1980s, to be resolving Indonesia's dire economic problems.

Greater mobility of population revealed the riches of the elite to everyone's eyes. Fenced golf courses occupied once fertile rice fields; huge villas behind high walls topped with broken glass took over the living space of urban squatters; international hotels provided clubs for the jet set where once Batavians had developed an Islamic folk culture. Ordinary Indonesians became the con-

Symbols of Java, Bali, and Islam at President Sukarno's burial site. Photo courtesy of Iskandar P. Nugraha.

cern of nongovernmental organizations dedicated to eradicating maternal mortality, creating safe workplaces, and defending the individual's rights against big government.

Beneath the New Order facade of stability and development there was huge change, social ferment, competing interests, and few lawful outlets for public debate and public disagreement. Indonesian intellectuals and activists carried their questions overseas to Western universities. There, in academic forums, they debated the course of New Order Indonesia. Others continued the debate as they made the pilgrimage to Mecca and experienced politics in Islamic countries. Wherever they journeyed, Indonesia's intellectuals found Indonesian settlements of exile and Indonesian faces in the journals and websites of Western human rights' organizations.

Most Indonesians were concerned with more private matters: taking care of family, educating children, and getting through a day. For them government was something to avoid, its police officers and officials people to whom they made small payments in return for the speedy resolution of modern problems such as getting a driving license, avoiding a traffic fine, or obtaining an identity card. Indonesia's former royals became businessmen, for their pedigrees won them lucrative licenses and contracts. Yogyakarta's Sultan Hamengkubuwono IX (r. 1940–1988), who had supported Indonesia's struggle for independence, served both Sukarno and Suharto as defense and economics minister and was, from 1973 to 1978, Indonesia's vice president. But most of Indonesia's royals were irrelevant to modern Indonesia dominated by secular government and its armed forces; they were relics of a past many called "golden" but few could describe in detail.

ROYAL RETURNS

In 1992 Indonesian royals, who had survived colonialism and republicanism, gathered in The Hague to exchange gifts with Dutch royals and attend an exhibition of court arts of Indonesia. In 1938 another set of princes had journeyed to Holland to present gifts and attend the wedding of Princess Juliana. In 1898 a delegation had attended the coronation in Amsterdam of Queen Wilhelmina. Queen Beatrix received Susuhunan Pakubuwono XII of Surakarta, Sultan Hamengkubuwono X, and Prince Puger of Yogyakarta, Prince Ide Anak Agung Gde Agung of Gianyar, Bali, Sultan Mudaffar Syah of Ternate, and their suites in the Indies Room of the Noordeinde Palace. The room had been designed by Dutch engineers and executed by Dutch and Indonesian craftsmen to evoke Indonesia through its Hindu-Buddhist (but not its Islamic) artistic traditions and to display gifts sent by the archipelago's kings for the wedding of Queen Wilhelmina in 1901. There were sculptures of Siva, carved kalas, heirloom krises, jewelry, a chandelier modeled on motifs from the Loro Janggrang Temple, curtains embroidered with lotus flowers, models of Minangkabau buildings in silver and gold, and an illustrated Javanese manuscript. Many of these treasures of Indonesian artistry had been gifts of the 1992 delegation's forebears or were objects from their own collections.

On previous visits, archipelago royals had worn ceremonial costumes, signifying their elevated rank and prerogatives in Indonesian societies. In 1992, archipelago royals wore casual Western dress of slacks and jackets, signifying their status as privileged citizens in a country that had removed royalty from decision-making. The pilgrimage to Holland suggested lingering nostalgia for past alliances and the importance of royal families.

Martial law and the doctrine of Dual Function brought the armed forces into Indonesian streets. Dual Function gave the armed services responsibilities not only for the external and internal defense of the nation but also for its welfare. Officers were involved in every facet of public life as managers of nationalized businesses, as partners with private businessmen, as members of the nation's cabinets and consultative assemblies, and as administrators of provinces, districts, and towns. Uniformed soldiers manned checkpoints, sat in ticket booths at tourist sites, and assisted in village road building projects. Tanks cruised streets and were stationed in the house compounds of senior ministers. When students poured out of campuses and staged demonstrations, army units were mobilized.

Through the 1970s, scholars treated Indonesia's armed forces as a monolith. Suharto was the great manipulator, assigning units far from their home bases to control different ethnic groups and rotating commanding officers. In the 1980s, analysts saw the armed forces as representing the many contrary trends in Indonesian politics. Senior commanders played politics and were willing to unleash militias against their enemies or to thwart state policies. Speculation turned to when President Suharto would withdraw from politics, how he would retire, and who would succeed him.

Indonesia's first two presidents claimed to represent Indonesia's people, but they always unleashed armed force to eliminate opposition, to intimidate, to ensure popular compliance. In some instances they sent regular units of the army to suppress dissent. At other times, militias armed, trained, and financed by the nation's army were used to achieve a Jakarta solution. Militias had their own uniforms and insignia, their own leaders, and their own local angers, vendettas, and causes. They were descended from jago gangs and inherited from the colonial era the application of force to solve problems. They were heirs to the revolution and a national history that uncritically celebrated resistance fighters, freelancers, and *pemudas.*

PEMUDA: A LEGACY OF VIOLENCE

In Indonesian history the term *pemuda,* meaning (male) youth, has a specific significance, for it designates young people devoted to the cause of national independence. Pemuda first had the connotation of privileged urban youth, students of the newly established Dutch university faculties and vocational training schools. Upon graduation they chose teaching in nationalist, private schools over jobs with the colonial government; their leisure hours were filled with debating clubs and political action. When Japan ruled Indonesia, young nationalist men had their first experience of mass organization and paramilitary training.

During the course of the revolution, *pemuda* came to mean any young man with a gun and developed the connotation of breaking free from established codes of conduct. Official versions of the revolution produced a sanitized history of devotion, fervor, unity of purpose. Novels, short stories, and memoirs of women who lived through these times stressed the civilian population's fear of young men with guns who gathered at train stations and markets. Pemuda, in these depictions, carried meanings of extortion, arbitrary arrest, and rape.

Pemuda added to its meanings those of thug, hired vigilante, and urban terrorist during the New Order and in the years since its collapse. Pemuda organizations, such as Pemuda Panca Sila, can put thousands of hired men on to the streets to intimidate parliament, politicians, Chinese, Christians, or any group they are paid to threaten or attack. Their weapons are numbers, fire, knives, guns, and the media.

Many features of modern Indonesia seemed to flow together in East Timor. Seen from Jakarta, East Timor was part of the archipelago's wild fringe. It had been a tributary of Majapahit. European colonialists had cut East Timor out of Indonesian histories, dividing island and communities between the Dutch in the west and the Portuguese in the east. The nationalist elite, gathered in the Committee to Investigate Indonesian Independence in 1945, had voted to incorporate East Timor into the state emerging out of World War II. In the 1950s, the republic that had been born in Java expanded its power west, north, and east into Majapahit's claimed territories, secured its hold on the Dutch state, and redefined the meaning of "Indonesian." By 1966 Indonesia meant a place without communists or communism. It had prevented breakaway movements from dismembering the republic, and it had put down attempts to transform Indonesia into an Islamic state. In 1975 the state was ready to expand into East Timor, to bring its peoples "home." The immediate causes were the sudden withdrawal of Portuguese colonial rule in 1974, the strategic importance of the deep waters and oil of the Timor Gap, and the victory of a communist-leaning Revolutionary Front for the Independence of East Timor (known by its acronym, Fretilin) in a war pitting East Timorese against each other.

There was no consultation of East Timorese. To Jakarta's ruling elite a shared heritage of Majapahit and colonial rule were compelling reasons for completing the republic. There was no free expression of opinion in New Order Indonesia, so there was no reason to extend such a privilege to East Timorese. And, in an Indonesia that had attacked communism, there was every reason to prevent the birth of a communist state along a land border. Jakarta was practiced in incorporating territories by force and in using the national history curriculum to explain the naturalness of this Indonesian solution to its citizens. East Timor became a new field for applying the policies of development, a new arena through which Indonesians could pass in the course of government, army, and business careers. East Timor also became a new arena where national strife was played out, where sections of the armed forces employed army units and pemuda militias to advance their particular strategies for the control of Jakarta.

Most published material on East Timor places its beginnings in the Portuguese colonial empire. Such texts document a history of colonial neglect and backwardness, followed by decolonization in 1974, invasion by Indonesia in December 1975, brutal occupation, an East Timorese diaspora in Portugal and Australia, popular resistance and hopes led by Fretilin, a historic vote for independence on August 30, 1999, the revenge destruction of East Timor by Indonesia's military and its militias, international claims of genocide, the late arrival of United Nations forces, and the slow beginnings of the new country of Timor Leste or Timor Loro Sa'e.

The maps which accompany such material generally show the island of Timor alone, or indicate its position in relation to Australia, or present it in a simplified map of Indonesia without indicating Timor's many island neighbors. With no acknowledged pre-colonial past or links of any kind to Indonesia, East Timor becomes the site of Indonesian, and more specifically, Javanese imperialism; East Timorese become a single ethnic group facing genocide from Indonesian militias whose own ethnic origins are not identified.

Timor is not an isolated island. It is the largest in the Lesser Sunda chain and one of the clusters of islands that lie between Java and New Guinea. Timorese origin myths recount that ancestors arrived by sea, sailing around the eastern end of Timor to land in the south. In some origin stories Timorese ancestors journey from the Malay Peninsula or the Minangkabau highlands of Sumatra. Anthropologists identify eleven distinct ethnolinguistic groups on Timor. The two largest are the Atoni of west Timor and the Tetum of central and parts of east Timor. Most Timor languages belong to the Austronesian family of languages spoken throughout Indonesia. Timor's non-Austronesian languages are related to languages spoken in Halmahera and Irian. Both language families link Timorese to the modern Indonesian state.

Timorese were land peoples in east Indonesia's water world. They did not make or maintain contact with other islands and peoples by sea. Contact with further worlds was the work of outsiders in Timor's history. Timor was part of a region of small islands and small populations, of land peoples served by sea peoples. At different points, networks of sea traders penetrated the entire region. Outside products, such as metal goods, rice, fine textiles, and coins were exchanged for the region's spices, sandalwood, deer horn, bees' wax, and slaves. Timorese slaves became rowers for Ternate and Banda navies and farmers on their spice plantations.

While trading patterns link Timor to specific Indonesian provinces of eastern Indonesia, Timor kin systems and political patterns link Timorese to a great arc of societies from Borneo, Sumatra, and east Indonesia. Timor cultural patterns, such as the symbolism of numbers, colors, and compass points, link islanders to all Indonesia. From the point of view of groups dominant in the archipelago at different times—Javanese, Portuguese, Dutch, Indonesian—Timorese participated in a culture of violence. Powerful outsiders described them as headhunters, their societies constantly entangled in tribal warfare. This characteristic links Timorese, in the writings of dominant outsiders, to other Indonesian peoples of the fringe: Dayaks, Bataks, Torajas, Irianese.

Timur means "east" in Indonesian languages; Timor Island lies east of Java. It is recorded as a vassal state of the Javanese kingdoms of Kediri and Majapahit. Timorese live in old Javanese inscriptions as awed offerers of homage. Communities on the eastern half of the island became cut off from their common, ancient base in Indonesian worlds in the sixteenth century when they were fitted into a Portuguese world of ports, forts, and churches strung along the coasts of Europe, Africa, South America, and Asia. Their strongest ties were to each other, their weakest to their immediate neighbors. Within the Indonesian archipelago, branches of the Portuguese sea highway led into Melaka, Banten, Makasar, Ternate, Tidore, Ambon, Solor, Flores, and Timor. During the seventeenth century these branch terminals and the western end of Timor became caught up in the Dutch sea network. East Timor ended up as a backwater of Portugal overseas.

From the sixteenth century, Portuguese filled the role of outsider for East Timor communities. They took over from Java the role of recorder of Timor society. They introduced a new food crop, maize, and a new export crop, coffee. They preserved Timor systems of tax and labor control. Until the end of Portuguese rule in 1974, Timorese paid their taxes through their labor and a portion of their harvests of sandalwood and coffee. The Portuguese injected mercenaries into Timor communities. Timor chiefs hired Portuguese soldiers for their wars against neighboring tribes. The Portuguese musket transformed Timorese men into deer hunters and suppliers of deer horn and hides for export.

Portugal also introduced a world religion, the Roman writing system, the printing press, and formal schooling. The new ruler injected two new groups into East Timor: men from Portugal and Portuguese Asians. Portuguese in church and state introduced the Latin and Portuguese languages; Portuguese Asians used Malay as well as the Portuguese language. A new Timorese elite emerged that was Portuguese-speaking and Roman Catholic. Officials and clerics traveling through the Portuguese sea empire span a web of common consciousness. Colonial policy offered citizenship of Portugal to men who assimilated Portuguese language, literacy, and religion. By 1970, twelve hundred East Timorese out of a population of seven hundred thousand had acquired citizenship of Portugal. They were members of aristocratic families, residents of the colonial capital, Dili, or of district towns. When Portugal withdrew from East Timor in 1974, 30 percent of the population were practicing Roman Catholics. The majority venerated local spirits of land and sky.

Portuguese Timor shared a land border with the much larger colony of the Netherlands East Indies. The Dutch half of Timor was at the terminus of Dutch sea highways and of a Muslim world focussed by colonial grids of government, transport, communications, schooling, and business on Batavia. The Dutch inherited the Majapahit view of the archipelago as consisting of Java plus a zone of head hunting, widow-burning societies, where there were mobile populations of traders, raiders, pirates, rantau peoples, and wandering Islamic teachers. Colonial policy used military expansion to bring this unruly zone under administrative control, block other European powers, and pacify it through colonial culture.

In 1914 Dutch and Portuguese authorities agreed on the positioning of borders in Timor. The decisions of European colonial powers had no special mandate for the Japanese. During their occupation of Indonesia, they assigned Timor Island as a single unit to the army's zone of administration. In February 1942 Japanese troops landed in both Kupang (West Timor) and Dili. East Timor was a site of Allied resistance and commandos. Japanese policy was to subdue East Timor through Japanese soldiers and militias raised in West Timor. Approximately forty thousand East Timorese died in the process of incorporation into Japan's Indonesian empire.

In the first twenty-five years of independence, East Timor remained outside the concern of Jakarta. In April 1974 Portugal stripped itself of its colonies. Three parties formed in East Timor in May of that year to make a bid for control of the former colony's scattered communities. The Timorese Democratic Union stood for union with Portugal and aimed to cement their leadership role by making Portuguese the new state's official language. Fretilin saw itself as part of Portugal's colonial world; its models included Angola. Its leaders also favored retention of Portuguese as the national language. The third party, the Timorese Popular Democratic Association, saw its future in an Indonesian world. It advocated eliminating the colonial-imposed separation of East from West Timorese communities and making Indonesian the official language. Each political party formed its own armed wing. In August 1975 when supporters of continuing links with Portugal took over government institutions, fighting broke out. Fretilin claimed victory and began the ouster of its rivals. East Timorese who saw their future inside the larger state of Indonesia supported Jakarta's decision to end civil war inside East Timor.

East Timor came into the Indonesian state through military conquest. Over four years, units of Indonesia's armed forces hunted down opponents, attacked civilians, and destroyed houses and farm plots. Approximately one hundred thousand East Timorese died as casualties of war and war-induced famine and disease. By 1979 around 80 percent of Fretilin's troops were dead, their leaders killed or captured, their weapons seized, and their bases overrun. In the wake of conquest, Fretilin abandoned bases in favor of mobile columns with support groups in villages inside East Timor. It also exported its fight outside Timor to Western human rights groups, the Western media, and the United Nations. East Timorese refugee communities secured the support of the Roman Catholic Church; unlike the Christian Ambonese fifty years earlier, they developed a powerful international lobby that had links into prestigious international forums such as the Nobel Peace Prize awards committee. Indonesia eventually lost the public relations battle in the Western press.

In East Timor the Portuguese language was banned and Indonesian became the language of government, school, and public business. The Indonesian school system was introduced along with the national curriculum. Panca Sila became the new province's official ideology. Appointment to government jobs was restricted to Indonesian-speakers who had certificates of Panca Sila training. The border between West and East Timor was opened, bringing an influx of West Timorese farmers. In January 1989 the twenty-seventh province was opened to private investment. Buginese and Makasar immigrants soon controlled the economic life of towns; army officials entered business contracts with Indonesian partners for the export of East Timor products; Balinese rice farmers were resettled as transmigrants in central Timor.

Incorporation into the Panca Sila state had another consequence. East Timorese animist belief system was not acceptable to Indonesia's ministry of religion. In order to meet the state's requirement of monotheistic belief, there were mass conversions to Christianity. By the 1980s, 80 percent of East Timorese were registered as Roman Catholics. The Catholic section of the ministry of religion targeted them for intensive induction. There had been few Timorese priests and no seminary. Priests from Indonesia, who moved in to take over from departing Portuguese clergy, began establishing an Indonesian Catholicism. They substituted Indonesian for the Portuguese and Latin mass. For these men committed to an Indonesian state, East Timor represented an expansion of Christian space within Muslim Indonesia.

A new elite of Indonesia-speakers formed in East Timor's Indonesian school system and in Indonesia's universities. By 1998, one thousand East Timorese had graduated from Indonesian universities, their studies financed by Jakarta. But Indonesian-educated East Timorese often found themselves shut out of jobs in government because they were not Muslim. Indonesian-speaking East Timorese also found themselves at odds with East Timorese who were developing an opposition identity based on Tetum language. In 1981, the senior Portuguese-trained bishop chose Tetum over Indonesian as the language for the mass. Businesses owned by immigrant Indonesians and army men shut Indonesian-speaking East Timorese out of the prosperity promised by New Order economic planners. East Timorese lacked the Jakarta connections that controlled licenses and contracts. "Do-good" projects conceived in Jakarta to transform East Timorese into Indonesians made many acutely aware of their status in the republic as backward and inferior. Indonesian official views presented East Timor as a province receiving a disproportionate share of national development funds. For many East Timorese, existence as Indonesia's twenty-seventh province was a brutal form of colonial rule. They were Natives exposed to the military might of a foreign government with no restraining judicial authority.

The insistence of East Timorese on a state independent of Indonesia was the product of personal experience of Indonesian rule. But independence became a possibility only when a host of Indonesian organizations brought down Suharto's government in May 1998. Groups that under the New Order's rules had had no chance to learn the civic arts of compromise took unyielding positions. Backed by armed vigilante groups they stormed the streets of Indonesia's cities. The transitional government of President Habibie was beset by daily demonstrations in the nation's capital staged in front of the world's cameras; it was harassed by rumors of military coups, demands for decentralization, and the threat of rebellion in Aceh, Riau, and Irian. In July 1998 Habibie sought temporary respite in one corner of the state by offering autonomy to East Timorese and then, in January 1999, by offering the choice of cutting loose from Indonesia altogether.

Across the archipelago, unemployed youth, that floating male mass detached from domestic circle, jobs, and a future, offered their services of anger, courage, and soldiering to men politicking to control Indonesia. They were organized into militias and equipped with the modern weapons of Indonesia's armed forces. They also brought the common man's machetes, knives, fire, and fists. East Timor became the stage for great causes—decolonization, socialism Cuba-style, United Nations-sponsored assemblies—and for gangs competing for control. East Timorese women, children, and older men seemed destined for a life in refugee lines. They were stampeded out of their villages; many were deported to camps across Indonesia. After the vote, when 78.5 percent chose independence over autonomy within Indonesia, Indonesia's army sent in militias to destroy the territory's public buildings and private housing, its industries and plantations. By the time Indonesia's People's Congress revoked its 1978 order of integration in October 1999, not much was left.

In 2002 East Timor began a new stage in its history as the new country of Timor Loro Sa'e. For Indonesia the exodus of East Timor marked the change fifty years had brought. In the 1950s, when rebellious provinces had to be subdued, the scale of violence was determined by the weapons and communications equipment at hand. There was also the sense that Muslim Indonesians were fighting each other, so officers who led rebellions were forgiven, and Sukarno was ready to bring together, rather than tear apart. In the last years of the twentieth century, Indonesia's armed forces and militias could unleash violence on a scale never possible before, and they had years of experience in dealing with opponents. When the New Order collapsed, army violence against civilian populations in Aceh and Irian was revealed, and there was grief or outrage over East Timor. Indonesia appeared to be a chaos of opposing groups with intentions both noble and sinister.

Indonesia's communications industry had also changed by the late 1990s. In the 1950s and 1960s Sukarno could direct censors to paint black ink over offending political commentary in imported magazines. Suharto employed state violence to intimidate human rights groups, but he could not isolate Indonesians from independent sources of information. Indonesia entered the electronic communications age with the rest of the world. It was impossible for government to censor the Internet and e-mail. Outlets appeared in the capital and smaller cities across the archipelago for web users to search for information and to launch their own views into cyberspace. When the West took notice of Indonesia at intervals, its press and television depicted a savage army run wild and fanatic Muslims torching and killing. Such coverage aroused shame or anger among Indonesians who routinely drew on satellite news sources, traveled overseas, or tracked the growing number of web sites devoted to Indonesian affairs. Electronic communications brought many mirrors to Indonesians struggling to realize new social and political visions.

In forums all over the world and inside Indonesia, Indonesians debate their future. Should Indonesia become a federation of states, choosing union because of sentiment, religion, and colonial experience? Can Indonesians be democrats and Muslims? Can Muslim and Christian Indonesians share the same space? Should ethnic groups assert ancestral rights to land and resources in a nation of migrants? Does Papua (Irian Jaya) have the right to secede? Should there be a national reckoning with the past? Should women hold public office? How should Indonesia's economy be restructured following the Asian economic crisis that began in 1997? How can ordinary Indonesians be protected from international capital and the corruption of power elites? Does the myth of glorious Majapahit justify Javanese domination in the twenty-first century? How can violence be contained? How can the constitution be rewritten to ensure justice, harmony, and prosperity? What place should the armed forces hold in public life? Are there Asian values to be pitted against Western values, or are there universal human values?

The civilian politician, Sukarno, adopted military uniform to project his image of modern-day Majapahit's greatness. The military general, Suharto, discarded his uniform for civilian dress to impose his view of Majapahit domination. The past holds many Indonesian histories. Java, Islam, origin myths, mobility, foreign rule, violence, and affinity link archipelago societies that today struggle to agree on how they can coexist, in justice, prosperity, and peace.

TWO INSTANCES OF RECONCILIATION: ABDUL HAMID AND ABDURRAHMAN WAHID

In 1601 Sultan Ala ud-Din Riayat Syah of Aceh selected seventy-one-year-old Abdul Hamid to head an embassy to Holland. Hamid reached the southern port of Middelburg in July 1602. The East Indies Company was formed that year in Amsterdam; Frederik de Houtman was already compiling the first Dutch-Malay word list in his Aceh prison. Aceh's ambassador died before he could accomplish his mission. He was the first Indonesian to die on Dutch soil, and his burial caused debate. As ambassador, Hamid stood in place of his king. State honors were due him. He was also Muslim, and it struck the Dutch that it was their duty to bury him with Islamic rites. Seventeenth-century Dutch theologians were virulent in their condemnation of Islam, but in Middelburg Abdul Hamid was given a Muslim funeral in St. Peter's church. There, in a building that had been wrested from its Roman Catholic priests and congregation and transformed into a Reformed house of worship, Arabic prayers were recited by the ambassador's companions, and his body laid on its right side facing Mecca.

St. Peter's fell into ruins in the nineteenth century and its old graves were lost. In 1978, Dutch and Acehnese again came together in a Middelburg church to unveil a plaque in Abdul Hamid's memory and to recall a moment when Dutch and Indonesians had treated each other as equals.

Four centuries later, in February 2000, Indonesia's Muslim President Abdurrahman Wahid flew into the new country of Timor Loro Sa'e. He toured sites of destruction in Dili and came to the Santa Cruz cemetery. There, he paid tribute to Christian East Timorese and to Muslim Indonesians who had met their death battling each other; he expressed sorrow and apology. At the end of the twentieth century, with its history of violence, few leaders had acknowledged the evil committed in their time or by their forebears. Indonesian histories flow into the twenty-first century around this shining moment.

GLOSSARY

adat—custom, lore, way of the ancestors, existing in oral and written form; sometimes thought of as older than Islamic law and in conflict with it.

babad—chronicle, epic, composed in Javanese verses, sung or recited, also preserved in written form with richly embellished and illustrated text; product of Muslim Java.

brahmin—Sanskrit specialist, man of superior caste in occupation related to literacy; in Indonesian histories a mobile specialist employed by government.

caliph—deputy of God and Muhammad; title taken by rulers of the Muslim community following the death of Muhammad and subsequently by Muslim kings; in Indonesian histories a title taken by kings on their conversion to Islam, and by rebels leading armies to unseat a ruling king.

dakwah—effort to improve thought and behavior to conform to Islamic ideals and standards.

Darul Islam—House of Islam, territory where a Muslim government implements and enforces Islamic law; a form of government proposed as an alternative to colonial and secular forms, a rallying cry, a form of government implemented by groups rebelling against the authority of secular politicians.

datu—hereditary chief, lineage head; title of vassal in kingdoms of southern Sulawesi.

fatwah—ruling issued by senior religious scholars clarifying whether an action or belief is lawful for Muslims; a ruling binding on Muslims.

Hadith—sayings of Muhammad, stories illustrating his life and teaching, verified by contemporaries and close associates, compiled in the ninth century C.E.; key source with the Koran for establishing Islamic principles.

haji—person who has made the pilgrimage to Mecca; title assumed by a man following completion of the pilgrimage.

hikayat—history, chronicle, composed in Malay language in Arabic script, existing in both written and oral forms, preserved in manuscripts, performed by chanting accompanied by musical instruments.

imam—Islamic leader, head of a mosque, often a leader combining book study and mystical practices; a title given a holy man by his followers, head of a dissenting Islamic community.

jago—head of a roving gang of robbers, bully, thug, head of vigilantes; often believed to possess magical powers or weapons, romantic and charismatic figure of mysterious origins.

Jawi—pilgrims to Mecca from Southeast Asia; Malay written in Arabic script.

jihad—holy war, war for extension of territory under Muslim government, a duty imposed on Muslim men and regulated in the Koran and in Islamic law.

kafir—pejorative term applied by Muslims to non-believers in Islam.

kala—head of a monster, guardian spirit, carved in wood or stone, usually over an entrance to a temple; feature of architecture in Hindu temples and entrance gates.

kawi—Javanese script derived from Indic writing systems; poet.

kiai, ki—title given to a man by followers who regard him as learned in Islam, pious, holy, radiating blessing; title for a holy or magically charged object.

kora-kora—warship; a ship with outriggers, powered by rowers, with platforms for soldiers, usually patrolling in fleets.

Koran—revelations delivered to Muhammad assembled in written form under the direction of the first two caliphs, mid-seventh century C.E.; holy text of Islam.

kris (krises)—dagger with curved blade, used as a weapon and in ceremonial costume; heirloom weapon with magical powers belonging to a kingdom's regalia; the possession of a circumcised male.

lingga—symbol of the god Siva; phallic symbol; a feature of temple architecture.

lontar—palm leaf prepared as a medium for writing; a text with writing, sometimes illustrated; text of many leaves tied together with covers in book form; handwritten texts containing chronicles, treatises, regulations, lists, and poetry.

madrasah—college for advanced study of Islam.

maharaja—supreme ruler; in Indonesian histories a title of royalty borrowed from Indian rulers.

merdeka—freedom, independence, also free, independent; used as a greeting during the war for independence.

nanyang—regions lying south of China, zone of Chinese offshore production.

Panca Sila—Five Pillars, the philosophical basis of the Republic of Indonesia; formulated by Muhammad Yamin and Sukarno in 1945 and presented by Sukarno as the way to draw all Indonesian communities into a nation; decreed the sole allowable charter for all Indonesian organizations by Suharto in 1985.

pemuda—youth, usually meaning young men (female form: *pemudi*); an ardent nationalist, a fighter during the war for independence; a paid member of a militia, a vigilante.

pesantren—Islamic school, often a boarding school, a tax-free establishment; often headed by families with connections to royal houses; center of Muslim Javanese culture; site of opposition to Java's royalty, to Dutch colonial government, and to the central government of the Republic of Indonesia.

raja—ruler, king, prince; a title of royalty borrowed from Indian rulers.

rantau—journey, usually by a man for trade or study; in Indonesian histories rantau connects mobile men to home bases of women and children.

sayyid—title of Arab man claiming descent from Muhammad.

sharia—laws and regulations derived from the Koran governing Muslim belief and practice.

stupa—bell-shaped symbol of the Buddha in temple architecture, sometimes housing a relic or an image of the Buddha; prominent feature of the Borobudur temple.

sultan—Muslim king, king who assumes responsibility for enforcing Islamic law in his kingdom; in Indonesian histories a title taken by Muslim kings on conversion or following an embassy to Mecca, an inherited title, or a title taken by a rebel leading armies to unseat the ruler.

sultanah—Muslim queen, queen who assumes responsibility for enforcing Islamic law; title taken by queens of Aceh and Bugis states.

sunan—title given to the nine legendary Muslim saints who brought Islam to Java.

surah—section of the Koran with a title or symbol as heading.

susuhunan—full form of sunan; title taken by kings of Mataram and Surakarta.

ulama—scholars of Islam, teachers, interpreters of Islamic doctrine and law; in Indonesian histories a title applied to a man recognized for his Islamic learning and piety, teacher.

uleebalang—tax collector, administrator of agricultural lands and villages; an office inherited in families in Aceh; a class eliminated during the war for independence.

wali—Islamic saint; in Javanese history a missionary bringing Islam to Java, a warrior prince, an advisor to kings, a holy man with connections to Javanese royalty, a descendant of Muhammad, or a traveler from an Arab country, a worker of miracles.

wayang—play, performance, using flat or round puppets, or human actors and dancers, with stories drawn from Sanskrit literature, Javanese and Balinese folklore; flat puppets are displayed against a lighted screen and their shadows may be viewed from the other side; texts belong to oral and written traditions; performance is both entertainment and a ritual act with a spiritual dimension.

BIBLIOGRAPHY

ESSENTIAL TEXTS FOR INDONESIAN HISTORIES

Cribb, Robert (2000). *Historical Atlas of Indonesia.* Honolulu: University of Hawaii Press.

——— (1992). *Historical Dictionary of Indonesia.* Metuchen, N.J.: Scarecrow Press.

Indonesian Heritage. 15 vols. Singapore: Editions Didier Millet, 1996– .

Kumar, Ann, and John H. McGlynn (eds.) (1996). *Illuminations: The Writing Traditions of Indonesia.* Jakarta: Lontar Press.

Ricklefs, M. C. (2001). *A History of Modern Indonesia Since c. 1200.* Basingstoke: Palgrave, 3rd ed.

SOME VALUABLE WEBSITES

Royal Institute of Linguistics and Anthropology, Leiden: www.kitlv.nl/Images

VOC Collection: www.atlasmutualheritage.nl/general.html

www.nla.gov.au/asian/indo/indsites.html

CHAPTER 1

Bellwood, Peter (1997). *Pre-History of the Indo-Malaysian Archipelago.* Honolulu: University of Hawaii Press, rev. ed.

Bosch, F. D. K. (1961). "The Problem of the Hindu Colonization of Indonesia," in F. D. K. Bosch, *Selected Studies in Indonesian Archaeology.* The Hague: M. Nijhoff, pp. 1–22.

Bronson, Bennet (1979). "The Archaeology of Sumatra and the Problem of Srivijaya," in R. B. Smith and W. Watson (eds.), *Early South East Asia.* New York: Oxford University Press, pp. 395–405.

——— (1992). "Patterns in the Early Southeast Asian Metals Trade," in Ian Glover et al. (eds.), *Early Metallurgy, Trade and Urban Centres in Thailand and Southeast Asia.* Bangkok: White Lotus, pp. 63–114.

Caldwell, Ian (1997). "A Rock Carving and a Newly Discovered Stone Burial Chamber at Pasemah, Sumatra." *Bijdragen tot de Taal-, Land- en Volkenkunde,* 153, no. 2: 169–182.

Christie, Jan Wisseman (1995). "State Formation in Early Maritime Southeast Asia: A Consideration of the Theories and the Data." *Bijdragen tot de Taal-, Land- en Volkenkunde,* 151, no. 2: 235–288.

——— (1990). "Trade and State Formation in the Malay Peninsula and Sumatra, 300 BC–AD 700," in J. Kathirithamby-Wells and John Villiers (eds.), *The Southeast Asian Port and Polity, Rise and Demise.* Singapore: Singapore University Press, pp. 39–60.

Coedès, G. (1968). *The Indianized States of Southeast Asia.* Canberra: Australian National University Press.

Diamond, Jared (1997). *Guns, Germs, and Steel: The Fates of Human Societies.* New York: Norton.

Gianno, Rosemary (1990). *Semelai Culture and Resin Technology.* New Haven: Connecticut Academy of Arts and Sciences.

Glover, I. C. (1979). "The Late Prehistoric Period in Indonesia," in R. B. Smith and W. Watson (eds.), *Early South East Asia.* New York: Oxford University Press, pp. 167–184.

Hall, Kenneth R. (1985). *Maritime Trade and State Development in Early Southeast Asia.* Sydney: Allen & Unwin.

Higham, Charles (1989). *The Archaeology of Mainland Southeast Asia from 10,000 B.C. to the Fall of Angkor.* Cambridge: Cambridge University Press.

——— (1996). *The Bronze Age of Southeast Asia.* Cambridge: Cambridge University Press.

Horridge, Adrian (1985). *The Prahu: Traditional Sailing Boat of Indonesia.* Singapore: Oxford University Press, 2nd ed.

Kulke, Hermann (1986). "The Early and the Imperial Kingdom in Southeast Asian History," in David G. Marr and A. C. Milner (eds.), *Southeast Asia in the Ninth to the Fourteenth Centuries.* Singapore: Institute for Southeast Asian Studies, pp. 1–22.

Manguin, Pierre-Yves (1980). "The Southeast Asian Ship: An Historical Approach." *Journal of Southeast Asian Studies,* 11, no. 2: 266–276.

——— (1993). "Palembang and Sriwijaya: An Early Malay Harbour-City Rediscovered," in *Journal of the Malaysian Branch of the Royal Asiatic Society,* 66, part I: 23–46.

McPherson, Kenneth (1993). *The Indian Ocean: A History of People and Sea.* Delhi: Oxford University Press.

Pluvier, Jan M. (1995). *Historical Atlas of Southeast Asia.* Leiden: Brill.

Reid, Anthony (1997). "Inside Out: The Colonial Displacement of Sumatra's Population," in Peter Boomgaard, Freek Colombijn, and David Henley (eds.), *Paper Landscapes: Explorations in the Environmental History of Indonesia.* Leiden: KITLV Press, pp. 61–89.

Schnitger, F. M. (1989). *Forgotten Kingdoms in Sumatra.* Singapore: Oxford University Press, reprint. Originally published as *The Archaeology of Hindoo Sumatra, 1938.*

Sellato, Bernard (1994). *Nomads of the Borneo Rainforest: The Economics, Politics, and Ideology of Settling Down.* Honolulu: University of Hawaii Press.

Slamet-Velsink, Ina E. (1995). *Emerging Hierarchies. Processes of Stratification and Early State Formation in the Indonesian Archipelago: Prehistory and the Ethnographic Present.* Leiden: KITLV Press.

Wolters, O. W. (1967). *Early Indonesian Commerce: A Study of the Origins of Srivijaya.* Ithaca, N.Y.: Cornell University Press.

——— (1970). *The Fall of Srivijaya in Malay History.* London: Lund Humphries.

——— (1983). "A Few and Miscellaneous Pi-Chi Jottings on Early Indonesia." *Indonesia,* 36, October: 49–65.

Yesner, David R. (1987). "Life in the 'Garden of Eden': Causes and Consequences of the Adoption of Marine Diets by Human Societies," in Marvin Harris and Eric B. Ross (eds.), *Food and Evolution: Toward a Theory of Human Food Habits.* Philadelphia: Temple University Press, pp. 285–310.

CHAPTER 2

Boechari (1979). "Some Considerations on the Problem of the Shift of Mataram's Centre of Government from Central to East Java in the Tenth Century," in R. B. Smith and W. Watson (eds.), *Early South East Asia.* New York: Oxford University Press, pp. 473–491.

Boomgaard, Peter (1997). "Hunting and Trapping in the Indonesian Archipelago, 1500–1950," in Peter Boomgaard, Freek Colombijn, and David Henley (eds.), *Paper Landscapes: Explorations in the Environmental History of Indonesia.* Leiden: KITLV Press, pp. 185–212.

Casparis, J. G. de (1979). "Palaeography as an Auxiliary Discipline in Research on Early South East Asia," in R. B. Smith and W. Watson (eds.), *Early South East Asia.* New York: Oxford University Press, pp. 380–394.

Casparis, J. G. de (1986). "Some Notes on the Oldest Inscriptions of Indonesia," in C. M. S. Hellwig and S. O. Robson (eds.), *A Man of Indonesian Letters: Essays in Honour of Professor A. Teeuw.* Dordrecht: Foris, pp. 242–256.

Casparis, J. G. de (1986). "Some Notes on Relations Between Central and Local Government in Ancient Java," in David G. Marr and A. C. Milner (eds.), *Southeast Asia in the Ninth to Fourteenth Centuries.* Singapore: Institute for Southeast Asian Studies, pp. 49–63.

Christie, Jan Wisseman (1983). "Raja and Rama: The Classical State in Early Java," in L. Gessick (ed.), *Centers, Symbols and Hierarchies,* Yale Monograph No. 26, pp. 9–44.

——— (1991). "States Without Cities: Demographic Trends in Early Java." *Indonesia,* 52, October: 23–40.

——— (1992). "Trade and Settlement in Early Java: Integrating the Epigraphic and Archaeological Data," in Ian Glover et al. (eds.), *Early Metallurgy, Trade and Urban Centres in Thailand and Southeast Asia.* Bangkok: White Lotus, pp. 181–198.

Creese, Helen (1993). "Love, Lust and Loyalty: Representations of Women in Traditional Javanese and Balinese Literature." Paper presented to Fourth Women in Asia Conference, University of Melbourne, 1–3 October.

Drakard, Jane (1999). *A Kingdom of Words: Language and Power in Sumatra.* New York: Oxford University Press.

Dumarçay, Jacques (1987). *The House in South-East Asia.* Singapore: Oxford University Press.

Ensink, J. (1967). *On the Old-Javanese Cantakaparwa and Its Tale of Sutasoma.* The Hague: M. Nijhoff.

Gallop, Annabel Teh (1995). *Early Views of Indonesia: Drawings from the British Library.* London: British Library.

Goody, Jack (1982). *Cooking, Cuisine and Class.* Cambridge: Cambridge University Press.

——— (1986). *The Logic of Writing and the Organization of Society.* Cambridge: Cambridge University Press.

Goody, Jack, and Ian Watt (1975). "The Consequences of Literacy," in Jack Goody (ed.), *Literacy in Traditional Societies.* Cambridge: Cambridge University Press, pp. 27–68.

Hyams, Edward (1971). *Plants in the Service of Man: 10,000 Years of Domestication.* London: J. M. Dent & Sons.

Jones, Antoinette M. Barrett (1984). *Early Tenth Century Java from the Inscriptions.* Dordrecht: Foris.

Jordaan, Roy E., and Robert Wessing (1996). "Human Sacrifice at Prambanan." *Bijdragen tot de Taal-, Land- en Volkenkunde,* 152, no. 1: 45–73.

Miksic, John N. (1990). *Borobudur: Golden Tales of the Buddhas.* Boston: Shambala.

Miksic, John N. (ed.) (1996). *Ancient History.* Singapore: Archipelago Press.

Noorduyn, J. (1965). "The Making of Bark Paper in West Java." *Bijdragen tot de Taal-, Land- en Volkenkunde,* 121, no. 4: 472–473.

Rubinstein, Raechelle (1996). "Leaves of Palm: Balinese Lontar," in Ann Kumar and John H. McGlynn (eds.), *Illuminations: The Writing Traditions of Indonesia.* Jakarta: Lontar Press, pp. 129–154.

Schoterman, J. A. (1981). "An Introduction to Old Javanese Sanskrit Dictionaries and Grammars." *Bijdragen tot de Taal-, Land- en Volkenkunde,* 137, no. 4: 419–442.

Sears, Laurie J. (1996). *Shadows of Empire: Colonial Discourse and Javanese Tales.* Durham, N.C.: Duke University Press.

Setten van der Meer, N. C. van (1979). *Sawah Cultivation in Ancient Java: Aspects of Development During the Indo-Javanese Period, Fifth to Fifteenth Centuries.* Canberra: Australian National University.

Soejono, R. P. (1979). "The Significance of the Excavations at Gilimanuk (Bali)," in R. B. Smith and W. Watson (eds.), *Early South East Asia.* New York: Oxford University Press, pp. 185–198.

Soekmono (1979). "The Archaeology of Central Java before 800 A.D.," in R. B. Smith and W. Watson (eds.), *Early South East Asia.* New York: Oxford University Press, pp. 457–472.

Suryohudoyo, Supomo (1996). "The Sovereignty of Beauty: Classical Javanese Writings," in Ann Kumar and John H. McGlynn (eds.), *Illuminations: The Writing Traditions of Indonesia.* Jakarta: Lontar Press, pp. 13–32.

Swadling, Pamela (1996). *Plumes from Paradise: Trade Cycles in Outer Southeast Asia and Their Impact on New Guinea and Nearby Islands Until 1920.* Papua New Guinea National Museum.

Zoetmulder, P. J. (1974). *Kalangwan: A Survey of Old Javanese Literature.* The Hague: M. Nijhoff.

CHAPTER 3

Abdullah, Taufiq (1989). "Islam and the Formation of Tradition in Indonesia: A Comparative Perspective." *Itinerario,* 13, no. 1: 17–36.

Ali, Abdullah Yusuf (1981). *The Holy Qur-an: Text, Translation and Commentary.* Lahore: Sh. Muhammad Ashraf.

Broeze, Frank (ed.) (1989) *Brides of the Sea: Port Cities of Asia from the Sixteenth to Twentieth Centuries.* Kensington: University of New South Wales Press.

Bruinessen, Martin van (1994). "Najmuddin al-Kubra, Jumadil Kubra and Jamaluddin al-Akbar: Traces of Kubrawiyya Influence in Early Indonesian Islam." *Bijdragen tot de Taal-, Land- en Volkenkunde,* 150, no. 2: 305–329.

Daniel, Norman (1962). *Islam and the West: The Making of an Image.* Edinburgh: Edinburgh University Press.

Dhofier, Zamakhsyari (1980). "Islamic Education and Traditional Ideology on Java," in J. J. Fox (ed.), *Indonesia: Australian Perspectives.* Canberra: Australian National University Press, vol. II, pp. 263–271.

Drakard, Jane (1989). "An Indian Ocean Port: Sources for the Earlier History of Barus." *Archipel,* 37: 53–82.

Geertz, Clifford (1960). *The Religion of Java.* Glencoe, Ill.: Glencoe Free Press.

Johns, A. H. (1961). "Sufism as a Category in Indonesian Literature and History." *Journal of Southeast Asian History* 2, no. 2: 10–23.

Jones, Russell (1979). "Ten Conversion Myths from Indonesia," in Nehemia Levtzion (ed.), *Conversion to Islam.* New York: Holmes and Meier, pp. 129–158.

Leur, J. C. van (1967). *Indonesian Trade and Society: Essays in Asian Social and Economic History.* The Hague: W. van Hoeve, 2nd ed.

Levathes, Louise (1994). *When China Ruled the Seas: The Treasure Fleet of the Dragon Throne, 1405–1433.* New York: Simon & Schuster.

Lewis, Bernard (1993). *The Arabs in History.* Oxford: Oxford University Press, rev. ed.

——— (1995). *The Middle East: A Brief History of the Last Two Thousand Years.* New York: Scribner.

Lindholm, Charles (1996). *The Islamic Middle East: An Historical Anthropology.* Oxford: Blackwell.

Lovric, Barbara (1987). "Bali: Myth, Magic and Morbidity," in Norman G. Owen (ed.), *Death and Disease in Southeast Asia.* Singapore: Oxford University Press, pp. 117–141.

Mills, J. V. (1979). "Chinese Navigators in Insulinde about A.D. 1500." *Archipel,* 18: 69–93.

Reid, Anthony (1989). "Elephants and Water in the Feasting of Seventeenth Century Aceh." *Journal of the Malaysian Branch of the Royal Asiatic Society,* 62, part II: 25–44.

Ricklefs, M. C. (1979). "Six Centuries of Islamization in Java," in Nehemia Levtzion (ed.), *Conversion to Islam.* London: Holmes & Meier, pp. 100–128.

Ricklefs, M. C. (ed.) (1984). *Chinese Muslims in Java in the Fifteenth and Sixteenth Centuries: The Malay Annals of Semarang and Cerbon.* Melbourne: Monash University Papers on Southeast Asia no. 12.

Southall, Aidan (1998). *The City in Time and Space.* Cambridge: Cambridge University Press.

Wertheim, W. F. (1959). *Indonesian Society in Transition: A Study of Social Change.* The Hague: W. van Hoeve, 2nd rev. ed.

CHAPTER 4

Aelst, Arjan van (1995). "Majapahit Picis, the Currency of a 'Moneyless' Society, 1300–1700." *Bijdragen tot de Taal-, Land- en Volkenkunde,* 151, no. 3: 357–393.

Behrend, T. E. (1996). "Textual Gateways: The Javanese Manuscript Tradition," in Ann Kumar and John H. McGlynn (eds.), *Illuminations: The Writing Traditions of Indonesia.* Jakarta: Lontar Press, pp. 161–200.

Blussé, Léonard (1986). "Trojan Horse of Lead: The *Picis* in Early Seventeenth Century Java," in Léonard Blussé, *Strange Company: Chinese Settlers, Mestizo Women and the Dutch in VOC Batavia.* Dordrecht: Foris, pp. 35–48.

Boomgaard, Peter (1991). "The Javanese Village as a Cheshire Cat: The Java Debate Against a European and Latin American Background." *Journal of Peasant Studies,* 18, no. 2, January: 288–304.

Breman, Jan (1980). *The Village on Java and the Early Colonial State.* Rotterdam: Erasmus University.

Caldwell, Ian (1995). "Power, State and Society among the Pre-Islamic Bugis." *Bijdragen tot de Taal-, Land- en Volkenkunde,* 151, no. 3: 394–421.

Casparis, J. G. de (1986). "Some Notes on Relations Between Central and Local Government in Ancient Java," in David G. Marr and A. C. Milner (eds.), *Southeast Asia in the Ninth to Fourteenth Centuries.* Singapore: Institute for Southeast Asian Studies, pp. 49–63.

Chambert-Loir, Henri (1996). "Bima on the Edge of Tradition," in Ann Kumar and John H. McGlynn (eds.), *Illuminations: The Writing Traditions of Indonesia.* Jakarta: Lontar Press, pp. 74–75.

Christie, Jan Wisseman (1991). "States Without Cities: Demographic Trends in Early Java." *Indonesia,* 52, October: 23–40.

Day, A. (1988). "Islam and Literature in South-East Asia: Some Pre-Modern, Largely Javanese Perspectives," in M. B. Hooker (ed.), *Islam in South-East Asia.* Leiden: Brill, pp. 130–159.

Geertz, Clifford (1963). *Agricultural Involution: The Process of Ecological Change in Indonesia.* Berkeley: University of California Press.

Hall, Kenneth R. (1991). "Coinage, Trade, and Economy in Early South India and Southeast Asia," in Amal Kumar Jha (ed.), *Coinage, Trade and Economy.* Bombay: Indian Institute of Numismatic Studies, pp. 99–107.

Milner, A. C. (1983). "Islam and the Muslim State," in M. B. Hooker (ed.), *Islam in South-East Asia.* Leiden: Brill, pp. 23–49.

Noorduyn, J. (1978). "Majapahit in the Fifteenth Century." *Bijdragen tot de Taal-, Land- en Volkenkunde,* 134, nos. 2–3: 207–274.

Padmapuspita, Ki J. (1966). *Pararaton. Teks Bahasa Kawi Terdjemahan Bahasa Indonesia.* Jogjakarta: Penerbit Taman Siswa.

Prapanca, Mpu (1995). *Desawarnana (Nagarakrtagama).* Translated by Stuart Robson. Leiden: KITLV Press.

Proudfoot, Ian, and Virginia Hooker (1996). "Mediating Time and Space: The Malay Writing Tradition," in Ann Kumar and John H. McGlynn (eds.), *Illuminations: The Writing Traditions of Indonesia.* Jakarta: Lontar Press, pp. 49–78.

Ras, J. J. (1994). "Geschiedschrijving en de legitimiteit van het koningschap op Java." *Bijdragen tot de Taal-, Land- en Volkenkunde,* 150, no. 3: 518–538.

Reid, Anthony (ed.) (1995). *Witnesses to Sumatra: A Travellers' Anthology.* Kuala Lumpur: Oxford University Press.

Robson, S. O. (1981). "Java at the Crossroads: Aspects of Javanese Cultural History in the Fourteenth and Fifteenth Centuries." *Bijdragen tot de Taal-, Land- en Volkenkunde,* 137, nos. 2–3: 259–292.

Sedyawati, Edi (1994). "The State Formation of Kadiri," in G. J. Schutte (ed.), *State and Trade in the Indonesian Archipelago.* Leiden: KITLV Press, pp. 7–16.

Soebardi, S. (1975). *The Book of Cabolek.* The Hague: M. Nijhoff.

Supomo, S. (1979). "The Image of Majapahit in Later Javanese and Indonesian Writing," in A. Reid and D. Marr (eds.), *Perceptions of the Past in Southeast Asia.* Singapore: Heinemann, pp. 171–185.

Teeuw, A., and S. D. Robson (1981). *Kunjarakarna Dharmakathana: Liberation Through the Law of the Buddha. An Old Javanese Poem by Mpu Dusun.* The Hague: M. Nijhoff.

Teeuw, A., et al. (1969). *Siwaratrikalpa of Mpu Tanakun.* The Hague: M. Nijhoff.

Wicks, Robert S. (1992). *Money, Markets, and Trade in Early Southeast Asia: The Development of Indigenous Monetary Systems to A.D. 1400.* Ithaca, N.Y.: Cornell Southeast Asia Program.

CHAPTER 5

Abdurachman, Paramita R. (1988). "'Niachile Pokaraga': A Sad Story of a Moluccan Queen." *Modern Asian Studies* 22, no. 3, July: 571–592.

Andaya, Leonard Y. (2000). "A History of Trade in the Sea of Melayu." *Itinerario,* 24, no. 1: 87–110.

Brierley, Joanna Hall (1994). *Spices: The Story of Indonesia's Spice Trade.* Kuala Lumpur: Oxford University Press.

Brissenden, Rosemary (1976). "Patterns of Trade and Maritime Society Before the Coming of Europeans," in Elaine McKay (ed.), *Studies in Indonesian History.* Melbourne: Pitman, pp. 98–123.

Cipolla, Carlo M. (1970). *European Culture and Overseas Expansion.* Harmondsworth: Penguin.

Ellen, Roy F. (1979). "Sago Subsistence and the Trade in Spices: A Provisional Model of Ecological Succession and Imbalance in Moluccan History," in P. C. Burnham and R. F. Ellen (eds.), *Social and Ecological Systems.* London: Academic Press, pp. 43–74.

Fraasen, Ch. F. van (1994). "Ternate and Its Dependencies," in Leontine E. Visser (ed.), *Halmahera and Beyond.* Leiden: KITLV Press, pp. 23–33.

Guillot, Claude (1989). "Banten en 1678." *Archipel,* 37: 119–151.

Kathirithamby-Wells, J. (1986). "The Islamic City: Melaka to Jogjakarta, c. 1500–1800." *Modern Asian Studies,* 20, no. 2: 333–351.

——— (1990). "Banten: A West Indonesian Port and Polity During the Sixteenth and Seventeenth Centuries," in J. Kathirithamby-Wells and John Villiers (eds.), *The Southeast Asian Port and Polity: Rise and Demise:* Singapore: Singapore University Press, pp. 107–125.

Lapian, A. B. (1994). "Bacan and the Early History of North Maluku," in Leontine E. Visser (ed.), *Halmahera and Beyond.* Leiden: KITLV Press, pp. 11–22.

Leirissa, R. Z. (1994). "Changing Maritime Trade Patterns in the Seram Sea," in G. J. Schutte (ed.), *State and Trade in the Indonesian Archipelago.* Leiden: KITLV Press, pp. 99–114.

——— (1997). "The Myth of the Eternal Return in the Early Modern History of Maluku." Seminar on Indonesian Social History, University of Indonesia, Depok, 8–11 December.

Leong, Swo-Theng (1997). *Migration and Ethnicity in Chinese History: Hakkas, Pengmin, and Their Neighbors.* Stanford, Calif.: Stanford University Press, 1997.

Lewis, Dianne (1995). *Jan Compagnie in the Straits of Malacca, 1641–1795.* Athens: Ohio University Monographs in Southeast Asian Studies, No. 96.

Lombard, Denys (ed.) (1970). *Le "Spraeck ende Woord-Boek" de Frederick de Houtman.* Paris: Ecole Française d'Extrême Orient.

Mills, J. V. (1979). "Chinese Navigators in Insulinde about A.D. 1500." *Archipel,* 18: 69–93.

Reid, Anthony (ed.) (1993). *Southeast Asia in the Early Modern Era.* Ithaca, N.Y.: Cornell University Press.

Russell-Wood, A. J. R. (1992). *A World on the Move: The Portuguese in Africa, Asia, and America, 1415–1808.* New York: St. Martin's Press.

Sollewijn Gelpke, J. H. F. (1994). "The Report of Miguel Roxo de Brito of His Voyage in 1581–1582 to the Raja Ampat, the MacCluer Gulf and Seram." *Bijdragen tot de Taal-, Land- en Volkenkunde,* 150, no. 1: 123–145.

Thrower, Norman J. W. (1996). *Maps and Civilization: Cartography in Culture and Society.* Chicago: University of Chicago Press.

Villiers, John (1990). "The Cash Crop Economy and State Formation in the Spice Islands in the Fifteenth and Sixteenth Centuries," in J. Kathirithamby-Wells and John Villiers (eds.), *The Southeast Asian Port and Polity.* Singapore: Singapore University Press, pp. 83–105.

CHAPTER 6

Abeyasekere, Susan (1987). *Jakarta: A History.* Singapore: Oxford University Press.

Andaya, Barbara Watson (1993). *To Live as Brothers: Southeast Sumatra in the Seventeenth and Eighteenth Centuries.* Honolulu: University of Hawaii Press.

Andaya, Leonard Y. (1979). "A Village Perception of Arung Palakka and the Makassar War of 1666–69," in Anthony Reid and David Marr (eds.), *Perceptions of the Past in Southeast Asia.* Singapore: Heinemann, pp. 360–378.

——— (1981). *The Heritage of Arung Palakka: A History of South Sulawesi (Celebes) in the Seventeenth Century.* The Hague: M. Nijhoff.

Blussé, Léonard (1979). "Chinese Trade to Batavia During the Days of the VOC." *Archipel,* 18: 195–213.

——— (1992). "In Praise of Commodities: An Essay on the Cross-Cultural Trade in Edible Birds'

Nests," in Roderich Ptak and Dietmar Rothermund (eds.), *Emporia, Commodities and Entrepreneurs in Asian Maritime Trade, c. 1400–1750.* Stuttgart: Franz Steiner Verlag, pp. 317–335.

——— (1996). "No Boats to China: The Dutch East India Company and the Changing Pattern of the China Sea Trade, 1635–1690." *Modern Asian Studies,* 30, no. 1, February: 51–76.

Curtin, Philip D. (1989). *Death by Migration: Europe's Encounter with the Tropical World in the Nineteenth Century.* Cambridge: Cambridge University Press.

Emmer, P. C. (1992). "European Expansion and Migration. The European Colonial Past and Intercontinental Migration: An Overview," in P. C. Emmer and M. Morner (eds.), *European Expansion and Migration: Essays on the Intercontinental Migration from Africa, Asia, and Europe.* Oxford: Berg.

Fell, R. T. (1988). *Early Maps of South-East Asia.* Singapore: Oxford University Press.

Gaastra, F. S., and J. R. Bruijn (1993). "The Dutch East India Company's Shipping, 1602–1795, in a Comparative Perspective," in J. R. Bruijn and F. S. Gaastra (eds.), *Ships, Sailors and Spices: East India Companies and Their Shipping in the Sixteenth, Seventeenth and Eighteenth Centuries.* Leiden: KITLV Press, pp. 177–208.

Goens, Rijklof van (1995). *Javaense Reyse: De bezoeken van een VOC-gezant aan het hof van Mataram, 1648–54.* Amsterdam: Terra Incognita (1667).

Goor, J. van (ed.) (1986). *Trading Companies in Asia, 1600–1830.* Utrecht: HES.

Grijns, Kees, and Peter J. M. Nas (eds.) (2000). *Jakarta-Batavia: Socio-Cultural Essays.* Leiden: KITLV Press.

Haan, F. de (1910). *Priangen: De Preanger-Regentschappen onder het Nederlandsch Bestuur tot 1811.* Vol. II: Personalia, Batavia: Bataviaasche Genootschap van Kunsten en Wetenschappen.

Hoadley, Mason C. (1990). "State-sponsored Migration: Java in the Seventeenth Century," in Robert R. Reed (ed.), *Patterns of Migration in Southeast Asia.* Berkeley, Calif.: Center for South and Southeast Asian Studies, pp. 25–42.

Houben, V. J. H. (1994). "Trade and State Formation in Central Java Seventeenth to Nineteenth Century," in G. J. Schutte (ed.), *State and Trade in the Indonesian Archipelago.* Leiden: KITLV Press, pp. 61–76.

Kartodirdjo, Sartono (1987). *Pengantar Sejarah Indonesia Baru: 1500–1900.* Jakarta: Gramedia.

Knaap, G. J. (1986a). "Coffee for Cash: The Dutch East India Company and the Expansion of Coffee Cultivation in Java, Ambon and Ceylon, 1700–1730," in J. van Goor (ed.), *Trading Companies in Asia, 1600–1800.* Utrecht: HES, pp. 33–49.

——— (1986b). *Shallow Waters, Rising Tide: Shipping and Trade in Java Around 1775.* Leiden: KITLV Press.

Knaap, Gerrit, and Luc Nagtegaal (1991). "A Forgotten Trade: Salt in Southeast Asia 1670–1813," in R. Ptak and D. Rothermund (eds.), *Emporia, Commodities, and Entrepreneurs in Asian Maritime Trade, c. 1400–1750.* Stuttgart: Franz Steiner Verlag, pp. 127–157.

Lombard, Denys (1978). "Agon, Sultan de Bantan: Tragédie en 5 Actes et en Vers." *Archipel,* 15: 53–64.

——— (1981). "Questions on the Contact Between European Companies and Asian Societies," in Léonard Blussé and Femme Gaastra (eds.), *Companies and Trade.* Leiden: Leiden University Press, pp. 179–187.

Mansurnoor, Iik A. (1995). "Rato and Kiai in Madura: Are They Twins?" in Kees van Dijk et al. (eds.), *Across Madura Strait: The Dynamics of an Insular Society.* Leiden: KITLV Press, pp. 25–48.

Meilink-Roelofsz, M. A. P. (1962). *Asian Trade and European Influence in the Indonesian Archipelago Between 1500 and About 1630.* The Hague: M. Nijhoff.

Pelras, Christian (1985). "Religion, Tradition and the Dynamics of Islamization in South Sulawesi." *Archipel,* 29, 1: 107–135.

Reid, Anthony (1993). *Southeast Asia in the Age of Commerce, 1450–1680.* Vol. 2, New Haven: Yale University Press.

Sollewijn Gelpke, J. H. F. (1995). "Afonso de Albuquerque's Pre-Portuguese 'Javanese' Map, Partially Reconstructed from Francisco Rodrigues' Book." *Bijdragen tot de Taal-, Land- en Volkenkunde,* 151, no. 1: 76–99.

Taylor, Jean Gelman (1983). *The Social World of Batavia: European and Eurasian in Dutch Asia.* Madison: University of Wisconsin Press.

Tooley, R. V. (1952). *Maps and Map-Makers.* New York: Crown.

Trocki, Carl A. (1997). "Chinese Pioneering in Eighteenth Century Southeast Asia," in A. Reid (ed.), *The Last Stand of Asian Autonomies.* London: Macmillan, pp. 83–101.

Velde, Pieter van de (1988). "On an Early Salt Industry on Java's South Coast," in David S. Moyer and Henri J. M. Claessen (eds.), *Time Past, Time Present, Time Future: Essays in Honour of P. E. de Josselin de Jong.* Dordrecht: Forris, pp. 78–84.

Villiers, John (1990). "Makassar: The Rise and Fall of an East Indonesian Maritime Trading State, 1512–1669," in J. Kathirithamby-Wells and John Villiers (eds.), *The Southeast Asian Port and Polity: Rise and Demise.* Singapore: Singapore University Press, pp. 143–159.

Vos, Reinout (1994). *Gentle Janus, Merchant Prince: The VOC and the Tightrope of Diplomacy in the Malay World, 1740–1800.* Leiden: KITLV Press.

CHAPTER 7

Ammarell, Gene (1999). *Bugis Navigation.* New Haven: Yale University Southeast Asia Monograph Series, No. 48.

Andaya, Barbara Watson (1997). "Adapting to Political and Economic Change: Palembang in the Late Eighteenth and Early Nineteenth Centuries," in A. Reid (ed.), *The Last Stand of Asian Autonomies.* London: Macmillan, pp. 187–215.

Black, Ian (1985). "The 'Lastposten': Eastern Kalimantan and the Dutch in the Nineteenth and Early Twentieth Centuries." *Journal of Southeast Asian Studies,* 16, no. 2, September: 281–291.

Blussé, Léonard (1986). "Batavia 1619–1740: The Rise and Fall of a Chinese Colonial Town," in Léonard Blussé, *Strange Company: Chinese Settlers, Mestizo Women, and the Dutch in VOC Batavia.* Dordrecht: Foris, pp. 73–96.

Dijk, Kees van et al. (eds.) (1995). *Across Madura Strait: The Dynamics of an Insular Society.* Leiden: KITLV Press.

Djaja, Tamar (1965). *Pusaka Indonesia: Riwajat Hidup Orang-Orang Besar Tanah Air.* Djakarta: Bulan Bintang, 4th ed., 2 vols.

Graaf, H. J. de (1987). *Disintegrasi Mataram di bawah Mangkurat I.* Jakarta: Penerbit P. T. Pustaka Grafitipers.

Groot, Hans (1997). "Society of Arts and Sciences (1838–1848)." Seminar on the Social History of Indonesia, University of Indonesia, Depok, 8–11 December.

Hadisutjipto, S. Z. (1971). *Pieter Erberveld mentjoba meraih bintang.* Jakarta: Dinas Museum dan Sedjarah.

Heidhues, Mary F. Somers (1992). *Bangka Tin and Mentok Pepper: Chinese Settlement on an Indonesian Island.* Singapore: Institute for Southeast Asian Studies.

Heuken, Adolf (1982). *Historical Sites of Jakarta.* Jakarta: Yayasan Cipta Loka Caraka.

Houben, V. J. H. (1994). "Trade and State Formation in Central Java Seventeenth to Nineteenth Century," in G. J. Schutte (ed.), *State and Trade in the Indonesian Archipelago.* Leiden: KITLV Press, pp. 61–76.

King, Victor T. (1993). *The Peoples of Borneo.* Oxford: Blackwell.

Kumar, Ann (1976). *Surapati, Man and Legend: A Study of Three Babad Traditions.* Leiden: Brill.

——— (1979). "Javanese Historiography in and of the 'Colonial Period': A Case Study," in Anthony Reid and D. Marr (eds.), *Perceptions of the Past in Southeast Asia.* Singapore: Heinemann, pp. 187–206.

——— (1987). "Literary Approaches to Slavery and the Indies Enlightenment: Van Hogendorp's *Kraspoekoel.*" *Indonesia,* 43, April: 43–65.

——— (1997). *Java and Modern Europe: Ambiguous Encounters.* London: Curzon.

Lombard, D., and C. Salmon (1993). "Islam and Chineseness." *Indonesia,* 57, April: 115–131.

Moeis, Abdoel (1979). *Surapati.* Jakarta: Balai Pustaka, 5th printing.

Nagtegaal, Luc (1986). "The Dutch East India Company and the Relations Between Kartasura and the Javanese North Coast, c. 1690–c. 1740," in J. van Goor (ed.), *Trading Companies in Asia, 1600–1830.* Utrecht: HES, pp. 51–81.

——— (1994). "Diamonds Are a Regent's Best Friend: Javanese Bupati as Political Entrepreneurs" in G. J. Schutte (ed.), *State and Trade in the Indonesian Archipelago.* Leiden: KITLV Press, pp. 77–97.

——— (1996). *Riding the Dutch Tiger: The Dutch East Indies Company and the Northeast Coast of Java, 1680–1743.* Leiden: KITLV Press.

Nieuhof, Johan (1988). *Voyages and Travels to the East Indies, 1653–1670.* Singapore: Oxford University Press, reprint (1669).

Noorduyn, J. (1986). "The Bugis Auxiliaries from Tanete in the Chinese War in Java, 1742–1744," in C. M. S. Hellwig and S. O. Robson (eds.), *A Man of Indonesian Letters: Essays in Honour of Professor A. Teeuw.* Dordrecht: Foris, pp. 271–292.

Onghokham (1984). "The Jago in Colonial Java, Ambivalent Champion of the People," in A. Turton and S. Tanabe (eds.), *History and Peasant Consciousness in Southeast Asia.* Osaka: Senri Ethnological Studies No. 13, pp. 327–343.

Pelras, Christian (1996). *The Bugis.* Oxford: Blackwell.

Remmelink, W. (1988). "Expansion Without Design: The Snare of Javanese Politics." *Itinerario,* 12, no. 1: 111–128.

——— (1994). *The Chinese War and the Collapse of the Javanese State, 1725–1743.* Leiden: KITLV Press.

Ricklefs, M. C. (1974). *Jogjakarta Under Sultan Mangkubumi 1749–1792: A History of the Division of Java.* London: Oxford University Press.

——— (1978). *Modern Javanese Historical Tradition: A Study of an Original Kartasura Chronicle and Related Materials.* London: School of Oriental and African Studies, 1978.

——— (1992). *War, Culture and Economy in Java, 1677–1726: Asian and European Imperialism in the Early Kartasura Period.* Sydney: Allen & Unwin.

——— (1998). *The Seen and Unseen Worlds in Java, 1726–1749: History, Literature and Islam in the Court of Pakubuwono II.* Sydney: Allen & Unwin.

Saleh, M. Idwar (1978). "Pepper Trade and the Ruling Class of Banjarmasin in the Seventeenth Century," in *Papers on the Dutch-Indonesian Historical Conference,* May 1976. Leiden: Bureau of Indonesian Studies, pp. 203–221.

Salmon, Claudine (1980). *Les Chinois de Jakarta: Temples et vie collective.* Paris: Eds. de la Maison Sciences de l'Homme.

Schoorl, J. W. (1994). "Power, Ideology and Change in the Early State of Buton," in G. J. Schutte (ed.), *State and Trade in the Indonesian Archipelago.* Leiden: KITLV Press, pp. 17–59.

Taylor, Jean Gelman (1990). "Politics and Marriage in VOC Batavia," in Fia Dieteren and Els Kloek (eds.), *Writing Women into History.* Amsterdam: University of Amsterdam Historical Series, No. 17, pp. 97–110.

Tio Ie Soei (1982). "Pieter Elberveld: Satoe kedjadian jang betoel di Betawi," in Pramoedya Ananta Toer (ed.), *Tempo Doeloe.* Jakarta: Hasta Mitra, pp. 91–115.

Velthoen, Esther J. (1997). "'Wanderers, Robbers and Bad Folk': The Politics of Violence, Protection and Trade in Eastern Sulawesi, 1750–1850," in Anthony Reid (ed.), *The Last Stand of Asian Autonomies.* London: Macmillan, pp. 367–388.

CHAPTER 8

Ahmad, Raja Ali Haji Ibn (1982). *The Precious Gift (Tuhfat al-Nafis).* Kuala Lumpur: Oxford University Press.

Andaya, Barbara Watson, and Virginia Matheson (1979). "Islamic Thought and Malay Tradition: The Writings of Raja Ali Haji of Riau (ca. 1809–ca. 1870)," in Anthony Reid and David Marr (eds.), *Perceptions of the Past in Southeast Asia.* Singapore: Heinemann, pp. 108–128.

Andaya, Leonard Y. (1975). *The Kingdom of Johor, 1641–1728.* Kuala Lumpur: Oxford University Press.

Bayly, C. A. (1986). "Two Colonial Revolts: The Java War, 1825–1830, and the Indian 'Mutiny' of 1857–1859," in C. A. Bayly and D. H. A. Kolff (eds.), *Two Colonial Empires: Comparative Essays on the History of India and Indonesia in the Nineteenth Century.* Dordrecht: M. Nijhoff, pp. 111–135.

Barnard, Timothy P. (1997). "The Timber Trade in Early Modern Siak." Paper presented at the Association of Asian Studies, Chicago, March.

Carey, P. B. R. (1977). "The Sepoy Conspiracy of 1815 in Java." *Bijdragen tot de Taal-, Land en Volkenkunde,* 133, nos. 2–3: 294–322.

——— (1979). "Aspects of Javanese History in the Nineteenth Century," in Harry Aveling (ed.), *The Development of Indonesian Society.* St. Lucia: University of Queensland Press, pp. 45–105.

——— (1981). *Babad Dipanagara: An Account of the Outbreak of the Java War (1825–30).* Kuala Lumpur, *JMBRAS* Monograph No. 9.

——— (1984). "Changing Javanese Perceptions of the Chinese Communities in Central Java, 1755–1825." *Indonesia,* 37, April: 1–47.

——— (1986). "Waiting for the 'Just King': The Agrarian World of South-Central Java from Giyanti (1755) to the Java War (1825–30)." *Modern Asian Studies,* 20, no. 1: 59–137.

Carey, Peter (ed.) (1992). *The British in Java, 1811–1816: A Javanese Account.* Oxford: Oxford University Press.

Crawfurd, John (1820). *History of the Indian Archipelago.* Edinburgh: A. Constable.

Durie, Mark (1996). "Poetry and Worship: Manuscripts from Aceh," in Ann Kumar and John H. McGlynn (eds.), *Illuminations: The Writing Traditions of Indonesia.* Jakarta: Lontar Press, pp. 79–100.

Florida, Nancy K. (1995). *Writing the Past, Inscribing the Future: History as Prophesy in Colonial Java.* Durham, N.C.: Duke University Press.

Gallop, Annabel Teh (1995). *Early Views of Indonesia: Drawings from the British Library.* London: British Library.

Houben, V. J. H. (1994). *Kraton and Kumpeni: Surakarta and Yogyakarta, 1830–1870.* Leiden: KITLV Press.

Ismail, Muhammad Gade (1994). "Trade and State Power: Sambas (West Borneo) in the Early Nineteenth Century," in G. J. Schutte (ed.), *State and Trade in the Indonesian Archipelago.* Leiden: KITLV Press, pp. 141–149.

Kathirithamby-Wells, J. (1997). "Siak and Its Changing Strategies for Survival, c. 1700–1870," in Anthony Reid (ed.), *The Last Stand of Asian Autonomies.* London: Macmillan, pp. 217–243.

Lombard, Denys (1967). *Le sultanat d'Atjeh au temps d'Iskandar Muda, 1607–1636.* Paris: Ecole Française d'Extrême Orient.

——— (1989). "Une description de la ville de Semarang vers 1812 (d'après un manuscrit de l'India Office)." *Archipel,* 37: 263–277.

Marsden, William (1966). *The History of Sumatra.* Kuala Lumpur: Oxford, reprint (1783).

Putten, Jan van den, and Al Azhar (eds.) (1995). *Di dalam Berkenalan Persahabatan. "In Everlasting Friendship": Letters from Raja Ali Haji.* Leiden: Leiden University Press.

Raffles, Thomas Stamford (1830). *The History of Java.* 2nd ed. London: John Murray.

Reid, Anthony (ed.) (1983). *Slavery, Bondage and Dependency in Southeast Asia.* St. Lucia: University of Queensland Press.

CHAPTER 9

Alexander, Paul, Peter Boomgaard, and Ben White (eds.) (1991). *In the Shadow of Agriculture: Non-Farm Activities in the Javanese Economy, Past and Present.* Amsterdam: Royal Tropical Institute.

Baardewijk, Frans van (1994). "Rural Response to Intensifying Colonial Exploitation: Coffee, State and Society in Central and East Java, 1830–1880," in G. J. Schutte (ed.), *State and Trade in the Indonesian Archipelago.* Leiden: KITLV Press, pp. 151–176.

Bachtiar, Harsja (1978). "Raden Saleh: Aristocrat, Painter, and Scientist," in *Papers of the Dutch-Indonesian Historical Conference,* May 1976. Leiden, Jakarta: Bureau of Indonesian Studies, pp. 46–63.

Bengal Civilian (1987). *Rambles in Java and the Straits in 1852.* Singapore: Oxford University Press, reprint, 1852.

Bigalke, T. (1983). "Dynamics of the Torajan Slave Trade in South Sulawesi," in Anthony Reid (ed.), *Slavery, Bondage and Dependency in Southeast Asia.* St. Lucia: University of Queensland Press, pp. 341–363.

Boomgaard, Peter (1987). "Morbidity and Mortality in Java, 1820–1880: Changing Patterns of Disease and Death," in Norman G. Owen (ed.), *Death and Disease in Southeast Asia.* Singapore: Oxford University Press, pp. 48–69.

——— (1989a). *Between Sovereign Domain and Servile Tenure. The Development of Rights to Land in Java, 1780–1870,* Amsterdam: Free University Press.

——— (1989b). *Children of the Colonial State: Population Growth and Economic Development in Java, 1775–1880.* Amsterdam: Free University Press.

——— (1994). "Colonial Forest Policy in Java in Transition 1865–1916," in R. Cribb (ed.), *The Late Colonial State in Indonesia.* Leiden: KITLV Press, pp. 117–137.

Boomgaard, P., et al. (eds.) (1990). *Changing Economy in Indonesia,* vol. 10: *Food Crops and Arable Lands, Java 1815–1942.* Amsterdam: Royal Tropical Institute.

Breman, Jan (1989). *Taming the Coolie Beast: Plantation Society and the Colonial Order in Southeast Asia.* Delhi: Oxford University Press.

Breman, Jan, and E. Valentine Daniel (1992). "Conclusion: The Making of a Coolie." *Journal of Peasant Studies,* 19, nos. 3–4: 268–295.

Bustaman, Soekondo (1990). *Raden Saleh, Pangeran di antara para pelukis romantik.* Bandung: Abardin.

Campo, J. N. F. M. à (1994). "Steam Navigation and State Formation," in R. Cribb (ed.), *The Late Colonial State in Indonesia.* Leiden: KITLV Press, pp. 11–29.

Ellen, Roy F. (1983). "Practical Islam in South-East Asia," in M. B. Hooker (ed.), *Islam in South-East Asia.* Leiden: Brill, pp. 50–91.

Elson, Robert E. (1979). "Cane-burning in the Pasuruan Area: An Expression of Social Discontent," in Francien van Anrooij (ed.), *Between People and Statistics: Essays on Modern Indonesian History.* The Hague: M. Nijhoff, pp. 219–234.

——— (1990). "Peasant Poverty and Prosperity Under the Cultivation System," in Anne Booth et al. (eds.), *Indonesian Economic History in the Dutch Colonial Era.* New Haven: Yale Southeast Asia Monograph Series No. 35, pp. 34–48.

——— (1994). *Village Java Under the Cultivation System, 1830–1870.* Sydney: Allen & Unwin.

Emmer, P. C. (1992). "European Expansion and Migration: The European Colonial Past and Intercontinental Migration, An Overview," in P. C. Emmer and M. Morner (eds.), *European Expansion and Migration.* Oxford: Berg, pp. 1–12.

Fasseur, Cornelis (1992). *The Politics of Colonial Exploitation: Java, the Dutch, and the Cultivation System.* Ithaca, N.Y.: Cornell University Southeast Asia Program.

Fernando, [M.] Radin (1980). *Famine in Cirebon Residency in Java from 1844–1850: A New Perspective on the Cultivation System.* Melbourne: Monash Working Paper No. 21.

——— (1996). "Growth of Non-Agricultural Economic Activities in Java in the Middle Decades of the Nineteenth Century." *Modern Asian Studies,* 30, no. 1, February: 77–119.

Gooszen, Hans (1999). *A Demographic History of the Indonesian Archipelago, 1880–1942.* Leiden: KITLV Press.

Gouda, Frances (1995). *Dutch Culture Overseas: Colonial Practice in the Netherlands Indies, 1900–1942.* Amsterdam: Amsterdam University Press.

Harris, Marvin, and Eric B. Ross (1987). *Death, Sex, and Fertility: Population Regulation in Preindustrial and Developing Societies.* New York: Columbia University Press.

Headrick, Daniel R. (1981). *The Tools of Empire: Technology and European Imperialism in the Nineteenth Century.* Oxford: Oxford University Press.

——— (1988). *The Tentacles of Progress: Technology Transfer in the Age of Imperialism, 1850–1940.* Oxford: Oxford University Press.

Henley, David (1995). "Minahasa Mapped: Illustrated Notes on Cartography and History in Minahasa, 1512–1942," in Reimar Schefold (ed.), *Minahasa Past and Present: Tradition and Transition in an Outer Island Region of Indonesia.* Leiden: KITLV Press, pp. 32–57.

Knight, G. R. (1992). "The Java Sugar Industry as a Capitalist Plantation: A Reappraisal." *Journal of Peasant Studies,* 19, nos. 3–4: 68–85.

——— (1994). "Gully Coolies, Weed-Women and *Snijvolk:* The Sugar Industry Workers of North Java in the Early Twentieth Century." *Modern Asian Studies,* 28, no. 1: 51–76.

——— (1999). "Coolie or Worker? Crossing the Lines in Colonial Java, 1780–1942." *Itinerario,* 23, no. 1: 62–77.

Kraan, Alfons van der (1980). *Lombok: Conquest, Colonization and Underdevelopment, 1870–1940.* Singapore: Heinemann.

——— (1994). *Bali at War: A History of the Dutch-Balinese Conflict of 1846–49.* Melbourne: Monash Asia Institute Paper No. 34.

Kumar, Ann (1985). *The Diary of a Javanese Muslim: Religion, Politics and the Pesantren 1883–1886.*

Canberra: Australian National University, Faculty of Asian Studies Monographs, New Series No. 7.

——— (1997). "Java: A Self-Critical Examination of the Nation and Its History," in A. Reid (ed.), *The Last Stand of Asian Autonomies.* London: Macmillan, pp. 321–343.

Lombard, Denys (1990). *Le carrefour javanais: Essaie d'histoire globale,* vol. 1. Paris: Editions de l'Ecole des Hautes Etudes Sociales.

Marasutan, Baharudin (1973). *Raden Saleh, 1807–1880: The Precursor of Painting in Indonesia.* Jakarta: Dewan Kesenian.

McDonald, Peter (1980). "An Historical Perspective to Population Growth in Indonesia," in J. J. Fox (ed.), *Indonesia: Australian Perspectives.* Canberra: Australian National University, vol. I, pp. 81–94.

Moor, J. A. de (1989). "Warmakers in the Archipelago: Dutch Expeditions in Nineteenth Century Indonesia," in J. A. de Moor and H. L. Wesseling (eds.), *Imperialism and War.* Leiden: Brill, pp. 50–71.

O'Malley, William J. (1990). "Plantations 1830–1940: An Overview," in Anne Booth et al. (eds.), *Indonesian Economic History in the Dutch Colonial Era.* New Haven: Yale University Southeast Asia Monographs, No. 35, pp. 136–170.

Onghokham (1984). "The Jago in Colonial Java, Ambivalent Champion of the People," in A. Turton and S. Tanabe (eds.), *History and Peasant Consciousness in Southeast Asia.* Osaka, Senri Ethnological Studies No. 13, pp. 327–343.

Reid, Anthony (1969). *The Contest for North Sumatra: Atjeh, the Netherlands and Britain 1858–1898.* London: Oxford University Press.

Reid, Anthony (ed.) (1993). *The Making of an Islamic Political Discourse on Southeast Asia.* Clayton, Victoria: Monash Papers on Southeast Asia No. 27.

Ricklefs, M. C. (1986). "Some Statistical Evidence on Javanese Social, Economic and Demographic History in the Later Seventeenth and Eighteenth Centuries." *Modern Asian Studies,* 20, no. 1: 1–32.

Schoffer, I. (1978). "Dutch Expansion and Indonesian Reactions: Some Dilemmas of Modern Colonial Rule (1900–1942)," in H. L. Wesseling (ed.), *Expansion and Reaction: Essays on European Expansion and Reaction in Asia and Africa.* Leiden: Leiden University Press, pp. 78–99.

Schulte Nordholt, Henk, and Margreet van Till (1999). "Colonial Criminals in Java, 1870–1910," in Vincent L. Rafael (ed.), *Figures of Criminality in Indonesia, the Philippines, and Colonial Vietnam.* Ithaca, N.Y.: Cornell University Southeast Asia Program, pp. 47–69.

Selosoemardjan (1962). *Social Changes in Jogjakarta.* Ithaca, N.Y.: Cornell University Press.

Steenbrinck, Karel (1993). *Dutch Colonialism and Indonesian Islam: Contacts and Conflicts, 1596–1950.* Amsterdam: Rodopi.

Stoler, Ann Laura (1985). *Capitalism and Confrontation in Sumatra's Plantation Belt, 1870–1979.* New Haven: Yale University Press.

Tagliacozzo, Eric (2000). "Kettle on a Slow Boil: Batavia's Threat Perceptions in the Indies." *Journal of Southeast Asian Studies* 31, no. 1: 70–100.

Van Niel, Robert (1992). *Java Under the Cultivation System.* Leiden: KITLV Press.

Vreede-de Stuers, Cora (1996). "Adriana, een kroniek van haar Indische jaren, 1809–1840." *Bijdragen tot de Taal-, Land-en Volkenkunde,* 152, no. 1: 74–108.

Wachlin, Steven (1994). *Woodbury and Page, Photographers Java.* Leiden: KITLV Press.

Wiener, Margaret J. (1995). *Visible and Invisible Realms: Power, Magic and Colonial Conquest in Bali.* Chicago: University of Chicago Press.

Wolters, Willem (1994). "From Corvee to Contract Labour: Institutional Innovation in a Central Javanese Village Around the Turn of the Century," in Robert Cribb (ed.), *The Late Colonial State in Indonesia.* Leiden: KITLV Press, pp. 173–189.

Yen Ching-hwang (1985). *Coolies and Mandarins: China's Protection of Overseas Chinese During the Late Ch'ing Period (1851–1911).* Singapore: Singapore University Press.

CHAPTER 10

Abeyasekere, Susan (1987). "Death and Disease in Nineteenth Century Batavia," in Norman G. Owen (ed.), *Death and Disease in Southeast Asia.* Singapore: Oxford University Press, pp. 187–209.

Aburrachman Surjomihardjo (1978). "National Education in Colonial Society," in H. Soebadio and C. A. du Marchie Sarvaas (eds.), *Dynamics of Indonesian History.* Amsterdam: North Holland Publishers, 277–306.

Anderson, B. R. O'G. (1993). "Census, Map, Museum," in *Imagined Communities: Reflections on the Origin and Spread of Nationalism.* London: Verso, rev. ed., pp. 163–185.

Benda, H. J. (1972). "The Samin Movement," in *Continuity and Change in Southeast Asia: Collected Journal Articles of Harry J. Benda.* New Haven: Yale University Southeast Asian Studies, Monograph No. 18, pp. 23–36.

Boomgaard, Peter (1993). "The Development of Colonial Health Care in Java; An Exploratory Introduction." *Bijdragen tot de Taal-, Land- en Volkenkunde,* 149, no. 1: 77–93.

——— (1996). "Dutch Medicine in Asia, 1600–1900," in David Arnold (ed.), *Warm Climates and Western Medicine.* Amsterdam: Rodopi, pp. 42–64.

——— (1986). "The Welfare Services in Indonesia, 1900–1942." *Itinerario* 10, 1: 57–81.

Brown, Colin (1981). "Sukarno on the Role of Women in the Nationalist Movement." *Review of Indonesian and Malaysian Affairs* 15, no. 1: 68–92.

Coppel, Charles (1997). "Emancipation of the Indonesian Chinese Woman," in Jean Gelman Taylor (ed.), *Women Creating Indonesia: The First Fifty Years.* Clayton, Victoria: Monash Papers on Southeast Asia, No. 44, pp. 22–51.

Cote, Joost (ed. and trans.) (1992). *Letters from Kartini, An Indonesian Feminist, 1900–1904.* Clayton, Victoria: Monash Asia Institute: Hyland House.

Cote, Joost J. P. (1997). "The 'Education' of Java: A Modern Colonial Discourse, 1860–1905." Ph.D. diss., Monash University.

Djelantik, A. A. M. (1997). *The Birthmark: Memoirs of a Balinese Prince.* Hong Kong: Periplus.

Drooglever, P. J. (1980). *De Vaderlandsche Club 1929–1942. Totoks en de Indische Politiek.* Franeker: T. Wever.

Fasseur, C. (1994). "Cornerstone and Stumbling Block: Racial Classification in the Late Colonial State in Indonesia," in R. Cribb (ed.), *The Late Colonial State in Indonesia.* Leiden: Brill, pp. 31–56.

Fernando, M. R. (1995). "The Trumpet Shall Sound for Rich Peasants: Kasan Mukmin's Uprising in Gedangan, East Java, 1904." *Journal of Southeast Asian Studies* 26, no. 2: 242–262.

Horikoshi, Hiroko (1975). "The Dar-Ul-Islam Movement in West Java (1948–1962): An Experience in the Historical Process." *Indonesia* 20, October: 58–86.

Hugo, Graeme J. (1980). "Population Movements in Indonesia During the Colonial Period," in J. J. Fox (ed.), *Indonesia: Australian Perspectives.* Canberra: Australian National University Press, vol. I, pp. 95–135.

Hull, Terence H. (1987). "Plague in Java," in Norman G. Owen (ed.), *Death and Disease in Southeast Asia.* Singapore: Oxford University Press, pp. 210–234.

Husken, Frans (1994). "Declining Welfare in Java: Government and Private Enquiries, 1903–1914," in R. Cribb (ed.), *The Late Colonial State in Indonesia.* Leiden: KITLV Press, pp. 213–227.

Ingleson, John (1986). *In Search of Justice: Workers and Unions in Colonial Java, 1908–1926.* Singapore: Oxford University Press.

Kartini, R. A. K. (1981). *Surat-Surat Kartini: Renungan tentang dan untuk Bangsanya.* Bandung: Djambatan, 2nd ed., translated by Sulastin Sutrisno.

——— (1992). *Letters from Kartini, An Indonesian Feminist, 1900–1904.* Trans. Joost Cote Clayton. Victoria: Monash Asia Institute.

——— (1995). *On Feminism and Nationalism: Kartini's Letters to Stella Zeehandelaar, 1899–1903.* Trans. Joost Cote Clayton. Clayton, Victoria: Monash Asia Institute.

Kartodirdjo, Sartono (1972). "Agrarian Radicalism in Java: Its Setting and Development" in Claire Holt (ed.), *Culture and Politics in Indonesia.* Ithaca, N.Y.: Cornell University Press, pp. 71–125.

Kuntowidjojo (1986a). "The Indonesian Muslim Middle Class in Search of Identity, 1910–1950." *Itinerario* 10, no. 1: 177–196.

——— (1986b). "Islam and Politics: The Local Sarekat Islam Movements in Madura, 1913–20," in Taufik Abdullah and Sharon Siddique (eds.), *Islam and Society in Southeast Asia.* Singapore: Institute for Southeast Asian Studies, pp. 108–138.

Larson, George D. (1987). *Prelude to Revolution: Palaces and Politics in Surakarta, 1912–1942.* Dordrecht: Foris.

Leirissa, Richard (1995). "Dynamics of the History of Manado," in Reimar Schefold (ed.), *Minahasa Past and Present: Tradition and Transition in an Outer Island Region of Indonesia.* Leiden: KITLV Press, pp. 107–116.

Maier, H. M. J. (1993). "From Heteroglossia to Polyglossia: The Creation of Malay and Dutch in the Indies." *Indonesia* 56, October: 37–65.

Mobini-Kesheh, Natalie (1999). *The Hadrami Awakening: Community and Identity in the Netherlands East Indies, 1900–1942.* Ithaca, N.Y.: Cornell Southeast Asia Program.

Nakamura, Mitsuo (1980). "The Reformist Ideology of Muhammadiyah," in James J. Fox (ed.), *Indonesia: Australian Perspectives.* Canberra: Australian National University Press, vol. I, pp. 273–286.

Noer, Deliar (1973). *The Modernist Muslim Movement in Indonesia, 1900–1942.* Singapore: Oxford University Press.

——— (1979). "Yamin and Hamka: Two Routes to an Indonesian Identity," in A. Reid and D. Marr (eds.), *Perceptions of the Past in Southeast Asia.* Kuala Lumpur: Heinemann, pp. 249–262.

Nugraha, Iskandar P. (1995). "The Theosophical Educational Movement in Colonial Indonesia (1900–1947)." M.A. thesis, School of History, University of New South Wales.

Onghokham (1978). "The Pulung Affair: A Tax-Payers Revolt from Patik. Aspects of Rural Politics in Java," in *Papers in the Dutch-Indonesian Historical Conference,* May 1976. Leiden: Bureau of Indonesian Studies, pp. 64–78.

Penders, C. L. M. (1977). *Indonesia: Selected Documents on Colonialism and Nationalism: 1830–1942.* St. Lucia: University of Queensland Press.

Reid, Anthony (1998). "Merdeka: The Concept of Freedom in Indonesia," in David Kelly and Anthony Reid (eds.), *Asian Freedoms: The Idea of Freedom in East and Southeast Asia.* New York: Cambridge University Press, pp. 141–160.

Rush, James (1991). "Placing the Chinese in Java on the Eve of the Twentieth Century." *Indonesia,* Special Issue: 13–24.

Shiraishi, Takashi (1990). *An Age in Motion: Popular Radicalism in Java, 1912–1926.* Ithaca, N.Y.: Cornell University Press.

Siegel, James T. (1997). *Fetish, Recognition, Revolution.* Princeton, N.J.: Princeton University Press.

Sjahrir, Sutan (1969). *Out of Exile.* New York: Greenwood.

Suryadinata, Leo (ed.) (1979). *Political Thinking of the Indonesian Chinese, 1900–1977.* Singapore: Singapore University Press.

Sutherland, Heather (1979). *The Making of a Bureaucratic Elite.* Kuala Lumpur: Heinemann.

Svensson, Thommy (1983). "Peasants and Politics in Early Twentieth Century West Java," in Th. Svensson and Per Sorensen (eds.), *Indonesia and Malaysia. Scandinavian Studies in Contemporary Society.* London: Curzon Press, pp. 75–138.

Taylor, Jean Gelman (1984). "Education, Colonialism and Feminism: An Indonesian Case Study," in Philip G. Altbach and Gail P. Kelly (eds.), *Education and the Colonial Experience.* New Brunswick, N.J.: Transaction Books, 2nd rev. ed., pp. 137–151.

——— (1989). "Kartini in Her Historical Context." *Bijdragen tot de Taal-, Land- en Volkenkunde,* 145, nos. 2–3: 295–307.

——— (1993). "Once More Kartini," in Laurie Jo Sears (ed.), *Autonomous Histories, Particular Truths.* Madison, Wis.: Center for Southeast Asian Studies, pp. 155–171.

Vreede-de Stuers, Cora (1960). *The Indonesian Woman: Struggles and Achievements.* The Hague: Mouton.

Wal, S. L. van der (1961). *Some Information on Education in Indonesia up to 1942.* The Hague: Nuffic.

CHAPTER 11

Anderson, B. R. O'G. (1961). *Some Aspects of Indonesian Politics Under the Japanese Occupation, 1944–1945.* Ithaca, N.Y.: Cornell Modern Indonesia Project.

——— (1972). *Java in a Time of Revolution: Occupation and Resistance, 1944–1946.* Ithaca, N.Y.: Cornell University Press.

Benda, Harry J. (1958). *The Crescent and the Rising Sun: Indonesian Islam Under the Japanese Occupation 1942–1945.* The Hague: Van Hoeve.

——— (1965). *Japanese Military Administration in Indonesia: Selected Documents.* New Haven: Yale University Southeast Asia Monographs.

——— (1972a). "The Communist Rebellions of 1926–27 in Indonesia," reprinted in *Continuity and Change in Southeast Asia: Collected Journal Articles of Harry J. Benda.* New Haven: Yale University Southeast Asia Monographs, No. 18, pp. 23–36.

——— (1972b). "Democracy in Indonesia," in *Continuity and Change in Southeast Asia: Collected Journal Articles of Harry J. Benda.* New Haven: Yale University Southeast Asian Studies, Monograph No. 18, pp. 162–169.

Cribb, Robert (1991). *Gangsters and Revolutionaries: The Jakarta People's Militia and the Indonesian Revolution, 1945–1949.* Honolulu: University of Hawaii Press.

Dijk, C. van (1981). *Rebellion Under the Banner of Islam: The Darul Islam of Indonesia.* The Hague: M. Nijhoff.

Djajadiningrat, Roswitha T. (1974). *Herinneringen van een vrijheidsstrijdster.* The Hague: M. Nijhoff.

Djojohadikusumo, Margono (1973). *Reminiscences from Three Historical Periods.* Jakarta: P. T. Indira.

Feith, Herbert (1962). *The Decline of Constitutional Democracy in Indonesia.* Ithaca, N.Y.: Cornell University Press.

Frederick, William (1989). *Visions and Heat: The Making of the Indonesian Revolution.* Athens: Ohio University Press.

Fusayama, Takao (1993). *A Japanese Memoir of Sumatra 1945–1946: Love and Hatred in the Liberation War.* Ithaca, N.Y.: Cornell Modern Indonesia Project.

Goto, Kenichi (1996). "Indonesia Under the 'Greater East Asia Co-Prosperity Sphere,'" in Donald Denoon et al. (eds.), *Multicultural Japan: Paleolithic to Postmodern.* Cambridge: Cambridge University Press, pp. 160–173.

Hanifah, Abu (1972). *Tales of a Revolutionary.* Sydney: Angus & Robertson.

Hatta, Mohammad (1981). *Mohammad Hatta, Indonesian Patriot: Memoirs.* Singapore: Gunung Agung.

Hicks, George (1995). *The Comfort Women.* Tokyo: Yenbooks.

Hillen, Ernest (1993). *The Way of a Boy: A Memoir of Java.* Toronto: Viking.

Hirschman, Charles (1994). "Population and Society in Twentieth Century Southeast Asia." *Journal of Southeast Asian Studies,* 25, no. 2: 381–416.

Huie, Shirley Fenton (1992). *The Forgotten Ones: Women and Children Under Nippon.* Sydney: Angus & Robertson.

Kahin, Audrey R. (1996). "The Communist Uprising in Sumatra: A Reappraisal." *Indonesia* 62, October: 19–36.

Kahin, George McT. (1959). *Nationalism and Revolution in Indonesia.* Ithaca, N.Y.: Cornell University Press.

Krancher, Jan (ed.) (1996). *The Defining Years of the Dutch East Indies, 1942–1949.* London: McFarland.

Kurasawa, Aiko (1991). "Films as Propaganda Media on Java Under the Japanese," in G. K. Goodman (ed.), *Japanese Cultural Policies in Southeast Asia During World War 2.* New York: St. Martin's Press, pp. 36–92.

Legge, John D. (1988). *Intellectuals and Nationalism in Indonesia: A Study of the Following Recruited by Sutan Sjahrir in Occupation Jakarta.* Ithaca, N.Y.: Cornell Modern Indonesia Project, Monograph Series.

Lindsey, Timothy (1997). *The Romance of K'tut Tantri and Indonesia: Text and Scripts, History and Identity.* Kuala Lumpur: Oxford University Press.

Lucas, Anton (1977). "Social Revolution in Pemalang, Central Java, 1945." *Indonesia* 24, October: 86–122.

——— (1997). "Images of Indonesian Women During the Japanese Occupation 1942–1945," in Jean Gelman Taylor (ed.), *Women Creating Indonesia: The First Fifty Years.* Melbourne: Monash Asia Institute, pp. 52–90.

Mangkupradja, Raden Gatot (1968). "The Peta and My Relations with the Japanese." *Indonesia,* 5: 105–134.

McIntyre, Angus (ed.) (1993). *Indonesian Political Biography: In Search of Cross-Cultural Understanding.* Melbourne: Monash Papers on Southeast Asia No. 28.

McVey, Ruth T. (1965). *The Rise of Indonesian Communism.* Ithaca, N.Y.: Cornell University Press.

Mortimer, Rex (1980). "The Place of Communism," in James J. Fox (ed.), *Indonesia: Australian Perspectives.* Canberra: Australian National University Press, vol. III, pp. 615–631.

Mrazek, Rudolf (1994). *Sjahrir: Politics and Exile in Indonesia.* Ithaca, N.Y.: Cornell University Southeast Asia Program.

——— (1996). "Sjahrir at Boven Digoel: Reflections on Exile in the Dutch East Indies," in Daniel S. Lev and Ruth McVey (eds.), *Making Indonesia: Essays in Honor of George McT. Kahin.* Ithaca, N.Y.: Cornell University Southeast Asia Program, pp. 41–65.

National Federation of Kenpeitai Veterans' Associations (1986). *The Kenpeitai in Java and Sumatra.* Ithaca, N.Y.: Cornell Modern Indonesia Project, Translation Series No. 65.

O'Malley, William J. (1980). "Second Thoughts on Indonesian Nationalism," in James J. Fox (ed.), *Indonesia: Australian Perspectives.* Canberra, Australian National University Press, vol. III, pp. 601–613.

Reid, Anthony (1974). *The Indonesian National Revolution, 1945–1950.* Melbourne: Longman.

——— (1979). *The Blood of the People: Revolution and the End of Traditional Rule in Northern Sumatra.* Kuala Lumpur: Oxford University Press.

——— (1980). "Indonesia: From Briefcase to Samurai Sword," in A. W. McCoy (ed.), *Southeast Asia Under Japanese Occupation.* New Haven: Yale University Southeast Asia Monographs.

Reid, Anthony, and A. Oki (eds.) (1986). *The Japanese Experience in Indonesia: Selected Memoirs of 1942–1945.* Athens: Ohio University Center for International Studies.

Said, Salim (1991). *Genesis of Power: General Sudirman and the Indonesian Military in Politics, 1945–1949.* Singapore: Institute for Southeast Asian Studies.

Sastroamidjojo, Ali (1979). *Milestones on My Journey.* St. Lucia: University of Queensland Press.

Sato, Shigeru (1994). *War, Nationalism and Peasants: Java Under the Japanese Occupation, 1942–1945.* Sydney: Allen & Unwin.

Simatupang, T. B. (1972). *Report from Banaran: Experiences During the People's War.* Ithaca, N.Y.: Cornell Modern Indonesia Project.

Smail, J. R. W. (1964). *Bandung in the Early Revolution.* Ithaca, N.Y.: Cornell Modern Indonesia Project.

Swift, Ann (1989). *The Road to Madiun: The Indonesian Communist Uprising of 1948.* Ithaca, N.Y.: Cornell Modern Indonesia Project Monograph No. 69.

Tantri, K'tut (1960). *Revolt in Paradise.* New York: Harper.

Taylor, Jean Gelman (1996). "Images of the Indonesian Revolution," in Jane Drakard and John Legge (eds.), *Indonesian Independence Fifty Years On, 1945–1995.* Monash Asia Institute, Annual Indonesia Lecture Series No. 20, pp. 13–36.

Ueno, Fukuo (1988). *Desa Cimahi: Analysis of a Village on Java During the Japanese Occupation (1943).* Rotterdam: Erasmus University Comparative Asian Studies Program.

Wild, C., and P. Carey (eds.) (1988). *Born in Fire: The Indonesian Struggle for Independence: An Anthology.* Athens: Ohio University Press.

Yamin, Muhammad (1959). *Naskah Persiapan Undang-Undang Dasar 1945.* Jakarta: Jajasan Prapantja.

Zainu'ddin, Ailsa Thomson (1997). "Building the Future: The Life and Work of Kurnianingrat Ali Sastroamijoyo," in Jean Gelman Taylor (ed.), *Women Creating Indonesia: The First Fifty Years.* Clayton, Victoria: Monash Asia Institute, pp. 156–202.

CHAPTER 12

Abaza, Mona (1993). *Changing Images of Three Generations of Azharites in Indonesia.* Singapore: Institute for Southeast Asian Studies Occasional Paper No. 88.

Adam, Ahmat (1995). *The Vernacular Press and the Emergence of Modern Indonesian Consciousness.* Ithaca, N.Y.: Southeast Asia Program.

Anderson, B. R. O'G. (ed.) (2001). *Violence and the State in Suharto's Indonesia,* Ithaca, NY: Cornell University Southeast Asia Project, 2001.

Anderson, B. R. O'G., and A. Kahin (eds.) (1982). *Interpreting Indonesian Politics: Thirteen Contributions to the Debate.* Ithaca, N.Y.: Cornell Modern Indonesia Project.

Anderson, B. R. O'G., and R. T. McVey (1971). *A Preliminary Analysis of the October 1, 1965 Coup in Indonesia.* Ithaca, N.Y.: Cornell Modern Indonesia Project.

Bourchier, D. (1984). *Dynamics of Dissent in Indonesia: Sawito and the Phantom Coup.* Ithaca, N.Y.: Cornell Modern Indonesia Project.

Bourchier, David, and John Legge (eds.) (1994). *Democracy in Indonesia 1950s and 1990s.* Clayton, Victoria: Monash Papers on Southeast Asia, No. 31.

Budiman, Arief (ed.) (1990). *State and Civil Society in Indonesia.* Clayton, Victoria: Monash Centre of Southeast Asian Studies.

Chauvel, Richard (1990). *Nationalists, Soldiers and Separatists: The Ambonese Islands from Colonialism to Revolt, 1880–1950.* Leiden: KITLV Press.

Coppel, Charles (1983). *Indonesian Chinese in Crisis.* Kuala Lumpur: Oxford University Press.

——— (1997). "Emancipation of the Indonesian Chinese Woman," in Jean Gelman Taylor (ed.), *Women Creating Indonesia: The First Fifty Years.* Melbourne: Monash Asia Institute, pp. 22–51.

Cribb, Robert (ed.) (1990). *The Indonesian Killings of 1965–1966: Studies from Java and Bali.* Melbourne: Monash Papers on Southeast Asia No. 21.

Cribb, Robert, and Colin Brown (1995). *Modern Indonesia: A History Since 1945.* London: Longman.

Crouch, Harold (1978). *The Army and Politics in Indonesia.* Ithaca, N.Y.: Cornell University Press.

Dake, Antonie C. A. (1973). *In the Spirit of the Red Banteng: Indonesian Communists between Moscow and Peking, 1959–1965.* The Hague: Mouton.

Dijk, Kees van (1995). "From Colony to Independent State," in Reimar Schefold (ed.), *Minahasa Past and Present: Tradition and Transition in an Outer Island Region of Indonesia.* Leiden: KITLV Press, pp. 72–91.

Emmerson, Donald K. (ed.) (1999). *Indonesia Beyond Suharto.* Armonk, N.Y.: M. E. Sharpe.

Federspiel, Howard M. (1994). *Popular Indonesian Literature of the Qur'an.* Ithaca, N.Y.: Cornell Modern Indonesia Project.

Feith, Herbert, and L. Castles (eds.) (1970). *Indonesian Political Thinking, 1945–1965.* Ithaca, N.Y.: Cornell University Press.

Grimes, Barbara Dix (1994). "Buru Inside Out," in Leontine E. Visser (ed.), *Halmahera and Beyond.* Leiden: KITLV Press, pp. 59–78.

Harsono, Ganis (1977). *Recollections of an Indonesian Diplomat in the Sukarno Era.* St. Lucia: University of Queensland Press.

Harvey, Barbara S. (1977). *Permesta: Half a Rebellion.* Ithaca, N.Y.: Cornell Modern Indonesia Project.

Hefner, Robert W. (1985). *Hindu Javanese: Tengger Tradition and Islam.* Princeton, N.J.: Princeton University Press.

——— (2000). *Civil Islam: Muslims and Democratization in Indonesia.* Princeton, N.J.: Princeton University Press.

Hill, Hal (ed.) (1994). *Indonesia's New Order: The Dynamics of Socio-Economic Transformation.* Sydney: Allen & Unwin.

Hobsbawm, Eric (1983). "Introduction", Eric Hobsbawm and Terence Ranger (eds.), *The Invention of Tradition.* Cambridge: Cambridge University Press, pp. 1–14.

Hugo, Graeme J., Terence H. Hull, Valerie J. Hull, and Gavin W. Jones (1987). *The Demographic Dimension in Indonesian Development.* Singapore: Oxford University Press.

Jenkins, David (1984). *Suharto and His Generals: Indonesian Military Politics, 1975–1983.* Ithaca, N.Y.: Cornell Modern Indonesia Project.

Kahin, Audrey R. (ed.) (1985). *Regional Dynamics of the Indonesian Revolution.* Honolulu: University of Hawaii Press.

Kell, Tim (1995). *The Roots of Acehnese Rebellion, 1989–1992.* Ithaca, N.Y.: Cornell Modern Indonesia Project.

Legge, John (1972). *Sukarno: A Political Biography.* London: Allen Lane.

Lev, Daniel (1966). *The Transition to Guided Democracy: Indonesian Politics 1957–1959.* Ithaca, N.Y.: Cornell Modern Indonesia Project.

Locher-Scholten, Elspeth (ed.) (1987). *Indonesian Women in Focus.* Dordrecht: Foris.

Lowry, Robert (1996). *The Armed Forces of Indonesia.* Sydney: Allen & Unwin.

O'Neill, Hugh (1993). "Islamic Architecture Under the New Order," in Virginia Matheson Hooker (ed.), *Culture and Society in New Order Indonesia.* Kuala Lumpur: Oxford University Press, pp. 151–165.

Parkin, David, and Stephen C. Headley (eds.) (2000). *Islamic Prayer Across the Indian Ocean: Inside and Outside the Mosque.* London: Curzon.

Penders, C. L. M., and Ulf Sundhaussen (1985). *Abdul Haris Nasution: A Political Biography:* St. Lucia: University of Queensland Press.

Reeve, David (1985). *Golkar of Indonesia: An Alternative to the Party System.* Singapore: Oxford University Press.

Reid, Anthony (ed.) (1996). *Sojourners and Settlers: Histories of Southeast Asia and the Chinese.* Sydney: Allen & Unwin.

Reid, Anthony (1998). "Political 'Tradition' in Indonesia: The One and the Many." *Asian Studies Review,* 22, no. 1: 23–38.

Riddell, Peter (2001). *Islam and the Malay-Indonesian World.* London: Hurst.

Robinson, Geoffrey (1995). *The Dark Side of Paradise: Political Violence in Bali.* Ithaca, N.Y.: Cornell University Press.

Robison, Richard (1986). *Indonesia: The Rise of Capital.* Sydney: Allen & Unwin.

Schwarz, Adam (1994). *A Nation in Waiting: Indonesia in the 1990s.* Boulder, Colo.: Westview Press.

Sjamsuddin, Nazaruddin (1985). *The Republican Revolt: A Study of the Acehnese Rebellion.* Singapore: Institute for Southeast Asian Studies.

Sudisman (1975). *Analysis of Responsibility: Defence Speech Before the Special Military Tribunal, Jakarta, 21 July 1967.* North Melbourne: Workers Co-operative.

Sukarno (1965). *An Autobiography As Told to Cindy Adams.* New York: Bobbs-Merrill.

Sundhaussen, Ulf (1982). *The Road to Power: Indonesian Military Politics.* Kuala Lumpur: Oxford University Press.

Tjandrasasmita, Uka (1985). "Le rôle de l'architecture et des arts décoratifs dans l'islamisation de l'Indonésie." *Archipel,* 29, no. 1: 203–212.

Toer, Pramoedya Ananta (1999). *The Mute's Soliloquy.* New York: Hyperion.

Wassing-Visser, Rita (1995). *Royal Gifts from Indonesia: Historical Bonds with the House of Orange-Nassau (1600–1938).* Zwolle: Waanders.

Wessel, Ingrid, and Georgia Wimhofer (eds.) (2001). *Violence in Indonesia.* Hamburg: Abera.

White, Benjamin (1976). "The Economic Importance of Children in a Javanese Village," in David Banks (ed.), *Changing Identities in Modern Southeast Asia.* The Hague: Mouton, pp. 269–289.

Wolf, Diane Lauren (1992). *Factory Daughters: Gender, Household Dynamics and Industrialization in Rural Java.* Berkeley: University of California Press.

Woodward, Mark R. (1989). *Islam in Java: Normative Piety and Mysticism in the Sultanate of Yogyakarta.* Tucson: University of Arizona Press.

INDEX